CARB WARS

SUGAR IS THE NEW FAT

A COOKBOOK BY
JUDY BARNES BAKER

CARB WARS

SUGAR IS THE NEW FAT

A COOKBOOK BY
JUDY BARNES BAKER

Book design and cover design by Kovacevich Design, Seattle, Washington
Preliminary layout by Glenda Gertz
Index by Roberts Indexing Service

ISBN 0-9792018-0-2
ISBN13 978-0-9792018-0-6

Printed in the United States of America

TABLE OF CONTENTS

To my mother, Irene Watson Barnes, whose greatest joy
was cooking for her family.
1916–2006

Special thanks to my family for their patience and help.

INTRODUCTION

Do we have to choose between good health and good food? Food is more than sustenance; it is one of life's greatest pleasures. We first experience love in the form of the person who feeds us. All our memories of childhood and happiness include food. My mother's buttermilk biscuits and fried apple pies are as much a part of me as my green eyes and crooked nose. The first meal I cooked for my husband and the birthday cakes I made for my children are part of the bond that connects us as a family. Shared meals are the heart of home life and the center of good times and celebrations. Food gives us our ethnic identity, our sense of belonging, and it defines who we are. It is music for our mouths and comfort for our souls.

But many of us, indeed most of us, if you believe the latest statistics, are going to have to change the way we eat. Something has gone horribly wrong in America. Something changed that has made us the fattest and most medicated country on Earth. Whatever it was, it started to go wrong in the late '70s and has been getting worse every year. It has been called an "epidemic" of obesity and diabetes.

On the wall of a local restaurant, there is a photograph from the 1930s of P. T. Barnum with the sideshow cast of the Barnum and Bailey Circus. It shows the standard lineup of what they called "freaks" in a less compassionate era: the tattooed man, the bearded lady, the Siamese twins, the man with three legs, a midget, and a giant, among others. But the most astonishing person in the picture is the one seated in the middle, a cherubic woman in a satin dress who would have been billed as "The Fat Lady." What I find astonishing is that people would have paid money to see her. Just walking from the parking garage to the restaurant, I passed people on the street who could have taken her place. Obesity has become so commonplace that we forget how rare it used to be.

The owners of Goliath caskets shipped four or five triple-wide models (44 inches across with a capacity of 700 pounds) a month in 2003; now they expect to sell 800 per year. When they started the company in the '80s, they sold one per year.[1] They recently added a 52-inch supersized casket, which is wider than the bed of a standard pickup truck and has a capacity of 1,200 pounds.

So how do we explain this precipitous decline in health? Let's start at the beginning.

If you go back far enough, all of us are descended from people who lived on low-carb diets. Agriculture is a recent invention, generally dated to the end of the last ice age, when many large game animals became extinct. The major climate change may have favored plants that produced dormant seeds, capable of surviving long dry seasons or

---

1 Warren St. John, "Obesity presents a grave problem for funeral directors across nation," *The New York Times,* September 28, 2003.

cold winters. Humans gathered and stored the seeds for their own use and eventually learned to plant and harvest grain crops. There are a few societies that still practice a hunting and fishing lifestyle, but they are rapidly changing.

Note: Jonny Bowden, in *Living the Low Carb Life*,[2] gives more details on the history and origins of low-carb diets than I have time or space to go into here. His well-researched book is informative, entertaining, and full of useful advice to make your low-carb life more enjoyable.

The Inuit in Greenland live the same way as their ancestors who have lived there since 2500 B.C.E. They eat sea birds and the meat and blubber of marine mammals. No vegetables or fruit grow in this Arctic land, and the nearest place to buy bread and tea is in Denmark, yet heart disease is unknown to these people. "Traditionally, this marine diet has made the people of the Arctic Circle among the world's healthiest. A 70-year-old Inuit man in Greenland has coronary arteries as elastic as those of a 20-year-old Dane eating Western foods," according to Dr. Gert Mulvad of the Primary Health Care Clinic in Nuuk, Greenland. "Some Arctic clinics do not even keep heart medications like nitroglycerin in stock." This is in spite of the fact that these people now live in the most toxic environment on Earth. Pollutants from the industrialized world are carried north by prevailing winds and ocean currents where they are preserved by the extreme cold and lack of sunlight. Sea animals ingest the contaminants and pass them on to the humans who hunt them. Public health officials are reluctant to advise them to limit their consumption of their traditional foods. "In part, doctors fear the Inuit will switch to processed foods loaded with carbohydrates and sugar." Dr. Mulvad continues, "The level of contamination is very high in Greenland, but there's a lot of Western food that is worse than the poisons."[3]

In 1918, Vilhjalmur Stefansson, an anthropologist who had lived with the Copper Inuit in Alaska for a total of five years, wanted to see if he had suffered any ill effects from living on a diet of meat, fat, and water. The results of his examinations were published in *The Journal of the American Medical Association* on July 3, 1926, in an article titled "The Effects of an Exclusive Long-Continued Meat Diet." The committee that examined Stefansson failed to find any trace of evidence of the expected harmful effects of the diet. The news was greeted with skepticism. One critic reportedly said, "You are likelier to meet a thousand liars than one miracle." A colleague, Dr. Karsten Anderson, volunteered to join Stefansson in a scientific experiment, under strict supervision, to determine the effects of a eating a diet consisting of only protein and fat for one year. He was not trying to prove anything, he stated, only to discover the facts. The two men checked into the dietetic ward of the Bellevue Hospital in New York City. Stefansson estimated that their diet was 80% animal fat and 20% animal protein.[4] At the end of the year, it was reported that Stefansson had lost 10 pounds of excess weight and his cholesterol was lower than when he started. Neither man had suffered from scurvy or any other deficiency disease, nor had they damaged their circulatory systems or kidneys as had been predicted.[5]

---

2   Jonny Bowden, M.A., C.N.S., *Living the Low Carb Life, Controlled-Carbohydrate Eating for Long-Term Weight Loss*, Sterling Publishing Co., Inc., New York, 2004.

3   Marla Cone, *Silent Snow: The Slow Poisoning of the Arctic*, Grove Press, New York, 2005.

4   Vilhjalmur Stefansson, *The Fat of the Land*, The Macmillan Company, New York, 1957.

5   Vilhjalmur Stefansson, "Adventures in Diet," *Harper's Monthly Magazine*, December, 1935.

Fast forward twenty years, and Stefansson had suffered a cerebral thrombosis, gained weight, developed arthritis, and according to his wife, become unhappy and grouchy. He decided to go back to his stone-age diet. After just a few weeks, he experienced startling improvements in his health. Mrs. Stefansson wrote "The stone-age all-meat diet is wholesome. It is an eat-all-you-want reducing diet that permits you to forget that you are dieting—no hunger pangs remind you. Best of all, it improves the temperament. It somehow makes one feel optimistic, mildly euphoric."[6]

I am not advocating that anyone should revert to an all-meat diet, but it is clear that we could, and that should put to rest most of the arguments that a much less restricted low-carb diet is dangerous or unhealthful. Stefansson believed that the meat had to be fresh or at least not over-cooked in order to contain the necessary vitamins. He also pointed out that during his time with the Eskimos, they had eaten fish bones and chewed the cartilage on the ends of larger bones and that this may have provided calcium and "bulk." (The Copper Inuit died of accidents and old age rather than disease, but they matured earlier and lived, on average, ten years less than their European contemporaries. Stefansson speculated that an all-meat diet accelerates the metabolism.)[7]

Note: *Eskimo* is the name given by the Algonquians to the tribes north of them. It means "eaters of raw flesh." To the Cree it was *askimowew,* "he eats it raw."

Low Carb Diets in Modern Times:
We tend to think that low-carb diets are a new "fad." Nothing could be further from the truth. The famous French epicure and gastronome, Jean Anthelme Brillat-Savarin, wrote his "Meditation XXII on Obesity" from *The Physiology of Taste* in 1825. He predicted that his readers would find him cruel for denying them all the good things made with sugar, eggs, and flour and allowing neither potatoes nor macaroni. (His advice to those who wanted to gain weight was to eat lots of fresh bread, take care not to throw away the crumbs, and go to bed early.)

In 1869 an English carpenter and undertaker named William Banting published *Letter on Corpulence*. A good-hearted and grateful man, he published his book at his own expense in order to spare

The Darwin of Nutrition
In the 1930s, Weston A. Price, who has been called the Darwin of nutrition, traveled the world to research the diets and health of isolated primitive peoples while such societies still existed. He sought out people who were continuing to live as their ancestors had lived with little outside influence. He found them to be a "picture of perfect health." They had superb physiques, perfect teeth, no arthritis, no heart disease, no cancer, and they were cheerful and happy. He found that all healthy populations included animal fat and protein in their diets, such as fatty fish, wild game, organ meats, eggs, and butter. He also studied less isolated people from the same groups. In his book, *Nutrition and Physical Degeneration,* he charts their catastrophic decline in health as they came in contact with "trade foods."[8]

---

6   Evelyn Stefansson, Preface, *Eat Fat and Grow Slim*, Richard MacKarness, Havill Press, London, 1958.

7   Vilhjalmur Stefansson, "Adventures in Diet," *Harper's Monthly Magazine,* January, 1936.

8   Weston A. Price, DDS, *Nutrition and Physical Degeneration,* McGraw-Hill, 1939.

others from suffering as he had as a result of obesity. He describes how doctor after doctor had failed to help him. They prescribed vigorous exercise, steam baths, and starvation diets, but he continued to get fatter and sicker. Eventually, when he started to lose his hearing, he consulted Dr. William Harvey, an ear, nose, and throat specialist, who had recently returned from a trip to Paris. Dr. Harvey diagnosed that all his health problems were the result of obesity and put him on a low carbohydrate diet. Banting's book gives the details of a diet that is very much like the ones later promoted by Dr. Robert Atkins, Drs. Michael and Mary Dan Eades, and others. He wrote, "I can confidently state that quantity of diet may safely be left to the natural appetite; and that it is quality only which is essential to abate and cure corpulence," in other words, it is *what* you eat and not *how much* that matters. (Banting avoided butter because he thought it contained sugar. He also drank copious amounts of alcohol, which he apparently believed to be medicinal.)

In the Preface to its fourth edition, he said his book had already sold 63,000 copies in England and attained worldwide circulation. His system was so popular that a new word was added to the dictionary. The Oxford Dictionary still lists "bant: [short for bantingize to reduce by bantingism, *fr.* banting + ize] to practice banting: Diet."

Although Banting has been called the father of low-carbohydrate dieting, he contradicts the claim. "I have been told, again and again, that the system was as old as the hills. I will not deny it, because I cannot; but I can say for myself and my many correspondents, that it was quite new to us; or some of us would doubtless have been recommended to practice it by medical advisers, as I have no doubt they are now, and as they surely will be hereafter more extensively." So here we are, over 130 years later, and what are most of our medical advisers recommending? Calorie restriction and exercise.

> "It is now proved that, by proper diet alone, the evils of corpulence may be removed without the addition of those active exercises, which are impossible to the sickly or unwieldy patient." *Letter on Corpulence,* by William Banting.

In the '50s and '60s, two British obesity researchers, Prof. Alan Kekwick and Dr. Gaston Pawan, observed that people who lost weight slowly on a very low-calorie diet that consisted mainly of carbohydrates, lost weight easily when the same amount of calories came mainly from protein and fat. A subsequent study conducted by Frederick Benoit and his associates at the Oakland Naval Hospital in California found that subjects who ate a diet low in carbohydrates but high in fat, lost fat at almost twice the rate of those who ate *nothing at all*.[9] This clinical evidence suggested that there is a metabolic advantage to burning fat instead of sugar for energy.

Dr. Robert Atkins, a cardiologist and graduate of the Cornell University School of Medicine, was reading a series of articles about low-starch and sugar diets in the October 1963 issue of the *Journal of the American Medical Association*[10] when he decided to do

---

[9] F. L. Benoit, R. L. Martin, R. H. Watten, "Changes in Body Composition During Weight Reduction in Obesity: Balance Studies Comparing Effects of Fasting and a Ketogenic Diet," *Annals of Internal Medicine,* 63(4), 1965, pp. 604-612.

[10] E. S. Gordon, M. Goldberg, G. J. Chosy, "A New Concept in the Treatment of Obesity," *Journal of the American Medical Association,* Oct 5, 1963, Volume 186, pp. 50-60.

something about the triple chin he was developing. Atkins was a man with a large appetite who had never been on a diet before. He lost 28 pounds in six weeks and found that it was easy, he was never hungry, he had more energy, and he liked the food. He stayed on the diet for the rest of his life and started to prescribe it for the patients in his clinic with the same success he had experienced. In 1972, he published *Dr. Atkins' Diet Revolution*, which sold almost a million copies. Eat until you're full, forget calories, limit only the carbs, was his message.

Purchased Food Replaced Home-Cooked:
As an art student in 1964, I designed the cover for a brochure advertising a talk by a new writer named Betty Friedan.[12] Her book, *The Feminine Mystique*, championed the rights of women to seek fulfillment outside the home. Her message: educated women do not make happy housewives. By the 1970s there was a dramatic increase in the number of working women. The kitchen became fallow ground as we stopped cooking and started to eat mass-produced food in restaurants and prepackaged foods from the grocery store. With both partners in a household bringing home a paycheck, we had the resources to spend on prepared food, soft drinks, and snacks.

The Atkins Revolution
Almost from the start, Atkins' diet was dismissed as a fad and a fraud that couldn't possibly work, and if it did, it must be dangerous. (Banting had been denounced in the same way almost one hundred years earlier.) To the low-fat camp, he was the devil incarnate; his system was the antithesis of the austerity, self-discipline, and deprivation they were preaching, and they attacked him with religious fervor. Most of the medical community refused to even consider looking into the science that would confirm or refute his convictions. According to his wife, he took on his detractors with the attitude "Okay, I'll be the best enemy you ever had." The sparring continued during his life and the controversy continues still. Atkins' widow, Veronica, has established a research foundation in his name; "I'll beat them through research," she says. The theme of Robert Atkins' memorial service was "To Dream the Impossible Dream."[11]

High Fructose Corn Syrup Replaced Sucrose:
In the late 1960s, manufacturers developed a way to make high fructose corn syrup by treating cornstarch with altered enzymes. It was cheaper and sweeter than cane sugar, and its liquid form made it easier to use. Between 1970 and 1990 the consumption of high fructose sweetener in the United States increased by 1,000 percent. It became the only caloric sweetener used for soft drinks. Fructose is not digested, absorbed, or metabolized like other sugars. It stimulates the

"To cereal manufacturers." Dr. Robert Atkins, in answer to the question: "But aren't whole grains important?"

formation of fat cells and bypasses the body's regulatory processes that reduce appetite: the release of insulin and the production of leptin.[13]

---

11 "The Diet Martyr," *New York Magazine*, March 15, 2004

12 Betty Freidan, *The Feminine Mystique*, W. W. Norton and Company, Inc., 1963.

13 George A. Bray, Samara Joy Nielson, and Barry M. Popkin, "Consumption of high-fructose corn syrup in beverages may play a role in the epidemic of obesity," *American Journal of Clinical Nutrition*, April, 2004, Vol. 79, No.4, pp. 537-543.

Polyunsaturated and Hydrogenated Fats Replaced Natural Fats in Commercial Products:
Consumption of trans fats, which have been around in the form of margarine and shortening since the early 1900s, skyrocketed as the amount of purchased cookies, crackers, bread, chips, cereal, donuts, fast food fries, and fried chicken displaced home-cooked meals. Margarine and shortening replaced butter and lard because they were cheap and "healthy." Trans fats were *shelf stable.* A bakery cake iced with Crisco® and powdered sugar doesn't need to be refrigerated, and it lasts for days.

Trans fats are liquid oils that have been partially hydrogenated to prolong their shelf life or to make them solid at room temperature. Trans fats have been linked to many serious health problems, including heart disease, stroke, type 2 diabetes, obesity, and cancer. The Nurses' Health Study, of 85,095 women, found that women who ate 4 teaspoons of margarine a day (about 4 grams of trans fat) increased their risk of heart disease by fifty percent.[14] (McDonald's® web site lists 8 grams of trans fats in a large order of fries.) In 1994, the Center for Science in the Public Interest petitioned the FDA to require label disclosure of trans fat content and to prevent misleading health claims. In 2002 the Institute for Medicine reviewed the scientific evidence and reported that the Tolerable Upper Intake Level for trans fats was zero.[15] Since January of 2006, food companies have been required to list trans fat content on all their labels.

However, there are loopholes in the disclosure law. For products with a small serving size, like peanut butter, the label may legally say the level of trans fat is "zero" if it is 0.5 grams or less per serving. Many labels now proclaim "no trans fats" when the contents have not changed at all. You must check the ingredients to see if partially hydrogenated oils are included.

There is another loophole, and it is a big one: restaurants are not required to disclose the amount of trans fat in the foods they sell. Many still use partially hydrogenated vegetable oil for frying to save money because it doesn't spoil, and it can be used over and over.

The Slippery Slope—The Government Recommended Fats Be Cut to 30% or Less:
In the late '70s we were told that it was dietary fats that caused weight gain and heart disease and that a healthy diet consisted of lots of carbohydrates and as little fat as possible. We now know about *good fats* and *bad fats;* back then they were all bad. As the consumption of the natural fats in eggs, dairy products, and meat were reduced, the impact of the trans fats was amplified. What was a body to do? With no alternative, it had to use the alien fats to build cell walls, to make hormones, to insulate brain and nerve tissue, and to cushion and protect organs. We *partially-hydrogenated* ourselves, and we are now experiencing the consequences.

---

14 "Fats and Cholesterol: The Nutrition Source, Knowledge for Healthy Eating," Department of Nutrition, Harvard School of Public Health (web site: www.hspnharvard.edu/nutritionsource/fats.html/).

15 "Letter Report on the Dietary Reference Intakes for Trans Fatty Acids," Food and Nutrition Board of the Institute of Medicine, July 10, 2002.

"In the 1940's, researchers found a strong correlation between cancer and the consumption of fat—the fats used were hydrogenated fats, although the results were presented as though the culprit were saturated fats. In fact, until recently, saturated fats were usually lumped together with trans fats in the various U.S. databases that researchers use to correlate dietary trends with disease conditions. Thus, natural saturated fats were tarred with the black brush of unnatural hydrogenated vegetable oils." Sally Fallon, *Nourishing Traditions,* 1995.

It was Ancel Keys, a University of Minnesota physician and government consultant, who introduced the theory that dietary fats, especially saturated fats, raise cholesterol and cause heart disease. He noted an alarming increase in coronary deaths among American men after World War II. (Ironically, each of the K-rations, designed by Keys to feed the army, included a pack of cigarettes, addicting a whole generation of returning soldiers. Smoking has been linked to coronary heart disease.) The conclusions he reached in his study of seven countries, which ran from 1958 to 1970, became the basis for the low-fat orthodoxy that continues to this day. The United States, Italy, Finland, the Netherlands, the Greek Island of Crete, Japan, and Yugoslavia were included in his study.[16]

Keys, with his wife, Margaret, originated the very popular *Mediterranean Diet*, which emphasized bread, pasta, beans, fruits, vegetables, and olive oil.[17] Although the common perception is that it was an almost vegetarian regimen, according to the 1961 Times issue[18] that featured Key's picture on the cover, he and his wife ate "carving meat—steaks, chops, and roasts" up to three times a week, and in addition to fish, they also included chicken, Canadian bacon, and liver on the diet—the latter because the Cretans, one of the two healthiest groups in his study, were very fond of organ meats like liver, kidney, and spleen. The Cretans also consumed more snails than anyone in the world and copious amounts of a wild plant called purslane, which has high levels of omega-3 fatty acids (the kind found in fatty fish).[19]

"I have seen the ravages of the low-fat, no-fat diet craze, and they are alarming." Dermatologist Dr. Nicolas Perricone, *The Perricone Prescription,* 2002.

Dr. Uffe Ravnskov points out many fallacies in the Seven Countries Study. Keys picked 7 countries from a potential list of 22. According to Ravnskov, he chose the ones that supported his hypothesis and ignored the ones that did not. For example, Finland and Mexico had similar rates of fat consumption, but Finland had seven times as many coronary deaths as Mexico. Finland was selected for the study; Mexico was not, even though data was available for both countries.[20] Subsequent studies have also found enormous differences in heart disease rates within countries, despite consistent cholesterol levels.[21] Recent research has

---

16 A. Keys, *Seven countries: a multivariate analysis of death and coronary heart disease,* Harvard University Press, London, 1980.

17 Ancel and Margaret Keys, *Eat Well, Stay Well,* 1959, *The Benevolent Bean*, 1967, and *Eat Well, Stay Well the Mediterranean Way,* Doubleday, 1975.

18 "The Fat of the Land," *Time Magazine,* January 13, 1961, Vol. LXXVII No.3.

19 William Hoffman, "Meet Monsieur Cholesterol," *University of Minnesota Update,* Winter, 1979.

20 Uffe Ravnskov, M.D., Ph.D., *The Cholesterol Myths: Exposing the Fallacy that Satuurated Fat and Cholesterol Cause Heart Disease,* 2003.

21 "Ancel Keys," *The Daily Telegraph,* London, December 17, 2004.

discovered that the level of C-reactive protein, a marker for inflammation, which is believed to cause damage to the lining of the blood vessels, and the level of homocysteine, which is related to the buildup of plaque in the arteries and the tendency to form clots, seem to be better indicators of risk for coronary events than cholesterol.[22]

It's Not the Pasta!

It looks like the mystery of the Mediterranean diet has finally been solved. Researchers at the Monell Chemical Senses Center report that freshly pressed olive oil contains a natural anti-inflammatory agent, which they named *oleocanthal.* The name is derived from *oleo* (olive) and *canth* (sting) because it is the chemical that gives premium olive oil its distinctive, throat-irritating sting. It has the same medicinal effect as ibuprofen and other non-steroidal anti-inflammatory drugs that inhibit the COX enzymes. Only very fresh, extra-virgin olive oil contains the compound, since it disappears quickly with age and when heated.[23] The Cretans ate freshly-pressed olive oil daily. The other group who came out on top in Key's study was the Japanese, whose diet included large quantities of fish. Fish oil has also been shown to reduce inflammation.

Note: Ancel Keys presented his theory about saturated fats at a meeting of The World Health Organization in 1955. According to colleague, Harry Blackburn, his ideas were challenged "in a way that only a distinguished British Intellectual could do it…He cited a piece—destroyed. He got up from being knocked to the ground and went out saying, 'I'll show those guys,' and designed the Seven Countries Study."[24]

Over the next 20 years the National Institutes of Health spent millions of dollars trying to prove the hypothesis put forth by Keys, the man who was nicknamed "Mr. Cholesterol." Five major studies failed to show any connection. A sixth study concluded that cholesterol-lowering *drugs* could help prevent heart disease. "According to Basil Rifkind, the man who oversaw the trials for the NIH, they had failed to demonstrate, at great expense, that eating less fat had any health benefits, but if a cholesterol-lowering *drug* could prevent heart attacks, then a low-fat, cholesterol-lowering *diet* should do the same. 'It is an imperfect world. The data that would be definitive is ungettable, so you do your best with what is available.' "[25]

In 1977 a Senate committee headed by George McGovern published its *Dietary Goals for the United States* and, as might be expected when politicians interpret science, politics prevailed. They recommended that all Americans over two years of age reduce their fat intake. The press picked up on the recommendations as if they were based on scientific

---

22 Sally Fallon with Mary G. Enig, Ph.D., *Nourishing Traditions: The Cookbook that Challenges Politically Correct Nutrition and the Diet Dictocrats,* Second Edition, 1999, New Trends Publishing, Inc.

23 Gary K. Beauchamp, Russell S. J. Keast, Diane Morel, Jianming Lin, Jana Pika, Qiang Han, Chi-Ho Lee, Amos B. Smith, and Paul A. S. Breslin, "Phytochemistry: Ibuprofen-like activity in extra-virgin live oil," *Journal Nature,* September, 2005, p. 45.

24 Harry Blackburn, quoted in *Health Revolutionary: The Life and Work of Ancel Keys,* 2002, Hall—Foushee Productions, Minneapolis, MN.

25 Gary Taubes, "What if It's All Been a Big Fat Lie?" *The New York Times,* July 7, 2002.

proof, rather than the opinions of a few staff members of a Senate committee, and the American public swallowed it, hook, line, and sinker. (Whistle blower, Gary Taubes, after reviewing the tapes of the hearings, exposed the lack of scientific evidence and the absence of consensus behind the Senate's guidelines in his March, 2001, article in the journal *Science*, "The Soft Science of Dietary Fats," [26] and a 2002 article in The New York Times, "What if It's All Been a Big Fat Lie?" [27]

> "...dieting may be the major cause of obesity."
> Jean-Paul Deslypere, Professor of Human Nutrition, University of Ghent

There were many dissenters to the Senate recommendations. Among them, E. H. "Pete" Ahrens, chairman of the Diet-Heart Review Panel of the National Heart Institute and his panel of ten experts who feared that changing the ratio of fats in the human body could have negative consequences. They warned, "The brain, for instance, is 70% fat, which chiefly serves to insulate neurons. Fat is the primary component of cell membranes. This could conceivably change the membrane permeability, which controls the transport of everything from glucose, signaling proteins, and hormones to bacteria, viruses, and tumor-causing agents into and out of the cell. The relative saturation of fats in the diet could also influence cellular aging as well and the clotting ability of blood cells."[28]

> "As if things weren't bad enough after we started harvesting grains in the Fertile Crescent, sometime in the early eighties we got it in our fool heads that we should eat less fat."
> Ariel Levy, "Carb Panic," *New York Magazine*, December 16, 2002.

Low-Fat No-Fat Frenzy:

It didn't take long for food manufacturers to learn that they could replace the expensive proteins and fats in their products with cheap sugar and starch. As long as it was labeled "fat-free" we would buy it. According to USDA agricultural economist, Judith Putnam, the major trends in the American diet since the late '70s have been a decrease in the percentage of fat calories and a "greatly increased consumption of carbohydrates. (Annual grain consumption has increased almost 60 pounds per person and caloric sweeteners, primarily high-fructose corn syrup, by 30 pounds.)"[29]

> "They say, 'You really need a high level of proof to change the recommendations,' which is ironic, because they never had a high level of proof to set them." Dr. Walter Willett, of the Harvard School of Public Health, on why government agencies did not change their guidelines to fit the data from three National Institutes of Health studies.[30]

The beginning of the obesity epidemic in America coincides with the flood of low-fat propaganda from government agencies in the late '70s. Exercise became an obsession. Gyms started to spring up everywhere, and early morning joggers took to the pavement as people tried to outrun their potbellies and love handles.

---

26   Gary Taubes, "The Soft Science of Dietary Fats," the journal *Science*, March, 2001.

27   Gary Taubes, "What if It's All Been a Big Fat Lie?" *The New York Times*, July 7, 2002.

28   Gary Taubes, "The Soft Science of Dietary Fats," *Science*, March, 2001.

29   Gary Taubes, "What if It's All Been a Big Fat Lie?" *The New York Times*, July 7, 2002.

30   Gary Taubes, "The Soft Science of Dietary Fats," *Science*, March, 2001.

A "Healthy" Diet for America:

In 1992 the USDA published its *Food Guide Pyramid* as a guide to a "healthy" diet. We were encouraged to eat six to nine servings of bread, pasta, rice, and cereal per day and to use fats "sparingly." Dietary guidelines from the American Heart Association and other nutritional groups recommended that we should get at least half of our calories from carbohydrates and no more than 30 percent from fat. According to an article in *Scientific American*, there was no scientific evidence that showed *any* health benefits that could be attributed to a low-fat diet. "The 30 percent limit was essentially drawn from thin air."[31] From 1991 to 2001, our obesity rate increased from 12 to 20 percent and the diabetes rate doubled.[32]

The American Heart Association's "Heart-Check" seal of approval can be displayed on any food that is low in fat, saturated fat, cholesterol, and salt as long as one serving contains ten percent of the daily value of *any one* of the following: protein, vitamin A, vitamin C, calcium, or fiber. There is no mention of the sugar or trans fat content. It could be 90 percent sugar and 10 percent sawdust and still qualify. A quick scan for products bearing the AHA symbol at my local grocery disclosed that Cocoa Puffs®, which lists sugar as the first ingredient, qualifies as "heart-healthy." Bruce's Whole Yams in Heavy Syrup was also deemed worthy to sport the red-heart-with-a-white-checkmark symbol. But for shear audacity, nothing tops Kellogg's® new Heart Start® Healthy Heart cereal which lists various kinds of sugar *twelve* times on the nutrition label and comes in at a whopping 46 grams of carbohydrate per serving—it also contains partially hydrogenated oil.

In January of 2005, the USDA released the *New Dietary Guidelines for Americans 2005*. It is an improvement over the 1992 Pyramid, but we are still being told that the largest part of our diet should come from grains, half of which can be refined starches. The old pyramid recommended 6 to 11 servings per day; the new one says 5 to 8 ounces of grain, which translates to 5 to 8 cups of cereal, 2½ to 4 cups of rice or pasta, or 5 to 8 slices of bread. Add the recommended 3 cups of milk (33 grams of lactose, the equivalent of 8.25 teaspoons of table sugar) and you will understand why the little man has to run up the stairs.

Three Quotes from the Harvard School of Public Health's web site:
"The USDA's MyPyramid also had many builders. Some are obvious—USDA scientists, nutrition experts, staff members, and consultants. Others aren't. Intense lobbying efforts from a variety of food industries also helped shape the pyramid."

"Released in early January 2005, the Dietary Guidelines for Americans 2005 continues to reflect the tense interplay of science and the powerful food industry."

"The guidelines suggest that it is fine to consume half our grains as refined starch. That's a shame, since refined starches behave like sugar. They add empty calories, have adverse metabolic effects, and increase the risks of diabetes and heart disease."

---

[31] Walter C. Willet and Meir J. Stampfer, "Rebuilding the Food Pyramid," *Scientific American*, January 2003.

[32] Anne Underwood, "New Ideas About Diabetes," *Newsweek*, January 20, 2003.

Where we are:

We are both lucky and unlucky enough to be living in a time and a place of unprecedented abundance. We can choose what we eat and eat only the things we like best. We are the end result of survival. For thousands of years the human race survived through feast and famine, through floods and droughts, through wars and devastation. Glaciers advanced and receded, and volcanic eruptions blocked out the sun for years at a time. The biggest challenge our stone-age parents faced was getting enough to eat (that, and not being eaten themselves). Who survived? Those who could sock away the most in reserve during the fat times to get them through the lean. We are programmed to gorge ourselves when food is available so we'll have fat to burn when it's gone. But we are caught in an endless summer of prosperity.

I've often wondered how something that has as much reward value as sugar could be bad for us. The answer is that it was *not* bad for us; in fact it could have been a lifesaver in the old days, but we were never meant to get so much of it and in such concentrated form. (Now even kids are suffering from what used to be the ills of middle age. What was once called "adult onset diabetes" is now called "type 2 diabetes." One in three children born in 2000 will become diabetic if the current trend continues.)[33] We have consumed more starch and sugar in the first few decades of life than our bodies are equipped to handle in a lifetime. Our cells become resistant to the huge amounts of insulin necessary to process it. Our overworked insulin-producing cells tire and eventually wear out, no longer able to keep up with the daily onslaught of fries, pizza, soft drinks, doughnuts, and Oreos®.[34]

The good news is that the tide may be turning. I have known very few people who lost weight on low-fat diets, and what they did lose usually came back with baggage. But in the last few years, a lot of people have lost large amounts of weight. You probably know some of them (or you may *be* one of them); and we have all seen celebrities who have slimmed down dramatically. Some have become poster children for bariatric surgery, but many relate that they were finally able to shed the pounds by eliminating "white foods" (bread, rice, pasta, potatoes, flour, and sugar). Apparently, people are taking matters into their own hands, emboldened by the constant stream of articles and news stories about study after study that consistently report that low-carbohydrate diets surpass low-fat diets in every comparison and with none of the dire consequences that were predicted. After years of being relegated to the lunatic fringe, low-carb dieting has at last gained some respect.

The Weight of the Evidence:

The medical establishment continues to have a hard time accepting a concept so diametrically opposed to the stand they have held for three decades, although, to their credit, many doctors are learning from their patients when they witness such dramatic results. New studies are validating that low-carb dieting works, that subjects lose more fat and less muscle than those on a high-carb/low-fat diet. It produces more weight loss on the same number of calories. It consistently improves blood lipid profiles, lowers blood pressure, and reduces cardiovascular and diabetes risk factors. Subjects experience a drop

---

33   Janet McConnaughey, "1 in 3 children Born in 2000 at Risk for Diabetes," *The Seattle Times*, June 15, 2003.

34   Michael R. Eades, M.D. and Mary Dan Eades, M.D., *Protein Power*, 1999, p. 311.

in cholesterol and they report that they feel better. (In one recent study, directed by Penelope Greene of the Harvard School of Public Health, a group who ate 300 calories more per day on a low-carb diet lost more weight than the low-fat dieters who were following the guidelines of the American Medical Association.) Interestingly, when the newspapers report the test results, they continue to include disclaimers, such as, "long-term effects unknown," "more study needed," "caution advised," and usually a quote from a nutritionist at the end insisting, "It's calories, calories, calories." The medical establishment seems to be advocating that we should choose to be sick now, rather than risk becoming sick 20 years from now.

> Weight loss has become an extreme sport on reality TV. If low-calorie and low-fat dieting don't work, and low-carb is anathema, then the only thing left is—exercise. That way, if the diet doesn't work, then you can blame the dieter. I actually had a window washer, standing on top of a ladder washing skylights, tell me that he couldn't lose weight because he didn't get enough exercise.

On February 8, 2006, the *Journal of the American Medical Association* reported the results of a huge government study, involving 49,000 women, designed to show the effects of a low-fat diet on women's health. After eight years, the women who both significantly reduced the amount of fat in their diet and increased their consumption of fruits, vegetables, and grains, had the same rates of breast cancer, colon cancer, strokes, and heart disease as those who ate whatever they pleased.[35] But old convictions are tenacious, even among scientists. The researchers expressed disappointment with the findings and made excuses: the test may not have lasted long enough; the participants may have started too late; they may not have reduced the fats low enough; they may have eaten the wrong fats; and they remained obese, which is, in itself, a risk factor. Did I get that right? They are explaining away the test results by blaming the fact that the women were still fat? After eight years on a low-fat diet? (According to Dr. Michael R. Eades' analysis of the data, all the women in the study also ate fewer calories. They reported that they ate 300 fewer calories a day, which over eight years should have resulted in a loss of 250 pounds each, "which would have been difficult since they started with an average weight of 170 pounds."[36]

The picture that accompanied the article in my local paper showed one of the participants eating a healthful meal. It consisted of a banana, a low-fat fruit yogurt, and what appeared to be canned peaches. By my calculations, that "healthy" meal contained over six tablespoonfuls of sugar.

Berkeley statistician, Dr. David A. Freedman, said that the overall message from the study was clear: "We, in the scientific community, often give strong advice based on flimsy evidence. That's why we have to do experiments."[37]

---

35 "The Women's Health Initiative Randomized Controlled Dietary Modification Trial," *Journal of the American Medical Association*, February 8, 2006, Vol. 296 No.

36 Posted by Michael R. Eades, M.D. on February 9, 2006 11:57p.m., www.proteinpower.com/drmike/archives/2006/02/man_bites_dog_i_html.

37 Gina Kolata, "Low-Fat Diet Does Not Cut Health Risks, Study Finds," *The New York Times*, February 8, 2006.

A recent study of people with Type 2 diabetes showed that restricting carbohydrates resulted in significant improvement in weight and glycemic control. The small study compared two groups of diabetics, a control group on a diet with 55 to 60 percent carbohydrate, and one with 20 percent carbohydrate. After six months, two thirds of the people on the high-carb diet switched sides when they saw how much better the low-carb faction was doing. Twenty-two months later, most of the low-carb subjects were continuing the regimen and still improving. More than half of the people who stayed in the high-carb group experienced "episodes of cardiovascular disease," but there were none among the patients who continued on or switched to the low-carb diet.[38]

When a spokesman for the American Diabetes Association was questioned about why his organization continues to recommend a high-carb diet, he replied that people don't like low-carb diets and won't stick to them, so they don't ask them to.[39]

> The most common criticism of low-carb diets is that they don't include enough fruits and vegetables. What would happen if you cut out *all* of the sugar and refined starch in your diet and replaced it with low-carb fruits and vegetables? The average American gets 4.6 servings of fruits and vegetables per day (and this includes *potatoes* which were counted as a vegetable), rather than the five to nine recommended by the USDA.[40] It is a rare day when I don't exceed the recommended number of servings of fruit and vegetables on my low-carb regimen (and not one of mine is potatoes).
>
> "I eat more vegetables than the average vegetarian." Dr. Robert Atkins

"Many people are essentially cured of their [type 2] diabetes by low-carbohydrate diets, but that message is not getting out....even organizations that claim to be opposed to low-carb diets are backing into acceptance with the approximations of diets based on glycemic index and the notion of avoiding refined sugars and starch....Even the ADA [American Diabetes Association] is probably trying to back into carbohydrate restriction with a minimum of losing face." Dr. Richard C. Feinman, Professor of Biochemistry at the State University of New York Downstate Medical Center, Brooklyn, New York, and Editor in Chief of the journal *Nutrition & Metabolism.*

I frequently say that low carb saved my vanity, but it saved my husband's life. When the results of his first post-diet medical checkup arrived in the mail, the doctor had written, "Way to go!" across the bottom. That was six years ago. Still, when I call the doctor's office and get put on hold, I hear a taped message that warns against "low carb *fad* diets that tend to resurface every ten years or so—because they don't work." Sorry, voice, but the cat won't go back in the bag so easily this time. Too many of us have tried it and experienced the benefits first hand. It's the scare tactics that no longer "work."

How low-carb diets work:
There are many gurus, many systems. New books are hitting the shelves and reaching the

---

38 Jørgen Vesti Nielsen and Eva Joensson, "Low-carbohydrate diet in type 2 diabetes. Stable improvement of bodyweight and glycemic control during 22 month follow-up," *Nutrition and Metabolism*, 2006, 3:22 (article available at http://www.nutritionandmetabolism.com/content/3/1/22).

39 Nielsen, J. V., *Nutrition and Metabolism*, June 14, 2006; *online open access journal*, Richard Feinman, Ph.D., professor of biochemistry, SUNY Downstate Medical Center, Brooklyn, N.Y., Nathaniel G. Clark, M.D., vice president for clinical affairs and youth strategies, American Diabetes Association.

40 Geoffrey Cowley, "A Better Way to Eat," *Newsweek*, January 20, 2003, p. 52.

top of the best-seller list every day. They vary in the details, but what they all have in common is that they all restrict starch and sugar consumption in order to control insulin, the hormone that triggers fat storage. I suggest that everyone read one of these books. In fact, you should probably read more than one, and then you can pick and choose what suits you best. They are all based on the same basic premise: that controlling blood sugar by restricting carbohydrates is the key to good health and weight control. To put it in a nutshell, carbohydrates cause the pancreas to release insulin. Insulin is required to store fat. So—eat fewer carbohydrates—store less fat.

> "The whole principle, the reason we restrict carbs, is so that fat becomes your source of energy. What the critics are really saying is, burning your fat is dangerous. Well, saying that if a person is 80 pounds overweight it's dangerous for him to lose fat is just about as stupid as it sounds." Dr. Robert Atkins

The body prefers to burn carbohydrates and to hang on to all the fat it has stored up as insurance against starvation. Once the starches and sugars are no longer available, the metabolism switches to "famine mode" and starts to burn fat. Bread, pasta, rice, corn, potatoes, and sugar are the bad guys. (Starch is converted to sugar when it is digested, so all of these are, in effect, sugar.) Protein, natural fats, low-starch vegetables, and low-sugar fruits are the good guys.

Nutritionists have been taught to believe that man is a machine fueled by calories; that the only way to lose a calorie is to burn a calorie. But nature is flexible; nature adjusts; nature compensates. We have hormones to act as modulators. Anyone who has ever been on a diet knows about "plateaus," those stalemate situations that happen when your body adjusts your metabolism to maintain the *status quo*. You are taking in less, but your weight doesn't budge. It has also been well established that when we reduce our total intake of food and restrict fat consumption, our metabolism reacts by slowing down and storing fat, rather than burning it, to help us through a perceived season of want. When the diet is over, we have to eat less than we did before to stay at our original weight. We have been *starvation proofed* by Mother Nature. To nature, it is not a problem; it is a solution to a problem.

It stands to reason that if calories can be conserved, then they can also be squandered. Until we are willing to go hungry for half the year (or until some real calamity forces us to), we have to convince our bodies that it's OK to use up our energy reserves. We can do this the same way our ancestors did, by cutting down on carbohydrates as though we were living through a dry season in the Kalahari Desert or a frigid winter in Siberia.

"Use your common sense," we hear, "fat makes you fat." And it is true that we have heard this for so long and from so many sources, that it has become part of our core belief system; one that we accept in spite of overwhelming evidence that what we've been doing for the last 30 years doesn't work. It requires a real leap of faith to say, "What if we've been wrong? What if it's sugar that makes you fat?" and to take that first bite of the forbidden food.

Improve your anatomy with surgery?
I find it incredible that many medical professionals are advising patients to have their digestive systems surgically redesigned. Do they really believe that there is something

THE PROCRUSTEAN SOLUTION

Bariatric surgery has become big business. It is being promoted as the only reliable solution for morbid obesity. Malabsorptive operations are the most common type used. In these procedures, most of the stomach is sealed off and the small intestine is rearranged in order to reduce the amount of food that can be absorbed. One in five patients have complications, one in twenty have serious cardiovascular complications (heart attacks, strokes, or severe high blood pressure), and one in 200 patients dies. Lawsuit settlements are generally not publicized but have been as high as $1.6 million and have raised the cost of malpractice insurance.[41]

Although the long-term risks are not fully known, many patients suffer from nutritional deficiencies, osteoporosis, and anemia, and 5 percent regain all the lost weight. If food addiction was the cause of obesity, it may be replaced by an even more destructive addiction, such as alcohol or drugs.

Gastric bypass surgery is the equivalent of cutting off your feet to fit the bed. If you correct the shortcomings of your diet, you shouldn't need to shorten your intestinal tract.

physically wrong with the anatomy of Americans? Something that changed in a very short span of time? According to the American Society for Bariatric Surgery, over 170,000 people in the United States had stomach reduction surgery in 2005. These horrendous procedures work by causing the patients to become physically ill when they eat. Couldn't they just take a pill that makes them sick and skip the surgery? I would hope these people have tried a low-carb diet and that such a drastic measure is a last resort. Even when this is the case, it might have been the fact that they were unable to stick to the regimen that caused the failure, not that it didn't work.

What works:

I have had many friends tell me that they have tried a low-carbohydrate diet, and that *it was the only one that ever worked for them*, but they couldn't stay on it because they missed their favorite foods too much. What we need is a "New *Cuisine* Revolution" to provide appetizing food that doesn't leave us feeling deprived, even if we must stay on the diet forever—a fact of life for many of us. Boring food ensures failure for any long-term weight-control plan. The urge to binge will become increasingly irresistible. The diet that works is the one that keeps us satisfied. We don't have to be disciplined, but we do have to be clever and inventive.

"Will power lasts about two weeks and is soluble in alcohol."
Mark Twain

My purpose in writing this book is to provide alternatives for the starches and sweets that make up such a large part of our traditional fare. I have scoured the supermarkets, scrutinized labels, and researched every source I could find to make it possible to continue to enjoy the foods that I love. I have been cooking this new way for more than six years now, and many of my friends have been urging me to share some of my more successful dishes so that we don't all have to start from scratch to reinvent healthful, natural food.

---

41   Milt Freudenheim, "Bariatric surgery risks raise malpractice insurance," *The New York Times,* May 27, 2005.

> "Foreigners cannot enjoy our food, I suppose, any more than we can enjoy theirs. It is not strange; for tastes are made, not born." Mark Twain from *A Tramp Abroad*

I invite you to be adventurous. Keep an open mind. So what if we have to give up a few foods? There's no reason to feel deprived. The world is a big place with an inexhaustible diversity of flavors, tastes, and textures to be explored. I've put some strange dishes on the table in the last few years, but we've found many delicacies that we would never have known about if we were still having the same old bread and potatoes. (Did you know that when potatoes were first introduced to Europeans, they didn't like them? The English considered them "trash food" and the Irish preferred their oat porridge; even the pigs didn't eat them.)[42] Much of what makes up our likes and dislikes depends on familiarity. Babies are born with a preference for sweet; everything else is an acquired taste. Dinner is an adventure at my house these days. Fortunately, my husband is a courageous man!

PubMed Central (PMC) is the U.S. National Institutes of Health (NIH) free digital archive of biomedical and life sciences journal literature. Abstracts or full articles about research studies are available on the PubMed web site: www.pubmedcentral.nih.gov.

---

[42] Larry Zuckerman, *The Potato, How the Humble Spud Rescued the Western World*, North Point Press, New York, 1998.

GETTING STARTED

CHOOSE A PLAN

Here are my summaries of some of the more popular low-carb diet books. I suggest that you read several of them so that you understand the basic concepts and can then tailor your own regimen to your taste. Each author has a particular point of view as well as certain peccadilloes, but I have found something useful from nearly every one.

Robert Atkins, M.D. *Dr. Atkins' New Diet Revolution,* **Avon Books, New York, 1992.**
Dr. Robert Atkins, the much-maligned alternative thinker, dared to challenge the medical establishment with his *Diet Revolution,* first published in 1972. He was hauled before Congress to defend his radical and "potentially dangerous" advice on nutrition.

Fortunately, he lived long enough to see the beginnings of his vindication in the media, although his many followers already had no doubts, having proved the effectiveness of his system for themselves. Many people learned about it by word of mouth, as I did, from friends who can only be described as "giddy with relief" to discover that they were not, after all, lazy, undisciplined gluttons because low-fat dieting and exercise did not work for them.

The Atkins plan starts with an Induction Diet phase that lasts a minimum of two weeks. Carbohydrates are limited to 20 grams per day. This extremely low level is designed to induce ketosis, a state in which the body burns stored fat for energy. The next stage is the Ongoing Weight-loss Diet, in which carbohydrates are added in increments of 5 grams per week. When you are within 5 to 10 pounds of your goal weight, you move to Pre-maintenance and the carb allowance goes up 10 grams per week as long as weight loss continues. When your target weight is reached, you begin the Maintenance Diet. When you have maintained your goal weight for at least a month, you have found your Atkins Carbohydrate Equilibrium or ACE. If you go above this level, you gain weight, so this is your maximum. Your ACE may range from 40 to 120 or more Net Carbs per day, depending on your metabolism, age, gender, and activity level.

The Atkins' plan sets no limit on the amount of food you can eat, excluding hunger as a factor. Vitamin and mineral supplementation is encouraged. Caffeine and alcohol are not allowed on the Induction Diet and are limited in the other phases. Sugar, refined starches, and trans fats are never allowed.

Michael R. Eades, M.D., and Mary Dan Eades, M.D., *Protein Power,* **Bantam, 1996, and** *Protein Power Lifeplan,* **Warner Books, Inc., New York, 2000.**
Dr. Michael Eades and his wife Dr. Mary Dan Eades endeavor to explain why our modern day diet is neither natural nor healthy for the human race. According to the authors, 99.995 percent of our genes are identical to humans who lived 10,000 years ago. We are virtually the same as our hunter/gatherer forebears. It was agriculture that opened a Pandora's box of human woes. Grain-based diets, while freeing mankind for the first time from dependence on wild game and vegetation, brought with it the many diseases of civilization. They cite as an example the ancient Egyptians, who had one of the earliest agricultural civilizations. Their health can be diagnosed through the examination of

thousands of mummies, as well as from their written documents, and although their diet was very similar to the one currently recommended by the American Medical Association, they suffered from arthritis, diabetes, heart disease, obesity, horrific dental problems, gum disease, and many of the same ills that plague us today.[1] A similar decline in health is evident throughout the world, whenever people changed from a high-protein to a high-carbohydrate diet.

The authors contend that most of us need more protein and a more natural balance of fats than we are currently getting. They advocate a return to the basic diet of our ancestors, one high in meat, fish, poultry, fruits, berries, and vegetables, but low in grains, refined sugars, and concentrated starches (which were unknown to early humans). The typical American diet consists mainly of carbohydrates and fat. The fat is not a problem except in combination with carbohydrates.

The cornerstone of the Protein Power plan is the minimum protein requirement. They include a formula for determining your individual daily protein need, based on your Lean Body Mass index. This is a minimum; you may have more but not less.

The Eadeses devote about the same amount of space in their books to explaining why we also need a balance of the different kinds of natural fats (including saturated fats) in our diets. (They could just as appropriately have called their book *Fat Power*, but perhaps they wouldn't have sold any!) They do warn, however, about excessive amounts of fat; if there is a constant supply of fat in the diet, the body won't bother to burn stored fat.

Intervention, Transition, and Maintenance make up the three levels of the diet, but you may also choose whether to be a Purist, a Dilettante, or a Hedonist, depending on your health needs and lifestyle. The Purist is the person who needs to adopt the most stringent regimen in order to reap the most benefits; the Dilettante follows a middle-of-the-road philosophy, while the Hedonists are the people who want to improve their health with a minimum of sacrifice. Regardless of which plan you choose, your carbohydrate limit and your minimum protein requirement will be the same at each level.

Intervention Level starts at 40 grams of carbohydrate a day in order to induce the metabolic shift to burning fat for energy. For some, Intervention may take only a few days, for others, it will be until their underlying health problems have been resolved. Transition Level, at 60 carbs per day, can last a few months. If everything remains stable, you may move to Maintenance with a carb allowance of 80, then gradually increase the amount up to 120.

The Eadeses were the first to introduce the concept that the fiber content of foods can be subtracted from the carb total, since it is indigestible. They coined the term Effective Carbohydrate Content, or ECC. Atkins adopted the concept, but he called it the Net Carb Count, the term that is now most widely used.

The Eadeses consider the glycemic index (the rate at which foods are digested) to be of little value since foods are seldom eaten alone, and the fiber, protein, and fat of other foods eaten at the same time will affect how quickly all are absorbed.

---

[1] Aidan Cockburn, *Mummies, Disease and Ancient Cultures,* Cambridge University Press, U.K., 1980.

Christian B. Allan, Ph.D., and Wolfgang Lutz, M.D., *Life Without Bread: How a Low-carbohydrate Diet Can Save Your Life,* **McCraw-Hill, New York, 2000.**
The first edition of *Leben ohne Brot (Life without Bread)* was published in German in 1967, five years before Atkins published his *Diet Revolution.* The book, now in its ninth printing, is based on the clinical experience of Dr. Lutz, an Austrian physician who has successfully treated thousands of patients over several decades.

You won't find a more simple diet than this one. The authors' take-home message about low-carbohydrate eating is this: "Restrict all carbohydrates to 72 utilizable grams per day. Eat as much of everything else as you want." Lutz and Allan explain that low-carb nutrition is not just for weight loss, but for the prevention and treatment of many health problems, like heart disease, diabetes, and Crohn's disease.

The foods that are restricted are the usual suspects: all carbohydrate foods (breads, pastas, cereals, grains, potatoes, pastries, bagels); sweet fruits; sweetened foods (yogurt, drinks, desserts, candy); and dried fruits.

The science behind the diet is explained clearly; all carbohydrates are simply different kinds of sugar. Simple carbohydrates, such as sugar and honey contain one or two sugar molecules. Complex carbohydrates, like bread and potatoes, contain many. Although it takes a little longer, they are broken down into simple sugars by digestive enzymes. "When you eat any carbohydrate you are essentially eating sugar." They state that your body is capable of making everything it needs out of fat and protein and that there is no such thing as an essential carbohydrate.

In addition, they warn, "Don't skimp on fat." Since most people are addicted to carbohydrates, one must eat plenty of fats to kill the urge for more and more carbohydrates. The authors point out that, contrary to popular wisdom, saturated fats are very healthful. Research has repeatedly emphasized the value of antioxidants, yet seems to have overlooked the important fact that, unlike unsaturated fat, saturated fat alone can resist oxidation. Saturated fat does not require a secondary molecule, such as an antioxidant, to eliminate the negative effect of oxidation.

Dr. Richard F. Heller and Dr. Rachael F. Heller, *The Carbohydrate Addict's Lifespan Program,* Plume, New York, 1998.
The authors don't claim that their diet works for everyone, only the ones who are addicted to carbohydrates. According to them, it is the insulin that is produced in response to carbohydrate consumption that triggers cravings. Their regimen consists of two very low-carb "craving-reducing meals" and one "reward meal" each day. When you eat carbohydrates, insulin is released in two waves. The Hellers believe the amount of insulin your body releases at the beginning of each meal is preset at a level determined by the amount of carbohydrate you have eaten in the last 12 to 24 hours. By keeping the preceding meals low in carbohydrates, this initial wave of insulin will be kept to a minimum. A second wave of insulin, released about 70 minutes after the first bite of the current meal, would normally compensate for any difference. If you finish your reward meal within one hour, however, you short circuit the process and prevent the release of the second wave of insulin and the resulting cravings for more carbs.

The reward meal starts with two cups of salad, followed by equal portions of protein, low-starch vegetables, and carbohydrate-rich foods, including desserts. You may have as much of any one kind of food as you want as long as you also eat an equal portion from the other two categories. You cannot have more dessert, for example, without eating more protein and vegetables as well.

The Hellers contend that for carbohydrate addicts, just the sensation of sweetness is enough to cause a surge of insulin in anticipation of sugar, even if the sweet taste comes from a sugar substitute. For this reason, they recommend that all sweets, even sugar-free ones, be limited to the reward meal only.

The second part of their plan is Options for Life. After the initial two weeks on the diet, you select from a list of options, such as adding exercise or eliminating caffeine.

Steven Rosenblatt, M.D., Ph.D., and Cameron Stauth, *The Starch Blocker Diet,* **Harper Collins, New York, 2003.**
On this have-your-cake-and-eat-it-too diet, an extract from white kidney beans is used as a way to neutralize dietary starch. It selectively joins with the enzyme, alpha amylase, and prevents it from breaking down starch. The effect lasts for about an hour, during which two-thirds to three-fourths of the starch that is eaten will pass through the digestive system as whole molecules, just as fiber does. The author states that the extract has no significant side effects and that it doesn't prevent the absorption of vitamins, minerals, enzymes, and proteins from the starchy foods.

Dr. Rosenblatt believes that low-fat diets don't work because people cannot hold out against hunger for very long, and he condemns low-carb diets as being dangerous and ineffective, although it is unclear why an artificial reduction in starch would be safer than not eating the starch in the first place. The author actually advocates that we should eat *more* starchy foods to "maximize the power of the new way to lose weight," and the book contains 100 high-starch recipes. (Like we need that!)

As you might have guessed by now, philosophically, Dr. Rosenblatt and I part company early on, but I think he missed the greatest potential market for the product, which is as an aid to those of us who embrace a low-carb system. My own very unscientific test, with a sample of one (myself), seems to bear out the claims for the product; they do seem to help. I try not to consider it a license to binge, but there are times when you have to eat what is available to keep from going hungry or offending a host, for example, as well as those times when you give in to temptation. Some starch will still be digested by saliva, and that will not be affected. Remember, a starch blocker can only prevent the conversion of starch to sugar, so any sugar you eat still counts.

There are several brands of starch blockers on the market; look for one that lists only the extract of northern white kidney beans as an active ingredient, without stimulants or added sugar (the one with Dr. Rosenblatt's picture on the label contains sugar).

Arthur Agatston, M.D., *The South Beach Diet,* **Random House, New York, 2003.**
This plan attempts to be both low-carb and low-fat (the author denies that it is either), so it is a popular choice among the faint of heart who can't kick their fat phobia. Dr. Agatston's system eliminates saturated fats, uses low-fat cuts of meat and poultry, and calls for low-fat and fat-free versions of cheese, cream cheese, sour cream, milk, and

yogurt. It sacrifices some carb reduction (and some health benefits, in my opinion) by using low-fat products. Foods low on the glycemic index are emphasized. There is no counting calories or carbs and no measuring portions; you just limit your foods to the ones on his list.

The diet has three phases; the first one is similar to the Induction phase of Atkins—very low carb. No fruits, no dairy products (except low-fat cheese), no bread, cereal, or starches are allowed. You can spend 75 calories per day on "treats" (such as sugar-free gelatin, sugar-free Popsicles, and cocoa powder). After the first two weeks, you progress to Phase 2 when beans, fruits, and low-fat milk and yogurt are added. Whole-grains are allowed "sparingly" in Phase 2. Phase 3 has no food list; after you reach your desired weight, you add back additional carbs. Whenever you regain some weight, you switch back to Phase 1. The author says some people will fail on his diet—he attributes their failure to boredom with the food. He says they get bored and start to cheat.

Suzanne Somers, *Eat, Cheat, and Melt the Fat Away*, Crown Division of Random House, New York, 2001.

Suzanne Somers' books are not usually mentioned with the other low-carb diet books, the Bimbo factor may be to blame for that, but her diet is basically low-carb. She admits that it is the low-carb part that works for weight loss.

Her system involves separating foods into three categories, which are never eaten together. Proteins and fats are eaten with low-starch vegetables but not with carbohydrates. Complex carbohydrates are eaten with low-starch vegetables but not with fats or proteins. Fruit is in a third category and can only be eaten alone, on an empty stomach. After eating fruit, you must wait 20 minutes before eating carbohydrates or one hour before eating fats and proteins. There is also a time-lapse requirement when changing from a carbohydrate meal to a protein/fat meal and vice versa. Some foods, such as avocados and nuts, are prohibited since they contain both protein and/or fat combined with carbs and cannot be separated. Some others (bananas, coconut, buttermilk, all sweeteners except stevia and her own brand, and refined starches) are prohibited as "funky foods."

Her system is similar to the "Hay Diet" developed by Dr. William Hay in 1911. Dr. Hay blamed all illness on excess acid. I haven't found any convincing scientific research to back up the food separation theory, but you can try it and see if it works for you. Having several hours a day when you can't eat anything might make up for the extra carbs in her diet.

Dr. Diana Schwarzbein, *The Schwarzbein Principle, The Truth About Losing Weight, Being Healthy, and Feeling Younger*, Health Communications, Deerfield Beach, FL, 1999.

Although Dr. Schwarzbein endorses Suzanne Somers' diet and has written forwards for some of her books, her own book contradicts key elements of Somers' advice. Dr. Schwarzbein states that it is vital that fats, proteins, non-starchy vegetables, and carbohydrates be eaten together at every meal to slow down the digestion of the carbohydrates and prevent the release of excessive amounts of insulin. She cautions against eating carbohydrates alone because the body has no mechanism to prevent overindulgence for carbohydrates as it does for fats and proteins.

She advises dieters who need to lose weight to eat 15 to 30 grams of carbohydrates per meal, depending on their current weight and activity level. They should choose only natural, unprocessed carbohydrates, such as whole grains, legumes, vegetables, and fruits, which should be eaten in their natural state or cooked by simple methods. She recommends choosing fruits and vegetables that are low on the glycemic index. Non-starchy vegetables should be eaten at every meal and they can be excluded from the carb allowance totals.

She believes it is not necessary to limit the amount of protein in the diet and that it is un-natural and unhealthy to limit the consumption of healthy fats. Her list of good fats includes all natural fats that have not been modified by man. Bad fats are those that have been hydrogenated, oxidized, or damaged by heat.

The USDA food pyramid encourages excessive carbohydrate consumption and does not include enough fat and protein, according to Dr. Schwarzbein. She replaces it with the Schwarzbein Square in order to achieve a balance between insulin and glucagons, the hormones that regulate whether fat is stored or burned. She warns against severe carb restriction because she believes that very low insulin levels are dangerous and lead to hormonal imbalances and depression.

Dr. Peter D'Adamo, *Eat Right for Your Type,* G. P. Putnam's Sons, New York, 1996.
Naturopathic physician, Dr. Peter D'Adamo, believes that people's blood types determine what foods they should eat. He believes the different blood types originated at different times in human evolution. The O blood type is the oldest, so people with O blood should follow a low-carb diet like the early hunter/gatherers. Next came the A type, who were farmers, so they should be vegetarians. Then came the B type, who were herdsmen, so they may include dairy products. The AB group came last, and they are a combination of the A and B blood groups.

For each blood type, there are lists of foods described as *highly beneficial, neutral,* or *avoid,* based on Dr. D'Adamo's research into how each food reacts with the blood from the different groups. He provides a list of foods that promote weight gain and a list of foods that promote weight loss for each type.

Dr. D'Adamo also believes he can determine the personality of an individual by blood type and that he can prescribe the best kind of exercise for each: strenuous aerobic for *O*s; yoga and meditation for *A*s; moderate, like swimming and walking, for *B*s; and calming exercises and relaxation for *AB*s.

Since there are more type O people in the world, and we already know that low-carb diets work, his plan will look as if it is effective for the majority of people who try it, whether or not the science behind it is correct.

Barry Sears, Ph.D., *The Zone,* Harper Collins, New York, 1995.
"The Zone" is the metabolic state at which the body works at peak efficiency. Dr. Sears' system was designed as a way to use food to produce optimal performance for athletes. He recommends that the three different kinds of foods, carbohydrates, proteins, and fats, be eaten as blocks to provide hormonal balance. Too many carbohydrates produce excess insulin and take you out of the "zone."

On this plan, your weight, your percentage of body fat, and your level of physical activity serve as the basis for calculating the amount of protein you need. This amount is divided into blocks consisting of 7 grams of protein each. You must get this amount of protein, no more, no less. For each protein block, you should consume one carb block (of about 9 grams) and one fat block. There is an emphasis on low-glycemic carbohydrates and unsaturated fats.

To be in the "zone," forty percent of your calories should come from carbs, thirty percent from protein, and thirty percent from fats. Although lower in carbohydrates than the standard American diet, this plan is probably not low enough to produce weight loss for many people, and with the restrictions on the amount of food you are allowed, it may also leave you hungry, a definite negative.

Ray Audette, *Neander Thin: Eat Like a Caveman to Achieve a Lean, Strong, Healthy Body*, St. Martin's Press, New York, 1999.
The author developed his diet plan, also called the Paleolithic Diet, after becoming frustrated with the medical treatment he was receiving for diabetes and arthritis. After researching the causes of autoimmune disorders and diabetes, he concluded that our modern high-carbohydrate diet, with its highly processed foods, is to blame for many illnesses and diseases. By switching to a pre-agricultural, natural diet, he experienced dramatic improvement in his arthritis, his blood sugar levels returned to normal, and he lost 25 pounds.

Basically, his diet consists of limiting what you eat to foods that could be hunted or gathered from nature without benefit of technology. He has a list of foods that should never be eaten. The forbidden foods are:
- Grains—because they are not edible in their natural state, they must first be milled and processed, and also because they include two of the most common allergens, corn and wheat.
- Beans and potatoes—because they contain toxic alkaloids.
- Dairy products—because they are highly processed, and milk is the third most common allergen, after wheat and corn.
- Sugar—because, except for honey, it would not have been available to Paleolithic man.
- Additionally, he bans alcohol and coffee. He considers all of these foods to be addictive and harmful.

His list of foods that should be eaten include:
- Meat and fish—he considers these to be essential since all primates are carnivorous.
- Fruits—he recommends that low carbohydrate fruits, such as melons and tomatoes, be eaten fresh and raw. He cautions that selective breeding has produced fruit that is much larger and sweeter now than it was for early man.
- Vegetables—Mr. Audette recommends that vegetables make up a significant portion of the diet, although some vegetables, like corn and yams, are not allowed.
- Nuts and seeds—he believes these are important as sources of fat and calories. He excludes peanuts and cashews from the list since they are not tree nuts.
- Berries—Mr. Audette believes raw berries are good for weight loss.

- Fat—he believes fat should be the primary source of calories, and it is important to include sources for the essential fatty acids such as those found in meat, seafood, avocados, olive oil, and nuts.

Dr. Michael Eades, coauthor of *Protein Power*, wrote the forward to *NeaderThin,* and he clearly agrees with Mr. Audette, although his own plan is much more lenient.

Fred Pescatore, M.D., *The Hamptons Diet: Lose Weight Quickly and Safely with the Doctor's Delicious Meal Plans,* **John Wiley & Sons, New York, 2004.**

Dr. Pescatore promises: "Atkins results, Hampton's style, Mediterranean science." Dr. Pescatore was an associate medical director at the Atkins Center for five years. His program is definitely low in carbohydrates, but he has adopted an "if you can't beat 'em, join 'em" position on saturated fats.

The "Mediterranean science" refers to the use of monounsaturated oil, although the classic Mediterranean diet uses olive oil, and Pescatore prefers Australian macadamia nut oil (which he sells). It contains a higher concentration of monounsaturates than olive oil, and it has a higher smoke point. He puts no limit on the amount of fat in the diet as long as it is monounsaturated. (I'm not sure about the *Hampton's style* part; perhaps it's a warning that his oil is expensive.)

On this diet, you are to eat lots of fish (especially salmon), vegetables, nuts, some fruits, and lean protein. There is an emphasis on minimally processed whole foods, organic if possible. You avoid trans fats and limit saturated fats. Moderate consumption of alcohol is allowed; caffeine is not mentioned.

The Hampton's diet has three levels, based on how much weight you need to lose. The levels are called the *A list,* the *B list,* and the *C list.* *A* is for people with 10 pounds or more to lose, and it limits carbs to 30 a day. *B* is for people with fewer than 10 pounds to lose, and the carb limit is 40 to 60 grams a day. *C* is for maintenance, and the carb allowance ranges from 55 to 85 grams. There is a list of appropriate foods for each level.

Gary Heavin with Carol Coleman, *Curves: Permanent Results Without Permanent Dieting,* **Putnam, New York, 2003.**

The Curves program is more about exercise than diet, but it does have two different diet plans. (I have a friend who is a member who didn't even know a diet was part of the program.) Thirty minutes of exercise three times a week is supposed to be a realistic goal for "real women."

The book for members outlines two different eating plans. Both plans have three phases: the first one lasts one to two weeks, the second lasts until you reach your goal weight.

The low-carb diet plan is for women who have been overweight since childhood. It is very much like Atkins or *Protein Power* for the first two phases, with the exception that you do not have to count the carbs in low-starch vegetables or the 20 carbs in a daily protein shake (they don't say why the shake doesn't count). It starts with 20 grams of carbohydrate a day and increases up to 60 grams in the second phase.

The second diet plan is for everyone else; it is low calorie. It starts with 1,200 calories a day, then increases to 1,600. It calls for precise portion control.

Phase three for both plans is no dieting at all; in fact, the book recommends a whopping 2,500- to 3,000-calorie "tune-up" plan. Founder, Gary Heavin, believes that exercise will build muscle and allow you to eat without restriction. Eating the larger amount is supposed to rev up the metabolism, since the body has to burn more calories. (Sounds good, doesn't it? Burning all those extra calories will keep you from gaining weight—in your dreams!) When you regain the weight, you return to phase one. Supplements are encouraged, including vitamins, antioxidants, and essential fatty acids.

Jack Goldberg, Ph.D., and Karen O'Mara, D.O., *GO-Diet: The Goldberg—O'Mara Diet Plan, the Key to Weight Loss & Healthy Eating,* **Go Corp, 1999.**
Dr. Goldberg is a biochemist and research scientist. Dr. O'Mara is a specialist in intensive care medicine. They put the blame for excess weight on the combination of sugar and saturated fat and claim that their plan is a safe low-carbohydrate way to lose weight.

Basics of the GO-Diet:
- Cut down on carbohydrates (less than 50 grams per day, no more than 12 to 15 per meal).
- Eat more fiber (25 to 50 grams per day). Fiber is subtracted to produce net carbs.
- Eat 5 servings of high phytochemical-antioxident low-carb vegetables daily.
- Be sure that at least half of the daily fat intake is monounsaturated.
- Eat probiotic foods, like yogurt and kefir (8 ounces per day).
- Eat natural nutrients such as nuts, seeds, and wheat bran.
- Exercise if you choose; it is optional.

The 3-stage plan starts with a 3-day Induction. Carbs are cut to 50 per day, and you may eat only the listed foods. From days 4 to 7, you add more foods and increase the monounsaturated fats. Phase 3 lasts from day 7 on. Fiber intake is increased to 25 grams per day, and the list of permitted foods is increased.

Goldberg and O'Mara feel that ketosis is a safe and normal part of weight loss, but they do not advocate the use of the urine testing strips, which according to them, measure only one of several types of ketones and so will not give an accurate measure of all the ketones being burned.

One important contribution of this book concerns fermented dairy products. According to his own experiments, Dr. Goldberg found that in every cup of yogurt (made with live cultures), 8 grams of the sugar has been eaten by the lactobacillus bacteria. So even though the label must reflect the number of carbs in the milk that went into it, only about 4 grams per cup will remain. Cultured dairy products provide "good" bacteria for the digestive system that can usually be tolerated even by those who are allergic to lactose.

RECOMMENDED READING

Bowden, Jonny, M.A., C.N.S., *Living the Low Carb Life: Controlled-Carbohydrate Eating for Long-Term Weight Loss,* Sterling Publishing, New York, 2004, revised 2005.

Cordain, Loren, *The Paleo Diet: Lose Weight and Get Healthy by Eating the Food You Were Designed to Eat,* New York: John Wiley and Sons, 2002.

Donaldson, Blake F., M.D., *Strong Medicine,* Originally Published: 1960, Doubleday, New York, Subsequent Publication: 1962, Cassell, London.

Enig, Mary G., Ph.D., *Know Your Fats: The Complete Primer for Understanding the Nutrition of Fats, Oils and Cholesterol,* Bethesda Press, 2000.

Enig, Mary G., Ph.D., and Sally Fallon, *Eat Fat, Lose Fat: Lose Weight and Feel Great With The Delicious, Science-based Coconut Diet,* Hudson Street Press, 2004.

Fallon, Sally with Mary G. Enig, Ph.D, *Nourishing Traditions: The Cookbook that Challenges the Politically Correct Nutrition and the Diet Dictocrats,* New Trends Publishing, Inc., 1999.

Groves, Barry, *Eat Fat Get Thin,* Vermillion, 2000.

McCully, Kilmer S. and Martha McCully, *The Heart Revolution: the Extrodinary Discovery That Finally Laid the Cholesterol Myth to Rest,* Harper Paperbacks, 2000.

Mercola, Joseph, *The No-Grain Diet: Conquer Carbohydrate Addiction and Stay Slim for the Rest of Your Life,* Dutton, New York, 2003.

Moore, Jimmy, *Livin' La Vida Low-carb: My Journey from Flabby Fat to Sensationally Skinny in One Year,* Booklocker.com, 2005.

Price, Weston A., D.D.S., *Nutrition and Physical Degeneration,* McGraw-Hill, New York, 1939.

Ravnskov, Uffe, M.D., Ph.D., *The Cholesterol Myths: Exposing the Fallacy that Saturated Fat and Cholesterol Cause Heart Disease,* New Trends Publishing, Inc, 2000.

TIPS FOR EATING OUT

Many restaurants offer protein plates, and most will replace starchy side dishes with extra vegetables, fruit, cottage cheese, or salad if you ask. It's a lot easier if the rice, pasta, and potatoes are not there to tempt you. Bread is another matter, since in this country, there's usually a basket of bread placed on the table before you order, while you are hungry. My rule is: if it's ordinary cold bread, I push it away. If it's really good hot bread, I have one or two bites (with lots of butter).

Here are some other tips for eating out:

- The all-you-can-eat buffet restaurants are good for people with some will power. They usually have roast beef and chicken, baked fish, vegetables, and salads, but you have to show some restraint at the dessert bar (that's a lot easier to do if you have sugar-free ice cream and cake or pie waiting for you at home).

- Many sandwich shops will make any sandwich into a salad, and some have a low-carb wrap as a bread option.

- Many fast-food restaurants offer main-dish salads with meat and cheese.

- I put a low-carb tortilla in my pocket when I'm going shopping or on an outing with family or friends. I can order any sandwich without a bun and turn it into a wrap. Fajitas at a Mexican restaurant taste just as good on my own tortillas, and I save 17 carbs for each one. At a pizza place, I can invert a pan pizza onto my tortilla and peel off the crust. (The last time I served on a jury, pizza was brought in for lunch while we were sequestered; fortunately, I had taken a tortilla along so I made a pepperoni-pizza taco. It was delicious!) The tortillas need to be stored in the refrigerator, otherwise I would just leave some in my car.

- You can have Mu Shu Pork or Peking Duck at a Chinese restaurant if you take along a few Crêpes to use rather than the traditional Mandarin pancakes. Low-carb flour tortillas also work.

- Here in the Northwest we have Ivar's seafood bars, which offer crab or shrimp cocktails as fast food.

- Tony Roma's restaurants have discontinued their wonderful Nada Carb barbecue sauce, but you can still get the ribs with no sauce.

- TCBY stores usually have one flavor of soft-serve, low-carb frozen yogurt. You can have it in a cake cone for only four additional grams of carbohydrate.

- The more expensive restaurants are less likely to serve lots of starchy fillers.

- Souvlaki or a Greek salad with gyro meat are possibilities at a Greek place. Moussaka is not too bad, and it doesn't usually come with rice. Check to be sure that it is made with eggplant, not potatoes. Either way, it will still have milk and a little flour in the custard.

- French food tends to be lower in carbs; Italian tends to be higher, since it usually includes both bread and pasta. American food is as bad, with both bread and potatoes.

- Mexican food generally comes with *three* starches: beans, rice, and tortillas. I seem to tolerate the beans if I skip the rice and bring my own low-carb tortillas.

- Chinese food tends to *look* innocent, if you avoid the rice, since there are lots of vegetables, seafood, and meats, but most of the dishes have sauces containing sugar and starch. A safer choice would be the Mongolian wok-type places where you can choose your ingredients, which are then cooked for you on a large round grill.

- Thai food tends to have lots of sugar in addition to the rice and noodles.

- Sometimes you have to eat what is provided to keep from going hungry or offending a host. In this situation, you may find a starch-blocker helpful. It works by counteracting the digestive enzyme (alpha amylase) that converts starch into sugar (glucose) so that it can be used by the body. The active ingredient is an extract of white kidney beans, *phaseolus vulgaris*, or phase II for short. There are several of these on the market; look for one that lists only the extract of northern white kidney beans as an active ingredient, without stimulants or added sugar. The instructions for using them vary as to exactly how much starch they can handle, and some starch is digested in your mouth anyway, so exercise some restraint. Remember, they can only prevent the conversion of starch to sugar, so any sugar you eat still counts.

  I like the capsule form of *Carb Intercept Phase 2 Starch Neutralizer*. It also comes in tablet form, but the tablets must be taken 30 minutes before eating. The capsules dissolve faster and are taken with the food—much easier. For more information, see p. 26.

- If all else fails, the impact of a high-carb meal might be moderated by finishing it within a one-hour time period. This idea comes from *The Carbohydrate Addict's Diet*, by Drs. Richard F. and Rachael F. Heller.[1] They postulate that your body anticipates that your next meal will be similar to your last one. It will release an initial amount of insulin based on the carbohydrate content of your most recent meal, and then make up the deficit with a second wave of insulin that comes a little over an hour later. Insulin is the fat-storage hormone, so less is better. If you finish eating within an hour, you can avoid the second surge of insulin. So save the bread until the rest of your meal comes, eat the salad first, and watch the time if you plan to include a dessert. I doubt that you would lose weight this way, but it may keep you from gaining as much as you otherwise would. (Two high carb meals in a row would negate this advantage.) To read more about this plan, see p. 25.

---

1   Richard F. and Rachael F. Heller, *The Carbohydrate Addict's Diet, The Lifelong Solution to Yo-Yo Dieting,* New York: E P Dutton, 1991, Reprint, New York: New American Library, 1999.

HIDDEN SUGAR AND STARCH

Lots of things that don't have labels, such as meat and seafood from the deli or meat counter, are loaded with sugar and starch. If there is no label on a product, I've learned to ask to see the ingredient list. I assumed I could safely buy a roast chicken from the deli counter, but when I happened to get one that had been prepackaged and labeled, I was in for a shock. A chicken roasted at home would have no carbohydrates; this one listed the carbs per serving as two, but claimed that this one little chicken made eleven servings, which means that the two of us who shared it got eleven grams of carbohydrate each. When I checked the label to find the source of all those carbs, I discovered: corn syrup solids, sugar, dextrose (listed twice), maltodextrine (listed three times), and lactose, which are all forms of sugar.

Other examples:

Shopping for a Thanksgiving turkey last year, I discovered that all the turkeys at the grocery store, both fresh and frozen, had been injected with a solution of sugar and salt.

I expected surimi (artificial crabmeat) to be just fish with crab flavoring, but on checking the ingredients, this is what I found: wheat starch, sugar, cornstarch, tapioca starch, and yam flour. It had *sixteen* grams of carbohydrate in a one-half-cup serving! Real crab meat has almost none. If I want to splurge on that many carbs, I'll have cake!

A local gourmet ice cream chain recently added a sugar-free ice cream to their menu. When my daughter inquired about the nutrition information, the clerk found a label from the carton to show her. Their regular ice cream had eighteen grams of carbohydrate per serving of one-half cup; the sugar-free had twenty. How is that possible? The regular was made with cream; the *diet* was made with non-fat milk, which has twelve carbs per cup (from lactose or milk sugar).

The moral of the story is *read the label!* If it doesn't have one, ask for the ingredients list and the nutrition information. If they can't give it to you, don't buy the product.

How to Use this Book

INGREDIENTS

FATS AND OILS

Your choice of the kind and quality of fats and oils you include in your diet is probably the most important diet-related decision you will make affecting your future health. This is not the place to skimp; saving money on cheap vegetable oil may eventually cost you more in medicine and doctor bills.

Rule Number One:
Avoid any oil, margarine, shortening, and any other product that lists "partially hydrogenated" oil as an ingredient. These are the unnatural trans-fatty acids that were once considered an improvement over the saturated fats in butter, beef fat, lard, and coconut oil but are now widely recognized as a danger to health. Consumption of partially hydrogenated fats is associated with cancer, atherosclerosis, diabetes, obesity, problems with the immune system, and many other diseases.[1]

> "...the only safe intake of trans fat is zero." from a report by the Institute of Medicine, a branch of the National Academy of Sciences, 2002.

We need the proper balance of natural fats for optimum health. All fats contain a mixture of saturated, monounsaturated, and polyunsaturated fatty acids. They are usually classified by the one that predominates.

Note: Fats are solid at room temperature; oils are liquid. The term *lipids* is used for both.

Saturated fats come mainly from animal sources and tropical plants like coconut and palm. Saturated fats are very stable: they don't go rancid easily; they don't break down at cooking temperatures; and they don't form free radicals, which cause damage by stealing atoms from other molecules. They transport fat-soluble vitamins and minerals, and they are needed for proper utilization of calcium in the bones. Saturated fats have antimicrobial and anti-fungal properties, and they stimulate the immune system.[2] Saturated fats like butter and coconut oil contain short- and medium-chain fatty acids, which can be used for quick energy and are less likely to cause weight gain than the long-chain fatty acids like olive oil and omega-6 polyunsaturated oils.

So why are we constantly warned about "artery-clogging" saturated fat when those of us on low-carb diets experience only positive changes in our blood chemistry? It is the carbs in the diet that determine what happens to the fat we eat. If the diet is low in fat and high in simple sugars, the body will make its own supply of saturated fat,[3] and the sugars will provide the insulin to put it into storage. When the carbs are low, the fat is burned for energy, not stored in the arteries or anywhere else.

---

1   Sally Fallon and Mary G. Enig, Ph.D., *Nourishing Traditions: The Cookbook that Challenges Politically Correct Nutrition and the Diet Dictocrats*, New Trends Publishing, 2000.

2   Stephen Byrnes, Ph.D., RNCP, "The Myth of Vegetarianism," *Nexus Magazine*, Volume 9, Number 2, April-May, 2002.

3   Lisa Cooper Hudgins, Marc Hellerstein, Cynthia Seidman, Richard Neese, Jolanta Diakun, and Jules Hirsch, "Human Fatty Acid Synthesis Is Stimulated by a Eucaloric Low Fat, High Carbohydrate Diet," *J. Clin. Invest.*, May, 1996, 97: pp. 2081–2091.

Monounsaturated oils are found in abundance in olive oil, avocados, macadamias, almonds, and peanuts, and they are also found in lard and poultry fat. Olive oil contains up to 75% oleic acid, an omega-9 monounsaturated oil. Peanut oil is also high in oleic acid, and new peanut varieties have been developed that produce oil that contains more of it than olive oil. Canola oil contains about 60% oleic acid and 10% omega-3 polyunsaturated fatty acids. It is often recommended as an inexpensive alternative to olive oil, but it may not be any better than the other refined vegetable oils. It is made from hybridized rape seed, and must be extracted with high-temperature mechanical pressing and chemical solvents. It must then be bleached, degummed, and deodorized. Some studies indicate that much of its omega-3 fatty acid content is converted into trans fats in the process.[4]

Olive Oil:

This is everybody's darling; even the low-fat camp has grudgingly conceded that some fat is necessary, and the one they endorse is olive oil. It would be hard to find fault with something that has been a staple food in so many cultures for thousands of years. It can be used with little processing, and in addition to its high oleic acid content, it also contains small amounts of both essential fatty acids, omega-6 and omega-3. Expeller-pressed extra-virgin olive oil is an excellent choice for flavoring, for dipping, for low-temperature cooking, and for dressing salads. Refined olive oil *extra light* can be

> "It seems plausible that oleocanthal plays a causal role in the health benefits associated with diets where olive oil is the principal source of fat." Paul Breslin, Monell Chamical Senses Center

The Secret of Olive Oil
In an article in the September, 2005 issue of the *Journal Nature*, a group of scientists reported that freshly-pressed olive oil contains a natural non-steroidal anti-inflammatory, called oleocanthal, which has the same medicinal effect as ibuprofen. Only the freshest extra-virgin olive oil contains the compound, since it is destroyed by heat and time. Inflammation has been linked to many chronic diseases, including coronary heart disease.[5]

heated to high temperatures, but it will have lost most of its healthful compounds. The bad news: the primary fatty acids in olive oil are the long-chain variety, which are more easily stored as body fat than medium- or short-chain fatty acids.

Polyunsaturated oils are less stable than monounsaturated and saturated lipids. They are easily damaged by heat, light, and oxygen if they are refined and again if they are heated for cooking. When ingested, these altered fats form free radicals, highly reactive molecules linked to a great many health problems. Polyunsaturated oils include the two essential fatty acids (EFAs): omega-3 and omega-6. They are called "essential" because they cannot be made in the body and must come from the diet. The ratio of EFAs is important because they are used to make substances, similar to hormones, that regulate many reactions in the body. Omega-6 oils promote blood clotting, muscle contraction, and inflammation, while omega-3s promote the opposite reactions: blood thinning,

---

4   Sally Fallon and Mary Enig, Ph.D., "The Great Con-ola," *Nexus Magazine*, Aug/September, 2002.
5   Gary K. Beauchamp, Russell S. J. Keast, Diane Morel, Jianming Lin, Jana Pika, Qiang Han, Chi-Ho Lee, Amos B. Smith, and Paul A. S. Breslin, "Phytochemistry: Ibuprofen-like activity in extra-virgin olive oil," *Journal Nature*, Sept, 2005, p. 45.

muscle relaxation, and an anti-inflammatory response. A high intake of omega-6, coupled with a low intake of omega-3, has also been associated with increased levels of depression and suicide.

Omega-6 oils include the heavily refined vegetable oils made from seeds and grains (soy, safflower, corn, cottonseed, and sunflower) that are found in most commercial products. Most of us get too much omega-6, which is usually highly processed, so we may still be deficient in this essential nutrient. Our reliance on oils made from grains and on grain-fed livestock has upset the *yin and yang* relationship of EFAs by greatly increasing our consumption of omega-6 in proportion to omega-3. Regular supermarket beef has a ratio of up to 13 parts omega-6 to one part omega-3, compared to a two- to one-ratio for wild game and pastured cattle.[8] Eggs from chickens fed on grain have up to 19 times the amount of omega-6 in eggs from free-range chickens.

Omega-3 oils are found in linseed (flax), fatty fish, and walnuts. They are also found in eggs and the meat, fat, bone marrow, and organs of animals. Omega-3 oils protect against cardiovascular disease, diabetes, and arthritis, but too much can increase the risk of strokes.

To get the maximum benefits from polyunsaturates, use oils that are cold pressed, not extracted with heat and chemicals. Unrefined oils retain more essential fatty acids. They should be stored in the refrigerator in opaque containers, and they should not be used for cooking.

Note: Purslane, an annual succulent, is the richest source of omega-3 oils in the plant kingdom. Thought to have originated in India, it is now common throughout the world. It is eaten raw and sautéed in Europe, especially in Greece. It can be dried to use as a thickener for stews and the stems can be pickled. It is possible to buy both plants and seeds for purslane, but if you look for it on the web, what you are likely to find is how to get rid of it or to prevent it from invading your lawn.

Cooking Fats—Fry if you must:
Heating fats to frying temperatures presents a minefield of potential dangers. For this

---

6   Dariush Mozaffrain, Eric B. Rimm, and David M. Herrington, "Dietary fats, carbohydrate, and progression of coronary atherosclerosis in postmenopausal women," *Am. J. Clin. Nutr.,* 2004, 80: pp. 1175–84.

7   C. V. Felton, D. Crook, M. J. Davies, M. F. Oliver, *Lancet,* 1995 Jan 28; 345(8944):256-7; author reply 257.

8   Bruce Watkins and Loren Cordain, M. Kehler, L. Rogers, "Fatty acid analysis of wild ruminant tissues: evolutionary implications for reducing diet-related chronic disease," *European Journal of Clinical Nutrition,* 2002, Mar; 56(3):181-91.

reason, many health advisers just say don't do it, and that is, of course, a safe choice. However, if you choose the right fats and treat them with respect, you can continue to enjoy the delicious crisp textures of fried foods without endangering your well being.

Smoke Point:

The smoke point is the temperature at which an oil begins to smoke and break down. Cooking oils should never be allowed to reach this temperature. Most unrefined oils (obtained with cold-extraction methods) have a lower smoke point than refined oils. Other factors that can lower the smoke point of an oil include: the length of time the oil has been heated; the number of times it has been used; exposure to light and heat during storage; and contamination with salt, food particles, and other impurities. It is important for both health and safety reasons to use fresh oil for frying. Oils deteriorate rapidly at high temperatures; even one use can reduce the smoke point for many oils so much that they can burst into flame at frying temperatures. Many oils give the smoke point on the label; call the company and ask, if in doubt, as the same kind of oil may differ from one brand to another.

(More information about the smoke points of various fats is available at www.goodeatsfanpage.com/CollectedInfo/OilSmokePoints.htm. Many companies include a toll-free number on their labels for consumer questions about specific products.)

Note: Omega Nutrition sells a blend of oils that can be heated to frying temperatures. Spectrum® Organics and Earth Balance make shortenings that can be used for frying.

Monounsaturated and saturated fats are best for cooking at higher temperatures. Rice bran oil and peanut oil are high in monounsaturates, relatively inexpensive, and have a neutral taste.

Rice bran oil, an omega-9 monounsaturated oil traditionally used in Japanese cooking, can be heated to high temperatures (490° F) without breaking down or absorbing flavors. (One manufacturer says it can be strained through a fine screen and reused, but I have reservations about doing that.) Asian markets should have it in stock. *Uwajimaya* (see Sources) in Seattle also sells it by mail order.

Peanut oil has a fatty acid composition very similar to olive oil, and some new varieties of peanuts have been developed that produce oil that contains up to 80% oleic acid, even more than olive oil. A small percentage of people are allergic to peanuts; refined peanut oil is less likely to provoke allergic reactions than unrefined.

Olive oil (refined), avocado oil, macadamia nut oil, and some other nut oils are monounsaturated oils that can take the heat, so they are also good for cooking, but a bit pricey to use in large amounts.

Tea oil, also called *tea seed oil* or *green tea oil,* is another gourmet oil that can withstand high heat. It is sometimes referred to as Asian olive oil because of its high oleic acid content. The Republic of Tea sells it through their catalog, and it can also be purchased or ordered from *Uwajimaya,* (see Sources). The Republic of Tea catalog states that tea oil can be used for cooking at up to 485° F without smoking or burning; it is rich in vitamin E and other antioxidants; it is unrefined and minimally processed; it has no trans-fatty acids, and it is not hydrogenated. (It's also not cheap.)

And, of course, there are the real champions of stability, the saturated fats; these include highly saturated palm and coconut oil and the animal fats, like clarified butter, goose and duck fat, and lard, which are part monounsaturated and part saturated.

Coconut Oil:

If even a fraction of the claims made for it are true, coconut oil is the best fat for all purposes, including cooking and baking. It was once a common ingredient in commercially produced foods. (It was what made movie popcorn smell so good!) The fear of saturated fats caused tropical oils to be replaced by polyunsaturated and hydrogenated oils, but coconut oil has recently regained popularity for cooking and as a nutritional supplement. Even unrefined virgin coconut oil is extremely stable and can be stored at room temperature for over a year because of its high levels of natural anti-oxidants. It contains large quantities of lauric acid, which has antibacterial, anti-viral, antifungal, and anti-protozoal properties. It reduces your chances of suffering a heart attack, improves cholesterol levels,[9] and raises the levels of antioxidant reserves in the cells. It is ideal for people with digestive disorders who have trouble digesting fats and for athletes who need quick energy.

According to Bruce Fife, author of *The Coconut Oil Miracle*, when coconut oil is used as a supplement, in cooking, or as a skin cream, it has been found to promote weight loss; protect against cancer, diabetes, arthritis, and many other degenerative diseases; prevent premature aging of the skin; strengthen the immune system; and improve digestion.[10] Studies sponsored by various health organizations have found that unrefined coconut oil prolongs the lives of AIDS patients by dissolving the lipid covering of the AIDS virus and other organisms responsible for opportunistic infections in patients. (Dr. Mary Enig, a biochemist recognized as an authority on fats, recommends a therapeutic dose of 3½ tablespoonfuls of coconut oil per day.)[11]

Coconut oil is solid below 76° F and liquid at higher temperatures. It's called coconut oil when it is liquid and coconut butter when it is solid. It can be used like butter or shortening in its solid state and like oil in its liquid state. A spokesman for Omega Nutrition's Virgin Coconut Oil told me it can be used for deep frying at 375° F (other sources give the maximum temperature for coconut oil as 350° or 365° F.)

---

9 G. L. Blackburn, et al., "A reevaluation of coconut oil's effect on serum cholesterol and atherogenesis," *The Journal of the Philippine Medical Association*, 1988, 65: pp. 144-152. Second Footnote: I. A. Prior, F. Davidson, et al., "Cholesterol, coconuts, and diet on Polynesian atolls: a natural experiment: the Pukapuka and Tokelau island studies," *American Journal of Clinical Nutrition*, Aug., 1981, 34(8): pp. 1552-61.

10 Bruce Fife, C.N., N.D., *The Coconut Oil Miracle*, Avery, New York, 1999, 2000, 2002, 2004. Previously published as *The Healing Miracles of Coconut Oil*.

11 *Nutrients and Foods in AIDS*, Edited by Ronald R. Watson, Ph.D., Chapter 5, written by Dr. Mary Enig, CRC Press, 1998, p. 81.

COCONUT OIL CANDY

Here's an easy way to add coconut oil to your diet—as a simple-to-make candy. Coconut oil makes candy with "snap" that still melts in your mouth. Chocolate also has health benefits; it contains flavonoids similar to those found in red wine and green tea. If you use walnuts, which are rich in omega-3 fatty acids, you will have candy that is delicious and also good for what ails you.

2 ounces of unsweetened chocolate, chopped
3 tablespoons of virgin coconut oil
2½ tablespoons of granular Splenda®
½ teaspoon of vanilla extract
A few grains of salt
Grated coconut and/or chopped nuts (optional)

Mix ingredients together in a microwave-safe dish and heat on low power just until melted, stirring every 30 seconds or so. Pour out onto a dish lined with plastic wrap. Chill until set. Peel off the plastic wrap and cut candy into pieces. Store in the refrigerator. Recipe makes about 8 ounces of candy.

PER SERVING OF 1/2 OUNCE:		
Total Carb: 1.2g	Fiber: 0.5g	Net Carb: 0.7g

VARIATION:

To lower the carb count even more, make this candy with purchased sugar-free chocolate chips. (Purchased chips, made with liquid Splenda®, will have no bulking agents, which add carbs.) See Sources. This version is sweeter than the one above.

Use two ounces of sugar-free chocolate chips and leave out the unsweetened chocolate and Splenda®.

PER SERVING OF 1/2 OUNCE:		
Total Carb: 2.0g	Fiber: 1.75g	Net Carb: 0.25g
When made with Eat Well, Be Well™ sugar-free chocolate chips.		

> "If you work out the numbers, you come to the surreal conclusion that you can eat lard straight from the can and conceivably reduce your risk of heart disease."
> Dr. Walter Willet, The Harvard School of Public Health, as quoted by Gary Taubes.[12]

Lard:
Lard is actually back in consideration for use. It is a natural fat that has been used as food for thousands of years. It makes an exceptional pastry crust (although some people prefer to limit its use to savory rather than sweet pies). The smoke point for lard may vary between 361° to 401° F, depending on the method used to render it and which part of the animal it comes from. It does contain some saturated fat, but we now know that saturated fat is not as bad as the trans fats like those in shortening or margarine. (Lard actually contains more monounsaturated than saturated fat.)

---

12 "What if It's All Been a Big Fat Lie?" *The New York Times*, July 7, 2002.

One word of caution: most of the lard that is currently on the shelves is partially hydrogenated. That means that it has been treated with hydrogen so that it will not melt at room temperature. It also means it contains the same trans-fatty acids as the unnatural fats, like shortening and margarine. (In my quest for natural lard, I made the mistake of asking for it at a health food store—the clerk almost went into shock.)

To purchase lard that is not partially hydrogenated, look for it in the cooler rather than on the shelf, and it should be refrigerated once you get it home. Because natural lard has become increasingly difficult to find, you may want to have a go at making it yourself. That way, you can be sure it's fresh and that it contains no trans fats or preservatives; however, you may also have difficulty buying the pork fat to make it. Grocery stores now receive their meat already trimmed with just a ¼-inch layer of fat left on. A butcher shop or an ethnic store (Chinese or Mexican) may be more likely to have it. The leaf fat from around the kidneys makes the best lard, but fatback or the fat trimmed from the loin or leg can also be used. If all else fails, you can put the fat trimmings from pork roasts and chops in the freezer and save it up until you have enough.

LARD

The crispy brown residue left in the pan after rendering lard is called cracklings. *It can be mixed into cornbread batter to make that old Southern delicacy,* cracklin' bread. *(If I close my eyes, I can still smell hot cracklin' bread, fresh out of a wood-fired oven, in my Grandma's kitchen.)*

2 pounds of unsalted pork fat

Preheat the oven to 225° F.

If you are using leaf fat, remove the papery filaments. Chop the fat: the smaller the pieces, the faster it will render. (Alternately, you can ask your butcher to grind it for you, or you can chop it into chunks and then pulse it briefly, in several batches, in a food processor.) Put some of the fat in a deep heavy kettle or skillet, being careful not to overfill the pan, and place it in the preheated oven. If you can fit more pans in the oven, you may be able to cook all of it at the same time. Cook at 225° F for an hour or so and then raise the temperature up to 250° or a maximum of 300°. Never let it get to 325° F or it may smoke and the lard will take on a dark color. Stir the pieces of pork fat occasionally so they don't stick. Continue to cook until only liquid fat and crisp brown bits remain in the pan: this will probably take 2 to 3 hours.

Let the pan cool a little and pour the lard through a strainer into containers, pressing the liquid fat out of the residue. Repeat with the rest of the fat until it is all rendered. Cover the containers tightly to prevent the absorption of off flavors and refrigerate. It will keep for several months.

Makes about 4 cups or 1½ pounds of lard.

Note: Lard has a higher fat content than butter, which contains some water. To substitute lard for butter in baked goods, reduce the amount by 20 to 25 percent.

OVEN BACON

When I was a kid, a coffee can full of bacon drippings had a permanent place on the back of the stove in every kitchen. Now that we have microwave ovens, this most flavorful of all cooking fats usually goes in the trash. Since I discovered uncured bacon, I have been reclaiming the rendered bacon fat to use for fried cornbread and okra and for flavoring green beans. Baking a pound of bacon at a time is the most efficient way to render the fat.

Place strips of nitrite-free bacon (see Sources) on a greased rack in an open roasting pan. Bake in a 350° F oven for 15 to 20 minutes or until bacon is almost crisp. Pour off fat as it accumulates and strain into a container. Cover the container and refrigerate for later use. Let bacon cool, wrap well, and refrigerate until needed, then microwave until crisp.

French Butter:

If you like duck as much as I do, you can have a supply of excellent cooking fat with little extra effort. Just pour off and strain the rendered fat from the pan when roasting a whole duck or searing duck breasts in a skillet. Duck fat is often called "French butter" because it is the preferred fat for many uses in France. Score the duck skin in a diamond pattern before cooking, cutting through the skin but not into the meat, to render more fat and make the skin crisper. Store the duck fat, covered, in the refrigerator.

Butter:

Butter has gotten a bad rap. It contains mostly saturated fat (66 percent saturated, the rest monounsaturated), but as it turns out, it is the trans fats that are the real villains and butter is actually good for us. It contains fat-soluble vitamins A (retinol), E, K, and D, and it is rich in minerals, including manganese, zinc, chromium, iodine, and especially selenium. It is a source for anti-microbial, anti-fungal, and anti-carcinogenic fatty acids; it strengthens the immune system and provides protection from heart disease, osteoporosis, and mental illness.[13] It has been suggested that the alarming increase in osteoporosis in this country is the result of replacing butter with margarine.

> "Julia was right all along."—Shirley O. Corriher, *Cookwise, The Secrets of Cooking Revealed,* Harper Collins, New York, 1997

> " . . . use as much good quality butter as you like, with the happy assurance that it is a wholesome—indeed, an essential food for you and your whole family." Sally Fallon and Mary G. Enig, Ph.D., *Nourishing Traditions: The Cookbook that Challenges Politically Correct Nutrition and the Diet Dictocrats.*

Note: Salt serves as a preservative in butter. Unsalted butter's only advantage is that it lets you control the amount of salt in your recipe more carefully.

Unsalted butter can be stored in the refrigerator for a month or frozen for six months. Butter wrapped in foil will not absorb off-flavors.

Nothing can compare with the taste of real butter, but it tends to burn easily. It can be combined with other oils to raise its smoke point, or clarified to use for sautéing and frying, although it will lose some flavor in the process.

---

13   Sally Fallon with Mary G. Enig, Ph.D., *Nourishing Traditions,* ProMotion Publishing, San Diego, CA, 1995.

CLARIFIED BUTTER

Clarified Butter is butter with the water and milk solids removed so that it can be stored at room temperature without spoiling and heated to higher temperatures without burning. Ghee is the Indian version; it is cooked until the milk solids are browned, giving it a nutty taste. Ghee will likely be found in a jar on the shelf in Indian food markets. At regular stores, you may find clarified butter on a shelf or packaged like fresh butter in the cooler. Better yet, you can make it yourself in a matter of minutes.

Cut unsalted butter into pieces and melt over low heat in a saucepan. Skim off the foam that rises to the surface and slowly pour off the clear liquid. Discard the milky residue in the bottom of the pan, or use it to flavor vegetables or eggs. Cool the butter, wrap well, and store in the refrigerator or freezer. One-half pound of butter will make three-quarters of a cup of clarified butter.

Shortening:
There are times when I prefer to use shortening rather than oil, as for pie crust. Spectrum® Organic Products makes an expeller-pressed palm oil shortening and Earth Balance® makes a shortening from expeller-pressed palm fruit, soybean, canola seed, and olive oils. Crisco® has introduced a no-trans-fat version; they have resolved the issue by fully hydrogenating one of the oils (cottonseed) in the formula so that it is completely saturated. It has about the same consistency as their standard shortening. You can use lard instead of shortening, if you can find one that is not partially hydrogenated, or use coconut butter.

SWEETENERS

I am optimistic that the perfect sugar substitute is on the horizon. One that tastes and performs like sugar, is beneficial to health, readily available, and reasonably priced. It will probably be made from a natural, prebiotic plant fiber, such as polydextrose, oligofructose, or inulin. In the meantime, there are many choices, each with advantages and disadvantages.

ASPARTAME is known as *Equal* in the little blue packets and as *NutraSweet*. One packet of Equal has four calories and 0.9 grams of carbohydrate. It is not heat-stable, so it cannot be used for cooking. There are some concerns about safety problems with this sweetener, possibly involving brain and nerve damage,[14] although the FDA continues to consider it safe. (A 2005 study by the Ramazzini foundation in Italy reported that aspartame induces lymphomas and leukemia in rats, although they found no higher incidence of brain cancer.[15]

SACCHARIN is the artificial sweetener known as *Sweet'N Low* in the pink packets and as *Sugar Twin*. (One teaspoon of Sugar Twin Brown Sugar Replacement has 0.4 carbs and one calorie.) It has a bitter aftertaste that becomes more pronounced when it has been heated. For many years, the FDA required saccharin products to carry a warning label because of its possible carcinogenic effects, but that requirement was removed in 2000. Sugar Twin makes a substitute for brown sugar, while Splenda® does not, so I occasionally use it in small amounts. It contains maltodextrin and saccharin.

ACESULFAME K (acesulfame potassium), sold as *Sunett®*, is chemically similar to saccharin. It does not break down when heated, so it can be used for cooking and baking; however, it has a bitter aftertaste like saccharin and may pose the same potential heath hazards. It is often blended with other sweeteners to enhance and sustain the sweet taste. It is the sweetener listed in DiabetiSweet®, which contains isomalt as a bulking agent and carries a warning that excessive consumption may cause stomach upset.

NEOTAME is a newer sweetener made by the Nutrasweet Company. It is similar to aspartame, but much sweeter (7,000 to 13,000 times as sweet as sugar), so only a tiny amount is needed. Neotame also has the ability to enhance other flavors, especially mint. It was approved by the FDA in 2002 and is said to be safe for children and pregnant women. It is being marketed to manufacturers of soft drinks, dairy products, and chewing gum rather than to the general public.

STEVIA, promoted as the natural no-calorie sweetener (one packet actually has one gram of carbohydrates and four calories) can legally be sold as a supplement in the U.S., but it does not have government approval to be sold as a sweetener. It has not been reported to have any toxic side effects, but some brands are very bitter. If you prefer to use stevia to cut your consumption of artificial sweeteners, shop around for one that is not bitter and use it in beverages or on fruit or cereal. You may also use a little for flavor enhancement in combination with other sweeteners in recipes.

---

14   Drs. Michael and Mary Dan Eades, *Protein Power Lifeplan*, 2000, pp. 166-167.

15   Morando Soffritti, et al., "Aspartame induces lymphomas and leukaemias in rats," Cancer Research Centre, European Ramazzini Foundation of Oncology and Environmental Sciences, Bologna, Italy, *Eur. J. Oncol.* vol. 10, n 2, pp. 107-116, 2005.

WHEY LOW® is a blend of three kinds of natural sugar: sucrose (table sugar), fructose (fruit sugar), and lactose (milk sugar). It can be substituted, measure for measure, for sucrose. It is real sugar, all sugar, and only sugar, so how can it be low carb? The manufacturer claims that two of the sugars cancel each other out and also prevent some starch from being metabolized so that it has one fourth the calories and impact carbs and one third the glycemic index of sucrose. Fructose is said to interfere with the absorption of lactose, and lactose with the absorption of sucrose, leaving just the fructose. (Does this mean that if you drink a cola and a glass of milk when you eat a candy bar, only the fructose in the cola will count? Any volunteers to test this theory?) At any rate, fructose and lactose have a lower glycemic index than sucrose, so that would slow down the insulin reaction, although fructose comes with a different set of potential problems. (The Drs. Michael and Mary Dan Eades, authors of *The Protein Power Lifeplan*, believe the increased consumption of fructose is largely to blame for the epidemic rise in obesity and diabetes as well as other problems, including even premature aging and wrinkles.)[16] Whey Low® has recently been approved for use on the South Beach Diet,[17] which emphasizes the glycemic index of foods.

> **Fructose**
> Two studies on sodas sweetened with high-fructose corn syrup by Penn State nutritionist Barbara Rolls suggest that fructose does not spur the production of insulin, which causes the body to process calories, or leptin, a hormone that reduces appitite, the way other foods do. She concludes that the extra sugar is added in without reducing the total food intake.[18]
>
> Large amounts of fructose have been implicated as contributing to nearly all of the classic manifestations of the insulin resistance syndrome, which leads to heart disease, diabetes, and hypertension, although small amounts, such as those that occur naturally in fruits and vegetables, may have a favorable metabolic effect.[19]

A number of clinical studies have been planned to determine the benefits of using Whey Low®, so for me, the jury is still out, but I do use it occasionally, in small amounts. It makes a fabulous meringue. (Use it in place of the Splenda® and superfine sugar in my recipe for soft meringue on p.154. Spread it on hot cream pie filling, seal it to the edge of the crust, and bake for 3 to 5 minutes in a 400° F oven.)

FRUCTOSE: Wax Orchard Fruit Sweet™ is a liquid fructose or fruit sugar that I use in small amounts in place of honey or molasses to moisten and sweeten cookies, cakes, and candies. It is sweeter than sugar or honey so you need less, and it has 7.5 carbs per tablespoon rather than the 15 to 17 in molasses, honey, or corn syrup.

---

16   Michael R. Eades, M.D. and Mary Dan Eades, M.D., *Protein Power Lifeplan*, 2000, pp. 159-162.

17   Arthur Agatston, M.D., *The South Beach Diet*, Random House, New York, 2003.

18   Marilynn Marchione, "Soda Targeted in Fight Against Obesity," *Seattle Post-Intelligencer*, March 4, 2006.

19   Sharon S. Elliott, Nancy L. Kein, Judith S. Stern, Karen Teff, and Peter J. Havel, "Fructose, weight gain, and the insulin resistance syndrome," *American Journal of Clinical Nutrition*, Vol. 76, No. 5, 911-922, November 2002.

The glycemic index is the ranking of carbohydrates by the effect they have on blood sugar and insulin levels. Glucose is generally used as the standard and given a value of 100; other foods are given a numeric value to show how they compare to glucose. (Some systems use white bread rather than glucose for 100.) Carbohydrates that break down rapidly have the highest glycemic index; those that break down slowly have the lowest. However, it is not as simple as it sounds. Many factors affect the index value of the same food, for example, mashed potatoes will be higher than cubed, because the digestive enzymes have contact with more surface area. Ripe fruit will rank higher than less ripe fruit, and cooked food will be higher than raw. The ranking will also be affected by other foods that are eaten at the same time; fiber, fat, and protein slow down the digestion of carbohydrates and lower their GI number.

While the *glycemic index* compares foods on a gram-for-gram basis to describe the potential of each to raise blood glucose levels, the *glycemic load* factors in the amount of carbohydrate in a standard serving. The glycemic index number, multiplied by the amount of carbohydrate in grams, divided by 100, gives the glycemic load.

SUGAR ALCOHOLS

These are the sweeteners that end in "-itol," like sorbitol, maltitol, manitol, and xylitol that have been used for many years to make products for people with diabetes. (They are not really sugars or alcohols.) They are now being widely used in low-carbohydrate products. The sugar alcohols are excluded when figuring the net carb counts for foods because they are thought to have little or no effect on blood sugar levels. Most of them have an unfortunate side effect, called osmotic diarrhea, and that's the reason they carry a warning against excessive consumption. Many low-carbohydrate products, like meal replacement shakes and bars, candy, and cereals contain sugar alcohols, especially maltitol. They may be used alone or to boost the sweetening power of more expensive sweeteners like sucralose. It is necessary to keep track of how much sugar alcohol you consume in all the different products that you eat within a given period of time; eat too much and the results are not at all pleasant, resulting in abdominal cramping, bloating, or worse.

XYLITOL, one of the sugar alcohols, may have health benefits, although it also has the laxative effect of the others. Studies have shown that chewing gum sweetened with xylityol can prevent ear infections and tooth decay.[20] Its similarity to sugar attracts and then "starves" harmful microorganisms, allowing for the re-mineralization of tooth enamel. It also appears to have potential as a treatment for osteoporosis. The US Army plans to include xylitol-sweetened gum in its MREs (meals ready to eat).

ERYTHRITOL has a higher digestive tolerance than the other sugar alcohols, and foods containing substantial amounts are unlikely to cause problems. It is 70% as sweet as table sugar, but a small amount of another sweetener, like sucralose, will boost its sweetening power by 30%. Since 1990 it has been added to commercially produced foods and

---

20　K. K. Makinen, et al, "Xylitol chewing gums and caries rates: a 40-month cohort study," *Journal of Dental Research*, vol. 74, 1904-1913, 1995.

beverages to provide sweetness and to improve taste and texture. The FDA granted GRAS (generally recognized as safe) status to erythritol in 1997.

MALTITOL causes more digestive problems than the other sugar alcohols, but it is probably the most widely used. It is available for home use in granular form from Steel's Gourmet Foods under the brand name *Nature Sweet*. It can be substituted measure for measure for granular and powdered sugar in recipes for candy and icing. It has 6 calories (half the calories of sugar) and 3 net carbs per teaspoon, but it is counted as zero carbs since it has a minimal impact on blood sugar levels.

SPLENDA®:
Splenda® became widely available in this country at just about the time I decided to curb my sugar-junkie life style. I knew the hardest part of low-carb dieting for me would be trying to cut down on the goodies. I had tried some of the other sweeteners and found them to be worse than no sweetener at all.

Splenda®, the brand name for sucralose, is a sweetener that is made from sugar (sucrose) by altering it so that it is not broken down by our digestive enzymes. Sugar is converted into sucralose by substituting three chlorine atoms for three hydroxyl groups on the sugar molecule. Is it a natural product? Not really, but it has been used for more than ten years in Canada (ironically, it was being manufactured in the U.S.) and is not required to carry any warning labels. It is even considered safe for nursing mothers and pregnant women. It comes in two forms, one in yellow packets for tea or coffee, and one in granular form that is fluffed up with bulking agents so it can be substituted, measure for measure, for sugar. It can be used for cooking like regular sugar since it holds up to heat, but the volume is much smaller since sucrolose is 600 times as sweet as sugar.

Commercial products made with sucralose have an advantage over any that we make

> ## Sugar Alcohols
> There is some controversy about sugar alcohols and glycerin. Most product labels exclude them from the nutrition counts, but for some people, they may be metabolized like other carbohydrates. It has been suggested that half the carbohydrate content listed on labels should be added to the total. My own opinion is that if you can eat a lot of maltitol or other sugar alcohols without getting sick, you are probably digesting at least some of it as if it were regular sugar. If your weight loss stalls, try cutting out all purchased sugar-free products that contain sweeteners other than Splenda® and see if that helps.

> ## Miracle Fruit
> Just one berry from the African miracle fruit plant (Synsepalum dulcificum) will make any sour food eaten for the next hour taste sweet. It stimulates the sweet taste buds on the tongue without affecting those that sense sour, so the sensation of both sweet and sour are experienced together. The Japanese have developed a way to freeze-dry the fruit, and have succeeded in genetically modifying lettuce plants to produce the miraculin protein, which they plan to use in diet foods. Miracle fruit juice and berries are not approved for sale in the United States, but the plants and seeds are available from many suppliers that specialize in tropical plants.

ourselves because they contain the liquid form, which has zero carbs and zero calories. Both the granular form and the packets of Splenda® that are sold retail contain a little sugar, either maltodextrin or dextrose, as a bulking agent. The labels say "no calories and no carbohydrates," but that is not strictly true. Government regulations allow products below a certain count to make that claim. Each packet, which replaces two teaspoonfuls of sugar, contains one gram of carbohydrate and four calories. One teaspoon of granular Splenda® contains one-half of a gram of carbohydrate and two calories. That doesn't sound like much, but one cup of granular Splenda® adds 24 grams of carbohydrates and 96 calories when used in recipes. Even so, that is only one-eighth the amount in regular sugar. Any time you can substitute sugar-free syrups, like Atkins or Da Vinci, made with liquid sucralose, for Splenda®, it is better to do so, as it really has zero carbs and zero calories.

Most of my sweet recipes are made and tested with Splenda®. You could use one of the other sweeteners that measures like sugar and holds up to cooking temperatures. There are other sweeteners on the horizon that may turn out to be better, but for now, Splenda® is readily available, it works, and it seems to be safe.

Tips for cooking with Splenda®:
- Splenda® is so lightweight that the beaters of an electric mixer or the rising air current from a heated pan can blow it away. Turn off the mixer before adding it to the mixing bowl and remove pans from the heat before adding Splenda®.

- Foods made with sugar substitutes will mold and spoil much faster than those with sugar, as sugar has a preservative effect. Refrigerate pies, cookies, and cakes if not using them within a day. To keep jams, jellies, and sauces, even in the refrigerator, you must reheat them occasionally. They can be frozen for longer storage.

- Foods made with Splenda® won't brown as well as those made with sugar. A light spray of nonstick vegetable oil can improve the browning (my cake recipes made with whey powder brown well without the spray).

- There are complex tastes to real sugar that aren't there with Splenda®, because the volume is so small. To avoid a flat or bland taste, you need to kick up the flavors in other ways; for example, I sometimes use extra vanilla or a small amount of a sweet liqueur which adds enough punch to justify the extra carbs. Adding a small amount of acesulfame K, sold as Sweet One® or DiabetiSweet®, is another way to improve the taste of Splenda®-sweetened recipes, especially plain vanilla ones.

POLYDEXTROSE:

A combination of sucralose and polydextrose makes an excellent replacement for sugar in some of my recipes. While polydextrose has only a slight sweetening effect, it provides many of the properties that are missing in high intensity sweeteners like Splenda®. It adds the missing bulk, and it thickens, stabilizes, caramelizes, and aids in moisture retention, while having little effect on insulin levels. It is a common ingredient in commercial low-carb and low-calorie products, and it can be purchased for home use. Polydextrose consists of long chains of double glucose molecules, a small amount (10%) of sorbitol (a sugar alcohol), and citric acid. Studies have shown that it passes through the digestive tract unchanged, like soluble fiber. Polydextrose dissolves best in warm or hot liquids, as it tends to form a gel when mixed with cold liquid. It contains 1 gram of carbohydrate and 25 grams of fiber per ounce. It was approved by the FDA in 1981 and is generally considered safe.

SUGAR-FREE SYRUPS:

I use Da Vinci Gourmet® sugar-free syrups (blue label) to sweeten and flavor many of my recipes. This is the coffee infusion used in many coffee shops and restaurants. Other brands, like Torani®, can be substituted, but Da Vinci and Atkins syrups are sweetened with just Splenda®, uncut with cheaper sweeteners like sorbitol or acesulfame potassium. The Atkins syrups are more widely available, but they are usually more expensive than Da Vinci and they come in only 6 flavors, compared to Da Vinci's 51.

The new *Simple Syrup* from Da Vinci is my dream come true! It is unflavored and can be used in any recipe that has enough liquid to be replaced with the syrup. Unlike the granular and packet forms of Splenda®, the syrups are truly calorie and carbohydrate free, since they are sweetened with liquid sucralose that contains no bulking agents. Anytime you can replace the Splenda® and some of the liquid in a recipe with one of the syrups, you will subtract both calories and carbohydrates. Like Splenda®, they are heat stable for cooking and safe for children and diabetics. If you live near one of a chain of discount stores called Cash and Carry, you are in luck. They specialize in Da Vinci syrups and carry a huge variety of sugar-free flavors at discounted prices.

Some of Da Vinci's 51 flavors are seasonal. Many groceries carry the sugar-free vanilla and hazelnut flavors, but all of them can be ordered from *www.DaVincigourmet.com* or by telephone by calling 1-800-640-6779. Some of the sizes are available in plastic bottles to facilitate shipping. (If you stock just one, get the Simple Syrup. You can always add a few drops of flavor extract.)

To substitute Splenda® and liquid for sugar-free syrup in recipes:
For each Tablespoon of syrup, use one tablespoon of water and one tablespoon (1½ packets) of granular Splenda®.

BLENDS: The latest approach to artificial sweeteners is the use of a complimentary blend. Using a combination of different sugar substitutes improves the taste and boosts the sweetening power of the mix. One such blend is Swiss Diet Shugr, a combination of erythritol, the most mild mannered of the sugar alcohols, maltodextrin, tagatose, and sucralose. Tagatose is similar to fructose, but its left-handed configuration prevents it from being fully digested. Shugr is sold in a shaker and in packets for use in tea or coffee, but it is probably too expensive to be used in the quantities needed for cooking.

X-W8

A sweetener called X-W8 has been in development for quite some time. It is made from inulin and a small amount of high-intensity sweeteners. Inulin is a sweet fiber found in chicory and other plants. Many traditional herbal medicines contain inulin and some studies indicate that it may have health benefits; it improves the balance of friendly bacteria in the lower GI tract and may help prevent osteoporosis and some cancers. X-W8 tastes like cane sugar and can be used in the same way. It is now available in candies and as a sugar replacement called D-Lish.

Note: Intestinal bacteria are necessary for a healthy digestive system. Both polydextrose and inulin are prebiotic, soluble fibers. A *prebiotic* is a non-digestible food ingredient that selectively nourishes the beneficial bacteria in the digestive tract.

STARCHES, FLOURS, AND THICKENERS

Note: All-purpose flour has 22 net carbs per ¼ cup. Whole-wheat flour has from 18 to 21 in the same amount.

WHITE WHOLE-WHEAT FLOUR:
Regular whole-wheat flour is made from red winter wheat. The white variety has the same nutritional values as the red, with the bran and germ intact, but it tastes more like white flour. It is available in many stores and by mail order from the King Arthur® Flour Company and from Bob's Red Mill®.

CARBALOSE™ is a low-carb flour substitute made by Tova Industries, LLC. It can be used like all-purpose flour in most recipes by making a few changes (the liquids may need to be adjusted and the yeast or leavening increased; the temperature needs to be lowered by 25° F, and the cooking time increased slightly). It works well as a coating for fried foods. Carbalose™ has 19 net grams of carbohydrate per cup.

CARBQUIK™ BAKE MIX is a low-carb biscuit mix (similar to Bisquik™) made with Carbalose™ flour. It contains 90% fewer net carbs than Bisquik™ and has no trans fats. It can be used to make pancakes, pizza, dumplings, sweet dough, batter for fried foods, and lots of other things. I tried the Cheese Biscuit recipe from the back of the box and a pound cake recipe I found on the www.lowcarbfriends.com web site. Both were very good. (Never one to leave well enough alone, I added ¼ cup of grated Parmesan to the biscuits and used a little extra Splenda® in the cake. Try toasting a slice of buttered pound cake and topping with ice cream and berries—yum!) I also use Carbquik™ to make Fried Apple Pies (see p. 285). The Carbalose™ web site, www.carbalose.com, has more recipes.

LITE WHITE FLOUR BLEND from Big Skies Farm has 6 net carbs per ¼ cup serving (24 per cup). It can be used cup for cup to replace all-purpose flour in most recipes. They also sell a **Lite Whole Wheat Flour Blend** with 6 carbs and a **Golden Flour** that has only 4 net carbs per serving, but the golden one contains soy flour, so it won't taste as good as the others. (For thickening gravies and sauces, they recommend their Cornstarch Blend, which is a blend of gums, fibers, and low-glycemic cornstarch, which has zero net carbs per serving.)

ATKINS QUICK QUISINE™ BAKE MIX can be used to replace up to one third of the flour in regular recipes. It can be used as a breading for fried foods or thickener for sauces. It has 15 grams of carbohydrate and 12 grams of fiber for a net count of 3 carbs per ¼ cup.

BOB'S RED MILL® has added a low-carb bread mix to their extensive line of products. It comes with a yeast packet and a recipe to use for making bread in a bread machine or by hand with 5 net carbs per slice. I have also used it as breading for cutlets, chicken, and vegetables even though it has a small amount of sugar in the mix, unnecessary for anything but yeast bread.

MAKE YOUR OWN low-carb flour replacement with my recipe on p. 116. It also makes delicious pie crust and hot cereal that tastes like cream of wheat.

POTATO FLOUR:

Potato *flour* is made from whole potatoes, as opposed to potato *starch*, which is just the extracted starch. Some manufacturers label their product as "potato *starch* flour," but here the word "starch" is just a milling term, and it is, in fact, potato flour. It is higher in carbohydrates than wheat flour, but you need only one-third the amount for thickening. It is also higher than cornstarch, but you need only one-half the amount, so it still has an advantage. I use it for pastry cream, pie filling, sauces, and soups.

SOY FLOUR:

Soy flour is a high-protein substitute for wheat flour. It behaves a lot like all-purpose flour in breads and cakes, but I don't use very much of it because I find the taste to be unpleasant. It contains no gluten, so it will not work for yeast-raised baked goods.

Note: An American Heart Association committee review of 22 studies found that soy foods and supplements did not lower cholesterol, prevent cancer, or relieve the symptoms of menopause.[21] The Center for the Evaluation of Risks to Human Reproduction (one of the National Institutes of Health) is reviewing the latest research about the effects of soy products and baby formulas on human development and reproduction. Soy contains Genistein, which mimics the effect of estrogen in humans. A spokesperson for the soy industry countered that animal studies cannot be extrapolated to humans and that soy-based baby formula has been used for over 35 years.[22] (Somehow, that doesn't reassure me very much, considering what has happened since the 1970s.)

OAT FLOUR:

Oat flour is whole-grain flour containing the germ, the oil, and the fiber of the oat kernel. It has 48 net grams of carbohydrate per cup compared to 88 for wheat flour. It is delicious and can be substituted in most recipes that do not depend on yeast to rise.

GLUTEN FLOUR:

Gluten flour, also called "high-gluten flour" or "vital wheat gluten," is wheat flour that has had most of the starch removed. Many groceries and health food stores sell gluten flour in packages or in bulk. Bob's Red Mill® Gluten Flour is widely available in supermarkets, or it can be ordered by mail. *The Baker's Catalog* of The King Arthur® Flour Company also sells gluten flour by mail order. See p.116 for directions for pre-baking the flour to deactivate the gluten proteins.

It has been estimated that 1 in 133 people in the United States suffers from gluten intolerance, also known as Celiac disease. Strict adherence to a gluten-free diet for life is the only way to prevent serious complications from the disease. More information is available at www.celiac.com.

---

21   Jamie Stengle, "Review casts doubt on soy's benefits," *The Associated Press, The Seattle Times,* January 23, 2006.

22   Rita Rubin, *USA Today,* March 15, 2006.

ALMOND FLOUR AND ALMOND MEAL:

Almond *Flour* is not just ground, blanched, almonds; it is a by-product from the process of making almond oil. If you try to make it yourself by grinding almonds in a food processor, you may get almond butter. It makes a delicious substitute for some of the flour in many of my recipes for breads, cakes, and pastries and for coating fried foods.

Almond *Meal* consists of the entire almond, oil and outer coating included, ground to a powder. It is not as fine as almond flour but can be substituted for it in most recipes. You can make nut meal from whole nuts if you have a flourmill. It is possible to grind the nuts for a recipe in a food processor if you include some of the dry ingredients along with the nuts to absorb the oil; you must be careful not to over-process the mixture.

VEGETABLE GUMS:

Vegetable gums are frequently used in commercial products and are now available for home use. They add no carbohydrates to the food, but they also add no flavor and are currently very expensive.

Xanthan gum, a thickener and emulsifier, is a very common ingredient in purchased products. It may seem expensive, but you need only a tiny amount, so one package will last a long time. Bob's Red Mill® Xanthan Gum is available in an 8-ounce package for home use in grocery and health food stores. Bob's Red Mill® is also available by mail order and it and other brands are available on-line.

Xanthan gum is derived from a microorganism called Xanthomonas camestris. It is composed of almost indigestible simple sugars, similar to peanut shells. It acts as a stabilizer and emulsifier with the ability to give foods a smooth texture and to hold food particles together. It is frequently used as a gluten substitute in bread for people with intolerance for gluten. It can be used to replace the flour, cornstarch, potato flour, etc., used to thicken many foods. I don't like to replace all the thickener with xanthan, however, because it can give a slimy texture if used in excess. My French Vanilla Ice Cream calls for a small amount in order to approximate the texture of ice cream made with sugar.

This information came from Bob's Red Mill®:
"Use one teaspoon of xanthan gum to replace one tablespoon of the original thickener in sauces. Use ⅛ to ¼ teaspoon per one cup of liquid to thicken salad dressings."

Guar gum is another thickener that is commonly used in commercial products. Bob's Red Mill® sells it for home use or it can be ordered from *The Baker's Catalog* of The King Arthur® Flour Company. It is a white powder made from an East Indian Seed. It can be used as a thickener for salad dressings, ice creams, puddings, gravies, sauces, and soups.

Information from Bob's Red Mill®:
"Use one to three teaspoons of powdered guar gum per recipe (about one loaf of bread, one cake, or up to one quart of liquid)."

Note: Both xanthan and guar gum have zero net carbs in one tablespoon.

A company called ThickenThin markets three products that are mixtures of vegetable gums (guar, xanthan, carob, and acacia) used to thicken and add volume and texture to foods. They are called Not/Sugar, Not/Cereal, and Not/Starch. The only one I regularly use is Not/Sugar, which improves hard meringues and allows me to make them with no sugar at all. It can also be used to make jam with less fruit and more water and to improve the texture of baked goods and candy.

This information came from the ThickenThin Company:
"Use 2 tablespoons of Not/Sugar per each cup of sugar replaced. For meringues, sponge cakes, and egg foams, use 4 tablespoons or more per cup of sugar replaced." Note that you must still add a sugar substitute, as this product does not contain any sweeteners.

"Not/Cereal can be used for hot cereal and to make vegetable purées taste more like mashed potatoes. Not/Starch can be used to thicken any liquid."

CHEESE FLOUR:

Cheese flour can be ordered from the King Arthur® Flour Company and from Spices etc®. It is dry, powdered cheese, useful for thickening purées and sauces and as an ingredient in breading for fried foods.

WHEY PROTEIN POWDER:

Whey powder is dried milk protein. It is sold in health food stores as well as other grocery stores. Whey powder is useful for protein shakes and in baked goods as a flour substitute. It can also make up for the missing bulk when replacing sugar in recipes. Unsweetened and unflavored whey is the most versatile. Check the label and find one that has no more than two grams of carbohydrate per serving. Trader Joe's sells Designer Whey Protein that has two net carbs in each one-quarter-cup serving.

CORN:

Iroquois Corn:
I learned about Iroquois corn from a book about diabetes prevention, *Stop Diabetes,* by Gretchen Becker.[23] It is a variety of corn that was domesticated and raised by the Iroquois in what later became the state of New York. It is high in fiber and protein and has a low glycemic index (it does not cause a sudden rise in insulin levels). The nutrition information is not yet available for it, but since controlling insulin release is the point of a low-carb diet, it seems reasonable to assume that it would be permissible on a low-carb regimen. My own experience with it seems to bear that out.

Iroquois corn is available by mail order from Pinewood Products in three forms: roasted white cornmeal, tamal flour, and hulled hominy. The first one I ordered was the roasted white cornmeal; the aroma of freshly roasted corn filled the room when I opened the box. Modern hybrids have lost that wonderful fragrance. I have just started to experiment with it, using it like stone-ground, whole-grain, cornmeal. I intend to try it in all my recipes that call for masa harina or corn meal on the grounds that it may help, it can't hurt, and the flavor is incredible. My Corn Muffins and Fried Cornbread are made with Pinewood Products' white corn flour, and my Tortillas and Corn Chips are made with their tamal flour. The muffins are wonderful, sweet and dense, with chewy

---

23 Gretchen Becker, *Stop Diabetes, 50 Simple Steps You Can Take at Any Age to Reduce Your Risk of Type 2 Diabetes,* Marlowe and Company, New York, 2002.

dried cranberries. The taste of the tortillas is authentic. The cornbread takes me back home.

MEXICAN STYLE HOMINY:

Juanita's® Mexican-style Hominy has 4 net grams of carbohydrate per ½ cup. Most corn products, and even other brands of hominy, have from 13 to 25 grams in the same ½-cup amount. It can be used as a side dish or chopped in a food processor to use as a substitute for rice, bulgur, barley, grits, or polenta. If you can't find Juanita's®, there are other brands of canned hominy that are almost as low, just be sure it says "Mexican Style" on the label.

TEPARY BEANS:

This is another product that I learned about from Gretchen Becker's book on diabetes prevention.[24] Native Seeds Search sells both the beans, and the seeds for growing them, from the kind of plants cultivated by Native Americans in the arid regions of the Southwest. They come in three varieties: white, which is described as being mild and sweet; brown, which has a more nutty flavor; and blue speckled, which is similar to brown, but with its own distinctive taste. All are high protein, high fiber, and have a low glycemic index (they do not cause a sudden rise in blood sugar levels). I have not been able to get a carb count for them, but since the purpose of controlling carb intake is to prevent excess insulin production, which is the body's response to a high blood sugar level, it makes sense that we should be able to include these in our diet.

CREAM:

Some cartons marked "heavy cream" contain milk, thickeners, and stabilizers, which add carbohydrates. Look for cream that says "zero carbohydrates," and lists only "cream" as an ingredient, or you may be adding as much as sixteen carbs per cup of cream to your recipe. You may be more likely to find a zero-carb cream on the organic foods aisle. If you live in dairy farm country, as I do, it may be possible to arrange delivery of fresh cream to your door.

Note: I use the low-carb trick of substituting cream and water in my recipes that would normally call for milk, such as Crêpes and Hot Chocolate. This cuts the carb count from 12 grams per cup of milk to zero, and cream and water are readily available. If you prefer to expend a few more carbs but cut the calories, you may use my Milk recipe on p. 336 or use Hood's Calorie Countdown 2% milk.

Tips for buying and using cream:

Treat fresh cream very gently. Buy it at a store near where you live, if possible, so it doesn't get overheated or rattled around in the car on the trip home. Look for the "use by" date; sometimes it has already turned to butter while still on the shelf. Keep it cold and beat it only to the soft-peak stage to reduce the risk of producing butter. If the cream will need to be beaten or stirred again when adding other ingredients, stop a bit sooner than you normally would. Even the churning of ice cream can produce butter.

---

[24] Ibid.

You can buy dispensers for whipped cream that let you put in fresh cream and sugar-free sweetener. They use N_2O cartridges, labeled as "cream chargers," to aerate the cream. (Even the whipped cream from the aerosol containers at the supermarket has almost no carbohydrates, or fat either, for that matter, since it is mostly air.)

You can buy canned cream, like Nestlé® Media Crèma (table cream), so that you always have it on hand when you need it. It is best used as a replacement for fresh cream in recipes that will be cooked, but in a pinch, it can be whipped, although it will not be as light and fluffy as fresh whipped cream. Look for it with the Mexican foods at the supermarket.

Sour Cream is a product that I use in some of my recipes. I haven't been able to find a zero-carb, real sour cream, now that the food industry is convinced that we only want the low-fat and artificial versions. There are some organic sour creams with one carb in two tablespoons that don't have a lot of thickeners and additives, but the first ingredient listed on the label is milk, not cream, so it still contributes 8 unnecessary carbs per cup. One option is to buy *crème fraîche* to use instead. It is milder, which means you can use it on desserts, but unfortunately it is much more expensive to buy. Don't despair; it is easy to make:

CRÈME FRAÎCHE

Crème fraîche *has the advantage that it can be whipped like cream, and it can be boiled without curdling, so it works well in sauces and in cream soups.*

Combine 1 cup of heavy cream with 2 tablespoons of buttermilk in a glass container. (Use cream that is not ultra pasteurized, if possible.) Cover and let stand at room temperature for 8 to 24 hours, or until thick. It should mound when dropped from a spoon, but not be as thick as commercial sour cream. Stir well, cover, and refrigerate for up to ten days.

PER SERVING OF 2 TABLESPOONS:		
Total Carb: 0.2g	Fiber: 0g	Net Carb: 0.2g

Note: For a quick substitute for *Crème Fraîche,* mix equal parts sour cream and heavy cream. If you use a zero-carb cream, this will cut the carb count in half compared to purchased sour cream.

FERMENTED DAIRY PRODUCTS:

The labels on fermented dairy products, with live cultures, must list all of the carbs from the milk that goes into them, but, according to Drs. Jack Goldberg and Karen O'Mara, authors of the *GO-Diet,* [25] most of the sugar (lactose) has been converted to lactic acid. The amount of carbohydrate remaining is about 4 grams per cup. Cultured dairy products such as buttermilk, yogurt, sour cream, and kefir, with live cultures, provide "good" bacteria for the digestive system that can usually be tolerated even by those who are lactose-intolerant.

---

[25] Jack Goldberg, Ph.D., and Karen O'Mara, D.O., GO-Diet: *The Goldberg—O'Mara Diet Plan, the Key to Weight Loss & Healthy Eating,* Go Corp, 1999.

EQUIPMENT

Nothing on this list is essential. (Some of them are still on my wish list.)

USEFUL THINGS TO HAVE:

BLENDER

CRÊPE PAN—a crêpe pan's low slanted sides make turning easier. Non-stick is a plus. A small pan makes small crepes, which are easier to turn without tearing.

DOUBLE BOILER—A bowl set over a pan of water works, but it's useful to have one with a tight-fitting lid.

DEEP FRYER—the kind with a wire basket that can be lifted while the lid is closed has a safety advantage. The Roto Deep Fryer, by DēLonghi, has a tilted basket and uses half as much oil, since the food rotates through the oil.

FOOD PROCESSOR—not essential, but it's a great convenience.

FOOD MILL—a food mill does some things that a food processor can't do, such as making tomato sauce while separating out the skins and seeds, or straining out the seeds from raspberries to make a sauce.

ICE CREAM MACHINE—the kind that requires ice and salt works better for sugar-free ice cream than the counter-top models that use a pre-frozen canister.

KITCHEN SCALE—a digital scale that measures in both ounces and grams and can be reset to zero while holding a container is preferred. The Salter Housewares Dream Scale from Sur La Table is a good one. Check their web site at www.surlatable.com or call 800-243-0852 for a catalog.

MANDOLINE—a mandoline is useful for cutting vegetables into thin slices.

MICROWAVE OVEN

OVEN THERMOMETER—enables you to check the accuracy of your oven temperature.

INSTANT READ THERMOMETER—choose one that can be used to test the doneness of meat and to measure the temperature of water for bread making.

ELECTRIC MIXER—I have two: a stand mixer and a hand-held one that I use with a copper bowl. Sometimes it's handy to use them simultaneously, one for egg whites, one for whipped cream, as when making ice cream.

UNLINED COPPER BOWL—used only for beating egg whites. Mine cost $3 dollars at a garage sale. (I had to scour off a lacquer coating.)

EXTRA FREEZER—gluten flour, whole-wheat flour, cornmeal, and many other ingredients keep longer if frozen. It is also convenient for freezing extra bread, cake, and cookies and to keep a supply of frozen fruits, vegetables, nuts, etc., on hand.

TIMER—Polder makes a digital timer/clock that hangs on a cord so you can wear it around your neck. I like this one because it frees me to do other things without worry about being out of hearing range. It's available from *The Baker's Catalog* of the King Arthur® Flour Company as well as other catalogs and in stores.

WAFFLE IRON

NUTRITION INFORMATION

The nutrition information for the recipes in this book is based on the information provided on the labels and packages of the designated products; the *USDA Nutrient Data Base for Standard Reference*; *The Complete Book of Food Counts* by Corinne T. Netzer;[1] *The Carbohydrate, Fiber, and Sugar Counter,* by Annette B. Natow and Jo-Ann Heslin;[2] and *Dr. Atkins' New Carbohydrate Gram Counter.*[3] Only the items on the ingredients list in the recipes are included in the nutrition counts. Suggested condiments, toppings, and garnishes are excluded or given in parentheses. Ingredients listed as "optional" are not included in the counts. If there is more than one option for an ingredient, the count may only reflect the first one listed.

Additional information about nutrients is available from the USDA National Nutrient Database for Standard Reference at http://www.nal.usda.gov/fnic/foodcomp/search. To search for a single nutrient, such as vitamin C, fat, or protein, go to the Nutrient Lists.

---

[1] Corinne T. Netzer, *The Complete Book of Food Counts,* Dell Publishing, New York, 2000.

[2] Annette B. Natow and Jo-Ann Heslin, *The Carbohydrate, Fiber, and Sugar Counter,* Pocket Books, New York, 1999.

[3] Robert C. Atkins, M.D., *Dr. Atkins New Carbohydrate Gram Counter,* M. Evans and Company, Inc., New York, 2002.

THE CARBS THAT COUNT

Foods are made up of three elements: fats, proteins, and carbohydrates. The government defines a carbohydrate as anything that is not a fat or a protein. This means that indigestible fiber must be included in the total carbohydrate counts on labels. The *net carb count* is the common way of designating the number of grams of carbohydrate contained in a food after subtracting the metabolically inactive grams of fiber. Drs. Michael R. and Mary Dan Eades (authors of *Protein Power*) use *effective carbohydrate count* or ECC;[1] Dr. Atkins used the term *net carbohydrate count.*[2] It means the same thing. At the end of each of my recipes you will find the carbohydrate count, the fiber count, and, in bold type, the net carbohydrate count, which is the first one minus the second one. The sugar alcohols are not included in the total or the net count, but are noted below.

---

[1] Michael R. Eades, M.D. and Mary Dan Eades, M.D., *Protein Power,* Bantam, 1996.

[2] Robert Atkins, M.D., *Dr. Atkins' New Diet Revolution,* Avon, New York, 1992.

MEASURES

All of my dry measures are what is called "dip, level, pour." That means you dip a measuring container in the ingredient and level it off with a straight-edged spatula or knife, so that it is not compacted. In many cases, I have also included the weight, since settling and moisture content can affect the volume.

EGGS

Eggs are large, unless otherwise specified. Yolks and whites are from large eggs.

RECIPES FOUND ELSEWHERE IN THE BOOK

Capitalized items are included elsewhere in the book; they can be located by referring to the Index.

APPETIZERS AND SNACKS

Tips and Notes

Low-carb appetizers needn't be limited to veggies and dip. Using low-carb bread, crackers, tortillas, and crêpes as the base gives us almost unlimited choices. See below to find many appetizers given as variations under other recipes throughout the book. See index.

Blini and Cocktail Crêpes.

Parmesan Lace Crisps.

Nachos and Quesadillas.

Faux Potato Chips and Sour Cream Dip.

Appetizer Puffs.

Oven-Dried Tomatoes. Make using small plum or cherry tomatoes. Serve alone, as a carrier for dips or cheese, or sprinkle them with oregano and use on Pepperoni Pizza Bites instead of the tomato sauce.

Macadamia Coconut Crusted Shrimp. Serve two or three per person with Sweet and Spicy Sauce for dipping.

Tamale Pancakes. Top them with cheese and salsa like tiny tacos.

Soup Shots. A tiny serving of soup makes an excellent appetizer. Try Vichyssoise using my recipe for Potato Soup. Serve it in a shot glass—no spoon needed!

ANTIPASTO TRAY

An antipasto tray should include a varied assortment of Italian style meats, cheeses, vegetables, and condiments. Choose from the following list or substitute others if you prefer. Make everything bite-size and arrange attractively on a large platter. Thin slices of meat and cheese can be rolled up or cut into strips. All of the pickled and marinated items can be purchased ready-made, either in jars or from the deli.

Marinated artichoke hearts
A variety of Italian olives
Sardines
Anchovies
Marinated roasted eggplant
Pickled cherry peppers
Hot peppers
Marinated mushrooms
Roasted red peppers, cut into strips (purchased, or made by
    directions on p.162)
Fresh red or yellow peppers, cut into strips
Pepperoni
Prosciutto
Salami
Provolone cheese
Mozzarella cheese

Ancient Ayurvedic Proverb:
"When the diet is wrong,
medicine is of no use.
When the diet is correct,
medicine is of no need."

GRILLED ARTICHOKES

Serve these as a convivial appetizer or side dish, beautiful to see, with wonderful flavor and aroma. What a great way to get a party started!

- Two large fresh artichokes
- Lemon slice or juice (to prevent cut edges from darkening)

2 or 3 cloves of roasted garlic

¼ cup of butter, melted

1 tablespoon of parsley, minced

¼ teaspoon of salt

- Freshly ground black pepper to taste

Cut artichoke stems to about one inch in length. Remove and discard small lower leaves; cut off top one-third of each artichoke. Use kitchen shears to trim tips of leaves to remove thorns. Cut artichokes in half. Rub cut surfaces with lemon slice or drop in a bowl of water with lemon juice added. Put an inch or two of water in a steamer or large pot with a rack and bring to a simmer. Place artichoke halves on rack; cover pot with a lid. Steam for 25 minutes or until tender and leaves pull out easily. Remove, drain, and let cool. Use a paring knife or spoon to scrape out the choke (the furry white fibers in the center). Remove the small purple leaves above the choke, being careful of the thorns on the tips.

Meanwhile, remove the papery outer layer from a bulb of garlic, leaving cloves intact. Cut off ½ inch from the top of the bulb. Rub generously with olive oil and wrap in foil. Bake at 400° F for 35 minutes or until very soft. Let cool. Squeeze garlic cloves out of skins. Mash into melted butter with a fork. (Use extra garlic for another purpose.) Add parsley, salt, and pepper. Baste artichoke halves with garlic butter, spooning down between leaves.

Heat grill or broiler to medium/high.

Grill Artichokes, cut side down, or place under broiler, cut side up, until brown, about 4 minutes. Turn and baste with garlic butter. Grill until outer leaves are charred. Sprinkle with coarse salt and serve with cold Mustard Dressing for dipping (see p. 92). To eat, pull off leaves, dip base in dressing, and scrape off the fleshy lower part of each leaf between teeth. (Provide a receptacle for discarded leaves, as they will make quite a pile.) Then cut up the heart and dip in dressing also.

Makes four servings of ½ artichoke each.

PER SERVING:		
Total Carb: 3.1g	Fiber: 1.6g	Net Carb: 1.5g

Tips and Notes

Artichokes are generally considered incompatible with wine because they affect the taste buds and can change the taste of whatever food or drink follows. The chemical they contain, called cynarin, enhances sweet flavors, so some experts suggest pairing them with very dry, acidic wines, which might be improved by the sweetness. Most agree that it is better to reserve a really good wine to accompany a later course.

A cut artichoke will darken from exposure to air. To prevent this, rub the cut surfaces with lemon immediately after cutting. Use stainless steel or other non-reactive knives and cooking utensils for artichokes, or they will blacken.

Brown tips on artichokes may be caused by frost damage, which does not affect their flavor.

SUPER BOWL
PARTY MENU:

Bread Pretzels with hot
mustard

Buffalo Wings with Bleu
Cheese Dressing and
celery sticks

Soy Nuts

Buttered Popcorn

Tortilla Chips and salsa

Cold low-carb beer
Sugar-free Soft Drinks

*

BUFFALO WINGS

The original hot wings came from Buffalo, New York. They are messy and macho and the perfect low-carb, pig-out snack. They are traditionally served with cold celery sticks and Bleu Cheese Dressing to put out the fire.

20 to 25 chicken wing "drummettes" (the meaty first section of the wing)
- Oil for frying
1/4 cup butter (1/2 stick)
1 to 2 ounces Tabasco® sauce, or to taste

Serve with:
Celery sticks
Bleu Cheese Dressing, recipe follows.

Heat oil in a deep fryer or skillet to 370° F. Dry the wings well on paper towels, sprinkle them with salt, but do not use flour or breading on the chicken. Fry wings, in several batches, for 10 to 12 minutes or until golden brown and very crisp. Drain on paper towels.

Melt the butter in a small saucepan and stir in the hot sauce. Dip the wings in the butter mixture. Arrange them on a platter and serve hot with celery sticks and Bleu Cheese Dressing for dipping.

Servings: 20 to 25 wings

PER SERVING:		
Total Carb: Trace	Fiber: 0g	Net Carb: Trace

BLEU CHEESE DRESSING

1/2 cup real mayonnaise
1/2 cup sour cream
1 tablespoon lemon juice
1/4 cup bleu cheese, crumbled
- Salt and pepper to taste

Mix all ingredients together and chill.

Serving size: 2 tablespoons

PER SERVING:		
Total Carb: 0.5g	Fiber: 0g	Net Carb: 0.5g

Meatballs

Form the Meat Loaf mixture (see p. 201) into small meatballs. Fry, in several batches, in oil for 3 to 4 minutes until brown and firm. Serve on wooden picks with warmed sugar-free Barbecue Sauce (see p. 218) for dipping.

Servings: about 40 meatballs

PER SERVING:		
Total Carb: 0.8g	Fiber: 0.1g	Net Carb: 0.7g

Pepperoni Chips

Thin slices of pepperoni become crisp and delicious when heated in a microwave oven. These make a great, zero-carb substitute for potato or tortilla chips for snacking. Pile them onto a big platter, set a bowl of salsa or dip in the middle, and watch them disappear!

Place the pepperoni slices in a single layer between paper towels and heat in the microwave until crisp. In my microwave oven, eight slices take 1 minute and 10 seconds at full power; twenty-five slices take 2 minutes.

Use Pepperoni Chips in place of crackers for canapés, topped with a bit of cream cheese and a teaspoon of chutney. You can also crumble them on salads or soups or use them anywhere you would use bacon bits. Store in the refrigerator in an airtight container.

PER SERVING:		
Total Carb: 0g	Fiber: 0g	Net Carb: 0g

Protein on a stick

Anything that can be grilled on a skewer, like lamb kabobs, Sesame Pork (see p. 208), or chicken sates, makes for delicious nibbling. Meatballs and bacon-wrapped shrimp, served on wooden picks, with flavorful sauces for dipping, are sure to be crowd pleasers.

VARIATION

Pepperoni Pizza Bites

Make Pepperoni Chips. Spread each slice with ¼ teaspoon of pizza sauce (or tomato sauce mixed with a pinch of dried oregano) and top with 1 teaspoonful of shredded mozzarella cheese. Reheat briefly to melt the cheese. Serve hot.

Each Piece:
Total Carb: 0.1g,
Fiber: 0g,
Net Carb: 0.1g

RUMAKI

A perennial favorite that is about as low-carb as it gets!

1   pound chicken livers
1   tablespoon soy sauce
1   (8-ounce) can whole water chestnuts, drained
9   slices precooked or partially cooked bacon, cut in half

Preheat the oven to 400° F.

Cut each chicken liver into bite-size pieces and remove the connective tissue. Place in a bowl with the soy sauce, turn to coat, and refrigerate for 15 minutes. Cut the water chestnuts into ¼-inch slices. Wrap a piece of liver and a slice of water chestnut in each half-slice of bacon. Secure with a wooden pick. Place on a broiler pan and bake in a preheated 400° F oven for about 20 minutes, or until the liver is cooked and the bacon is crisp. Serve warm.

Servings: about 16

PER SERVING:		
Total Carb: 1.2g	Fiber: 0.3g	Net Carb: 0.9g

MELON WITH PROSCIUTTO

1   cantaloupe, honeydew, or other ripe melon
½   pound thinly sliced prosciutto
1   lime, quartered

Peel and seed the melon and cut into thin wedges. Arrange several wedges in a fan pattern on each of eight plates. Divide the prosciutto into eight portions and place over the melon slices. Serve with a lime wedge to squeeze over top.

Servings: 8

PER SERVING:		
Total Carb: 5.9g	Fiber: 1.0g	Net Carb: 4.9g

Tips and Notes

Using packaged, precooked bacon prevents excess shrinkage and fat accumulation. It should not be crisp, since it needs to be flexible enough to roll. If you prefer, you may use raw bacon: microwave it between paper towels until it is partially done but not crisp.

CANDLELIGHT DINNER MENU:

Melon with Prosciutto
- -
Pan Seared Duck Breast Brown Sauce

Candied Kumquats

Rutabaga Fried in Duck Fat

Sautéed Asparagus
- -
Browned Butter Rhubarb Almond Cake
*

STUFFED PEAS

The quick dip in boiling water makes the pea pods crisp-tender and brightens their green color. Prepare these on the day they will be served and chill until serving time.

25 (about 4 ounces) small, tender snow peas
• Boiling, salted water for blanching peas
¼ pound Boursin herb cheese or other soft cheese, flavored with pepper, garlic, or herbs

Bring the water to a boil in a large pot. Have ready a bowl of ice water.

Break the tip of the stem end of the peas and pull it down to remove the strings that run along the edges of the pod. Add the peas to the boiling water and cook for 15 seconds. Dip them out and plunge them into the ice bath. Let them sit for a few minutes to cool and stop the cooking. Drain and blot dry. Insert the tip of a small knife into the stem end and slit each pod open on the curved side so that the tiny peas are undisturbed. Use a pastry tube or a blunt knife to fill each pea with the cheese.

Servings: 25

PER SERVING:		
Total Carb: 1.8g	Fiber: 0.7g	Net Carb: 1.1g

Stuffed Vegetables

Bite-size stuffed vegetables make perfect finger foods. They're neat, they don't require toast, crackers, or chips (so you can save those carbs to spend later), and they won't spoil your appetite for dinner. Mushrooms, celery, artichoke bottoms, Belgian endive leaves, snow peas, sweet pepper wedges, and cherry tomatoes can be used as containers for pâté, curried chicken, herbed cheese, Crème Fraîche with caviar, or whatever suits your fancy.

"Leave your drugs in the chemist's pot if you can heal the patient with food."
—Hippocrates

- **Fennel:** Rinse the fennel and cut off and discard the stalks and fronds. Trim away about $1/8$ inch from the bottom of the bulb. Slice the bulb vertically into slices a little less than $1/2$ inch thick.
- **Asparagus:** Choose very fresh small asparagus with tightly closed tips. Break off and discard the lower part of the stalk. Pare away the outside skin of the stalk with a vegetable peeler. Rinse in cold water.
- **Celery:** Cut inner stalks into 3- to 4-inch sections.
- **Zucchini:** Choose small, firm zucchini. Trim off both ends and cut into thick strips.
- **Radishes:** Rinse in cold water and cut off the roots, but leave the tops on to use as handles for dipping.
- **Broccoli:** Use just the stalks, pared and cut into thick slices; save the florets for another use.
- **Scallion:** Rinse and trim roots and ends. Leave whole.
- **Red and yellow peppers:** Rinse, remove seeds and membranes, and cut into wedges.
- **Jicama:** Peel and cut into wide strips or slices.

BAGNA CAUDA

Bagna cauda means "hot bath" in Italian. It was traditionally served with winter vegetables like cardoons, artichokes, and scallions. The tangy dip must be kept hot to contrast with the cold, crunchy, raw vegetables for an authentic bagna cauda.

- Raw vegetables for dipping (see sidebar)

Hot Piedmontese Dip:
$3/4$ cup extra virgin olive oil
3 tablespoons butter
2 teaspoons garlic, finely chopped
8 to 10 anchovy filets, or about 2 ounces, finely chopped
- Salt

Prepare the vegetables (choose from the list at left, or use others in season). Keep them in ice water until serving time. Drain and arrange attractively on a platter.

Put $1/2$ inch of water in the bottom of a double boiler. Bring to a brisk simmer. Put the oil and butter in another pan and heat over a burner set on medium-low until the butter melts and just begins to foam. Add the garlic and sauté briefly but do not let it color. Put the mixture in the top pan of the double boiler and place over the simmering water. Add the anchovies and cook, mashing them with a fork or spatula, until they dissolve into a paste. Add salt to taste and place in a fondue pot or a serving pot set over a candle warmer. Serve with the vegetables. Makes about 1 cup of dip.

Serving size: 2 tablespoons

PER SERVING:		
Total Carb: 0.2g	Fiber: 0g	Net Carb: 0.2g
count is for dip only		

Basic Recipe for Hard-cooked Eggs

Cooking the eggs upright in an egg rack will help keep the yolks centered, a useful thing, both for esthetics and for a uniform container of egg white for stuffing. Another way to center the yolks: put a rubber band around the carton of raw eggs and store it on its side in the refrigerator

Place the eggs in a heavy pan and cover with water to a depth of 1½ inches over the top of the eggs. Place a lid on the pan so that it is partially covered and bring the water to a full boil. Immediately turn the heat to low and cover the pan. Continue to cook for 30 seconds, then remove the pan from the heat and let stand for 15 minutes. Drain eggs and hold under cold running water until they are cool. Roll them on a counter to crack the shells and peel them under running water.

Serving size: 1 egg

PER SERVING:		
Total Carb: 0.6g	Fiber: 0g	Net Carb: 0.6g

Stuffed Eggs

Always welcome at picnics and barbecues but also a perfect low-carb appetizer.

8   Hard-cooked Eggs (see Basic Hard-cooked Eggs), shelled and chilled
1   teaspoon dry mustard
3   tablespoons heavy cream (more or less as needed)
1   tablespoon shallot, minced
1   tablespoon lemon juice
1   tablespoon fresh chives, chopped, plus additional for garnish
¼   teaspoon salt
⅛   teaspoon pepper

Slice eggs in half lengthwise. Reserve the whites. Mash the yolks lightly with a fork. Add cream until yolk is moistened. Add other ingredients and blend. Fill the egg whites with the mixture and garnish with chopped fresh chives. Refrigerate until ready to serve. Makes 16 halves.

Serving size: ½ egg

PER SERVING:		
Total Carb: 0.5g	Fiber: 0g	Net Carb: 0.5g

Tips and Notes

For perfectly cooked eggs, I use an electric appliance called the Global Design Egg Cooker by Toastmaster. It accommodates six eggs at a time and they always turn out beautifully with shells that slip right off. I don't recall where I purchased mine, but you can check with the company at 1-800-947-3744 or www.toast-master.com for sources.

QUAIL EGGS IN A NEST

VARIATION

Break quail eggs into Appetizer Puff cases (see p. 120). Bake, season, and garnish as directed for Quail Eggs in a Nest.

Serving size: 1 piece
Total Carb: 1.7g
Fiber: 0.5g
Net Carb: 1.2g

Clean fresh medium- to large-sized mushrooms (about 2½ inches across) and remove the stems. Sprinkle them with salt and brush with melted butter. Place the mushrooms, rounded side up, on a baking sheet and bake at 425° F for 10 minutes. Remove from the oven and drain on paper towels. Blot the mushrooms with additional paper towels, pressing down into the cap with the towels to soak up excess moisture. Reduce the oven temperature to 325° F. Arrange the mushroom caps, hollow side up, on the pan and break a quail egg into each one. Spray the eggs with no-stick spray or drizzle with oil or melted butter. Bake for about 8 minutes or until the whites are set. Remove from the oven and sprinkle with grated Swiss cheese. Return to the oven for a few minutes more until the cheese is melted and the yolks are cooked to your taste, creamy or firm. Sprinkle with salt and pepper. Garnish with snipped chives or crumbled crisp bacon or serve with Hollandaise Sauce (see p. 225). Serve hot.

Serving size: 1 piece

PER SERVING:		
Total Carb: 1.0g	Fiber: 0g	Net Carb: 1.0g

TEA EGGS

These beautiful eggs look like alabaster. I make them with The Republic of Tea's Blackberry Sage Tea, but you can try other flavors or just use regular black tea like the classic Chinese recipe.

6 hard-cooked eggs (see p. 65)
5 cups water
¼ cup black or flavored tea (loose, not in teabags)
3 star anise pods
1 stick cinnamon
1 teaspoon salt

Prepare hard-cooked eggs and cool them in cold water as in Basic Recipe for Hard Boiled Eggs. Roll them gently on the counter or tap them all over with a spoon until the shells are uniformly cracked but still intact. Bring the water to a boil in a medium-sized saucepan (the water should cover the eggs) and add the tea, spices, and salt. Carefully place the eggs in the water. Cover the pan and simmer on low heat for 1 hour. The shells will turn brown. Turn off the heat and let the eggs stand in the water for an additional 2 hours. Store the eggs, covered, in the refrigerator until ready to serve, then peel and slice lengthwise into quarters. They can be stored for up to a week, but they taste better if served within two or three days.

Servings: 24 slices

PER SERVING:		
Total Carb: 0.2g	Fiber: 0g	Net Carb: 0.2g

SESAME CHEESE BALLS

¼ cup sesame seeds (Using a bit more makes it easier to coat the cheese.)
1 (8-ounce) package cream cheese
2 ounces soy sauce

Toast the sesame seeds in a 350° F oven for 15 minutes or until golden. Let cool. Cut the cream cheese into twenty-four squares. Roll each square into a ball. Roll the cheese balls in sesame seeds until coated. Dip in soy sauce, drain, and serve on wooden picks.

Servings: 24

PER SERVING:		
Total Carb: 0.6g	Fiber: 0.2g	Net Carb: 0.4g

Tips and Notes

Buy sesame seeds from the bulk bins at the grocery if possible rather than in the expensive, small jars sold with the spices. You may be able to buy them already toasted.

HOT BRIE

Use triple-cream Brie if possible. Either my Shallot and Peach or Rhubarb Ginger Chutney (see pp. 230, 231) goes well with this.

1 small wheel ripe French Brie cheese (8 ounces)
¼ cup sliced almonds

Preheat oven to 350° F.

Place cheese on a baking sheet. Sprinkle almonds on top. Heat in the oven for 3 to 4 minutes until slightly melted. Place on serving platter and garnish with chutney and fresh fruit. Serve warm with Parmesan Sesame Crackers (see p. 136).

Servings: 10

PER SERVING:		
Total Carb: 0.5g cheese and almonds only	Fiber: 0.3g	Net Carb: 0.2g

In Spain, the tidbits that accompany drinks are called tapas, which means "cover," a name whose origin can be traced to the slices of ham or cheese that were placed on top of wine glasses to keep the flies out. The small plates of Greece are called meze, which means middle; mezethes (the plural of meze) are served, not as a prelude to a meal, but as nibbles to go with drinks and conversation in the middle of the after-noon

Fresh basil keeps better at room temperature than in the refrigerator.

I trim the stems and put it in a vase, changing the water every few days. Put a clear plastic bag over the top and you have a little green house. Sometimes it will even root in the water. I seem to have better luck growing it this way than in a pot with soil.

"Cheese—milk's leap toward immortality."

—Clifton Paul Fadiman

BRUSCHETTA

1   cup flavorful ripe tomatoes, chopped and drained
½   cup fresh sweet basil leaves, shredded
3   tablespoons olive oil
2   teaspoons red wine vinegar or balsamic vinegar
3   thin slices low-carb bread, cut in half
    (Mixed Flour Bread, see p. 144, or use purchased bread with 3 to 4 net carbs per slice.)
2   cloves fresh garlic, cut in half

Mix tomatoes and basil together and add 1 tablespoon of the olive oil and the vinegar. Place the remaining 2 tablespoons of olive oil in a skillet and sauté the bread slices until well browned, adding more oil if needed. Remove the bread from the pan and rub both sides with the cut cloves of garlic. Heap the tomato mixture onto the hot bread slices and serve.

Servings: 6

PER SERVING:		
Total Carb: 4.2g	Fiber: 1.0g	Net Carb: 3.2g

GRILLED HALLOUMI® AND VEGETABLE SKEWERS

This remarkable cheese doesn't melt which allows it to be grilled or fried without a coating of breading. It is a sheep's milk cheese from Cyprus with a taste and texture that is somewhere between feta and mozzarella.

Cut the cheese into 1-inch cubes and thread it onto skewers with onions, peppers, and mushrooms. Grill for 10 minutes or until cheese is golden brown. Sprinkle with dried oregano and serve.

A one-ounce serving of Halloumi® has one net gram of carbohydrate.

FRIED HALLOUMI®

Halloumi® can also be fried with no oil; it will still become brown and crisp.

Cut cheese into thin slices or ½- by ½-inch strips. Preheat 2 or 3 tablespoons of oil in a large skillet on medium heat. Fry cheese for about 2 minutes on each side until very brown and crisp. Serve with marinara sauce for dipping or sprinkle with capers and serve with lemon wedges as an appetizer. It can also be served as a side dish like french fries or slices can be used as a base for canapés or mini-pizzas.

A one-ounce serving of Halloumi® has one net gram of carbohydrate.

Tip: Halloumi® keeps well; it can be refrigerated, or even frozen, for up to one year. After opening, rewrap any remaining Halloumi® in plastic wrap to prevent it from drying out and store in the refrigerator.

DOUBLE GRILLED CHEESE SANDWICHES

Literally, grilled cheese sandwiches. *I was just being silly when I made these, but they are really good!*

Cut the Halloumi® into thin slices, as wide as possible. Cut Cheddar cheese into slices that are slightly smaller and sandwich between two pieces of the Halloumi®. Melt 1 or 2 tablespoons of butter in a skillet and fry for a minute or two on each side or until golden brown. Serve hot.

A one-ounce serving of Halloumi® has one net gram of carbohydrate. Cheddar cheese has zero carbs.

Tips and Notes

The name "Halloumi®" is derived from the ancient word "Halmi" which means "salty." The saltiness comes from the fact that the cheese was traditionally preserved in brine. "Halloumi®" is officially recognized as a distinctive cheese indigenous to Cyprus and bears trademark protection in the United States. The Cypriots actually have Halloumi® police who inspect stores and dairies to make sure the historical methods are used in the production of the cheese. See Sources.

Cotija, a dry, salty, Mexican cheese is similar to Halloumi® and can be used in much the same way.

THINGS THAT GO CRUNCH

NUTS

Nuts are tasty, healthful, and low in carbs—great for a quick snack or for munching in front of the TV. Buy walnuts in the shell and use a nutcracker so they last longer. Or roast some peanuts in the shell; just the smell is enough to make you feel like a kid again.

POPCORN

Popcorn has three grams of carbohydrate per cup. Buy plain popcorn and pop it yourself in an air popper or in a pan with peanut or coconut oil. Pour on melted butter and sprinkle with salt. Rent a movie and have a sugar-free cola with your hot buttered popcorn. Is this a great diet or what?

Alternative:
Soy Crisps made by GeniSoy Products are like little popcorn or rice cakes, but with only about ½ gram of carbohydrate each. See Sources.

BAKED KALE

Try this as a novelty for a bright green crunchy snack or garnish

Wash and dry fresh kale leaves, discarding the stems. Cut across the leaves to make shreds. Heat the oven to 350° F. Spread the kale on a greased or nonstick baking sheet. Bake for 8 to 15 minutes, stirring occasionally, or until dry but not brown. Sprinkle with salt and grated Parmesan cheese. The kale needs to be completely cooled before storing. It can be stored in an airtight container for one or two days.

Serving size: 1 ounce fresh kale

PER SERVING:		
Total Carb: 2.8g	Fiber: 0.4g	Net Carb: 2.4g

Pumpkin Seeds

Pumpkin Seeds are a super low-carb snack. They come in several flavors in expensive little bags from the health food store, but you can buy them from the bulk bins at the grocery store for less. Trader Joe's, always the best place to buy nuts, has them also. Check Sources. Get the green ones that don't have to be shelled. They come from pumpkins that have seeds without hulls. Usually these come already roasted and salted, but if not, you can do it yourself. (Don't bother to save the seeds from your pumpkins unless they are a variety that has naked seeds. If they have to be shelled, the tiny kernels are not worth the effort.)

2   tablespoons peanut oil
1   cup green pumpkin seeds
¼   teaspoon salt

Heat the oil in a nonstick skillet on medium heat. Add the pumpkin seeds and stir until they start to pop and turn brown, 4 or 5 minutes. Drain on paper towels. Sprinkle with salt and store in an airtight container.

Servings: 4 (¼ cup each)

PER SERVING:		
Total Carb: 5.0g	Fiber: 1.0g	Net Carb: 4.0g

Soy Nuts

Whole dried soybeans that have been soaked in water and roasted are called soy nuts. They taste like very crunchy peanuts. They can be eaten as a snack or used in salads or as a garnish. Soy nuts can be purchased salted or plain, in a variety of flavors, or coated with chocolate or yogurt.

To make soy nuts at home, cover dried soybeans with water and soak for 8 hours. Spread on a greased cookie sheet and bake at 350° F, stirring frequently, until brown and crisp. Store airtight.

Sources vary, but soy nuts contain about 5 net carbs per ounce.

Tips and Notes

Some tree nuts, like walnuts, almonds, pecans, and hazelnuts will soon be allowed to carry labels advertising their health benefits. Peanuts and cashews are not true nuts, and both are higher in carbs than tree nuts. (Peanuts are legumes, like peas; cashews are seeds that grow on the outside of the cashew fruit.)

SOUPS, CHOWDERS, AND CHILI

SOUPERHEROES

Soup can solo as a hearty lunch or supper, or it can add dimension and variety to a meal as a starter or a side dish.

> "It's good soup and not fine words that keeps me alive."
>
> —Molière

Tips and Notes

The rind of Parmesan cheese should not be grated, but it can be added to the simmering stock for extra flavor. Remove the rind before adding the egg mixture.

STRACCIATELLA SOUP

Stracciatelli, Italian for "little rags," refers to the shreds of egg in this Roman-style egg drop soup. The stock can be beef or chicken, but the success of the soup depends on the quality of the stock.

4   cups beef stock
4   eggs
1   ounce freshly grated Parmesan cheese, about ½ cup, but the volume may change depending on whether it is compacted or fluffy
1   tablespoon fresh parsley, chopped
•   Ground nutmeg
•   Pepper to taste and salt if needed

Bring the stock to a boil in a large saucepan and then reduce the heat to medium. Break the eggs into a bowl and beat with a whisk until well blended. Whisk the cheese, parsley, and a sprinkle of nutmeg into the eggs. Pour the egg mixture in a thin stream into the simmering stock. Let it cook for a few seconds and then whisk to break up the strands of egg. Continue to whisk for about 4 minutes until the egg is cooked. Add freshly ground pepper, but taste before adding salt, since the stock and cheese may provide enough. Serve the soup in heated bowls.

Servings: 4

PER SERVING:		
Total Carb: 0.6g	Fiber: 0.2g	Net Carb: 0.4g

CHICKEN AND VEGETABLE SOUP

Make lots of soup so you'll have leftovers; it's even better the next day. The baby corn I've used in this soup is the kind used in Chinese cooking. It is very low in carbohydrates compared to whole kernel corn.

1   small rutabaga, peeled and diced
1   walnut in the shell
1   lemon slice with peel
1   boneless, skinless chicken breast (about 1 pound)
2   tablespoons olive oil
4   cups chicken broth or water
1   onion, chopped (about 3/4 cup)
1   cup celery, chopped
2   (14.5-ounce) cans diced tomatoes, including juice
1   cup shelled green soybeans (edamame), frozen or fresh
1   cup shredded cabbage
1   (15-ounce) can baby corn, drained, and sliced horizontally into 1/4-inch slices
2   Turkish bay leaves
1   teaspoon dried thyme
1   tablespoon dried parsley
2   teaspoons Worcestershire sauce
•   Salt and pepper to taste

Cook the rutabaga in a generous amount of water with the walnut and the lemon slice for 15 to 20 minutes. Drain. Discard the walnut and lemon slice.

Cut the chicken into roughly 1-inch pieces. Heat the olive oil in a large, heavy pot. Sauté the chicken with the precooked rutabaga, the onion, and celery over medium heat until it is just starting to brown and the onion is soft. Add all other ingredients, cover, and simmer over low heat for 1 hour or more. Extra soup can be frozen for individual servings.

Servings: 16

PER SERVING:		
Total Carb: 7g	Fiber: 2.7g	Net Carb: 4.3g

Tips and Notes

Adding walnuts in the shell to the cooking liquid will neutralize the odor of cooking cabbage; I have discovered that it also helps counteract the turnip or cabbage flavor of similar vegetables, like cauliflower and rutabaga. Lemon also helps to neutralize strong flavors. Changing the water once while boiling makes them even milder.

Bay leaf is an aromatic herb that comes from the ever-green bay laurel tree, native to the Mediterranean. There are two main varieties of bay leaves that are dried to use for cooking. The Turkish bay has oval leaves, one to two inches long. The California bay has narrow, pointed leaves, two to three inches long. Turkish bay leaves are generally considered to be superior, with a more subtle taste, and a higher price tag. When substituting California bay leaves for Turkish, use half the amount. Be sure to remove the bay leaves from foods before serving, because the edges are hard and sharp.

VARIATION: ROASTED CHICKEN SOUP

I started making this soup using leftover chicken or turkey when my husband was in graduate school. We called it "carcass soup" back in those days. I remember vividly the first time I had the luxury of throwing away the turkey bones after Thanksgiving. It does make a delicious soup though, especially now that we have it because we want to.

Put the leftover chicken or turkey bones and any leftover meat in a large pot with 4 cups of water. Break the carcass apart if necessary so that it is covered with water. Add 1 peeled onion, 1 carrot, 1 stalk of celery with top leaves, 2 bay leaves, and salt and pepper to taste. Simmer on low heat for one hour. Take out the chicken and vegetables with a slotted spoon. Remove any bits of meat left on the carcass, and discard the bones and skin. Discard the onion, celery, carrot, and bay leaves used to flavor the broth. Strain the broth, and return the broth and the meat to the pot.

In another pan, sauté 1 chopped onion, 1 cup of chopped celery, and the precooked rutabaga in olive oil over medium heat until tender. Add to the soup pot and add the rest of the vegetables and seasoning ingredients as in the recipe for Chicken and Vegetable Soup. Simmer for an hour.

Servings: 16

PER SERVING:		
Total Carb: 7.0g	Fiber: 2.7g	Net Carb: 4.3g

CREAM OF CELERY ROOT SOUP

The "Dirty Hairy" of vegetables turns to silk and satin as a purée.

3³/₄ ounces shallots (³/₄ cup, chopped)
1   celery root (about 1 pound, trimmed, or 3¼ cups, peeled and chopped)
2   tablespoons butter
1   tablespoon oil
6   cups chicken stock or part water
•   A sprig fresh thyme
1   teaspoon salt
¼   teaspoon white pepper
½   cup heavy cream

Peel and chop the shallots. Put the chopped shallots in a large heavy pot with the butter and oil and cook on low heat until soft, about 5 minutes. Add celery root, chicken stock, thyme, and salt and pepper. Bring to a boil, reduce heat to low, and simmer uncovered for about 30 minutes or until celery root is very tender. Let cool for a few minutes. Remove the thyme. Purée the soup in batches in a food processor and return to the pot, or use an immersion blender. Stir in heavy cream. Taste and adjust seasoning. Reheat just before serving. Garnish with curls of crisp bacon and sprigs of fresh thyme.

Servings: 8

PER SERVING:		
Total Carb: 7.8g	Fiber: 1.0g	Net Carb: 6.8g

"If you're afraid of butter,
just use cream."
—Julia Child

Tips and Notes

Fried pork rinds, also called chicharrones, can be found with the chips or on the Mexican food aisle at the grocery store. They have no carbs and almost no fat, just a small amount of protein. They can be used for munching or as a replacement for crackers with soup or chili and as crunchy croutons for soup or salad, as well as breading for fried foods.

CLAM CHOWDER WITH RUTABAGA

This is also good without the rutabagas in place of the customary potatoes, but with them, it tastes like hearty traditional chowder.

1 cup diced rutabaga, cooked with walnuts and lemon, see p. 167 for Basic Faux Potato recipe, drained and rinsed
1 small onion, diced
2 stalks celery, diced
2 tablespoons butter
1 (10-ounce) can clams with juice
1 egg yolk
2 cups cream
2 teaspoons Worcestershire sauce
3 slices bacon, cooked and crumbled
• Salt and pepper to taste

Sauté the onion and celery in butter until soft. Add the clams, including the juice, and the pre-cooked rutabaga. In a small bowl, beat the egg yolk with a fork and blend in the cream. Stir the combined egg yolk and cream into the clam mixture. Add the Worcestershire sauce. Heat slowly over low heat, but do not boil. Add salt and pepper to taste. Top with bacon just before serving.

Servings: 4

PER SERVING:		
Total Carb: 9.4g	Fiber: 1.9g	Net Carb: 7.5g

Chinese Proverb:
"Broth to a cook is voice to a singer."

HAM AND TEPARY BEAN SOUP

As a rule, tepary beans need long slow cooking but the fresher they are, the faster they cook. You can make this soup with boneless ham, but the bone contributes a lot of flavor. A leftover ham with some meat left on it is ideal.

Tip: I simmer the ham first so I can separate the meat from the bones and strain the liquid without straining out the little beans.

1   cup brown tepary beans or lentils
•   Ham bone with at least 1 pound of meat or 2 or 3 pounds of ham hocks
4   cups water or part broth
½   cup onion, chopped
2   tablespoons butter
•   Salt, if needed, and pepper to taste

Rinse and pick over the beans. Cover with water to a depth of one inch over the top of the beans. Either soak the beans for 8 hours, or bring them to a boil, simmer for 3 minutes, then turn off the heat, and let them sit for an hour. Drain and reserve.

Meanwhile, cover the meat with the water in a deep pot and simmer for 1 hour or until very tender. Remove the meat from the bones and cut it into pieces. Discard the bone, skin, and gristle. Strain the cooking liquid, and return the broth and the meat to the pot. Add the beans and simmer for 1 to 2 hours or until the beans are tender. In a skillet, sauté the onion in the butter until softened. Stir the onion and butter into the soup and heat through. Taste and adjust the seasoning; salt may not be necessary depending on the saltiness of the ham.

Servings: 6

PER SERVING:
Total Carb: 8.5g   Fiber: 2.3g   Net Carb: 6.2g
when made with lentils, since the carbohydrate count for tepary beans is not available

Note: Tepary beans have been the subject of exhaustive research. Native Seeds Search provided me with pages of nutrition information about their protein and fat content, but the carbohydrate count was not included. They are certainly lower in starch than other beans or lentils because they retain their shape and do not break down into a thick soup when cooked.

Tepary Beans

The most exciting discovery in my quest for low-carb beans is a nonprofit company called Native Seeds Search. They sell both the beans and the seeds for growing them, from the kind of plants cultivated by early Native Americans. Their tepary beans come in three varieties: white, which is described as being mild and sweet; brown, which has a more nutty flavor; and blue speckled, which is similar to brown, but has its own distinctive taste.

All varieties are high protein, high fiber, and have a low glycemic index (they do not cause a sudden rise in blood sugar levels). The carbohydrate count for them is not available from the company, but their information states that they are digested more slowly and are useful for preventing diabetes. The Native Americans of the Southwest would eat a meal of tepary beans in preparation for a journey to keep them from becoming hungry on the trip.

I have tried all three kinds. The white ones are very much like navy or great northern beans, but they do not disintegrate or get soupy like beans with more starch. I use the white ones in my recipe for Baked Beans. The brown ones taste like lentils to me, so I put them in my favorite ham and lentil soup. It is very good and very filling.

Tips and Notes

Juanita's Mexican Style Hominy® has four net grams of carbohydrate per half-cup. Most corn products, and even other brands of hominy, have from thirteen to twenty-five grams in the same half-cup amount. Put it, straight out of the can, in soups instead of dumplings or noodles, and in chili instead of beans. Serve it with butter as a side dish or chop it in the food processor and use it in place of rice, bulgur, barley, grits, or polenta. If you can't find Juanita's®, there are other brands that are almost as low, just be sure it says "Mexican Style" on the label.

Cure 81® Hams have zero carbs; they are not injected with sugar-water like most other brands. The label for their spiral sliced hams will list a higher count because they come with a packet of sugar glaze, which you don't have to use. Even better, if you can find them, Maple Leaf® brand hams have zero carbs and no added nitrates or nitrites as well. See Sources. You may also find hams at the deli counter that have zero carbs, but you have to ask to see the label.

HAM AND HOMINY SOUP

This is a good way to use the ham left on the bone after all the neat slices are gone.

- Ham bone with meat
  (from a zero-carb ham, like Maple Leaf® or Cure 81® brand)
- Water to cover
- ½ cup onion, chopped
- Olive oil
- Salt and pepper to taste. (Salt may not be necessary, depending on the saltiness of the ham.)
- 1 teaspoon bottled onion juice (optional) I used Reese brand.
- 1 can (28-ounces) Mexican-style hominy

Cover the ham bone with water and simmer for 2 hours until the meat pulls away from the bone easily. Strain, reserving the broth. You need about 2 quarts of broth. Remove the meat from the ham bone and discard the bone, fat, and skin. (To eliminate some of the fat, you may refrigerate the broth and meat separately at this point. When the broth is cold, lift off the solid fat layer that rises to the top with a slotted spoon.) Return the meat to the broth. In another pan, sauté the onion in olive oil until soft and add to the soup. Stir in the onion juice and hominy and heat through.

Servings: 8

PER SERVING:		
Total Carb: 8.1g	Fiber: 4.6g	Net Carb: 3.5g

CHICKEN AND NO RICE SOUP

I miss the days when making lunch could be as easy as opening a can of soup. This is almost that easy, especially if you have extra hominy left over from another recipe.

- Butter
- ¼ cup chopped celery
- 1 (14.5-ounce) can chicken broth
- 1 cup canned or leftover chicken, cubed
- ½ cup Mexican-style hominy that has been chopped in the food processor (See p. 175 for Basic Recipe for Hominy "Rice")
- Salt and pepper to taste

Sauté the celery in butter. Add the broth, chicken, and hominy. Correct the seasoning, and heat through.

Servings: 2

PER SERVING:		
Total Carb: 5.6g	Fiber: 3.3g	Net Carb: 2.3g

QUICK CHILI

- 1 pound ground beef
- 1 cup water or broth
- 1 (15-oz) can enchilada sauce
- 1 (15-oz) can diced tomatoes with juice
- Salt, pepper, and chili powder to taste
- 1 cup Mexican-style hominy or 1 cup of cooked tepary beans (optional)

Brown ground beef and drain off the fat. Put meat, water or broth, enchilada sauce, and tomatoes in a large saucepan. Simmer for 30 minutes. Add optional beans or hominy; cook for five minutes more. Correct seasoning with salt and pepper and chili powder to taste. Serve with shredded Cheddar cheese, chopped green onion or chives, and sour cream or Crème Fraîche (see p. 51) for topping.

Servings: 6

PER SERVING:		
Total Carb: 6.8g	Fiber: 0.6g	Net Carb: 6.2g

Tips and Notes

Most canned broth and stock contains MSG and sugar. Check the labels for one that lists zero carbs, but you may have to make your own to eliminate the MSG. See Index for Chicken and Beef Stock recipes.

Glutamic acid, the flavor enhancer in monosodium glutamate (MSG) is made from hydrolyzed wheat or corn. Any ingredient label that lists hydrolyzed plant protein will contain some MSG, even if it also says "No MSG." Monosodium glutamate is a brain stimulating chemical that makes you think something tastes really good, the way alcohol makes you think you're having a good time.

Tips and Notes

Crème Fraîche can be whipped like cream, and it can be boiled without curdling, so it works well in sauces and in cream soups.

Crème Fraîche

Combine 1 cup of heavy cream with 2 tablespoons of buttermilk in a glass container. Cover and let stand at room temperature (about 70°) for 8 to 24 hours, or until very thick. Stir well, cover, and refrigerate for up to ten days.

For a quick substitute for Crème Fraîche, mix equal parts sour cream and heavy cream. If you use a zero-carb cream, it will cut the carb count in half compared to purchased sour cream.

CHILI

This is my husband's chili recipe. He likes it plain; I like mine topped with green onions, cheese, and sour cream. You can adjust the heat to your taste by using mild or hot enchilada sauce and by adding more or less chili powder.

1½ pounds lean pork, cut into cubes
2 tablespoons soy flour or Low-Carb Flour Replacement
1 teaspoon chili powder (or to taste)
1½ teaspoons salt
½ teaspoon pepper
½ teaspoon dried cumin
1 clove garlic, peeled and chopped
2 (15-ounce) cans mild or hot enchilada sauce
1 (15-ounce) can tomato sauce

Cook the pork in a heavy skillet on medium-high heat until it starts to color, stirring several times. Drain off any excess fat. Stir in the soy flour or flour substitute and chili powder. Continue to cook on medium heat until the meat is brown. Add the rest of the ingredients and bring to a boil. Reduce the heat, cover, and simmer for about 2 hours. Serve with sour cream or Crème Fraîche (see sidebar), cheese, and chopped onion or chives for topping.

Servings: 8

PER SERVING:		
Total Carb: 9.1g	Fiber: 0.8g	Net Carb: 8.3g

Proverb from Ghana:
"A good soup attracts chairs."

FRENCH ONION SOUP

I've always loved onion soup with soggy bread and stringy melted cheese on top, but I could never figure out how to eat it gracefully in public. This takes care of that problem and eliminates carbs as well.

2 ounces (about ½ cup) thinly sliced yellow onion
1 tablespoon butter
1 tablespoon olive oil
½ teaspoon potato flour (or use 1 teaspoon cornstarch and add 0.8 net carbs per serving)
• A pinch of salt
1 (14.5-ounce) can beef broth or 2 cups of stock
1 teaspoon bottled onion juice
1 tablespoon sherry or white wine
• Salt and pepper to taste (canned broth may already include enough salt)
2-3 large mushrooms, center slices only
¼ cup grated Swiss or Parmesan cheese

Place the onion in a large saucepan with the butter and oil. Cover the pan and heat on low for 15 minutes, stirring occasionally. Remove the cover from the pan, raise the heat to medium-low, and continue to cook until the onions are golden brown. Add the potato flour and salt; stir and cook 1 minute longer. (If using cornstarch, stir it into a little of the cold broth before adding it to the pan.) Remove the pan from the heat and gradually stir in the beef broth and wine. Season to taste. Simmer for 30 minutes more.

Preheat the broiler.

Meanwhile, slice the mushrooms vertically. Use only the center slices that have a slice of stem attached; reserve the side slices for another use. Arrange the mushroom slices on a paper towel, fitting them together as closely as possible. Sprinkle the cheese over the mushrooms. (Using the towel allows you to recover the excess cheese by shaking it into a bag from the folded towel.) Lift the slices carefully off the towel and place them on a baking sheet. Run under the broiler for a minute or two until the cheese is melted and browned.

Ladle the soup into hot bowls. Float three or four of the mushroom slices in each bowl and serve.

Servings: 2

PER SERVING:		
Total Carb: 5.4g	Fiber: 1.0g	Net Carb: 4.4g

Tips and Notes

If you chop onions near an open flame, they won't make you cry.

Potato flour turns out to be one of the best choices for thickening sauces. It is higher in carbohydrates than wheat flour, but you need only one third the amount. It is also higher than cornstarch, but you need only one half the amount, so there is still an advantage.

I find Dorot frozen garlic, ginger, and herbs to be great time savers—no more measuring, washing, peeling, and chopping, and although the herbs are not exactly like fresh, they will do in a pinch. They are sold at Trader Joe's stores in the US. Dorot sells frozen crushed garlic, chopped basil, chopped coriander, chopped dill, chopped parsley, and crushed ginger in trays of 20 cubes each. See Sources.

Use the kind of peanut butter that lists just peanuts and salt as ingredients. It usually says, "stir before using."

VARIATION:

Tortilla Soup

Use 1 low-carb tortilla for each 2 servings of soup. Cut tortillas into thin strips. Fry in hot oil until puffed, brown, and crisp. Place strips in bowls before adding soup or serve alongside.

PEANUT SOUP

Fragrant, earthy, and spicy, with echoes of exotic places. Add some Poached Chicken to make Peanut Stew.

2 tablespoons peanut or olive oil
½ cup chopped onion, about 2 ounces
2 teaspoons minced garlic
¼ teaspoon red pepper flakes
2 tablespoons yellow curry powder
3 cups chicken stock
1 (14.5-ounce) can diced tomatoes with juice
⅔ cup natural peanut butter
6 large fresh basil leaves, shredded (¼ cup)
1 cup canned coconut milk
¼ teaspoon salt or to taste

Sauté onion in a large saucepan on medium heat until softened. Add garlic, pepper flakes, and curry powder and cook and stir for two minutes more. Add tomatoes, including juice, and stock and bring to a boil. Stir in peanut butter and simmer for about 15 minutes. Add basil, coconut milk, and salt. Stir over low heat until smooth and hot. Puree, if desired, for a smooth soup. Garnish with chopped peanuts or toasted coconut flakes.

Servings: 8

PER SERVING:		
Total Carb: 9.3g	Fiber: 3.5g	Net Carb: 5.8g

CARNITAS SOUP

This is great to serve a crowd. A platter of chilled fruit goes well with this soup; watermelon slices and grapes are especially nice.

Make Carnitas recipe from page 199. Put some of the meat into the reserved broth and reheat. Prepare dishes of chopped onion, red or green bell pepper, chopped green onion, shredded lettuce, diced avocado, diced jicama, diced chilies, chopped tomato, sliced black olives, and shredded Jack cheese to be spooned into soup. Serve with sour cream and mild and hot salsa. Ladle soup into heated bowls and let guests add any or all of the fresh vegetables and toppings to their individual bowls.

CHICKEN STOCK

The chicken used to make this stock is too good to waste. It is tender and flavorful when made into soups, salads, and main dishes.

1   chicken, about 3 pounds (giblets, except liver, can be included)
3   quarts cold water
2   yellow onions, chopped
2   cups celery, some leaves included, chopped
2   cups carrots, chopped
5   whole black peppercorns
1   Turkish bay leaf
3   sprigs fresh parsley or 3 teaspoons, dried
3   sprigs fresh thyme or ½ teaspoon, dried
2   teaspoons salt

Put everything in a large stockpot and bring just to a boil. Reduce heat to low and simmer, uncovered, for 1 hour, skimming every 30 minutes to remove any foam that rises to the surface. Remove the chicken at this point and pick the meat off the bones to use for another purpose. Return the carcass to the pot and continue cooking, skimming every 30 minutes, for another hour.

Cool the stock quickly by setting the pot in a sink full of cold water. Strain stock into a large bowl and discard the solids. Refrigerate, leaving uncovered until completely cold. Cover with plastic wrap, and refrigerate for at least 4 hours. Remove the layer of fat that rises to the surface with a slotted spoon. Store the stock in the refrigerator for four days or freeze for up to three months. Bring stock to a boil before using.

Makes 2 quarts of stock.

PER SERVING:		
Total Carb: 0g	Fiber: 0g	Net Carb: 0g

Tips and Notes

To make clear stock, remove the foam that rises to the surface every 30 minutes, and keep the pot at a low simmer. Do not stir the pot until after the fat is removed to keep the fat from emulsifying, which makes a cloudy, fatty stock. This way, the fat will rise to the surface as the stock cools so it can be skimmed off.

BEEF STOCK

Tips and Notes

After the cooled layer of fat is removed, the stock can be boiled without causing it to become cloudy and greasy.

A basket-style coffee filter can be used as a fine strainer to make clear stock.

Most supermarkets sell bones to give your dog, not bones for making soup. Since meat is not butchered on site, they don't have the leftover marrowbones that used to find their way into the soup pot. However, they will probably have beef back ribs, which are meaty and full of flavor and cost about the same as the dog bones. You will find the rib meat gains as much flavor as it gives in its long slow cooking in the broth with the vegetables. It tastes like a really good pot roast and can make a fine supper for the family.

5	pounds beef back ribs
2	tablespoons oil
•	Salt and pepper
2	leeks
2	cups carrots, roughly chopped
4	stalks celery with some leaves, roughly chopped
2	yellow onions, peeled and cut into quarters
3	cloves garlic, peeled and crushed
½	cup tomatoes, chopped
4	quarts cold water
2	teaspoons salt
3	sprigs fresh parsley or 3 teaspoons, dried
3	sprigs fresh thyme or ½ teaspoon, dried
1	Turkish bay leaf
2	whole cloves
8	black peppercorns

Preheat the oven to 425° F.

Place the ribs in a large roasting pan. Brush them with some of the oil and sprinkle with salt and pepper on both sides. Bake for 30 minutes, or until just browned. Pour off the accumulated fat after the first 15 minutes, and turn them over for even browning.

Meanwhile, prepare the vegetables. Cut off the root ends and the green tops of the leeks. Split them lengthwise, chop into several pieces, and place in a bowl of cold water. Separate the layers and stir to allow the dirt to settle to the bottom of the bowl. Lift the leek pieces out with a slotted spoon and drain. Put leeks, carrots, celery, onions, and garlic in a bowl with the remaining oil and toss to coat. Add to roasting pan. (Set the bowl with oil aside.) Sprinkle vegetables with salt. Bake for another 25 minutes. Toss the tomato in the bowl with the oil. Stir the vegetables in the roasting pan, and add the tomatoes. Bake for 20 minutes more.

(continued on next page)

BEEF STOCK, CONTINUED

Transfer the meat and vegetables to a large stockpot. Set the roasting pan over two burners on the stovetop and turn heat to medium. Add 1 cup of water. Stir and scrape for a few minutes to incorporate the caramelized glaze and the browned bits from the bottom of the pan; pour into the stockpot. Add 4 quarts of water and the remaining ingredients to the pot. Bring just to a boil over high heat. Immediately reduce heat to low and simmer, uncovered, for about 4 hours, skimming every 30 minutes to remove foam. Never stir the pot and never let it come to a full boil. Remove the beef ribs and use for another purpose. Cool the stock quickly by setting the pot in a sink full of cold water. Strain the stock into a large bowl and discard the solids. Refrigerate, leaving uncovered until completely cold. Cover with plastic wrap and refrigerate for at least 4 hours. Remove the layer of fat that rises to the surface with a slotted spoon. The stock can now be boiled to reduce it further, if necessary. Store in the refrigerator for up to four days or freeze for three months. Bring stock to a boil before using.

Makes 2 quarts.

PER SERVING:		
Total Carb: 0g	Fiber: 0g	Net Carb: 0g

Yiddish Proverb:
"Worries go down better with soup."

SOUP FOR LUNCH:

MENU I

Chili
Quesadillas
Cole Slaw
Cantaloupe
*

MENU II

Ham and Tepary Bean Soup
Corn Muffins with butter
Sliced tomatoes
Chocolate Chip Cookies
*

MENU III

French Onion Soup
Parmesan Sesame Crackers
Waldorf Salad
Berry Custard Cake
*

MENU IV

Tortilla Soup
Shredded lettuce, diced avocado, tomato, onion, and jack cheese
Sour cream and salsa
Watermelon
*

See pages 222 and 223 for cream soup recipes.

SALADS

SALADS

This book does not contain many salad recipes because low-carb salads are easy to find in regular cookbooks. The classic recipes for Greek, Caesar (leave out the croutons), Cobb, and Chef's salads are usually fine. Caprese salad, made by alternating slices of tomatoes with fresh mozzarella and basil leaves, dressed with olive oil, is also a good choice. Most of the ones I have included in this chapter are here because they normally have a high-carbohydrate ingredient, like sugar, apples, or potatoes, which I have replaced.

Tips and Notes

Jicama is a root vegetable from Mexico. It has a smooth brown skin and crunchy, juicy, white flesh. It is low in carbohydrates and almost tasteless, so it can be flavored to imitate any crisp fruit or vegetable. (The Waldorf and the Celery Root and Jicama Salads in this chapter would normally be made with apple.) Jicama can also be used in Chinese dishes in place of water chestnuts.

WALDORF SALAD

Jicama has all the crunch of a crisp, fresh apple without all the carbs. Marinating it in cider vinegar and sweetener provides the apple taste. Other gourmet fruit-flavored vinegars can be used as well; I love to make it with pear vinegar, which makes the jicama taste like Asian pears.

2   cups peeled and cubed jicama
2   tablespoons apple cider vinegar
2   teaspoons granular Splenda® (add more if vinegar has more than 5 percent acidity)
1   cup sliced celery
⅓   cup real mayonnaise
•   A few thinly sliced red grapes (optional)
•   A generous dash of nutmeg
•   Salt and pepper to taste
½   cup walnuts

Toss the jicama with the vinegar and Splenda® and let stand for 5 to 10 minutes. Mix with celery, mayonnaise, grapes, nutmeg, salt, and pepper. Add walnuts just before serving.

Servings: 4

PER SERVING:		
Total Carb: 9.0g	Fiber: 4.7g	Net Carb: 4.3g

Celery Root and Jicama Salad with Garlic Mayonnaise

Salad:
1 cup celery root, peeled and cut into julienne strips
1 cup jicama, peeled and cut into julienne strips
1 cup baby spinach leaves, rinsed and dried

Garlic Mayonnaise:
¼ cup real mayonnaise
1 tablespoon lemon juice
1 clove garlic, chopped, or 1 teaspoon garlic paste
• Salt and pepper to taste

Place spinach in individual salad bowls. Toss celery root and jicama together and put on top of the spinach. Mix dressing ingredients together until smooth and serve with salad.

Servings: 4

PER SERVING:		
Total Carb: 7.2g	Fiber: 2.6g	Net Carb: 4.6g

Celery Root, also called Celeriac

Don't be intimidated by this weird-looking vegetable. Not really a root, it comes from a kind of celery grown for its edible corm. It is very popular in Europe where it is used both raw and cooked.

Choose firm, fresh celeriac and scrub it well to remove all the dirt that tends to cling to its hair-like roots. To prepare, slice it first and then peel it, so it is easier to get into all the convoluted spaces. Cut off the fibrous roots, but if some are large, you can peel and use them too.

"Let nothing which can be treated by diet be treated by other means."
—Maimonides

The whole chayote squash is edible, peel, seed and all.

Celery Root and Chayote Salad with Mustard Dressing

Salad:
1   cup celery root, peeled and cut into julienne strips
1   chayote squash
2   tablespoons fresh parsley, chopped

Mustard Dressing:
2   teaspoons Dijon mustard
2   tablespoons lemon juice
$2/3$ cup heavy cream
•   Salt and pepper

Cube the chayote and cook in boiling water for 10 minutes or microwave with ¼ cup of water for 7 to 8 minutes. Drain and cool. Blend the mustard with the cream and lemon juice. Toss the dressing with the celery root and chayote. Add salt and pepper to taste. Sprinkle with parsley and serve.

Servings: 4

PER SERVING:		
Total Carb: 7.2g	Fiber: 2.3g	Net Carb: 4.9g

Cole Slaw

½   head cabbage, shredded (about 4 ½ cups)
1   red or green pepper, seeded and finely sliced
1   tablespoon fresh chives, chopped
½   cup real mayonnaise
¼   cup apple-cider vinegar
½   teaspoon granular Splenda®
•   Salt and pepper to taste

Combine in a large bowl and toss.

Servings: 8

PER SERVING:		
Total Carb: 3.4g	Fiber: 1.5g	Net Carb: 1.9g

MIXED GREENS WITH GLAZED PECANS AND CRANBERRY DRESSING

Salad:
½   cup Glazed Pecans (see p. 267)
4   cups mixed salad greens (Boston lettuce and baby spinach are nice), rinsed, dried, and torn into small pieces
¼   cup sugar-free Dried Cranberries (see p. 105)
1   tablespoon granular Splenda®
¼   cup water

Cranberry Dressing:
1   tablespoon reserved cranberry and Splenda® liquid
1   tablespoon balsamic vinegar
6   tablespoons extra-virgin olive oil
•   Salt and pepper to taste

Make Glazed Pecans and let cool. Place Dried Cranberries, 1 tablespoon of Splenda®, and ¼ cup of water in a small saucepan. Heat to boiling and simmer until cranberries are softened and liquid is reduced, about 5 minutes. Drain cranberries, reserving liquid, and let cool.

Whisk together: 1 tablespoon of the cranberry liquid, the vinegar, and the oil. Add salt and pepper to taste and set aside.

Just before serving, toss the greens, cranberries, and pecans together in a bowl and place on serving plates. Whisk the dressing to re-blend and drizzle over the salads.

Servings: 4

PER SERVING:		
Total Carb: 9.7g	Fiber: 3.2g	Net Carb: 6.5g

Tips and Notes

Tossed salads are a staple for dieters, but the dressings can be a problem since most of them contain sugar and starch. Cream dressings would be fine, but most bottled dressings substitute milk and "modified food starch," whatever that is, for cream. When making your own, use real, zero-carb cream. Also use real, zero-carb mayonnaise rather than "salad dressing." When you eat in a restaurant, olive oil and vinegar are probably the safest choice. At home, indulge in some really special flavored vinegars and extra virgin olive oil or macadamia, hazelnut, or walnut oil.

The name, shallot, for this member of the onion family, is probably derived from Askalon, an ancient port city in Palestine; the "Ascalonian onion" was introduced to Europe by crusaders returning from the Holy Land. It looks like a cross between onion and garlic, but its taste is more delicate and subtle than either. The most common shallot in the US, the French red, has pink-tinged skin, but the gray shallot is said to be superior in flavor.

WARM ROASTED CAULIFLOWER OR CELERY ROOT SALAD

I made this warm "potato" salad with roasted cauliflower and with roasted celery root to see which was better, but couldn't decide.

1	small head cauliflower or 1 celery root, about 1 pound
•	Olive oil
•	Salt and pepper
¼	pound bacon
¼	cup shallots, peeled and chopped
¼	cup red wine vinegar
½	teaspoon granular Splenda®
2	tablespoons olive oil
¼	cup red onion or additional shallots, chopped
¼	cup fresh parsley, chopped

Heat oven to 400° F.

Wash and trim the cauliflower and separate into small florets, cutting large ones when necessary. If using celery root instead of cauliflower, peel and cut into ½-inch cubes. Put in a roasting pan and sprinkle with olive oil. Toss to coat. (You may also spray it with no-stick spray to be sure it is all coated.) Season with salt and pepper. Roast uncovered for 30 to 40 minutes, stirring occasionally, until brown.

Sauté the bacon in a skillet and set aside. Sauté ¼ cup of shallots in the bacon fat until soft but not browned. Stir hot cauliflower or celery root into the skillet with the shallots and add the vinegar, Splenda®, and olive oil. Transfer to a bowl. Add parsley and red onion or additional shallots and toss. Correct the seasoning and crumble reserved bacon over top. Serve warm.

Servings: 4

PER SERVING:

Total Carb: 11.8g	Fiber: 3.7g	**Net Carb: 8.1g**
when made with cauliflower		
Total Carb: 16.2g	Fiber: 2.3g	**Net Carb: 13.9g**
when made with celery root		

Celery Root "Potato" Salad

This is a potato salad substitute based on a baked potato salad that I found in the deli at the grocery store. You can also make it with cauliflower.

1   celery root, also called celeriac (about 1 pound)
1   small onion, peeled and chopped
3   Hard-Cooked Eggs, see p. 65
2   stalks celery, chopped
1   cup shredded Cheddar cheese
½   cup real mayonnaise
½   cup sour cream
¼   cup chopped fresh parsley
½   cup minced fresh chives or green onion tops
•   Salt and pepper to taste
6   strips bacon, cooked until crisp, and crumbled

Peel and cube the celery root. Cook in boiling, salted water until fork tender, about 15 to 20 minutes. Drain and dry the celery root on paper towels, pressing out as much water as possible. Mix in other ingredients, except bacon, in a large bowl. Correct seasoning. Toss with bacon just before serving.

Servings: 6

PER SERVING:		
Total Carb: 10.5g	Fiber: 2.2g	Net Carb: 8.3g

Tips and Notes

A low-carb potato, well, at least a *lower-carb* potato, is being marketed by a Florida cooperative. The new potato, called SunLite™, is said to have 30% fewer carbs than a Russet. A 5.2-ounce (148 grams) SunLite™ potato has 18 grams of carbohydrate and 4 grams of fiber (for a net count of 14) and 87 calories. Russets have 27 grams of carbohydrate, 117 calories, and 4 grams of fiber (a net of 23 grams). SunLite™ potatoes are available in groceries in the Southeast United States and can be ordered from the growers; see Sources.

This advice is from SunLite™ potatoes: Store SunLite™ potatoes in a cool dry place or in the crisper of your refrigerator. Never store onions or garlic with potatoes. Place a fresh, whole lemon with potatoes for prolonged storage and maximum flavor.

Pumpkin Salad

Tips and Notes

Other recipes using pumpkin can be found elsewhere in the book:

Baked Pumpkin, 153
Candied Pumpkin, 152
Pumpkin Chips, 157
Pumpkin Faux French Fries, 157
Pumpkin Fritters, 158
Holiday Pumpkin Casserole, 154
Pumpkin Hush Puppies, 158
Italian Pumpkin Casserole, 156
Pumpkin Mousse, 319
Pumpkin Pie, 295
Pumpkin Tamales, 172–74

Make this in the fall when fresh pumpkins are available. Buy one of the little ones meant for cooking, not for Jack-o-lanterns.

1   sugar baby or similar pie pumpkin (about 1½ pounds)
2   tablespoons olive oil
4   green onions tops, chopped
¼   cup onion, chopped
¼   cup red bell pepper, chopped
1   tablespoon granular Splenda®
1   tablespoon cider vinegar
•   Salt and pepper to taste
¼   cup crumbled crisp bacon

Heat oven to 400° F.

Cut the pumpkin into strips. Remove the seeds and fibers and peel the strips. Cut the pumpkin flesh into ½-inch cubes. Place in a baking dish and toss with the olive oil. Bake uncovered for 10 to 15 minutes, or until brown, stirring once. Stir in green onions, onions, red pepper, Splenda®, and vinegar. Add salt and pepper to taste. Top with bacon. Serve warm or at room temperature.

Servings: 6

PER SERVING:		
Total Carb: 4.2g	Fiber: 0.8g	Net Carb: 3.4g

GREEN PAPAYA SALAD

You may have to go to an Asian market for the green papaya for this salad. It must be very green and hard with very white flesh and pearly white seeds.

Dressing:
- Juice of 2 small limes
- 1 tablespoon soy sauce or Thai fish sauce (nam pla)
- 2 teaspoons granular Splenda®
- 2 tablespoons peanut oil
- ¼ teaspoon chili oil or more to taste

Salad:
- 2 cups shredded green papaya (about ½ pound as purchased)
- 2 green onions, white part only, sliced into thin slices
- ¼ cup peanuts, chopped
- Salt and pepper, if needed

To make the dressing, place the lime juice, soy sauce, and Splenda® in a large bowl. Add the peanut and chili oils and whisk together.

Peel the papaya, cut in half, and scrape out the seeds. Grate the papaya on the largest hole of a grater or use the shredding disk of a food processor. Add the papaya, peanuts, and onion to the bowl with the dressing and toss the salad together. Taste and add salt and pepper or more chili oil if needed. Let stand for 20 minutes and serve.

Servings: 4

PER SERVING:		
Total Carb: 10.4g	Fiber: 2.9g	**Net Carb: 7.5g**

Tips and Notes

Fish sauce is made from the liquid from salted, fermented fish. It is very pungent, salty, and strong. In Southeast Asia, fish sauce is used in much the same way that we use salt. It is part of almost every dish, even desserts. I used soy sauce in my Green Papaya Salad because I like it better (and I didn't have any fish sauce.)

FRUIT

BORN OF A FLOWER

Fruits and vegetables are usually referred to as if they were a single category. Not so. Technically, vegetables are the edible stems, leaves, and roots of plants. Fruits are the seeds and seed containing parts. However, we tend to define them according to usage; so tomatoes, cucumbers, peppers, and green beans are considered vegetables although they are really plant ovaries. We reserve the name fruit for the ones that taste sweet. Is it surprising then, that we can't eat an unlimited amount of fruit if we want to cut the amount of sugar in our diet? Still, fruits are a valuable source of antioxidants and important phytochemicals and certainly a better choice for a treat than candy or cookies; but not all fruits are created equal. Fortunately, the most beneficial ones are also the lowest in carbohydrates.

Some fruits that are fairly low in carbs are: avocados (1.2 net grams in 1 ounce for the Hass or California variety), blackberries (5.6 net grams in ½ cup), blueberries (6.2 net grams in ½ cup), cantaloupe (6.1 net grams in ½ cup, cubed) and most melons, coconut (1.7 net grams in 1 ounce, fresh), cranberries (4 net grams in ½ cup), red or white currants (5.3 net grams in ½ cup), gooseberries (3.4 net grams in ½ cup), kiwi (8.7 net grams in one medium), oranges (8.2 net grams in ½ cup of segments), papayas (5.6 net grams in ½ cup, cubed), peaches (8 net grams in a 4-ounce peach), plums (9.5 net grams in ½ cup, sliced), prickly pear or cactus fruit (8 net grams in a 5-ounce fruit), pumpkin (2.8 net grams in ½ cup, cubed, fresh), star fruit (6.5 net grams in a 4.7-ounce fruit), raspberries (2.9 net grams in ½ cup), and strawberries (3.5 net grams in ½ cup).

Rhubarb, although technically not a fruit, is one of the lowest on the list (1.7 net grams in ½ cup). Tomitillos, the little green tomato-like fruits from Mexico, are also very low (2.5 net grams in ½ cup) and can be used for jam or pies as well as the more familiar Mexican dishes and salsas. (They are sometimes called jamberries.) If you like fried green tomatoes, try making them with tomatillos, which are less tart and lower in carbohydrates (see p. 189).

AVOCADO

We usually see this buttery, delectable fruit in salads, sandwiches, and guacamole, but sweetened, it can become a very low-carb fruit to use in desserts. See the Index for a wonderful Avocado Mousse and for Avocado-lime Ice Cream.

Hass (rhymes with "pass") avocados are the lowest in carbs and by far the best variety for flavor and texture. They have pebbly skins that turn black when they are ready to eat. The stem end will yield to gentle pressure when ripe. Choose ones with no dents or flattened spots. They will ripen for you at home, so buy them green if you don't plan to use them for a day or two. Putting them in a paper bag will expedite the ripening process.

When perfectly ripe, avocados are difficult to peel the conventional way, since the pulp is very soft and the rind is rigid. Try doing it this way for beautiful halves or slices: Cut the avocado in half lengthwise, down to and around the seed, then twist to pull the halves apart. Hold the half containing the seed, skin-side down, with the seed facing up, in the palm of your hand. Smack the blade of a long knife across the seed, turn the knife, and the seed will pull out with the knife blade. To peel, hold one of the halves in your hand with the rounded side facing up. Make vertical cuts with a paring knife, just through the skin, but not into the flesh, about an inch apart. Pull the strips of skin away from the flesh. Slice or dice as desired.

BANANAS

Bananas are generally not a good choice for low carbohydrate dieting, since they are high in both starch and sugar. While just a few bites may be enough to satisfy a banana craving, it's hard to stop, especially when the rest of the banana will go to waste if you have no one to share it. One of the tiny finger bananas may provide the solution. They are as rich and creamy as the regular varieties, but only about three inches long. Like all bananas, you can buy them green and they will ripen beautifully. Buy just one if you are will-power challenged in regard to bananas as I am.

Other ways to get a banana fix:
• Use banana flavoring in a cream pie or pudding and slice one tiny banana on top.
• Add banana extract to a milk shake.
• Turn low-carb ice cream into a banana split by placing a few thin slices on the bottom and topping with strawberries, whipped cream, and chocolate sauce.
• Slice your tiny banana on top of a bowl of low-carb cereal for breakfast when your insulin is more sensitive and better able to handle it.

BLUEBERRIES

Blueberries top the list as the most valuable fruit for the carbohydrate expenditure. The beneficial compounds are concentrated in the dark-colored skins, so small wild blueberries will have more anti-oxidant-rich skin in proportion to the pale, sweet interior. Frozen wild blueberries are readily available year round.

Coconut

Unsweetened, dried coconut can be found in the health food section or the bulk bins at most grocery stores, from Bob's Red Mill® at retail stores, or by mail order. It can also be ordered from the King Arthur® Flour Company (see Sources). Check an Asian grocery store for frozen, grated coconut that can be used like fresh. Canned coconut cream is usually unsweetened and can be used for drinks, curries, and desserts. Fresh coconut requires more effort, but sometimes it is worth the trouble, especially for a dessert like Coconut Amaretto Cake (see p. 246).

Immature coconuts are sometimes available at regular or ethnic markets. They may be called white or young coconut. They are unripe coconuts with a white outer husk and meat that is white but still slightly gelatinous. I prefer to buy them at groceries that specialize in Thai and Asian foods because their stock is more likely to be fresh. Choose one that is heavy for its size; it should make a sloshing sound when you shake it. The husk should be very white with no discolorations or bruises. The raw food chefs shred the meat and use it like pasta. That's all I've done with it so far, other than drink the liquid, but there are probably more great recipes out there somewhere. See p. 166 for my recipe for Coconut "Pasta."

Kiwi

Kiwi fruit, or Chinese gooseberry, is a good source of potassium, vitamin C, and fiber. It is cultivated in both California and New Zealand, whose seasons are reversed, so kiwi fruit is available year round. The fuzzy, brown fruit is about the size and shape of an egg with a taste reminiscent of strawberries and pineapple. Its bright green flesh and striking pattern of crunchy black seeds add visual appeal to fruit salads and desserts. One medium kiwi (3.1 ounces) has 8.7 net grams of carbohydrate.

Prickly Pear Fruit

You will occasionally find these fruits, with the thorns already removed, in the supermarket or at a Mexican grocery. They may also be called tuna, Indian figs, or cactus pears. There are several varieties, but the best ones are large and rosy red. They are a carb bargain at six to eight net carbs in a 5- to 6-ounce fruit. Most sources reccomend eating them out of hand, like fresh fruit, or sliced and sweetened. I find them to be too full of annoying seeds for either of these methods and suggest blending or mashing them instead, and using the strained pulp for drinks, sorbet, or jelled desserts. Native Seeds Search (see Sources) sells bottled prickly pear nectar with a carb count of zero for a serving of 1 teaspoon.

RHUBARB

Yes, I know it's really a vegetable, but it is always sweetened and used like a fruit for compotes, pies, and sauces. Rhubarb is one of those foods that people either love or hate. I was in the latter group, having only encountered it in its sour, gray, mushy form, until I realized what a carb bargain it is; then I determined that I would find a way to make it palatable. Some of my favorite recipes are included. Strawberry Rhubarb Pie, Rhubarb Chutney, and Baked Rhubarb with Strawberry Sauce (see Index to locate recipes) should cure even the worst case of rhubarb aversion.

Rhubarb is available fresh in the spring and summer and frozen the rest of the year. Choose bright red stalks when buying it fresh. Cut them into 6-inch sections and soak them in cold water for 20 minutes before cooking. This will remove some of the astringency. Baking, rather than boiling, will help keep your rhubarb firm and rosy. Adding an acid like lemon juice or white wine helps it retain its color.

Rhubarb is very easy to grow, especially here in the Northwest, where it almost becomes a weed. Placed in a sunny spot, its large green leaves add drama to the landscape. One of the best varieties for home gardeners has green stalks with just a blush of rosy color at the base, but it is as beautiful and tasty as store-bought rhubarb.

Note: Rhubarb leaves are very toxic. Trim away any green leaves from the tops of the stalks.

STAR FRUIT

Star fruit is not naturally very sweet, but when sliced and sprinkled with Splenda®, it becomes a low-carb and healthful treat (only eight to ten net carbs in a whole medium-sized star fruit). In the initial phase of a low-carb diet, when fruit is a no no, a few slices of star fruit can reduce that feeling of deprivation.

When buying star fruit, look for firm fruit without soft or brown spots. If it is green, ripen it at home until it is turns yellow, then use or refrigerate it. Although the outside may darken after it is cut, the interior flesh does not turn brown, like many fruits, and it retains its unique crunchy texture for days.

To prepare star fruit, slice crosswise into "stars" and remove the seeds. I have heard that the seeds are so toxic that they can be used as a pesticide, so be sure to remove them. If there is a tough brown ridge that runs along the edge of each point, cut it away. This will be easier to do before slicing the fruit. Sprinkle with Splenda® and eat fresh or prepare according to the recipe for Sautéed Star Fruit or make the spectacular Star Fruit Pie (see Index for recipes).

CRANBERRIES

Fresh cranberries are readily available in the fall and winter. They are beautiful and tart to use in sauces and desserts and, when sweetened, they can be substituted for cherries. Packages of fresh berries can be put directly in the freezer without blanching, and frozen cranberries can be used in any recipe in place of fresh ones. When dried, they can be used as low-carb raisins. One-fourth cup of dried cranberries has ten net grams of carbohydrate compared to twenty-nine for an equal amount of raisins. Also check out the recipe for Candied Cranberries (see p. 113).

Cranberries were probably called "crane berries" by the first European settlers because the shape of the cranberry's flower resembled the heads of the cranes who lived in the New England bogs. They are also known as "bounce berries" because good berries will bounce. Modern day processors have machines designed to separate the berries by bouncing them over a barrier, leaving the bad ones behind.

Tips and Notes

To make a wonderful pie: place the rhubarb in a pre-baked Meringue or Pastry Shell (see Index), cover with the sauce, and serve with sugar-free ice cream.

BAKED RHUBARB WITH STRAWBERRY SAUCE

Baking rhubarb instead of simmering it in water keeps it firm and rosy—not mushy and gray. The rhubarb can also be served without the sauce as you would serve applesauce.

1   pound fresh rhubarb, rinsed, trimmed, and cut across
    the ribs into ½-inch slices
2   tablespoons granular Splenda®
10 ounces (1⅓ cups) frozen sugar-free strawberries, thawed,
    reserving juice
¼   cup granular Splenda®
3   tablespoons strawberry-flavored sugar-free syrup
    (or use 3 tablespoons water plus 3 tablespoons Splenda®)

Preheat the oven to 375° F.

Spread the rhubarb slices in a single layer in a shallow pan. Sprinkle with the 2 tablespoons of Splenda®. Bake for 20 to 25 minutes or until tender.

To make the strawberry sauce:
Purée the strawberries in the bowl of a food processor with ¼ cup Splenda®. Put in a bowl and stir in the reserved strawberry juice and syrup. Strain for a smooth sauce.

Spoon the sauce over the rhubarb and serve warm. Top with sugar-free ice cream if desired.

Servings: 8

PER SERVING:		
Total Carb: 6.1g	Fiber: 2.2g	Net Carb: 3.9g

DRIED CRANBERRIES

I have not been able to find sugar-free dried cranberries to purchase, so I make my own. I dry lots of them when they are available fresh in the fall and winter since it is easy and they keep extremely well. Leave out the Splenda® when drying them if you like, and sweeten them when you use them.

Rinse and pick over fresh cranberries. Place them in a bowl and pour boiling water over them. Let them sit until the skins crack, about 30 seconds, then immediately submerge them in cold water. Drain and blot dry on paper towels.

Spread the cranberries on a cookie sheet sprayed with no-stick spray or lined with a nonstick mat. Place in the freezer for 2 hours to help break down the cell walls and shorten the drying time. For sweetened cranberries, use ¼ cup of granular Splenda® for 3 cups of cranberries (one 12-ounce bag); push the berries together so they form a single-layered mass with no space between the berries and sprinkle with Splenda®.

Preheat the oven to 350° F. Put in the cranberries and immediately reduce the temperature to 135° F. Bake until dry. It will probably take about 6 hours. If any berries puff up, prick them with a knife. Stir occasionally. A convection oven speeds up the process, or you can use a dehydrator, if you have one, according to its directions. It may take 10 to 15 hours in a dehydrator. When dry, the cranberries should be shriveled and lightweight with no sign of moisture other than a slight stickiness. If they are not dry enough, continue to bake until they are.

Dried cranberries can be refrigerated for up to two years or frozen indefinitely. Use them as a substitute for raisins; they are much more tart, so add extra sweetener when using them in recipes, or plump them in the microwave with Da Vinci® sugar-free simple syrup or hot water and Splenda® before using. They have about one-third the carbohydrate count of raisins. The fresh berries will be reduced to about one-fourth their original weight.

PER CUP:		
Total Carb: 56g	Fiber: 16g	Net Carb: 40g
PER TABLESPOON:		
Total Carb: 3.5g	Fiber: 1.0g	Net Carb: 2.5g

VARIATION:

Dried Cranberries from Frozen Cranberries

Bring water to a boil in a large pan. Drop the frozen berries into the water and heat until they pop. Dip them out and drain on paper towels. Spread on a nonstick pan, sweeten if desired, and place in a 350° F oven. Immediately turn the heat down to 135° F, and leave for 6 hours or overnight or until the cranberries are shriveled and lightweight.

Tips and Notes

Don't throw away the liquid in which you heated the cranberries. Boil it down and add it to tea or sparkling water. Sweeten to taste for a delicious and healthful drink. (Recent research has shown that the folk remedy for treating bladder infections with cranberry juice has some basis in fact.)

Tips and Notes

Wax Orchard™ brand Fruit Sweet® is a liquid fructose or fruit sugar that I use in small amounts to help keep dried and candied fruit moist. It is sweeter than sugar or honey so you need less, and it has 7.5 carbs per tablespoon rather than the 15 to 17 in molasses, honey, or corn syrup. See Sources.

The scientific definition of a fruit is any structure that develops from a fertilized ovary and contains seeds of the plant. All fruits come from the ovaries of a flower. Therefore, many things that we consider to be vegetables are actually fruits. For example tomatoes, cucumbers, beans, peas, peppers, corn, eggplant, and squash are all fruits. Rhubarb is one of the few vegetables that are usually treated as fruit.

Tart, sweet, rosy-red, dried rhubarb can be used in muffins, fruitcake, candy, or any recipe that calls for raisins or dried cranberries.

1	pound rhubarb (4 cups after it is cut up)
½	cup dry white wine
¼	cup Da Vinci® sugar-free simple or strawberry-flavored syrup
½	cup granular Splenda®
2	teaspoons Wax Orchard™ Fruit Sweet® (see Sources) or use honey and add 6.7 net carbs per cup of rhubarb

Spray a baking sheet with no-stick spray or line with a nonstick mat.

Rinse the rhubarb and trim the ends. Cut it into ⅛-inch slices.

Mix the other ingredients together in a large saucepan and bring to a boil. Add the rhubarb and stir. Cover the pan with a lid and remove it from the heat. (Do not let the rhubarb cook or it will disintegrate.) Let it stand for an hour, stirring several times to recoat the fruit with the liquid. Remove the rhubarb with a slotted spoon and reserve. Bring the liquid back to a boil and cook until it is reduced to a thick syrup. Remove the pan from the heat; return the rhubarb to the pan and stir until it is coated with syrup. Spread the rhubarb out on a nonstick baking sheet and drizzle with any of the syrup left in the pan. Place in a pre-heated 135° F oven and bake for 1 hour. Stir the rhubarb and continue to bake, stirring once every hour, for 2 more hours or until it is lightweight and chewy. Store in the refrigerator or freeze. My 1-pound batch of rhubarb became 2½ ounces and measured a little less than 1 cup after it was dried.

PER CUP:		
Total Carb: 41.0g	Fiber: 12.2g	Net Carb: 28.8g
PER TABLESPOON:		
Total Carb: 2.6g	Fiber: 0.8g	Net Carb: 1.8g

CANDIED FRUIT

You can candy almost anything that is fairly firm and not too fragile. I have candied gorgeous rounds and stars of candied kiwi and star fruit, as well as cherries, cranberries, ginger, citrus peels, and watermelon rind. Use candied fruits in recipes or to embellish cakes and pastries. They make beautiful edible garnishes snuggled up to a roast turkey or tucked around a wheel of Brie. Other candidates for the treatment include plums, angelica, nopales, pumpkin, and rhubarb. Who knows what's next, maybe black olives or cucumbers?

Sugar-free candied fruits are a necessary ingredient for my Fruit Cake and Nutty Fruit Candy and can also be used in ice cream, cookies, compotes, chutneys, frostings, and fillings. It is not currently possible to buy sugar-free candied fruit and peel, but it is not hard to make. I've included three different ways to make it.

BASIC RECIPE FOR CANDIED FRUIT MADE WITH SPLENDA®

You can make candied fruit with just Splenda® and a little fructose syrup or honey to help keep it chewy. It will lose about 75 percent in volume and will not be as soft as fruit candied with polydextrose or maltitol, but it can be hydrated with hot water before using.

Prepare the fruit to be candied and put it in a shallow, heavy pan, just big enough to hold it in one layer. Put water in a measuring container and add enough to cover the fruit, making note of the total amount needed. Stir in 1 cup of granular Splenda®, 1 teaspoon of Fruit Sweet®, and a few grains of salt for each cup of water used. Cook over low heat, stirring, occasionally at first, and more often as the syrup thickens, until most of the water is evaporated, and the fruit is very sticky and glossy. Lift out with a slotted spoon and place on a nonstick baking sheet or waxed paper. Let fruit dry in an airy, warm place or in a warm oven, turning or stirring occasionally. You may sprinkle it with more Splenda®, with whey protein powder, or with powdered maltitol to keep it from sticking together. Store in an airtight container in the refrigerator or freeze.

Tips and Notes

A small amount of Fruit Sweet® (Wax Orchard™ brand's liquid fructose) helps keep candied fruit made with Splenda® moist and chewy. Honey would work as well but it will add more carbohydrates. Leave out the Fruit Sweet® if you prefer to completely dry the fruit; it will keep much longer, but you must heat it in liquid to soften it before using.

PER CUP OF SYRUP:

| Total Carb: 26.5g | Fiber: 0.1g | Net Carb: 26.4g |

PER TABLESPOON OF SYRUP:

| Total Carb: 1.7g | Fiber: 0g | Net Carb: 1.7g |

I have given the carb counts for the syrups used for candying and for those fruits and peels for which counts are available. It is difficult to give accurate nutrition information because there are so many variables, and an indeterminate amount of the sweeteners stays in the pan, so the counts may be considerably less than the totals for the ingredients. Consider the numbers as estimates for comparison only.

Polydextrose has the texture and mouth feel of sucrose and adds missing bulk in recipes made with high intensity sweeteners. It also browns and caramelizes like regular sugar, but it behaves like soluble fiber when ingested. It is widely used in commercial products to allow a reduction in the amount of sugar or fat needed and to add beneficial fiber. It has a total of 27 grams of carbohydrate and 25 grams of fiber for a net carb count of 2 grams per ounce. See Ingredients for more information and see Sources to order. My recipes were tested with Stay-lite® III polydextrose from Honeyville Grain.

BASIC RECIPE FOR CANDIED FRUIT MADE WITH SPLENDA® AND POLYDEXTROSE

Prepare the fruit to be candied and put in a shallow, heavy pan, just big enough to hold it in one layer. Put water in a measuring container and add enough to cover the fruit, making note of the total amount needed. Mix ¾ cup of granular Splenda®, a few grains of salt, and ¾ cup of polydextrose together until *thoroughly blended* for each cup of liquid needed to cover fruit. Stir into the pan. Cook over low heat, stirring, occasionally at first, and more often as the syrup thickens, until most of the water is evaporated, and the fruit is very sticky and glossy. Lift out with a slotted spoon and place on a nonstick baking sheet or waxed paper. Let fruit dry in an airy, warm place or in a warm oven, turning or stirring occasionally. You may sprinkle it with more Splenda®, with whey protein powder, or with powdered maltitol to keep it from sticking together. Store in an airtight container in the refrigerator or freeze.

PER CUP OF SYRUP:		
Total Carb: 180g,	Fiber: 150g	Net Carb: 30g
PER TABLESPOON OF SYRUP:		
Total Carb: 11.3g	Fiber: 9.4g	Net Carb: 1.9g

BASIC RECIPE FOR CANDIED FRUIT MADE WITH MALTITOL

Prepare the fruit to be candied and put in a shallow, heavy pan, just big enough to hold it in one layer. Put water in a measuring container and add enough to cover the fruit, making note of the total amount needed. Add 1 cup of powdered maltitol and a few grains of salt for each cup of liquid needed to cover fruit. Stir into the pan. Cook over low heat, stirring, occasionally at first, and more often as the syrup thickens, until most of the water is evaporated, and the fruit is very sticky and glossy. Lift out with a slotted spoon and place on a nonstick baking sheet or waxed paper. Let fruit dry for several hours in an airy, warm place or in a warm oven, turning or stirring occasionally. You may sprinkle it with whey protein powder, or with powdered maltitol to keep it from sticking together. Store in an airtight container in the refrigerator or freeze.

Orange Sauce

Don't waste all that lovely sweet goo left in the pan after making Candied Orange or Kumquat Peel. Use it to make sauce for Crêpes Suzette or roast duck.

PER CUP OF SYRUP:		
Total Carb: 0g	Fiber: 0g	**Net Carb: 0g**
Count excludes 144 grams of sugar alcohol		

PER TABLESPOON OF SYRUP:		
Total Carb: 0g	Fiber: 0g	**Net Carb: 0g**
Count excludes 9 grams of sugar alcohol		

Note: Maltitol, can be substituted measure for measure for sugar and for powdered sugar in recipes. Typically, the yield using maltitol will be double that with Splenda® and the fruit will not become hard and dry. The carb counts will also be lower since maltitol can be excluded. (All sugar alcohols carry a warning that excessive consumption may cause digestive distress.) See Ingredients and Sources.

CANDIED ORANGE PEEL

Use lemons instead of oranges to make Candied Lemon Peel.

Cut off a circle of peel from the top and bottom of each orange. Make vertical cuts just through the skin, but not into the flesh, about 1½ inches apart, down the sides of the fruit. Carefully pull the strips of peel away from the orange. Use the orange flesh for another purpose. Lay the peel on a flat surface and scrape away about half of the white pith with a sharp knife. You should be able to see a few speckles of orange rind showing through the white layer of pith. Cut the peel into long narrow strips, about ¼ inch wide.

Place the peel in a saucepan and cover with a generous amount of water. Bring to a boil. Drain, rinse, and repeat for a total of 3 times. Taste the peel to test for bitterness and repeat if necessary.

Proceed as in one of the Basic Recipes for Candied Fruit.

Add water to the skillet used for making candied citrus peel and stir on low heat until the glaze is dissolved and the liquid is like sauce. Stir in 2 tablespoons of butter, 1 tablespoon of Grand Marnier, and ½ teaspoon of grated orange zest for each ½ cup of sauce. Heat until slightly thickened and reduced. See p. 129 for recipe for preparing Crêpes Suzette.

Serving size: 2 tablespoons
Per Serving:
Total Carb: 2.2g
Fiber: 0g
Net Carb: 2.2g

PER TABLESPOON, ORANGE PEEL ONLY:		
Total Carb: 1.5g	Fiber: 0.6g	**Net Carb: 0.9g**

CANDIED GRAPEFRUIT PEEL

Use directions for Candied Orange Peel**,** except change the water and bring the peel to a boil 4 times rather than 3. Taste the peel to test for bitterness and repeat for as many times as necessary. Proceed as in one of the Basic Recipes for Candied Fruit.

VARIATION:

Chocolate Covered Citrus Peel

See recipe as a variation under Chocolate Dipped Strawberries. (See p. 261.)

CANDIED KUMQUAT PEEL

The easiest way to make candied citrus peel is with kumquats. They have no pith under the skin that needs to be cut away and the skins are not bitter so they do not need to be parboiled. The pulp can be pulled out easily and completely, leaving just the thin sweet skin. (They make wonderful cases to stuff with chopped nuts and candied fruit or with a Chocolate Truffle to make Sugar Plums.) The only problem is availability; so freeze extra when kumquats are in season in the fall and winter.

Wash kumquats and remove any stems. Slit lengthwise down one side. Pull out the pulp and seeds. Cut into slices or leave whole. Proceed as in one of the Basic Candied Fruit recipes.

KUMQUATS IN SYRUP, KUMQUAT PRESERVES, MARMALADE, AND CANDIED KUMQUATS

This can be a condiment, dessert topping, Preserves, Marmalade, or Candied Kumquats, depending on how you prepare the kumquats and how long you cook it.

FOR KUMQUATS IN SYRUP:

Wash the kumquats and remove any stems. The kumquats can be sliced and seeded or left whole. *To use whole:* cut down one side of the fruit so it can be spread open. Make a horizontal cut through the pulp and push the seeds out with your thumb. Or just cut a slit in each kumquat so the syrup can penetrate and let the person who eats it deal with the seeds.

Place the sweetener and water from one of the Basic Recipes for Candied Fruit in a shallow, heavy pan. Add kumquats and bring to a boil. Lower the heat and simmer until the kumquats are deep orange and glossy and the syrup is thickened. Serve as a dessert topping or condiment.

> **PER OUNCE OF KUMQUATS IN SYRUP:**
>
> Total Carb: 7.6g   Fiber: 1.8g   Net Carb: 5.8g
> when made with Splenda® and Fruit Sweet®

Tips and Notes

To prolong the storage life of sugar-free Kumquats in Syrup, Marmalade, and Preserves, reheat them to boiling every few days. (Polydextrose has some anti-microbial properties and recipes made with it may keep longer than ones made with just Splenda®.)

FOR KUMQUAT PRESERVES:

Seed kumquats and slice or leave whole. Prepare as in previous recipe, but cook until syrup is thick.

> **PER TABLESPOON OF PRESERVES:**
>
> Total Carb: 4.3g   Fiber: 1g   Net Carb: 3.3g
> when made with Splenda® and Fruit Sweet®

FOR MARMALADE:

Seed the kumquats and cut them into thin slivers. Use recipe for Kumquats in Syrup but continue to cook until the syrup is very thick. Store in the refrigerator.

> **PER TABLESPOON OF MARMALADE:**
>
> Total Carb: 4.9g   Fiber: 1.1g   Net Carb: 3.8g
> when made with Splenda® and Fruit Sweet®

FOR CANDIED KUMQUATS:

Glossy, sweet, whole fruits make gorgeous edible decorations and garnishes.

Wash the kumquats and remove any stems. Cut down one side of the fruit so it can be spread open. Make a horizontal cut through the pulp and push the seeds out with your thumb. Or just cut a slit in each kumquat so the syrup can penetrate and let the person who eats it deal with the seeds. Cook as in one of the Basic Candied Fruit recipes (the polydextrose formula is preferable) until all the water is evaporated. Fruit can be left glossy and sticky (messy but luscious!), air-dried, or placed in a warm oven for several hours. It can be coated with powdered maltitol to make it less sticky. (Don't use more polydextrose; it attracts moisture and keeps it sticky.) Store in refrigerator or freeze.

> **PER OUNCE, KUMQUATS ONLY:**
>
> Total Carb: 4.6g, Fiber: 1.8g, Net Carb: 2.8g

CANDIED GINGER

Use with discretion, as it can be very hot.

Cut or break fresh ginger root into pieces to facilitate peeling. Peel and dice. Follow one of the Basic Candied Fruit recipes. Store in an airtight container in the refrigerator or freeze.

> **PER SERVING OF 2 TABLESPOONS, GINGER ONLY:**
>
> Total Carb: 2.1g   Fiber: 0.2g   Net Carb: 1.9g

Ginger Syrup

After removing the ginger, add water to the skillet and simmer until the glaze sticking to the pan and the spatula is dissolved. Cook until reduced and thickened. Use ginger syrup to add to carbonated water to make ginger ale or to add to hot tea.

Cherries contain anti-inflammatory compounds and antioxidants but all cherries, even tart ones, contain a lot of sugar. Flavonoid Sciences,™ the makers of Cherry Flex™ capsules, have discovered a way to put the beneficial compounds of the whole fruit in a highly condensed softgel, while eliminating most of the sugar. Each capsule has 100 milligrams of anthocyanins and less than 1 gram of carbohydrate. They also make Blueberry IQ™, a softgel that contains the equivalent of ½ cup of blueberries, minus the sugar. For more information, see www.cherryflex.com.

CANDIED CHERRIES

Even drab, canned pie cherries take on a glossy, deep red color.

Use fresh, frozen, or canned, tart cherries. If using frozen cherries, thaw and drain. If using canned cherries, drain. Use whole cherries only, saving crushed or damaged ones for another use. Follow one of the Basic Recipes for Candied Fruit.

PER SERVING OF 2 TABLESPOONS, CHERRIES ONLY:		
Total Carb: 2.4g	Fiber: 0.2g	Net Carb: 2.1g

CANDIED WATERMELON RIND

I have added watermelon rind to the list of fruits and peels normally used; it is readily available, cheap, and with a little lemon juice added, it makes a good replacement for citron, which I can't find fresh. You'll need an old-fashioned watermelon for this, not one of the new thin-skinned varieties.

Cut the rind from a slice of watermelon into chunks. Pare away and discard the thin green outer rind with a vegetable parer and cut away all traces of the pink flesh. Dice the rind into medium to small chunks.

For each 2 cups of diced rind: Cover rind with water to which you have added 1 teaspoon of lemon juice. Let stand 8 hours or overnight. Drain and rinse. Place the rind in a saucepan, cover with fresh, cold water, and bring to a boil; simmer for about an hour. Drain and rinse. Proceed as in one of the Basic Candied Fruit recipes, but add 2 additional teaspoons of lemon juice a few minutes before the end of the cooking time.

Sprinkle with whey protein powder or maltitol, if desired, to keep rind from sticking together. (Polydextrose attracts moisture and would not help with the stickiness.)

CANDIED CRANBERRIES

This recipe is made with just Splenda®. The former methods don't work well for cranberries; the tough skins have to break before the syrup will penetrate and then the berries tend to disintegrate in the water. Use Candied Cranberries as a condiment for meat or poultry or in recipes that call for candied fruit. I sometimes use them (well drained) as a low-carb replacement for candied cherries in my Fruitcake and Nutty Fruit Candy recipes.

Preheat the oven to 350° F.

Wash and pick over 2 cups of fresh cranberries. Spread them in an even layer on a shallow, nonstick baking pan. Sprinkle the berries with ¾ cup of granular Splenda®. Cover tightly with foil and place in the oven for 10 minutes to crack the skins. Stir the berries, replace the foil, and return to the oven for about 10 minutes more, or until the berries are glossy but still whole. Let cool. Store in the refrigerator. Serve as a condiment like cranberry sauce or drain and blot dry to use like candied cherries.

Makes about 1½ cups.

PER SERVING OF ½ CUP:		
Total Carb: 7.6g	Fiber 1.3g	Net Carb: 6.3g

Tips and Notes

Candied fruit will retain more of its original weight and its texture will be more like that of fruit candied with sugar if it is made with maltitol rather then Splenda®. Typically, the yield using maltitol will be double that with Splenda® and the fruit will not become hard and dry. The net carb counts will also be lower since maltitol can be excluded. I've given directions for using both Splenda® and maltitol for some of the candied fruit recipes and you can substitute maltitol for Splenda® in all of them if you prefer. (See Ingredients and Sources.)

BREADS, TORTILLAS, AND CRACKERS

REDEEMED

> "Shun anything made with flour, no matter in what form it hides; do you not still have the roast, the salad, and the leafy vegetables?"
>
> —Jean Anthelme Brillat-Savarin

Some of the recipes in this chapter call for baked gluten flour. This is gluten flour that has been heated to deactivate the gluten proteins. By combining the baked and unbaked flours, you can control the amount of gluten necessary for the bread to rise without having so much that it becomes rubbery. I buy two packages of gluten flour at a time and bake one of them. Then I store them in separate canisters labeled "baked" and "unbaked."

To bake gluten flour:
Spread gluten flour in a large roasting pan and bake in a preheated 350° F oven for about 15 minutes, or until just slightly colored. Stir it well several times as it bakes. Watch it carefully or it will burn. The time it takes will vary depending on how much moisture is in the flour. Cool and store in an airtight container in the refrigerator or freezer.

Tips and Notes

This mixture also makes a delicious pie crust. (See p. 306.)

You'll have a gummy mess if you try to clean up spilled gluten flour with a wet towel. Vacuum it up or use a dry towel to wipe it away.

LOW-CARB FLOUR REPLACEMENT

What are the alternatives to wheat flour when you need a quick coating for a cutlet or for browning a roast? Straight gluten flour is too gummy; straight soy flour tastes terrible; whole-grain oat flour is delicious but at thirty-nine net carbs per cup, not low enough (although certainly better than regular flour at eighty-four). The solution is a mixture. There are several available that you can purchase, but it's a snap to mix up a batch at home. Most of the ingredients can be found at a local grocery or health food store, or you can order them from Bob's Red Mill® or the King Arthur® Flour Company. Feel free to make your own custom blend, but here's what I include:

For 1 cup:
¼ cup wheat gluten flour
¼ cup wheat bran
2 tablespoons whole grain oat flour
2 tablespoons flax meal
2 tablespoons soy flour
2 tablespoons almond flour

Stir together and place in an airtight container. Store in the refrigerator.

Serving size: ¼ cup

PER SERVING:		
Total Carb: 8.8g	Fiber: 4.5g	Net Carb: 4.3g

VARIATION:
HOT CEREAL

Use the Low-Carb Flour Replacement mix on the precious page to make cooked cereal that tastes like oatmeal or Cream of Wheat, only better.

Heat ¼ cup of water to boiling. Add ¼ cup of Low-carb Flour Mixture. Add a pinch of salt and sweeten to taste. Stir. Top with a pat of butter and a splash of cream. Other add-ins: Chopped nuts, a sprinkle of cinnamon, and sugar-free Dried Cranberries, see p. 105. (Add cranberries to the water before heating.)

Serving size: ¼ cup

PER SERVING:		
Total Carb: 8.8g	Fiber: 4.5g	Net Carb: 4.3g

GENERAL RECIPE FOR BREADED MEAT, FISH, SEAFOOD, AND VEGETABLES

Pork rinds make a very crisp, zero-carbohydrate breading for fried foods. They can be used alone, as in my recipe for Fried Chicken, or combined with other ingredients to make excellent crispy coatings. One of my favorites is a mixture of equal parts pork rinds, sesame seeds, and almond flour. Once you have tried this, you'll never go back to flour or cornmeal!

Measure equal amounts of pork rinds, sesame seeds, and almond or hazelnut flour. Process the pork rinds and sesame seeds in the food processor until fine. Stir in the nut flour. Season to taste with salt and pepper.

Dry the food to be fried well. Beat egg whites with a fork. Beat in one tablespoon of cream for each egg white. Dip the food in the egg white mixture and roll in the pork rind, sesame seed, and almond mixture until evenly coated. Let dry on a rack for 15 minutes. Fry in deep oil at 365° F until brown and crisp. Drain and serve.

This breading mixture will contain 1.5 net carbs per tablespoon. (Count only the amount that adheres to the food; some will be left over.)

Tips and Notes

Flax is an amazingly useful plant. We get linseed oil from the seeds and linen from the fibers. When the seeds are ground, they make flax meal, a powerhouse of nutrition. It contains high levels of antioxidants and alpha-linolenic acid, the plant version of Omega-3 oil. (The oil in flaxseed is 50% alpha-linolenic acid; canola and walnut oil, the next highest plant sources, have only 10%.) It also supplies calcium, iron, niacin, phosphorous, and vitamin E, and two tablespoons contain 4 grams of fiber, as much as a cup and a half of oatmeal.

When mixed with liquid, flax meal develops a texture similar to egg whites and is sometimes substituted for eggs or oil in recipes. Because of its high oil content, flax meal should be stored in the refrigerator or frozen.

Tips and Notes

Breads like popovers and soufflés that depend on eggs to rise, rather than yeast or baking powder, need bottom heat for maximum height. If there is heat from the top, it will set the batter too soon and limit its expansion. Use the bottom heating element only, if that's an option with your oven; if not, set the pan on an oven rack positioned in the lower third of the oven and shield it from above with a baking sheet placed on the upper rack. Be sure to leave enough headroom between the racks for the popovers to rise.

POPOVERS

If you're on a low-carb diet, I know what you want—a big, hot, crusty chunk of bread! Here it is.

Popovers should be crisp on the outside and hollow on the inside. I must have made these a hundred times trying to get that combination. I could get crisp; I couldn't get hollow. That is, until I tried combining the batter for the popovers with a technique used in making pâte à choux: boiling the liquid and combining it with the flour. Voilà!

Normally, this recipe would be made with 1 cup of bread flour. In order to reduce the carbohydrate count, I used ¹/₈ cup of gluten flour to get the amount of gluten in 1 cup of bread flour, and then I replaced the other ⁷/₈ cup with other flours.

- Butter for pan
- ¹/₈ cup gluten flour (about ¹/₂ ounce)
- ¹/₄ cup almond flour
- ¹/₄ cup white whole-wheat flour (1 ounce)
- ³/₈ cup oat flour (1³/₄ ounces)
- ¹/₂ teaspoon salt, slightly rounded
- ¹/₂ cup cream
- ¹/₄ cup plus 2 tablespoons water
- 2 whole eggs
- 3 egg whites (¹/₃ cup)

Preheat the oven to 300° F. Spray the blade of the food processor with no-stick spray so the batter will release easily.

Place 1 teaspoon of butter in each cup of a 6- or an 8-cup muffin pan or a 6-cup popover pan. A nonstick metal pan is best. Heat the pan in the oven for a few minutes just before filling it so that the butter is melted and the pan is hot. (Set the muffin pan on a cookie sheet, also preheated, to catch any butter drips.) Position an oven rack in the lower third of the oven. Use bottom heat only or place a baking sheet on the upper rack of the oven to shield the batter from top heat. Leave plenty of head room between the racks for the popovers to rise.

Measure the flours and the salt and whisk together. Set aside.

(continued on next page)

POPOVERS, CONTINUED

In a medium-sized, heavy saucepan, bring the water and cream to a boil. Add the flour mixture all at once and stir vigorously with a wooden spoon until the mixture forms a soft mass and pulls away from the sides of the pan. Turn off the heat and let the dough cool for 2 or 3 minutes.

Place the dough in the bowl of the food processor and run it for one minute. (The dough can be beaten by hand with a wooden spoon rather then in a food processor if necessary.) Remove the lid of the food processor and let the steam escape until the mixture has cooled enough so that it will not cook the eggs when they are added. Touch it with your fingers to be sure it is not too hot. Break one of the eggs into the processor bowl and run the machine until the egg is incorporated. Add the egg whites and process again until they are incorporated. Scrape down the bottom and sides of the bowl with a spatula. Add the last egg and process it until blended. The dough should be about the consistency of cake batter.

Remove the hot pan from the preheated oven and brush the melted butter around to coat the inside of the cups. Divide the batter evenly into the cups, filling about ¾ full. Place the pan on the oven rack in the lower third of the oven and immediately raise the oven temperature to 450° F. Bake for 10 to 15 minutes or until well risen and browned. No peeking! Don't open the oven door before the dough is well puffed and brown. Lower the heat to 300° F and continue to bake for an additional 10 to 15 minutes to dry out and set the popovers so they won't deflate. Remove the pan from the oven and pierce each popover with a sharp knife to release the steam. Return to the oven for 5 minutes more. (Cut the popovers open and pull out the soft centers to reduce the carb count even more.) Serve hot with butter.

Servings: 7

PER SERVING:		
Total Carb: 6.4g	Fiber: 1.4g	Net Carb: 5.0g

Tips and Notes

The volume of flour will vary depending on its moisture content. Sifting and settling also changes the volume. Whether the flour is sifted before or after measuring can also make a difference. The most accurate way to measure it is by weight, so for recipes where an accurate measurement is important, I have included the weight in grams and ounces, as well as the amount in cups. Package labels give you an accurate weight for a stated volume, so with a little math you can always figure out the weight for the amount called for. A digital kitchen scale that can be reset to zero after the container is weighed is ideal for dry ingredients.

VARIATION: APPETIZER PUFFS

To make Appetizer Puffs, bake Popover batter in buttered, nonstick mini-muffin pans, using about 1 tablespoon of batter in each cup. A whole recipe will make twenty-four small puffs. Bake as for Popovers, watching carefully so they don't burn. Cut off the tops of the hot puffs and pull out the soft centers with a fork. Spray the inside with no-stick spray or brush with melted butter and return to the 300° F oven for 5 minutes to dry. Let shells cool completely before storing. Store in an airtight container and fill just before serving so they stay crisp. Fill with creamed crabmeat or chicken or egg salad and replace the top. Shells can be reheated until crisp before filling, if necessary.

Servings: 24

PER SERVING:		
Total Carb: 1.7g	Fiber: 0.5g	Net Carb: 1.2g

VARIATION: TUNA MELTS

Tips and Notes

To use Popovers as cases, as in the Tuna Melt recipe, or to store for later use:

Split the hot popovers open, pull out the soft centers with a fork, brush the inside with melted butter, and bake for 5 more minutes until dry and crisp. Let cool completely and store airtight. If not using within a day or so, freezing is recommended.

1 large can tuna (12 ounces), drained
2 chopped green onions
1 cup shredded Cheddar cheese
½ cup celery, sliced
2 tablespoons diced red pepper
½ cup real mayonnaise
1 teaspoon prepared mustard
• A pinch of garlic powder
• A pinch of onion powder
• Salt and pepper to taste
4 Popovers, split in half, with the soft centers removed.

Preheat oven to 375° F.

Set popover shells in the cups of a muffin pan to keep them upright. Combine all other ingredients and spoon into popovers. Bake for 5 to 10 minutes or until hot and the cheese is melted.

Servings: 4

PER SERVING (FILLING ONLY):		
Total Carb: 6.7g	Fiber: 2.0g	Net Carb: 4.7g

VARIATION:
CREAM PUFFS

Add 1 tablespoon of granular Splenda® to the Popover batter. Bake in nonstick mini-muffin pans, using about 1 tablespoon of batter for each cup. Prepare and preheat the pans as in the recipe for Popovers. Place the pan on the oven rack in the lower third of the oven and immediately raise the oven temperature to 450° F. Bake for 10 to 15 minutes or until puffs are well risen and browned, watching carefully so they don't burn. Reduce the oven temperature to 300° F and continue to bake for another 6 minutes to set. Cut off the tops of the puffs and pull out the soft centers with a fork. Brush them inside with melted butter and return to the oven to dry out for a few minutes more. Let cool.

Fill puffs with chilled Pastry Cream or French Vanilla Ice Cream (see Index) and replace the tops. Pour a spoonful of Chocolate Glaze or Chocolate Sauce (see Index) over each puff. Fill the puffs just before serving so they stay crisp. Shells can be reheated until crisp if necessary before filling.

Servings: 24

PER SERVING:		
Total Carb: 4.9g	Fiber: 0.8g	Net Carb: 4.1g
count is for Cream Puffs with Pastry Cream and Chocolate Glaze		

VARIATION:
YORKSHIRE PUDDING FOR ROAST BEEF

Make Standing Beef Rib Roast (see p. 207). Make the Popover batter a few minutes before the roast is done. Remove the roast from the oven and tent it with foil to keep it warm. Reduce oven setting to 300° F. Heat ¼ cup of the pan drippings from the roast in a 9-inch square pan (add butter if necessary to make ¼ cup). Heat the pan in the oven until hot. Use bottom heat only if that is possible with your oven, or place a baking sheet on the top rack to shield the pudding from top heat. Pour the batter into the hot pan, place it on the oven rack in the lower third of the oven, and increase the temperature to 425° F. Bake for about 25 to 30 minutes, or until the pudding is puffed and brown. Cut it into nine squares and serve with the roast.

Servings: 9

PER SERVING:		
Total Carb: 4.5g	Fiber: 1.3g	Net Carb: 3.2g

"The proof of the pudding is in the eating."

—Miguel de Cervantes, Don Quixote de la Mancha

Toad in a Hole is one of those picturesque names the English have for common dishes, such as Bubble and Squeak (fried mashed potatoes with cabbage), Spotted Dick (boiled pudding with raisins), and Wet Nelly (bread pudding).

VARIATION:
TOAD IN A HOLE

Toad in a Hole served with cooked apples and sautéed cabbage was my son's favorite dinner when he was small. What little boy wouldn't love eating toads?

Position an oven rack in the lower third of the oven. Use bottom heat only or place a baking sheet on the upper rack of the oven to shield the batter from top heat. Preheat oven to 300° F. Prepare Popover batter.

Cut about 10 ounces of smoked sausage into 2-inch slices. Cook and turn the slices in a skillet with a little oil for 2 to 3 minutes on medium heat. Reserve the sausage. Add oil or butter to the grease in the skillet if necessary so that you have about ¼ cup of fat. Put some of the grease in each cup of a 6-cup popover pan or an eight-cup muffin pan. Set the pan on a baking sheet to catch drips. Heat both pans in the oven until hot. Remove the hot pan containing the grease from the oven and put a sausage slice in each cup. Pour the popover batter over the sausage and put the pan on the oven rack positioned in the lower third of the oven. Shield from above. Raise the temperature to 425° F. Bake for about 15 to 20 minutes or until well puffed and brown. Do not open the oven! Lower the heat to 300° F and continue to bake for an additional 10 to 15 minutes to dry out and set the popovers so they won't deflate.

Servings: 7

PER SERVING:		
Total Carb: 5.7g	Fiber: 1.6g	Net Carb: 4.1g
when made with zero-carb sausage		

WAFFLES

Use these as a base for eggs Benedict, shape them into bowls while they are hot and fill with ice cream, or top with berries and whipped cream for dessert. And, of course, you can serve them for breakfast with butter and sugar-free maple syrup.

- 4   eggs, separated
- ½   stick butter, softened
- ¼   cup oat flour
- 1   tablespoon cornstarch
- 1   tablespoon powdered egg white
- 1   teaspoon granular Splenda®
- ½   teaspoon salt
- 1   cup Crème Fraîche (see p. 51) or sour cream
- •   A pinch of cream of tartar (omit if beating in a copper bowl)

Preheat waffle iron while mixing the batter. Preheat oven to 200° F.

Separate the eggs and reserve the whites. Cream the butter with an electric beater and beat in the egg yolks one at a time. Sift together the oat flour, cornstarch, powdered egg white, Splenda®, and salt. Add the Crème Fraîche or sour cream and the flour mixture alternately to the yolk batter, beating after each addition. In a separate bowl, with clean beaters, beat the reserved egg whites with the cream of tartar (if using) to the stiff-peak stage. Fold one-fourth of the egg whites into the batter to lighten, and then gently fold in the rest of the whites. Follow manufacturer's directions for your waffle iron and bake until brown. Place the waffles in a 200° F oven for 10 minutes after removing them from the waffle iron to dry and crisp. Serve hot.

The waffles can be frozen. Separate them with layers of waxed paper and place in an airtight bag or container to freeze. Reheat frozen waffles until crisp in a toaster or in a 200° F oven.

Makes six servings of two (2 ½- by 5 ½-inch size) waffles each.

Servings: 6

PER SERVING:		
Total Carb: 3.9g	Fiber: 0.4g	Net Carb: 3.5g

see p. 51

VARIATION:

Chocolate Waffles

Omit the cornstarch in the Waffle recipe. Add 2 tablespoons of Dutch-process cocoa powder to the dry ingredients and increase the Splenda® to 2½ tablespoons. Add 1 teaspoon of vanilla with the Crème Fraîche or sour cream. Stir in ¼ cup of chopped nuts (optional), and bake as directed by the manufacturer of your waffle iron. Serve topped with fresh fruit and sugar-free whipped cream or with sugar-free ice cream. Makes six servings of two waffles each.

Per Serving:
Total Carb: 3.9g
Fiber: 0.7g
Net Carb: 3.2g

Tips and Notes

Your crêpe will be the same size as the bottom of your pan. Choose a crêpe pan with low, sloping sides and a nonstick finish. Having a proper pan makes a difference; it is worth the investment to have a pan for this one purpose. My experiment with an electric crêpe maker, the kind that you dip into a dish of batter, was not a success; this batter wouldn't stick to the pan's surface.

I found a classic French recipe for making 18 crêpes with only 3 tablespoonfuls of flour. Made with all-purpose flour, they would have less than two grams of carbohydrate each, but I've used oat flour to make the carb count even lower. This recipe makes 18 six-inch, paper-thin pancakes that can be used in many ways for appetizers, main dishes, and desserts.

The batter must be very thin, like fresh cream, and it should spread out to cover the entire bottom of the pan. Add more liquid if it does not. If the batter doesn't sizzle when it hits the pan, the pan is not hot enough. If your crêpes have little holes in them, the pan was too hot. Make the first crêpe as a trial to test the amount and consistency of your batter. Don't despair if you wreck a few at first, it's not difficult once you get into the rhythm of it.

- 3   level tablespoons oat flour
- •   A pinch of salt
- 3   eggs
- ½   cup heavy cream and ½ cup of water, mixed together
- 3   tablespoons butter that has been melted and cooled, or use olive oil
- •   Oil for the pan

Whisk the oat flour and the salt together in a mixing bowl. Add the eggs one at a time and whisk until each one is absorbed before adding the next one. Slowly add ⅔ cup of the liquid, stirring constantly. Stir in the butter or oil and add more of the liquid if necessary until the batter is the consistency of fresh cream. Let the batter rest for half an hour or more if possible.

Use about 2 tablespoonfuls of batter each to make 6-inch crêpes, 3 tablespoonfuls for 7-inch crêpes. (Smaller crêpes are easier to turn.) Measure the proper amount of batter into the ladle or cup that you will use for dipping. Notice the fill line so that you can gauge the same amount each time.

Use a heat resistant brush to coat the pan with oil. Set the pan on medium heat until hot. (You must use an oil that won't burn while you cook all the crêpes—olive oil or butter can't take the prolonged heat.) The "correct" way to make a crêpe is to lift the pan from the heat with your right hand and pour in the batter with the left, while tilting the pan to spread a thin film over the entire bottom of the pan. For me, pouring with my right hand is easier. Try it to see what feels natural to you.

(continued on next page)

CRÊPES, CONTINUED

Pour any batter that does not instantly adhere to the pan back into the bowl and use a little less next time. Return the pan to the heat for about 30 seconds. Holes and tears can be mended with a few drops of fresh batter.

Lift the edges of the crêpe with a narrow spatula and check to see if the underside is lightly browned. If so, slide the spatula underneath to loosen it, and flip it over. Don't attempt to turn it until it is completely loose. You can also flip it with your fingers if you're quick: push the loosened crêpe with the spatula so that it extends over the front edge of the pan. Grasp the edge with both hands, pull it up, and flip it over. Cook for 15 seconds more, or until the second side browns, then slide it out onto a cloth towel. Pour in the batter for the next pancake and repeat. Stir the batter just before pouring each time. The flour tends to settle to the bottom so you may need to add more liquid at some point. The pan will probably need to be greased again but not between every crêpe.

Let the cooked crêpes cool on a cup towel before stacking. Cover with a cloth so they don't dry out until all are cooked. The side of the crêpe that browned first should be the presentation side. It will be darker and more evenly browned than the second side. Use it as the outside for rolled or folded crêpes. The crêpes can be made ahead and reheated or frozen. Separate the crêpes with sheets of parchment or waxed paper before freezing them.

Servings: 18 (6-inch crêpes)

PER SERVING:		
Total Carb: 0.6g	Fiber: 0.1g	Net Carb: 0.5g

For appetizer-sized crêpes, use a tablespoon of batter for each and cook on a griddle or in a large skillet.

Servings: 72 (3-inch crêpes)

PER SERVING:		
Total Carb: 0.2g	Fiber: 0g	Net Carb: 0.2g

Tips and Notes

If you can't get your crêpes turned without tearing them, here are two suggestions that may help:

1. Preheat a second skillet or griddle. When the first side of the crêpe is done, invert the crêpe pan over the second pan so that the crêpe falls into it. Cook the reverse side of the crêpe until done, and then slide it out onto a cloth towel. (A pancake maker consisting of two pans that are hinged together has been for sale recently on TV and in stores. Mine didn't last long, but it worked great.)

or

2. Cook the crêpes on one side only. Cook them a little longer on the first side than you normally would and invert the pan or slide them out on the towel. When you roll or fold them, use the un-browned side as the inside.

VARIATION:
STUFFED CRÊPES AU GRATIN

Use chopped leftover meat or vegetables, moistened with a compatible sauce, to fill the crêpes. Roll them up and place in a baking dish, sprinkle with grated cheese, dot with butter, and bake at 375° F for 15 minutes.

VARIATION:
CRÊPES NICHOLAS

Put 2 tablespoonfuls each of chopped, cooked chicken and sautéed, chopped mushrooms on each pancake. Roll up and place in a baking dish. Pour Cheese Sauce (see p. 222) on top to cover and run under the broiler until browned.

Serving size: 1 crêpe

PER SERVING:		
Total Carb: 1.7g	Fiber: 0.2g	Net Carb: 1.5g

VARIATION:
CANNELLONI

Tips and Notes

Marinara-type pasta sauces that are imported from Italy are usually the lowest in carbohydrates. American ones tend to have added sugar.

1 recipe Crêpes
2 cups ricotta cheese (one 15-ounce container)
1 egg
1 recipe Tomato Sauce with Meat from Lasagna Casserole recipe (see p. 163), or use purchased Italian marinara sauce
1 cup shredded mozzarella cheese
• Grated Parmesan cheese

Mix ricotta and egg together. Fill the crêpes with the ricotta mixture and roll up. Place in a greased baking dish and cover with sauce. Sprinkle with mozzarella and Parmesan cheese. Bake at 350° F for 15 minutes. Makes six servings of three crêpes each.

Servings: 6

PER SERVING:		
Total Carb: 13.0g	Fiber: 1.9g	Net Carb: 11.1g

VARIATION:
COCKTAIL CRÊPES

Make tiny crêpes and wrap around cocktail sausages or fill with curried chicken or with seafood in Cream Sauce (see p. 221). Serve on wooden picks.

VARIATION:
BLINI

Make tiny Crêpes. Top each with a bit of Crème Fraîche (see p. 51) or sour cream and smoked salmon or caviar.

Serving size: 1 Blini

PER SERVING:		
Total Carb: 0.4g	Fiber: 0.1g	Net Carb: 0.3g

VARIATION:
JAM CRÊPES

Spread each crêpe with 1 tablespoon of sugar-free jam and roll up or fold into quarters. Serve warm with sugar-free whipped cream. If stacked and cut in wedges like a layer cake, this becomes Crêpes Napoleon.

Serving size: 1 crêpe

PER SERVING:		
Total Carb: 5.7g	Fiber: 0.8g	Net Carb: 4.9g

VARIATION:
CHOCOLATE CRÊPES

Spread each crêpe with 2 tablespoons of Pastry Cream (see p. 256). You will need about 1½ cups for twelve crêpes. Roll up or fold into quarters and place in an ovenproof dish. Sprinkle with finely chopped sugar-free chocolate chips. You will need about ¾ of a cup of chips for twelve crêpes. Place in a 350° F oven just until the chocolate melts.

Serving size: 1 crêpe

PER SERVING:		
Total Carb: 4.2g	Fiber: 1.1g	Net Carb: 3.1g

"I went on a diet, swore off drinking and heavy eating, and in 14 days I lost two weeks."

—Joe E. Lewis

The outermost layer of the peel of a citrus fruit is called the zest. Only the colored part, which contains the aromatic oils (not the white pith), is the zest. It can be removed with a zesting tool, a vegetable peeler, or a grater.

VARIATION:
CHEESE BLINTZES

For filling:
2   cups ricotta or moist cottage cheese
1   beaten egg or the equivalent amount of egg substitute (the egg may not get thoroughly cooked)
2   tablespoons granular Splenda® or less to taste
½   teaspoon ground cinnamon
½   teaspoon grated lemon zest
1   teaspoon vanilla extract
•   Butter for the pan

Beat together the cheese, egg, Splenda®, cinnamon, lemon zest, and vanilla. When making the crêpes, brown them on one side only. Invert the pan to turn them out, browned side up, onto a layer of towels. Put a spoonful of the cheese mixture on each one, fold in the sides, and roll up. Sauté the filled crêpes in butter until brown. Serve with sour cream or Crème Fraîche (see p. 51) and sugar-free jam.

Servings: 18

PER SERVING:		
Total Carb: 1.6g	Fiber: 0.1g	Net Carb: 1.5g

VARIATION:
CHOCOLATE HAZELNUT CRÊPES

The American version of the popular European spread called Nutella™, contains trans fats, fillers, and sugar. Here's something better to slather on your own fresh Crêpes. If this isn't decadent enough for you, add fresh strawberries or sugar-free jam.

2   cups raw hazelnuts
1   cup granular Splenda®
¼   cup Dutch process cocoa powder
½   teaspoon of vanilla extract
•   A few grains of salt
3   tablespoons peanut oil, more or less

Preheat oven to 400° F. Put hazelnuts in shallow roasting pan and toast for 10 to 15 minutes until skins are charred. Place hot nuts in a cup towel and rub off the skins. Process nuts in a food processor until they are liquefied, about 5 minutes, scraping down the sides of the bowl as necessary. Add Splenda®, cocoa, vanilla, salt, and some of the oil and process until thick and smooth, scraping down the bowl occasionally. Slowly pour in more oil with machine running, until mixture has the texture of thin peanut butter. (It will be warm from the friction of the blade; it will thicken as it cools.) Refrigerate until needed. Let it warm up to spreading consistency; spread on warm Crêpes; fold into quarters.

Serving size: 1 Crêpe with 2 tablespoons spread.

PER SERVING:		
Total Carb: 4.5g	Fiber: 1.7g	Net Carb: 3.2g

VARIATION:
CRÊPES SUZETTE

Delicious (and safe!) without the pyrotechnics, but if you must be dramatic, and your insurance is paid up, you can flambé the crêpes. I wouldn't try this at the table; do it on the stovetop with a hood overhead and stand back as far from the pan as possible. Use a long fireplace match or clicker-type fire starter. Turn your face the other way when pouring in the brandy and lighting the sauce. Don't pour the brandy directly from the bottle; it may ignite when it hits the hot pan and the flames could travel up to the bottle and set fire to the whole thing while it is in your hand.

12 six-inch Crêpes

For Suzette Sauce:
- Grated zest of one orange (1 tablespoon)
- ½ cup water
- ½ cup granular Splenda®
- 1 teaspoon Wax Orchard™ Fruit Sweet® (or use honey and add 0.6 net carbs per serving)
- 1 tablespoon Grand Marnier liqueur
- 2 tablespoons butter

- 1 teaspoon powdered sugar or powdered maltitol (optional)
- ¼ cup brandy to flambé (optional)

Place the orange zest (the thin orange-colored outer rind only), water, Splenda®, and Fruit Sweet® or honey in a large skillet over medium-low heat. Simmer, stirring occasionally, until the water is evaporated and the mixture starts to sizzle. Add the Grand Marnier and butter and stir until the butter is melted. Fold the crêpes into quarters and arrange in the pan with the sauce. Continue to cook for five minutes more, spooning the orange sauce over the crêpes. Place the crêpes on serving dishes and dust with a little powdered sugar or powdered maltitol (optional). Serve hot.

To flambé:
Warm ¼ cup of brandy. After adding the crêpes to the sauce, carefully pour the brandy into the pan, keeping your face averted. It may ignite by itself or you can touch it with a long match to flambé. Spoon the sauce over the crêpes after the flames die down and serve.

Servings: 12

PER SERVING:		
Total Carb: 2.5g	Fiber: 0.1g	Net Carb: 2.4g

Tips and Notes

Renowned chef, Henri Carpentier, claimed to have accidentally created Crêpes Suzette as an assistant waiter, when he was 14 years old. The truth of his account is not undisputed, but it makes a great story. In *Life A La Henri—Being the Memories of Henri Charpentier*, he tells how a chafing dish of cordials caught fire as he was preparing a dish to be served to Edward, the Prince of Wales, at the Maitre at Monte Carlo's Café de Paris in 1895. Thinking the dish was ruined, he tasted it and declared it to be the "most delicious melody of sweet flavors I had ever tasted." When the Prince asked the name of the dessert, Henri intended to name it in honor of the royal guest, who requested that it be named, instead, for a young lady who was present at the table, whose name was Suzette. "Thus was born and baptized this confection, one taste of which, I really believe, would reform a cannibal into a civilized gentleman. The next day I received a present from the Prince, a jeweled ring, a Panama hat and a cane."

Tips and Notes

Out of context, it is impossible to tell the difference between almond and cherry flavors. That's why I use almond extract and amaretto (almond) liqueur to intensify the cherry flavor in the Cherry Clafouti.

Peach, Cranberry, or Rhubarb Clafouti

For peach clafouti: replace the cherries with 1 cup of peeled, pitted, and sliced ripe peaches.

For cranberry or rhubarb clafouti: simmer one cup of fruit in ½ cup of water with 2 tablespoons of granular Splenda® for 5 minutes. Cool and drain. Substitute for cherries.

Serves 6.

Per Serving with
Cranberries:
Total Carb: 8.8g
Fiber: 2.4g
Net Carb: 6.4g

Per Serving with Rhubarb:
Total Carb: 7.5g
Fiber: 2.2g
Net Carb: 5.3g

Per Serving with Peaches:
Total Carb: 9.6g
Fiber: 2.2g
Net Carb: 7.4g

Clafouti, a rustic French confection that is part pancake, part soufflé, makes a wonderful breakfast with only ½ teaspoon of flour per serving. Chill the batter overnight so it can be assembled quickly in the morning. It is especially delicious made with fresh Bing cherries, but peaches, cranberries, or rhubarb can be used for a lower carbohydrate version.

½ cup almond flour (or substitute ground almonds)
1 tablespoon all-purpose flour
⅓ cup plus 1 tablespoon granular Splenda®
2 eggs
3 egg yolks
⅔ cup heavy cream
• A pinch of salt
• Butter for pan
1 cup pitted, fresh sweet cherries, cut into halves
1 tablespoon amaretto (optional) or use sugar-free amaretto-flavored syrup
⅓ cup sliced almonds

Whisk together the almond flour and 1 tablespoon of all-purpose flour. (If using nuts rather than nut flour, grind the nuts and the all-purpose flour together in a food processor to a fine powder. Don't over-grind, or the nuts will form a paste.)

Put in the bowl of an electric mixer: the Splenda®, eggs, egg yolks, cream, salt, and the nut and flour mixture. Beat the ingredients together thoroughly. Cover the bowl and refrigerate for a few hours or overnight.

Preheat the oven to 350° F. Remove the batter from the refrigerator. Butter an 8- or 9-inch round pan with sides at least one inch high.

In a bowl, mix the cherries with the amaretto or syrup and let sit for 10 minutes, stirring occasionally. Drain the cherries and place on paper towels to absorb the excess moisture. While the batter is still chilled, stir it with a whisk to blend, and then pour half of the batter into the prepared pan. Place the cherry halves in an even layer over the batter and pour the rest of the batter over to cover the cherries. Sprinkle the sliced almonds over the top. Bake for 25 to 30 minutes, or until the top is puffed and brown and the batter is set. Serve warm or cold with sugar-free Whipped Cream. Never refrigerate the clafouti. It is better if eaten the same day.

Servings: 6

PER SERVING:		
Total Carb: 9.8g	Fiber: 2.2g	Net Carb: 7.6g

FLOUR TORTILLAS

Tortillas made of whole-wheat and oat fiber from La Tortilla Factory™ are available by mail and at many supermarkets (see Sources). They come in two sizes and several flavors. At three net carbs and very little fat for one regular tortilla, they work for any kind of diet and make it much easier to stick to a low-carb diet. La Tortilla Factory™ has recently added a low-carb flour tortilla made with olive oil which is indistinguishable from a regular flour tortilla. (Be careful to get the low-carb version.) Other tortilla brands have also developed low-carb versions, just be sure to check for a count of no more than three to five net carbs for a regular size, five to seven for a large, and be sure they contain no trans fats.

Low-carb tortillas can be used for wrap sandwiches and Mexican dishes. Heat them in the microwave or place them, one at a time, directly on a gas burner for a few seconds to warm and soften. You can also spread them with butter and crisp them in a hot oven for a few minutes or fry them in a little oil or butter in a skillet until they get puffy and crisp. Cut them up and fry them in oil to use as crackers or chips. I'm including some of my favorite recipes for them.

Note: A common complaint about the initial phase of several of the low-carb diets is the lack of fiber. One regular size tortilla from La Tortilla Factory™ has eight grams of fiber; one packet of Metamucil® has five! Even on the most restrictive of the diets, it might be possible to include one three-net-carb tortilla a day without going over the carb limit.

INDIVIDUAL THIN CRUST PIZZAS

Preheat oven to 425° F.

Spread low-carb tortillas with purchased pizza sauce or with canned tomato sauce mixed with a little oregano. (Each regular size tortilla will take 2 to 3 tablespoons of sauce.) Sprinkle with about ½ cup of shredded mozzarella cheese. Add your choice of toppings: chopped red and green bell pepper, thinly sliced onion, sliced fresh mushrooms, sliced black olives, sliced or chopped fresh tomatoes, pepperoni slices, and precooked crumbled sausage. Put pizzas on a baking sheet and place in a hot oven for 7 to 10 minutes, or until the crust is brown and the cheese bubbles. Cut into wedges with a pizza wheel and serve hot. Count three to five net carbs for each 6- to 7-inch tortilla, about 1.5 net carbs per tablespoon for the sauce, plus whatever you put on top.

Tips and Notes

When I will be eating lunch on the run, I put a low-carb tortilla in a plastic bag in my pocket. Then I can order any sandwich or burger without a bun and make it into a wrap sandwich, or I can order a pan pizza, invert it onto a tortilla and peel away the crust.

In a Mexican restaurant, I put my tortilla on top of the hot ones in the warmer that comes with my order. Within a few minutes, I have a soft, warm, low-carb tortilla.

FAJITAS

Tips and Notes

Faja means sash, belt, or band in Spanish. The name *fajita* comes from the shape of the skirt steak, a long, flat piece of beef from the diaphragm muscle. Skirt steak is extremely flavorful and streaked with fat, but it must be marinated and cooked quickly to make it tender.

For the marinade:
- 2 cloves garlic, chopped
- 2 tablespoon lime juice
- 1 tablespoon Worcestershire sauce
- 3 tablespoons canned, diced chilies, hot or mild
- 1 cup oil
- Black pepper to taste

- 1 pound skirt steak
- 2 large red or green bell peppers
- 1 large white onion
- 1 tablespoon butter
- 2 tablespoons olive oil

Accompaniments:
- 2 limes
- 8 low-carb tortillas or my Corn Tortillas (see p. 142)
- 2 avocados, peeled and sliced
- ½ cup salsa
- ½ cup sour cream

Combine the marinade ingredients in a shallow dish and add the steak. Let stand for 10 to 15 minutes, turning once. Drain and blot dry.

Meanwhile, cut the onion and pepper into narrow strips. Sauté them in the butter and olive oil until tender.

Grill or broil the steak on high heat for 1 minute per side for rare; 1½ minutes per side for medium rare. Cover and let stand for 5 minutes, and then slice across the grain into thin slices. Place meat on a hot platter with the onions and peppers and squeeze the limes over top. Sprinkle with salt.

Serve in warm tortillas, topped with sliced avocados, salsa, and sour cream.

Servings: 8

PER SERVING:		
Total Carb: 21.1g	Fiber: 10.4g	Net Carb: 10.7g
count includes tortillas and toppings		

TACOS

Two cups of meat will make about ten tacos.

- Low-carb flour tortillas or my Corn Tortillas (see p. 142)
- Carnitas, shredded (see Index)
- Shredded Cheddar or cubed Monterey Jack cheese
- Shredded lettuce
- Chopped onion
- Chopped tomato
- Salsa, mild or hot
- Sour cream

Heat the tortillas on a griddle or in a skillet with a little oil until puffed and hot but still soft. Blot on paper towels. Place about ¼ cup of hot Carnitas down the center of each tortilla, add cheese, and then other ingredients as desired, and fold over.

MEXICAN LASAGNA

1½ pounds ground beef
1   teaspoon salt
1   (15-ounce) can mild or hot enchilada sauce
1   (4-ounce) can diced green chilies, drained
1   (14-ounce) container ricotta cheese
2   eggs
9   low-carb tortillas
2½ cups (10 ounces) shredded Jack cheese

Preheat oven to 350° F. Have ready a 9- by 13-inch baking pan.

Cook ground beef in a large skillet until it starts to brown. Drain off the fat. Add salt, enchilada sauce, and chilies. Simmer on low heat for 10 minutes.

Mix ricotta cheese and eggs with a fork until blended. Heat the tortillas on a greased griddle or in a pan with a little oil until they start to brown. Cut the tortillas into wide strips. Place half of the meat sauce in the bottom of the 9- by 13-inch baking pan. Cover with a single layer of the tortillas, using edge pieces to fill in the gaps. Drop half the ricotta mixture evenly over the tortillas and spread to cover. Sprinkle with half the Jack cheese. Spread the rest of the sauce over the cheese, cover with a second layer of tortillas, and another layer each of ricotta and Jack cheese. Bake at 350° F for 20 to 30 minutes. Let stand for 10 minutes. Cut into eight squares. Serve with sour cream, if desired.

Servings: 8

PER SERVING:		
Total Carb: 17.6g	Fiber: 9.0g	Net Carb: 8.6g

Tips and Notes

Salsa has surpassed ketchup as the most popular condiment in the US, and that's a good thing. Even purchased salsas are low in carbs and contain little or no sugar (ketchup usually has about 4 grams of carbohydrates per tablespoon; most brands of salsa have only 1 gram per tablespoon). You can eliminate even more carbs by using salsa verde, made with tomatillos instead of tomatoes.

SAUSAGE WRAPS

A quick and easy lunch or supper dish.

Nachos

Cut low-carb tortillas or Corn Tortillas (see p. 142) into strips or triangles. Fry in oil until crisp and brown. Sprinkle with shredded cheese and serve with salsa or taco sauce for dipping.

1   pound bulk pork sausage
1/4 cup chopped onion
5 or 6 fresh mushrooms, sliced, or use canned sliced mushrooms
1   egg
4   low-carb tortillas
1   cup shredded Cheddar cheese

Cook and stir the sausage in a skillet, breaking it up with a spatula, until it just starts to brown. Add the onion and mushrooms and cook until the onion is soft and the meat is well browned. Beat the egg in a small bowl with a fork. Stir the egg into the skillet, and cook until set. Warm the tortillas over a burner or in the microwave. Spoon one fourth of the sausage onto each tortilla, top with one fourth of the cheese and roll up.

Servings: 4

PER SERVING:		
Total Carb: 12.7g	Fiber: 8.3g	Net Carb: 4.4g

QUESADILLAS

Quesadillas are Mexican grilled cheese sandwiches, with tortillas instead of bread. These can be a snack, an appetizer, or a main dish, but I find them to be most useful as a quick and hearty side dish, especially good with chili.

2   low-carb tortillas
1/4 cup shredded Jack or Cheddar cheese
1   tablespoon chopped green chilies

Place one tortilla on a microwaveable dish and cover with the cheese. Sprinkle with the chilies and place a second tortilla on top. Heat in the microwave until the cheese is melted and the tortillas stick together. Cut the tortilla sandwich into six wedges. Fry the wedges in oil in a skillet until crisp; turn and fry the other side. Serve with salsa.

Servings: 2 (3 wedges each)

PER SERVING:		
Total Carb: 11.7g	Fiber: 8.0g	Net Carb: 3.7g

BUÑUELOS

Make these crisp, fried pastries using low-carb tortillas for a sweet treat.

Cut each low-carb tortilla into nine squares, roughly 2½ inches each. Heat about a quarter-inch of oil in a skillet. Fry the squares, turning every few seconds so they will puff up evenly. Fry until brown and very crisp. Drain on paper towels. Stir ½ teaspoon of cinnamon into ½ cup of granular Splenda® in a small bowl. Dip the hot squares into the Splenda® mixture. Serve hot or reheat in a 250° F oven for 5 minutes. (Recipe was tested with La Tortilla Factory™ low-carb tortillas.)

Serving size: one buñuelo

PER SERVING:		
Total Carb: 1.3g	Fiber: 0.9g	Net Carb: 0.4g

CHOCOLATE CINNAMON TACOS

For each serving:
1   low-carb tortilla
1 to 2 teaspoons softened butter
2   teaspoons granular Splenda®
¼   teaspoon ground cinnamon
1   tablespoon sugar-free Chocolate Chips (see p. 260)

Spread the tortilla with butter. Sprinkle with granular Splenda®, cinnamon, and sugar-free chocolate chips. Fold one end up and then fold in the sides to enclose the filling. Place in a buttered pan and bake in a 400° F oven until crisp, about 6 minutes. Serve warm.

PER SERVING:		
Total Carb: 14.1g	Fiber: 9.4g	Net Carb: 4.7g

Cinnamon Sugar Crisps

Melt butter in a skillet. Cut low-carb tortillas into strips and fry until crisp. Sprinkle generously with granular Splenda® and cinnamon. Serve hot.

PARMESAN SESAME CRACKERS

Tips and Notes

Buy sesame seeds from the bulk bins at the grocery if possible rather than in the expensive, small jars sold with the spices. You may be able to buy them already toasted.

Once you have assembled all the ingredients, these are a snap to make. I found the wheat gluten, wheat bran, oat flour, and egg white powder all at a regular grocery store. Some of it may be in the organic or health food section. I ordered the almond flour from www.netrition.com and the white whole-wheat flour from The King Arthur® Flour Company's catalog. I've also included sources for the other ingredients in case you have trouble finding them. (I used white whole-wheat flour, which I keep on hand for bread, but there is so little of it in this recipe that regular whole-wheat would be just fine.)

3 ounces grated Parmesan cheese (about 1 cup, but the volume may change depending on whether it is compacted or fluffy). It can be grated in the food processor before the other ingredients are added.
¼ cup plus 1 tablespoon wheat gluten flour (1⅓ ounces)
½ cup almond flour
¼ cup wheat bran
2 tablespoons white whole-wheat flour or use regular whole-wheat flour (½ ounce)
2 tablespoons oat flour (⅓ ounce)
2 tablespoons powdered egg white
½ teaspoon salt, plus more for sprinkling on crackers
¼ teaspoon cream of tartar
¼ teaspoon baking soda
¼ cup plus 3 tablespoons water
• Sesame seeds, about ½ cup, for rolling out the crackers

Preheat oven to 400° F.

Combine everything except the water and sesame seeds in the bowl of a food processor with the metal blade in place. Process to blend the dry ingredients and, with the motor running, pour in the water. Process until the dough starts to form a ball. Scrape down the bowl and process for a few seconds more. (Alternately, use an electric mixer with a dough hook attachment and mix on low speed until the dough is smooth and starts to form a ball, or knead by hand as for bread until mixed.) Gather the dough into a ball with your hands and wrap it in plastic. Refrigerate for at least an hour—overnight is better.

(continued on next page)

PARMESAN SESAME CRACKERS,
CONTINUED

Unwrap the dough and cut it into eight pieces. Flatten each piece into a disk shape. Place one piece on a layer of plastic wrap that has been sprinkled generously with sesame seeds and a small amount of almond or oat flour. Sprinkle more sesame seeds and flour on top of the dough and cover it with a second layer of wrap. Use a rolling pin to roll it out until very thin (no more than $1/16$-inch thick). Lift and turn the dough several times, adding more sesame seeds over and under it with each turn, so that the whole surface is covered with seeds on both sides.

After rolling it out, you may cut the dough into 2- by 2-inch squares with kitchen shears or a pizza wheel or you can leave it in large irregular pieces. Place the pieces on a nonstick cookie sheet or one with a nonstick liner. Sprinkle with salt. Bake one batch while you roll out the next. Bake for 6 to 7 minutes or until golden brown. If you left the dough in irregular pieces, the pieces will be brown on the edges, but the center of each section will be pale. At this point you will need to remove it from the oven, let it cool just long enough to handle, and break it into smaller pieces. Return it to the oven for 2 or 3 minutes longer so that it is golden brown and crisp all over. (This is really the easiest way to do it and I like the way it looks, very rustic and unpretentious.)

Let the crackers cool completely and store in an airtight container. These keep very well. If necessary to re-crisp, you can reheat them in the oven for a few minutes.

This recipe makes a big pile of crackers; it's difficult to say how many if you make them the second way so they are all broken up into irregular shapes. If you cut them into squares, there will be almost a hundred crackers.

Servings: 98 crackers

PER SERVING:		
Total Carb: 0.7g	Fiber: 0.3g	Net Carb: 0.4g

Tips and Notes

You can eliminate the cracker altogether and use Parmesan Lace Crisps (see p. 138), crunchy slices of pepperoni (see p. 61), or jicama as the vehicle to carry cheese, nut butters, dips, or spreads.

PARMESAN LACE CRISPS

Wonderful zero-carb cheese "crackers" to use as a base for an appetizer, to serve with soup or salad, or just for snacking.

1 ounce Parmesan Reggiano cheese (about ⅓ cup grated)

Preheat oven to 350° F.

Grate the cheese into medium-fine shreds. Place cheese by teaspoonfuls on a nonstick baking sheet. (One with a nonstick liner makes them easier to remove; just lift the liner and they will pop off.) Tap the mounds down slightly with your finger to even out the thickness. They do not spread, so you can place them fairly close together. Bake for about 5 minutes, or until golden brown. Let them cool until crisp before removing from the pan. Store in an airtight container.

Servings: 24

PER SERVING:		
Total Carb: 0g	Fiber: 0g	Net Carb: 0g

QUICK CRACKERS

Cut low-carb tortillas into nine squares each. Spread with butter or coat with no-stick spray; bake at 350° F until crisp.

Serving size: 1 cracker

PER SERVING:		
Total Carb: 1.3g	Fiber: 1.0g	Net Carb: 0.3g
when made with La Tortilla Factory™ tortillas		
(3 net carbs each)		

CORN BREADS

The English called it corn, a word that could refer to any grain, but the Indian name was maize, which means "our life."

I use a special heirloom corn for some of my cornbread recipes. This type of corn is digested more slowly and contains more protein and less starch than modern hybrid corn. Pinewood Products sells the kind of corn that was originally raised by the Iroquois in what is now New York State. It must be harvested and processed by hand, making it more expensive than regular corn flour, but once you've tried it, I think you'll agree that its worth it. See Sources.

The Three Sisters of Life

Corn has been domesticated in the Americas for at least 10,000 years. Native Americans developed an amazingly sophisticated method for the companion planting of corn with beans and squash, which they called "the three sisters of life." In Iroquois legend, the three plants are depicted as three loving sisters, daughters of the Corn Mother, and granddaughters of Sky Woman, the creator of everything that grows on the earth. The three sisters are dependent on one another and are only happy when they are together.

The elder sister (corn) grows strong and tall and provides support for the middle sister (beans) who twines around her. The youngest sister (squash) grows at their feet, providing shade and preventing weeds. Her prickly stems repel invaders, such a raccoons, who would ravage the crops.

The botanical needs of the three plants differed enough to insure that at least one food source was likely to survive. One plant would thrive in conditions that would cause another to languish; the high winds that would damage the corn and squash would not hurt the small leaves of the beans; the corn could withstand heat and drought, while beans could tolerate cold, wet weather. Beans fixed nitrogen in the soil, which fed the other plants, and the large leaves of the squash helped hold moisture in the ground.

Another thing that the early Americans knew, was that these three crops, eaten together, provided complete nutrition and could sustain life, not an easy feat for members of the plant kingdom.

"And those who came were resolved
to be Englishmen
Gone to the World's end,
but English every one,
And they ate the white corn-kernels,
parched in the sun,
And they knew it not,
but they'd not be English again."

—Stephen Vincent Benét, Western Star

This recipe will make about thirty-two mini muffins. Bake them for 12 to 15 minutes until well browned.

Per Serving:
Total Carb: 4.9g
Fiber: 1.9g
Net Carb: 3.0g
when made with Bob's Red Mill® stone-ground corn meal

I prefer to use Pinewood Products Roasted Iroquois White Corn Flour (see Ingredients and Sources) for these muffins. The carb count given at the bottom is what it would be with regular stone-ground corn meal since the nutrition information for the Iroquois corn is not yet available.

- ⅓ cup stone-ground corn meal or Pinewoods Products White Corn Flour
- ⅓ cup oat flour
- 1 cup soy flour
- ¼ cup wheat bran
- 1 cup almond flour
- ⅓ cup plus 2 tablespoons granular Splenda®
- ¾ teaspoon salt
- 1 teaspoon baking soda
- 1 cup sugar-free Dried Cranberries (see p. 105) (For a few more carbs, you can use part sugar-free dried apricots, cherries, or peaches.)
- ½ cup chopped walnuts
- • Grated zest of one orange
- 2 eggs
- 1 cup sour cream
- ⅓ cup oil
- 1 teaspoon vanilla extract

Preheat the oven to 350° F. Butter a 12-cup muffin pan or use paper liners.

Whisk the dry ingredients together and stir in the dried fruit, nuts, and orange zest. In another bowl, beat the eggs with a fork and combine with the sour cream, oil, and vanilla. Mix wet mixture into the dry ingredients, stirring just until blended but still lumpy. Divide the batter into the muffin cups. Bake for 20 to 25 minutes or until brown. Serve hot with butter. Store in the refrigerator or freeze. Reheat frozen muffins for a few minutes in a 350° F oven.

Servings: 12

PER SERVING:
Total Carb: 13.0g Fiber: 5.0g Net Carb: 8.0g
when made with Bob's Red Mill® stone-ground corn meal—the carb count when made with Iroquois corn may be lower

FRIED CORNBREAD

This is my mother's cornbread recipe. I've never seen it written down—my mother, my grandmothers, and my aunts all made cornbread and biscuits without measuring anything. By watching my mother, and interrupting her to measure the ingredients, I managed to get this down. It can be baked in a preheated iron skillet in the oven, but I fry it because I like more crispy outside than soft inside. (It's the special corn from Pinewoods Products that makes this low-carb.)

1   cup Pinewood Products Roasted White Corn Flour
1   teaspoon baking soda
½   teaspoon salt
1   egg
1   cup buttermilk
¼   cup oil, bacon grease, or a combination

Stir the dry ingredients together in a medium-sized mixing bowl. Break the egg into the bowl and add the buttermilk. Mix just until smooth. Heat a large, heavy skillet on medium-high heat. Add the oil or grease and heat until it shimmers in the pan. Drop the cornbread batter by scant tablespoonfuls into the hot pan. Cook until the cornbread starts to brown around the edges and bubbles form around the edges on the top. Turn and cook the other side until crisp and brown. Serve hot.

Servings: 20

```
PER SERVING:
   Total Carb: 6.0g          Fiber: 0.8g          Net Carb: 5.2g
when made with Bob's Red Mill® stone-ground corn flour —
Pinewood Products corn should be lower
```

VARIATION:

Replace the buttermilk with ⅔ cup of Crème Fraîche plus ⅓ cup of water. This will lower the carb count by 0.6 grams per serving.

"Perhaps no bread in the world is so good as Southern cornbread, and perhaps no bread in the world is quite so bad as the Northern imitation of it."

—Mark Twain, Autobiography, 1924

CORN TORTILLAS

Pinewood Products' corn doesn't have enough starch to make traditional kneaded and rolled tortillas, but if you thin the batter and add a little egg, you can make them like pancakes or crêpes.

½ cup Pinewood Products Tamal Flour
½ teaspoon salt
¼ cup plus 3 tablespoons water
1 large egg

Grease a skillet or crêpe pan or use a nonstick pan. Do not preheat the pan. (If the pan is too hot, the batter will set before it spreads enough and the tortillas will be too thick.) A second pan will allow you to make tortillas without waiting for the first pan to cool.

Whisk the ingredients together. Use 2 tablespoonfuls of batter for a 6-inch tortilla, more for larger ones. Measure the batter and pour into a cool skillet or crêpe pan. Tilt the pan to spread a thin, even layer that covers the bottom of the pan. Set the pan over medium heat for about a minute. The edges of the tortilla should come loose and lift up from the pan when it is ready to turn. Turn the tortilla and cook the other side until it is flecked with brown but still pliable. Remove and stack on a plate.

Let the pan cool between tortillas or alternate two pans. Stir the batter each time before dipping. Add more water if necessary, as the solids tend to settle to the bottom of the bowl. Grease the pan for each new tortilla unless you are using a nonstick pan. Cover the tortillas with a cloth to keep warm, or let them cool, and separate them with sheets of waxed paper and refrigerate.

Servings: 7

PER SERVING:		
Total Carb: 7.7g	Fiber: 1.1g	Net Carb: 6.6

when made with Bob's Red Mill® stone-ground corn flour—
Pinewood Products tamal flour should be lower

VARIATION:

Tortilla Chips

Cut each tortilla into eight wedges. Sprinkle with salt and spread on a baking sheet. Place in a 350° F oven for 5 to 10 minutes or until evenly golden brown. Sprinkle with powdered cheese or grated Parmesan, if desired. Let cool and store in an airtight container.

Makes 56 chips.
Per Chip:
Total Carb: 0.9g
Fiber: 0.1g
Net Carb: 0.8g
when made with Bob's Red Mill® stone-ground corn meal

YEAST BREAD

Good bread is the Holy Grail of low-carb cooking—searching for it has been the hardest thing I've attempted to do for this book. Most of the recipes for low-carb bread, as well as the packaged breads and mixes that you can purchase, are based on soy flour and they taste terrible. I tried using gluten flour since it is so much lower in carbs than regular flour, but the bread was so rubbery, it was more suitable for making tires than toast.

My breakthrough came after reading this passage in a book called *On Food and Cooking,* by Harold McGee. He was explaining that prehistoric people could make only flat breads because: "Wild wheats, with their characteristically adherent hulls, were parched in order to separate the grain, and heat denatures the gluten-forming proteins. Once a gruel of raw wheat could be made, the discovery of raised bread was only a matter of time."

I'm sure there must have been a light bulb over my head when I read that. I tried baking the gluten flour, and sure enough, the baked flour made a soft paste when kneaded with water, while the unbaked flour made bubble gum. After a lot of trial and error, I came up with the following recipe. The yeast is mostly for flavor; the baking powder boosts the lift without letting enough gluten develop to produce a rubbery texture.

Tips and Notes

White whole-wheat flour from the King Arthur® Flour Company (see Sources) is as nutritious as regular whole-wheat but tastes more like white flour. You may find it at your local store, or you can order it from The Baker's Catalogue® of the King Arthur® Flour Company. or from Bob's Red Mill®.

Gluten flour is usually available at supermarkets, where you may find it on the health food aisle or with the other flours. Bob's Red Mill® sells gluten flour in grocery stores as well as by mail order, and it can also be ordered from the King Arthur® Flour Company. See Sources for both gluten and white whole-wheat flour.

Never store bread in the refrigerator because it will become stale more quickly at temperatures close to, but slightly above, freezing. Keep it at room temperature or freeze it rapidly. Separate the slices with freezer paper when freezing to make it easy to defrost the amount you intend to use without damaging the rest of the slices.

Tips and Notes

The small amount of cinnamon in this recipe will keep the bread fresh longer without altering the taste.

To bake gluten flour: Spread gluten flour in a large roasting pan and bake in a preheated 350° F oven for about 10 minutes or until just slightly colored. Stir it well several times as it bakes. Watch it carefully or it will burn. The time it takes will vary depending on how much moisture is in the flour. Cool and store in an airtight container in the refrigerator or freezer.

French Toast

Beat 2 eggs with a fork. Add ½ cup of cream or low-carb Milk and ¼ teaspoon of salt. Mix well. Place in a dish, and soak slices of low-carb Mixed Flour Bread in the mixture until saturated. This is enough for about four slices of bread. Melt butter in a skillet. Fry slices on both sides until golden brown and firm. Serve hot with sugar-free maple syrup.

Makes 4 servings of one slice each.
Total Carb: 4.9g
Fiber: 1.5g,
Net Carb: 3.4g

MIXED FLOUR BREAD

Don't be intimidated if you've never made bread before. It's really very easy; if I can do it, you can do it!

½ cup unsifted gluten flour to be prebaked (2¼ ounces)
¼ cup unsifted, unbaked, gluten flour (1⅛ ounce)
1 cup water at 115° F
1 teaspoon active dry yeast (not a whole package)
1¼ cups almond flour
½ cup white whole-wheat flour (2¾ ounces)
½ cup oat flour (1½ ounces)
2 tablespoons sesame seeds
2 tablespoons wheat bran
¾ teaspoon baking powder
1¼ teaspoons salt
⅛ teaspoon ground cinnamon
2 teaspoons granular Splenda®
1 large egg
2 tablespoons butter, cut into small pieces and brought up to room temperature

Place the ½ cup of gluten flour in a shallow pan and bake in a preheated 350° F oven for 5 to 10 minutes, or until just slightly colored. Stir it well two or three times while it bakes so that it colors evenly. Watch it carefully or it will burn; the time it takes will vary depending on how much moisture is in the flour. Let it cool.

Measure 1 cup of warm water and test it with a thermometer for a temperature of 115° F. Stir the yeast into the warm water and let stand in a warm place for 10 minutes while assembling the other ingredients.

Spray the metal blade of the food processor with no-stick spray so the dough will release more easily. Place the baked gluten flour and all the other dry ingredients in the food processor bowl with the metal blade in place. Process for a few seconds to blend the dry ingredients. Remove and reserve ¼ cup of the dry mixture, plus a separate small amount for preparing the pan.

With the machine running, add the egg and the yeast/water mixture. Process until the dough forms a ball; add the softened butter and process for 30 seconds more. The dough should be moist and elastic. If it is too wet, add the remaining ¼ cup of flour mixture, a little at a time, processing after each addition, until it is the correct consistency.

(continued on next page)

MIXED FLOUR BREAD, CONTINUED

Move the dough to a bowl that has been oiled or sprayed with no-stick spray. Turn the dough over to coat the surface with oil, or spray the top of the dough as well. Place the bowl on a rack over (but not in) a pan of hot water. Cover the dough with a damp cloth and then with a layer of plastic film. Let rise until doubled in bulk, about 40 minutes. Punch down the dough and shape it into a loaf. Do not knead the dough.

Grease an 8½- x 4½- x 2½-inch loaf pan and sprinkle it with some of the reserved flour mixture to evenly coat the bottom and sides. Put the dough in the pan, place the pan on a rack over hot water, and cover as before. Let rise until almost doubled, about 30 minutes.

Position the oven rack in the center of the oven. Preheat the oven to 375° F. Have ready a spray bottle of water.

Cut several slashes across the top of the loaf with a razor-sharp blade or the metal blade from the food processor. To make the crust crisper, spray the walls of the oven with water just before putting in the bread. Bake the bread on the middle rack of the oven, being sure there is enough head room for it to rise. Bake for 30 to 35 minutes or until it is well browned and sounds hollow when rapped on the bottom of the loaf. Another way to check for doneness is to insert a thermometer into the center of the bread after it is removed from the pan. If it reads 200° F, the bread is done. If the bread is undercooked, it may start to fall. If this happens, return it to the hot oven and continue to bake for 5 to 10 minutes more. Cool the loaf on a wire rack for a few minutes after removing it from the pan. Slice the loaf into thin slices with a serrated or an electric knife. Serve warm, or let it cool completely and then wrap it; be sure it is completely cooled before wrapping, or the condensation will encourage mold development. Store at room temperature or freeze. Makes twenty-eight slices.

Servings: 28

PER SERVING:		
Total Carb: 4.6g	Fiber: 1.5g	Net Carb: 3.1g

Tips and Notes

Gluten flour, also called "high-gluten flour" or "vital wheat gluten," is wheat flour that has had most of the starch removed. Many groceries and health food stores sell gluten flour in packages or in bulk. Bob's Red Mill® Gluten Flour is widely available in supermarkets, or it can be ordered by mail. The Baker's Catalogue® of The King Arthur® Flour Company also sells gluten flour by mail order. See Sources. See p. 144 for directions for pre-baking the flour to deactivate the gluten proteins.

It has been estimated that 1 in 133 people in the United States suffers from gluten intolerance, also known as Celiac disease. Strict adherence to a gluten-free diet for life is the only way to prevent serious complications from the disease. More information is available at www.celiac.com.

One original Auntie Anne's™ pretzel has 72 grams of carbohydrate and 3 grams of fiber, for a net count of 69 grams.

Note: An Italian study reported in the December 2006 issue of the *International Journal of Cancer* (Volume 119, Issue 12, pp. 2916-2921), found a high correlation between bread consumption and renal cell cancer. Researchers found that those who ate the most bread increased their risk by 94 percent compared to those who ate the least. Rice and pasta increased the risk by 29 percent. Foods that reduced the risk included poultry, processed meat, and vegetables.

VARIATION: BREAD PRETZELS

My husband expressed a longing for a soft pretzel, so I took a little dough from the bread I was making and turned it into a pretzel for him. He pronounced it to be a success!

After the first rising, divide the dough into sixteen pieces. Roll each piece into a "snake" about a foot long and tie it into a pretzel-shaped knot. (Dust it with a little of the extra flour mixture or some oat flour if necessary to make it easier to handle.) Put on a greased baking sheet. Brush with beaten egg, thinned with a little water, and sprinkle generously with coarse salt. Let rise in a warm place until doubled in size.

Preheat the oven to 475° F. Spray the walls of the hot oven with water to produce a crisp crust. Bake for about 10 minutes or until brown.

Servings: 16

PER SERVING:		
Total Carb: 8.2g	Fiber: 2.7g	Net Carb: 5.5g

VARIATION: CINNAMON NUT BREAD

Increase the Splenda® to 2 tablespoons. Increase the cinnamon to 2 teaspoons. Add ¼ cup of chopped walnuts to the food processor bowl after you have finished processing the dough. Pulse two or three times to evenly distribute the nuts. Proceed as in the recipe for Mixed Flour Bread.

Servings: 28

PER SERVING:		
Total Carb: 5.0g	Fiber: 1.7g	Net Carb: 3.3g

Yiddish Proverb:
"Everyone is kneaded out of
the same dough but not
baked in the same oven."

DRESSING FOR ROAST TURKEY

Special occasions just wouldn't be the same without turkey and dressing. Here's a festive version that won't totally wreck your diet. You won't have to make two different kinds; this is one that everyone will enjoy.

- 2 cups cooked and drained wild rice (or 4 ounces uncooked)
- ½ cup dried peaches, chopped
- ½ cup sugar-free Dried Cranberries (see p. 105)
- 1 tablespoon finely chopped fresh ginger
- 2 tablespoons granular Splenda®
- 1 cup water or broth
- 3 tablespoons butter
- 1 small onion, chopped
- ½ cup celery, chopped
- 2 cups soft Mixed Flour Bread crumbs (see p. 144), or use purchased low-carb bread at 3 to 4 net carbs per slice
- ½ cup almonds or walnuts, chopped
- 1 tablespoon lemon juice
- 1 teaspoon grated lemon rind
- 3 tablespoons fresh parsley, chopped
- 1 large egg, beaten with a fork
- 1 (8-ounce) can water chestnuts, diced
- ¼ teaspoon dried sage
- ¼ teaspoon dried thyme
- • Salt and pepper to taste

Boil the wild rice in 2 cups of water or broth for 45 to 50 minutes, or according to the package directions. Drain.

Place peaches, cranberries, ginger, Splenda®, and 1 cup of broth or water in a saucepan. Simmer, uncovered, for about 10 minutes, until the fruit is plump and the liquid is reduced to ½ cup. Melt the butter in a large pan and sauté the onion and celery until softened. Stir in the breadcrumbs. Add the peaches, cranberries, and ginger, including the reduced liquid, and all other ingredients except the egg and wild rice. Let the mixture cool, then add the egg, and stir until well mixed.

Reserve about 1½ cups of the dressing mixture. Add all of the cooked wild rice to the rest of the dressing. Place the dressing in a greased 8 x 8 x 2-inch pan. Spread the reserved dressing mixture without wild rice, on top. Dot with butter, baste with turkey drippings, or spray with no-stick spray. Bake, covered, at 350° F for ten minutes, then remove the cover and bake until the top starts to brown, about 10 minutes more.

Servings: 12

PER SERVING:		
Total Carb: 16.8g	Fiber: 3.5g	Net Carb: 13.3g

Tips and Notes

The grains of wild rice would become dry and hard if they were on top. It is not necessary to reserve any of the mixture to put on top if you are cooking the stuffing inside the bird.

It's stuffing if it's baked in the bird; dressing if it's baked in a separate pan. The turkey will be more juicy and tender if it is baked without the stuffing inside. It also helps keep the white meat moist if you start the turkey breast-side down on a rack in the roasting pan and turn it upright to brown toward the end of the cooking time.

"You first parents of the human race...who ruined yourself for an apple, what might you have done for a truffled turkey?"

—Jean Anthelme Brillat-Savarin

STARCHY SIDE DISH REPLACEMENTS

THE AMAZING VANISHING ACT

Right before your eyes, starchy side dishes will disappear and carbs will vanish, as humble vegetables are transformed into mashed potatoes and spaghetti! Pumpkins magically turn into French fries, and squash becomes Lasagna! Your mouth will never notice (but your waistline will!)

VARIATION:

Fried Capers

Capers turn into spicy, crunchy, little flowers when deep fried.

Drain canned capers and blot dry. Fry in 360° F oil for about 30 seconds until crisp. Do not add additional salt. Serve at once or let cool and store in an airtight container. Use as a garnish or a snack.

Per tablespoon of Capers:
Total Carb: 0.4
Fiber: 0.3
Net Carb: 0.1

Tips and Notes

Artichokes are the flower buds of a thistle. Different-sized artichokes come from different parts of the plant. Large ones, weighing about 10 ounces, come from the top. Medium-sized ones, about 7 ounces, come from the side of the plant and ripen a week or so later. The baby ones, which sprout where the leaf meets the stalk, are the last to be harvested.

FRIED ARTICHOKES

These bloom out in the hot oil like a fan of crispy little chips. Serve them as a side dish in place of french fries.

- One 14-ounce can of artichoke hearts or 6-8 fresh baby artichokes
- (2 tablespoons lemon juice and a bowl of water for fresh artichokes)
- Oil for deep frying
- Salt

To use fresh baby artichokes:
Wash and cut off the stems from fresh baby artichokes. Cut off and discard the top third of each artichoke. Peel away the green outer leaves until only a yellow-colored cone remains. Trim the remaining leaves with kitchen shears to remove any tough tips or thorns. Drop the fresh artichokes in a bowl of water with 2 tablespoons of lemon juice to prevent browning.

To use canned artichoke hearts:
Trim away any tough stems, outer leaves, thorns, or tops.

Slice the fresh or canned artichoke hearts vertically into eight narrow wedges. The canned ones are usually available quartered so you only need one additional cut per piece. You want narrow wedges with the leaves intact. Drain and blot them between paper towels until they are as dry as possible, so they won't splatter.

Heat the oil to 360° F and fry the artichokes until brown and crisp. Drain on paper towels, sprinkle with salt, and serve hot.

Servings: 3

PER SERVING:		
Total Carb: 6.0g	Fiber: 4.0g	Net Carb: 2.0g

TWICE BAKED POTATOES AND POTATO SKINS

The only part of a potato that comes close to being low-carb is the skin. When my order in a restaurant comes with a baked potato, I scoop out the inside, pile on the toppings and eat just the skin. This is not something I could do often, but its a lot better than eating the whole thing. When I cook for guests, I often make twice-baked potatoes and prepare the skins for my husband and me. I've learned to make extra because everyone wants to share ours!

Scrub one large russet for each carb-eating guest. Prick with a fork. Bake at 350° F for 1 hour and 15 minutes or until soft. Remove the potatoes from the oven and immediately cut them in half to release the steam. Scoop out the centers, leaving just enough white to keep the sides rigid. Mash the potato pulp with 1 tablespoon of butter and heavy cream for each potato. Add salt and pepper to taste. Refill half of the empty shells with all of the pulp so that the inside of a whole potato goes into each. Drizzle with melted butter and set on a baking sheet.

Raise oven temperature to 450° F. Cut the empty potato skins in half lengthwise. Place on a baking sheet, brush with melted butter, and sprinkle with salt and pepper. Bake filled shells and skins at the same time for 8 to 10 minutes or until the filled potatoes are brown on top and the skins are very crisp. (The potato skins may brown more quickly than the other potatoes.) Remove from the oven. Sprinkle the potato skins with shredded cheese and bake for 3 or 4 minutes more to melt the cheese. Serve with butter, sour cream, crumbled bacon, and chives as toppings.

> **PER EACH STUFFED POTATO:**
> Total Carb: 54.9g   Fiber: 4.8g   **Net Carb: 50.1g**
>
> **PER SERVING OF TWO POTATO SKINS:**
> Total Carb: 6.3g   Fiber: 0.5g   **Net Carb: 5.8g**
> **The carb count will vary with the thickness of the skins; the numbers are approximate.**

Fried Potato Skins

These make it hard to feel sorry for ourselves!

Scrub and pare Russet potatoes, removing the peels in large pieces. Discard the potatoes or make french fries for friends or family members who want them. Trim the peels into uniform sized pieces. Dry well on paper towels. Heat oil in a deep fryer to 325° F. Fry skins until they just start to brown. Remove and spread out on paper towels. Wait until they are cool. They can be refrigerated for a few hours or overnight at this point.

Raise temperature of oil to 375° F and fry skins again, briefly, in batches (do not crowd the pan), until brown and crisp. Sprinkle with salt, place on a rack in a roasting pan and put in warm oven until all are fried. Serve with cheese, bacon, salsa, and sour cream.

The peel from one large potato makes 2 servings of fried peels.

Per Serving of Potato Skins:
Total Carb: 6.3g
Fiber: 0.5g
Net Carb: 5.8g
Carb counts are approximate depending on the thickness of the skins.

PUMPKINS

Not even Cinderella's pumpkin was this versatile!

I eagerly anticipate the fall season when fresh pumpkins show up at grocery stores and farmer's markets so I can use them to make "potato" chips and french fries and to replace sweet potatoes and yams in my favorite recipes. Pumpkins are similar in taste and texture but are much lower in carbohydrates. When sweetened with a sugar substitute, they fill that vacant spot on the dinner plate where the sweet potatoes used to be.

Small pie pumpkins are only available in the fall, when they are sold mainly for decorative use. (Many groceries now sell only gourds that look like pumpkins, probably because they last longer.) Stock up on these little fresh pumpkins when they are available.

Tips and Notes

If you can afford the extra carbs in sweet potatoes, just cut them like thick french fries and use instead of pumpkin. Be sure to get yellow-fleshed sweet potatoes, not red ones called yams which are just sweet potatoes with a higher sugar content. (A true yam is an entirely different vegetable.) You can always sweeten the yellow ones with a sugar substitute so they taste like "yams".

A grapefruit spoon with a serrated tip makes a handy tool for scraping out the seeds and strings of pumpkin or squash.

FAUX CANDIED YAMS (CANDIED PUMPKIN)

For Thanksgiving last fall I made our favorite candied yams in two batches, one with sugar for the rest of the family and one with Splenda® for my husband and me. Our non-sugar version was as good as the traditional recipe, but yams are naturally so sweet that they were still high in carbohydrates. This year, I have a recipe for a guilt-free version that we don't have to save for a holiday! It's good with ham, chicken, pork, and smoked sausage as well as turkey.

1   fresh pie pumpkin (about 1½ pounds)
4   tablespoons butter (½ stick)
2   slices lemon with peel (about ¼ of a small lemon)
½   cup granular Splenda®
½   teaspoon ground cinnamon
•   A pinch of salt
¼   cup sugar-free simple syrup or substitute ¼ cup of water and increase the Splenda® to ¾ cup (add 1 net carb per serving)

Cut the pumpkin in half, scrape out the seeds and fibers, and cut into slices. Pare the slices with a vegetable peeler. Cut the slices into ½-inch by 3-inch pieces, similar in size to fat french fries. Melt the butter in a skillet and add the pumpkin. Squeeze the lemon slices over the pumpkin, and then drop them into the pan. Mix the Splenda® with the cinnamon and salt and sprinkle over the pumpkin. Add the syrup or water. Cook, stirring and basting with the pan liquid, over medium heat until the pumpkin is tender and starting to brown and caramelize. Add more water if necessary. It will take about 20 to 25 minutes.

Servings: 6

PER SERVING:		
Total Carb: 4.8g	Fiber: 0.4g	Net Carb: 4.4g

FAUX BAKED YAMS (BAKED PUMPKIN)

I grew up in Arkansas where we would have a rich, sweet baked yam for dinner more often than a regular baked potato. The Texas version was topped with butter and brown sugar to further gild the lily. These pretend yams are very good and unbelievably easy.

1 (1 to 2 pound) pie pumpkin
2 tablespoons butter
2 tablespoons granular Splenda®
• Cinnamon and grated lemon peel (optional)
• Salt and pepper to taste

Cut the pumpkin into halves or quarters, depending on size. Scrape out the seeds and fibers but do not peel. Place an equal portion of butter and Splenda® in each cavity. Sprinkle with salt and pepper and with cinnamon and lemon peel if desired.

To microwave:
Place ¼ cup of water in a baking dish and add the pumpkin halves or quarters. Cover the dish with plastic wrap. Microwave until the pumpkin starts to soften. Uncover and pierce the pumpkin flesh all over (but not through the skin) with a fork. Baste with the hot butter from the "bowl" of the pumpkin. Replace the plastic wrap and microwave until tender.

To oven bake:
Place the pumpkin halves or quarters in a baking dish, add ¼ cup of water to the dish, and cover with a lid or foil. Bake at 325° F until the butter is melted and the pumpkin starts to soften, about 20 to 30 minutes. Pierce the pumpkin flesh all over (but don't puncture the skin) with a fork and baste with the liquid from the center of the pumpkin. Cover and continue to bake until tender, for a total cooking time of about 1 hour.

Serve one-half or one-fourth of a pumpkin to each person, to be eaten out of the shell with a spoon.

Serving size: ½ of a 1 pound pumpkin

PER SERVING:		
Total Carb: 6.9g	Fiber: 0.9g	Net Carb: 6.0g

VARIATION

Instead of the Splenda®, use 2 tablespoons of sugar-free Da Vinci's™ Simple Syrup and subtract 1.5 net carbs per serving. Use French-vanilla or caramel syrup for a brown sugar or caramel flavor.

To store pumpkins:
Wash them well with a solution of 2 tablespoons of chlorine bleach to a quart of water. Rinse well, dry thoroughly, and wrap them individually in newspaper. Keep them for a week or so in a warm room to harden the skins, then move them to an unheated garage, basement, or other cool place, but don't let them freeze. They will keep for several months. They can also be packed in sand or sawdust to extend the storage time. Don't set them directly on a concrete floor unless you put a wooden or cardboard base under them. Any hard squash can be stored this way, including spaghetti squash. Pumpkins can also be cut up, blanched and frozen.

HOLIDAY PUMPKIN CASSEROLE

Remember sweet potato casseroles, slathered with crusty, melted marshmallows? No holiday dinner or church potluck was complete without one. Not exactly haute cuisine, *but it was usually the first empty dish on the table! Here's my replacement for it, with no apologies. (I think this interpretation is much more sophisticated, however.)*

3   tablespoons butter
¼   cup granular Splenda®
1   teaspoon ground cinnamon
½   teaspoon ground ginger
¼   teaspoon ground nutmeg
¼   teaspoon salt
2   cups cooked, mashed pumpkin or one (15-ounce) can
1   egg, beaten with a fork
½   cup chopped pecans (optional)

For the meringue topping:
2   tablespoons cold water
1   teaspoon cornstarch
4   egg whites
•   A pinch of cream of tartar (omit if beating in a copper bowl)
¼   cup Splenda®
4   teaspoons superfine sugar

Preheat oven to 400° F. Butter a 9-inch square baking dish.

Melt the butter over medium heat or in the microwave. Let cool. Mix the Splenda®, spices, and salt together. Place the pumpkin in a bowl, stir in the beaten egg, and then blend in the melted butter, the spice and Splenda® mixture, and the salt. Stir in the pecans, if using. Spoon the pumpkin mixture into the baking dish. Cover with foil and heat in the oven for about 15 minutes. Prepare the meringue topping while the pumpkin is heating.

(continued on next page)

HOLIDAY PUMPKIN CASSEROLE, CONTINUED

Meringue topping:
Put the cold water in a small saucepan, sprinkle with the cornstarch, and let hydrate for 1 minute. Place the saucepan over low heat, and cook, stirring constantly, just until thickened. Let the cornstarch mixture cool slightly while beating the meringue. The cornstarch mixture should be liquid and lukewarm when added so it will blend smoothly. If it is too thick, stir in a little more water. (You may find it easier to double the amount of cornstarch and water, and then just use half of it — it's hard to control such a tiny amount.)

Beat the egg whites and cream of tartar (if using) to soft peaks with an electric mixer. Combine the Splenda® and sugar and add gradually, while beating. Add the cornstarch mixture a little at a time. Continue to beat until stiff peaks form. Spread the meringue over the top of the hot pumpkin, sealing completely around the edges, and bake at 400° F until lightly browned, 3 to 5 minutes. Serve warm.

Servings: 6

PER SERVING:		
Total Carb: 13.0g	Fiber: 4.0g	Net Carb: 9.0g

Tips and Notes

If you still want marshmallows on top of your faux sweet potatoes, try La Nouba® sugar-free marshmallows; see Sources. They won't look exactly the same (they are pink and white), but they will brown and melt just like your Aunt Polly's. (They brown quickly, so watch that they don't burn.)

You'll never know what you're missing!

Almond flour, made from blanched almonds, makes a delicious substitute for some of the flour in many of my recipes. It is a by-product from making almond oil, although some processors use whole blanched almonds. Almond Meal consists of the entire almond, oil and outer coating included, ground to a powder. It is not as fine as almond flour but can be substituted for it in most recipes. Check Sources for purchasing information. You can make nut meal from whole nuts if you have a flourmill. It is possible to grind the nuts for a recipe in a food processor if you include some of the dry ingredients along with the nuts to absorb the oil; you must be careful not to over-process the mixture.

ITALIAN PUMPKIN CASSEROLE

Unsweetened pumpkin, paired with almonds and Parmesan, makes an excellent savory side dish.

- ³/₄ cup almond meal or almond flour, divided in half
- 4 tablespoons butter, melted and cooled
- 1 (15-ounce) can pumpkin or 2 cups of cooked, mashed pumpkin
- 6 eggs
- ²/₃ cup plus an additional 1 cup grated Parmesan cheese
- ³/₄ teaspoon salt or more to taste
- • Pepper to taste

Preheat the oven to 400° F. Butter an 8-cup capacity baking dish.

Stir one half of the almond meal or almond flour (6 tablespoons) and one half of the melted butter (2 tablespoons) into the pumpkin. Beat the eggs with an electric mixer until fluffy. Stir ²/₃ cup of the Parmesan cheese into the eggs. Gradually stir in the pumpkin mixture. Add the salt and pepper and pour into the baking dish. Stir together the remaining 6 tablespoons of almond meal or almond flour and the remaining 1 cup of Parmesan cheese. Sprinkle evenly over the casserole. Drizzle with the remaining 2 tablespoons of butter. Bake for 30 minutes or until set and browned on top. Serve hot.

Servings: 10

PER SERVING:		
Total Carb: 5.6g	Fiber: 2.8g	Net Carb: 2.8g

PUMPKIN FAUX FRENCH FRIES

Pumpkin is one of the few non-starchy vegetables that will get brown and crisp without a coating of flour or batter. It has an amazing soft crunch that is quite addictive. Try making fries with the small white ghost pumpkins if you can find them at a farmer's market in the fall. They have a more neutral flavor and your fries will even look like french fries. (Not all pumpkins that are white on the outside are white on the inside.) Regular orange pumpkins will be fine if you can't find white ones.

Cut one ghost or sugar baby pumpkin in half; scrape out the seeds and fibers. Cut into wedges and peel. Cut the wedges into thin strips about ½-inch wide by 3 inches long. Fry in small batches in a deep fryer at 365° F until golden brown and crisp. When all the strips are cooked, return them to the hot fat briefly to reheat and crisp before serving. Drain on paper towels and sprinkle with salt. A 2-pound pumpkin will make about sixty fries.

Servings: 6

PER SERVING:		
Total Carb: 3.6g	Fiber: 0.6g	Net Carb: 3.0g

FAUX POTATO CHIPS (PUMPKIN CHIPS)

These have the same crunch as homemade potato chips with about a third of the carbohydrates. If I can find them, I use the very mild white pumpkins like ghost for these, but the orange ones are also delicious. Bet you can't eat just one!

Pare, seed, and cut a fresh pumpkin into several pieces. Slice very thinly on a mandoline, with the slicing blade of the food processor, or with a potato peeler. Aim for uniform slices; cut off any narrow points and discard or save for another use. Fry a few slices at a time in oil in a deep fryer heated to 365° F until golden brown and crisp, about 2 to 3 minutes. Watch them carefully; if they become too dark, they will taste bitter. Drain on paper towels and sprinkle with salt. Serve hot, or let cool and store in an airtight container. Serve with Sour Cream Dip (see p. 232) or salsa. One fourth of a 2-pound pumpkin will make about fifty chips.

Serving size: 10 chips

PER SERVING:		
Total Carb: 1.2g	Fiber: 0.2g	Net Carb: 1.0g

Tips and Notes

Make your own low-carb Ketchup to accompany your fries (see p. 232).

Pie pumpkins are small and thick walled, unlike the ones used for jack-o-lanterns. The most common one is called *sugar baby*, but there are others, like *ghost*, which is white. Alas, one of my favorites, the small tan colored *cheese* pumpkin is really a winter squash.

To save the day when potato hunger strikes, check out the recipe for Potato Soup on p. 223.

VARIATION:

Dessert Fritters

Serve these with sugar-free Whipped Cream (see p. 328) for dipping. They taste like crispy little doughnuts with pumpkin pie in the center. Yum!

Make pumpkin fritters as directed. Mix $1/4$ cup of granular Splenda® with $1/2$ teaspoon of cinnamon in a small bowl. Roll the hot fritters in the mixture and serve.

Makes about 34.

Per Fritter:
Total Carb: 1.5g
Fiber: 0.5g
Net Carb: 1g
Count includes all the Splenda®, but about half will be left in the bowl.

PUMPKIN FRITTERS

I love to serve these as a side dish. They are like a cross between hush puppies and doughnuts. If you let them get very brown they will be crunchy on the outside and melt-in-your-mouth creamy on the inside. Try the dessert version too, by rolling them in cinnamon and Splenda.®

1   cup canned pumpkin
$1/2$ cup ricotta cheese
1   egg white
$1/4$ cup granular Splenda®
1   teaspoon vanilla extract
$1/4$ cup oat flour
$1/4$ cup wheat gluten flour
$3/4$ teaspoon baking powder
•   A pinch of salt
•   Oil for frying

Place the pumpkin, ricotta cheese, egg white, Splenda®, and vanilla in the bowl of an electric mixer or a food processor and blend. Sift the remaining dry ingredients together and add. Beat or process until smooth.

Heat the oil in a deep fryer or an electric skillet to 365° F.

Shape the dough into balls the size of a small walnut using two spoons. Fry a few fritters at a time until they are deep golden brown. Turn them over in the hot oil so they brown evenly. Dip out with a slotted spoon and drain on paper towels. Serve hot.

Servings: 34

PER SERVING:		
Total Carb: 1.4g	Fiber: 0.5g	Net Carb: 0.9g

VARIATION:

PUMPKIN HUSH PUPPIES

Substitute stone-ground corn meal for the oat flour and add ¼ cup of finely minced onion to the batter. Fry as above.

Servings: 34

PER SERVING:		
Total Carb: 1.9g	Fiber: 0.5g	Net Carb: 1.4g

PASTA

There have been many failed attempts to make palatable low-carb pasta. Most of them are dreadful; one store owner said he couldn't *give* them away. But that was before the new Dreamfields™ pastas showed up. There should be dancing in the aisles for this one! It is made with regular semolina flour and a patent-pending fiber blend. It is slightly firmer but otherwise almost indistinguishable from regular pasta.

The nutrition information for Dreamfields™ pasta lists only four grams of fiber per serving, but the company claims that this fiber somehow attaches to the other carbohydrates and prevents them from being absorbed so that the carb count for a generous two-ounce serving is only five net grams. All of my pasta recipes can be made using Dreamfields™ low-carb pasta rather than spaghetti squash. However, it is my onerous duty to tell you that spaghetti squash counts as a vegetable and is allowed, even in the initial phases of most low-carb plans, while grains are forbidden until later, even though the Dreamfields™ pasta lists a slightly lower net carb count than the squash. You can decide how strictly you want to follow the rules.

I don't recommend any of the boxed low-carb macaroni and cheese products that I've tried (rubbery pasta and watery sauce, yuk!), but you can use Dreamfields™ macaroni to make a wonderful mac and cheese dish with my Cheese Sauce recipe on p. 222.

Note

Some ready-made spaghetti sauces are naturally low-carb. Look for ones that are imported from Italy; they will have no sugar. I have found some that are as low as two net grams of carbohydrates in ½ cup. If you avoid any that list sugar in the ingredients, and compare the carbohydrate content, you should find some that qualify. See Sources for Alessi® and Don Pomodoro® marinara pasta sauce.

Spaghetti Squash

This is a very mild-flavored, stringy squash that can be used in almost any pasta recipe. It doesn't have the taste or texture of pasta, but it has so little taste of its own that it can serve as the base for all your favorite sauces and toppings. It has a crisp texture and although it's a stretch to say it resembles *al dente* spaghetti, you may decide you like it as well as the real thing. Try it in place of rice with curry dishes too. I have included some of my favorite uses for it. I prefer to buy medium-sized squash, 2 to 3 pounds, because they are easier to handle than the very large ones and if they are much smaller than 2 pounds, the strands are too thin. Sometimes the market has only large ones, so you will have extra squash to put in the refrigerator for later use. It makes a quick lunch topped with sauce from a jar and Parmesan.

BASIC RECIPE FOR SPAGHETTI SQUASH "PASTA"

Pierce the spaghetti squash several times and microwave it for about 5 minutes or just until the skin is soft enough to cut. For a small squash, 2 or 3 minutes may be enough. Don't overcook the squash at this point; it is easier to remove the center fibers while the squash is still firm and raw. After it is cooked, the rest of the squash turns to fibers as well, and they tend to pull out along with the seedy ones.

Split the squash lengthwise. Remove the seeds and stringy fibers from the center. I use a grapefruit spoon with a serrated edge to scrape them out. Place the halves, cut side down, in a dish with ¼ cup of water, cover, and cook in the microwave until tender. This may take 4 or 5 minutes per half, but there are many variables, so check it several times for doneness. When it is ready, you should be able to squeeze the sides in and see the strands start to separate at the edges. (There is no *al dente* stage, it's crisp or it's mush.)

Let the squash cool enough to handle and tease out the strands, one layer at a time, from the shell using a combing motion with a fork. If you have a very cooperative squash, you may be able to loosen the strands around the edges with a fork, and then pull them out with your fingers. Use in the following recipes or any recipe that calls for spaghetti.

Note: Spaghetti squash will continue to weep each time it's heated. Drain it well and serve it with a slotted spoon, or blot up the excess liquid with a paper towel.

SPAGHETTI SQUASH AU GRATIN

3 cups cooked Spaghetti Squash Pasta
3 tablespoons butter, melted
2 tablespoons heavy cream
3 tablespoons Parmesan or Cheddar cheese, grated
• Salt and pepper to taste

Mix the spaghetti squash with the melted butter, heavy cream, and 2 tablespoons of the grated Parmesan or Cheddar cheese. Add salt and pepper to taste. Put in a greased baking dish; smooth the top, and sprinkle with the remaining 1 tablespoon of cheese. Coat the top with no-stick spray or melted butter, and bake at 400° F until brown, about 30 minutes.

Servings: 6

PER SERVING:		
Total Carb: 4.0g	Fiber: 0.7g	Net Carb: 3.3g

VARIATION:

Spaghetti Squash Au Gratin with Ham or Salami

Sauté ¼ cup of chopped onion in the butter before adding the squash. Stir in 1 cup diced ham or spicy salami before baking for a delicious lunch or supper dish.

Makes 8 servings.
Per Serving:
Total Carb: 3.4g
Fiber: 0.6g
Net Carb: 2.8g

SPAGHETTI SQUASH ALLA CARBONARA

4 cups cooked Spaghetti Squash Pasta
2 tablespoons olive oil
1 medium onion, chopped
½ pound bacon, cooked until crisp, and crumbled
3 eggs, lightly beaten
• Salt and pepper to taste
1 cup grated Parmesan cheese

Drain the cooked squash on paper towels. Sauté the onion in a skillet in olive oil until soft. Add the squash and bacon and stir until it is hot. Add the eggs, all at once, and stir briefly, until squash strands are coated and the eggs are slightly cooked. Add salt and pepper to taste, top with Parmesan, and serve.

Servings: 4 as a main dish, 8 as a side dish

PER SERVING:		
Total Carb: 10.8g as a main dish	Fiber: 1.8g	Net Carb: 9.0g
Total Carb: 5.4g as a side dish	Fiber: 0.9g	Net Carb: 4.5g

SQUASH PASTA WITH ROASTED PEPPERS AND SUN-DRIED TOMATOES

This is my version of the most popular dish served at a restaurant called Chameleon's in Los Angeles. The restaurant is long gone, but not forgotten.

2   tablespoons butter
2   tablespoons olive oil
8   sun-dried tomatoes packed in olive oil, finely chopped
¼   cup fresh basil, chopped
¼   cup fresh parsley, chopped
4   cloves garlic, about 4 teaspoons, minced
2   red and 2 green peppers (about 16 ounces total)
3   cups cooked Spaghetti Squash Pasta, p. 160
2   cups grated Parmesan cheese
•   Salt and pepper to taste

To roast the peppers: lay them, whole, on a gas burner grate or barbecue grill and turn them with tongs until the skins are blistered and completely black. Wrap them in plastic wrap or put in a plastic bag to sweat for ten minutes, and then use a paper towel to rub off the skins. Slice the peppers open, remove the seeds and membranes, and cut the peppers into strips.

Heat the butter and olive oil together in a large skillet. Add the sun-dried tomatoes, basil, parsley, garlic, red and green peppers, and salt and pepper. Sauté until heated through. Serve over spaghetti squash topped with Parmesan cheese.

Servings: 8 as a side dish, 4 as a main dish

PER SERVING:		
Total Carb: 9.3g if divided into 8 servings	Fiber: 2.4g	**Net Carb: 6.9g**
Total Carb: 18.6g if divided into 4 servings	Fiber: 4.8g	**Net Carb:13.8g**

SPAGHETTI SQUASH LASAGNA CASSEROLE

- Approximately 6 cups cooked Spaghetti Squash Pasta (1 ¾ pounds as purchased)

Tomato sauce with meat:
1   pound lean ground beef
½   cup onion, chopped
2   teaspoons garlic paste or 2 cloves of minced garlic
2   (8-ounce) cans tomato sauce
1   (15-ounce) can chopped tomatoes
4   tablespoons fresh parsley, minced, or 2 tablespoons dried
2   teaspoons fresh basil, minced, or 1 teaspoon dried
1   teaspoon salt
½   teaspoon pepper

2   cups (16 ounces) ricotta cheese
¾   cup, total, shredded Parmesan cheese, divided into ¼ cup and ½ cup
2   eggs
1½ teaspoons salt
2   cups shredded mozzarella cheese (8 ounces)

Preheat oven to 350° F. Grease a 9- by 13-inch pan.

Prepare the squash as directed for Spaghetti Squash Pasta (see p. 160). Cook the ground beef in a skillet until it is no longer pink. Add the onion (and fresh garlic, if using) and cook until the onion is softened and the meat is brown; drain. Add the tomato sauce and tomatoes, including the liquid, garlic paste (if using paste instead of fresh garlic), parsley, basil, and salt and pepper. Simmer, uncovered, stirring occasionally, for about 45 minutes or until thick (like spaghetti sauce).

Mix the ricotta with ¼ cup of the Parmesan, the eggs, and 1½ teaspoons of salt. Cover the bottom of the prepared pan with a layer of squash strands (about 3 cups). Spoon one-third of the sauce over top. Sprinkle with one-half of the mozzarella cheese. Using a spatula and a knife, drop one-half of the ricotta mixture over the top until evenly distributed. Repeat with another layer of squash, sauce, cheese, and ricotta. Top with the remaining sauce and sprinkle with the remaining ½ cup of Parmesan. Bake, uncovered, for about 40 minutes or until well browned. Let stand for 15 minutes before cutting. Lift out portions with a slotted spatula.

Servings: 10

> **PER SERVING:**
> Total Carb: 12.0g   Fiber: 1.7g   Net Carb: 10.3g

Dreamfields™ makes fabulous low-carb lasagna noodles as well as rotini, linguini, spaghetti, penne, and macaroni. It has a lower carb count (digestible carbs) than spaghetti squash. Although technically forbidden for induction on most diets, you can decide how strictly you want to adhere to the rules. Certainly once you graduate to a maintenance diet, you can enjoy the convenience of Dreamfields™ and the taste of authentic pasta.

I actually prefer spaghetti squash over Dreamfields™ low-carb pasta for Sukiyaki. It looks and tastes like Japanese bean thread noodles when cooked in broth.

"The only time to eat diet food is while you are waiting for the steak to cook."

—Julia Child

SUKIYAKI WITH SPAGHETTI SQUASH "NOODLES"

Use an electric skillet that you can put in the center of the table for this "Hot Pot" style meal. The spaghetti squash is very much like the bean thread noodles in the original recipe for Sukiyaki that we learned many years ago from some Japanese friends.

2 pounds thinly sliced tender beef, like sirloin
  (Place the meat in the freezer for 20 minutes to
  facilitate slicing.)
12 green onions, root tips trimmed and outer layer removed
½ pound mushrooms, sliced
1 (8-ounce) can sliced bamboo shoots
1 (8-ounce) can sliced water chestnuts
1 pound spinach, well rinsed, with stems removed
3 cups cooked Spaghetti Squash Pasta, p. 160
1 cup beef broth
1⅓ cups water
1 cup soy sauce
1 tablespoon granular Splenda®
4 eggs, slightly beaten (optional)

Arrange the beef and vegetables on a platter. Put the broth, water, soy sauce, and Splenda® in a large skillet and heat to 350º F. Put a portion of meat and vegetables for each person in the skillet and cook until the meat just loses its pink color. Do not over-cook, or the meat will be tough. Remove the meat and vegetables with a slotted spoon to individual plates and add more ingredients to the pan to cook until all are used. (Add more broth mixture if needed.)

Stir the eggs, one at a time, into the leftover broth and serve as soup at the end of the meal, if desired.

Servings: 4

PER SERVING:		
Total Carb: 15.4g	Fiber: 4.2g	Net Carb: 11.2g

BLACK "PASTA" (FRIED CHINESE BLACK MUSHROOMS)

I first encountered Chinese black mushrooms in a stir-fry at a luau in Hawaii. I had no idea what I was eating. It had a mild taste and a texture like crunchy pasta. On an expedition to an Asian grocery store, I found fresh Chinese black mushrooms: a likely candidate for the mystery ingredient. It required some research to know what to do with them. On my first attempt at preparing them, I had hot mushrooms exploding like little balloons all over the kitchen. Now I use dried ones rather than fresh, but I keep a spatter shield nearby just in case.

1   cup shredded, dried, Chinese black mushrooms
2   cups chicken stock
1   tablespoon peanut oil
5   slices peeled fresh ginger
•   A pinch of salt
•   A pinch of granular Splenda®
1   teaspoon soy sauce

Soak the mushrooms in cold water for 30 minutes and rinse. Put the chicken stock in a saucepan and simmer the mushrooms for 10 minutes. Drain, reserving 1 cup of the broth. Blot the mushroom pieces until dry on paper towels. Put the peanut oil in a skillet and fry the ginger slices until they are golden. Remove and discard the ginger. Fry the mushrooms in the oil for 2 minutes. Add the reserved stock and the salt, Splenda®, and soy sauce. Boil on high for about 10 minutes or until most of the liquid is evaporated.

Servings: 2

PER SERVING:		
Total Carb: 10.0g	Fiber: 7.0g	Net Carb: 3.0g

Chinese black mushrooms may also be called wood ears, cloud ears, or Chinese black fungus. Each mushroom segment is shaped like an ear or a trumpet. They are available dried at regular grocery stores, but I have found the price to be much more reasonable at Asian stores. See Sources to order them from Uwajimaya in Seattle.

Use a basket-style coffee filter made for drip coffee makers to strain out all the sand and dirt from the liquid when draining the soaking liquid from dried mushrooms. Reserve the liquid to add to the dish.

Tips and Notes

The coconut used here may be called young coconut, green coconut, or white coconut. It is an unripe coconut with a white outer husk and meat that is white but still slightly gelatinous. I prefer to buy them at groceries that specialize in Thai and Asian foods because their stock is more likely to be fresh. Choose one that is heavy for its size; you should hear a sloshing sound when you shake it. The husk should be white with no discolorations or bruises.

YOUNG COCONUT "PASTA"

The idea for using green (unripe) coconut meat for pasta originated with the raw food folks. It's soft and slippery like the rice noodles used for pad Thai. Power tools are not essential but will save you some time and effort.

Make two holes on opposite sides of the top of the coconut (use a drill with a $^3/_8$-inch bit or a nail and a hammer) and drain the liquid through a sieve into a bowl. Serve the coconut water as a beverage or save to use in a sauce or Panna Cotta.

Use a saw to cut the coconut in half. Loosen the coconut flesh from the shell with a spoon and remove it in large pieces. Scrape off any brown rind that adheres to it. Cut the coconut meat into thin strips. The "pasta noodles" can be served cold or heated in liquid until hot. They can also be sautéed quickly in butter or peanut oil.

One coconut makes about 1 cup of "pasta"

Servings: 2

PER SERVING:		
Total Carb: 6.0g	Fiber: 3.5g	Net Carb: 2.5g

"The doctor of the future will give no medication, but will interest his patients in the care of the human frame, diet and in the cause and prevention of disease."

—Thomas Edison

RUTABAGA

Rutabaga, sometimes called yellow turnip, is the potato pretender that I use most often. I cook it with walnuts and lemon just as I do cauliflower to neutralize its distinctive turnip-like taste. For other recipes that use rutabaga in place of potatoes, see Clam Chowder, Chicken and Vegetable Soup, and Pot Roast (see Index for recipes).

If you can find fresh pumpkin in the fall, you can substitute it for the rutabaga in all these recipes. It is so mild that you don't need to use the walnut and lemon trick and it cooks up softer so there is no need to precook it.

BASIC RECIPE FOR RUTABAGA FAUX POTATOES

Buy the smallest, freshest rutabagas you can find. Fresh ones will be heavy for their size and they will feel firm to the touch. Avoid ones that have been waxed to give them a longer shelf life; they may feel hard but the older they are, the stronger they will taste. Cook them my way and use them in the following recipes. They may not pass for russets, but they can definitely make you think you are eating Yukon gold potatoes!

3   small rutabagas (about 1 pound)
2   walnuts in the shell
1   slice lemon with the peel
•   Salt and pepper to taste
•   Splenda®, if needed

Peel the rutabaga and dice into ½- to 1-inch cubes. Simmer in a generous amount of water, to which you have added salt and pepper and the 2 whole walnuts for 10 minutes. Change the water if desired, add the lemon, and continue to cook for 10 to 15 minutes more or until fork tender. Drain well. Discard the walnuts and lemon. Return the rutabaga to the pan on low heat and stir a minute or two longer to dry. Taste the rutabaga and if it is bitter, sprinkle with a small amount of Splenda®. Use in one of the following recipes.

Note: If the recipe you will be using calls for cream, rinse the rutabaga well after draining to remove any trace of the lemon so the cream won't curdle.

> "I appreciate the potato only as a protection against famine, except for that, I know of nothing more eminently tasteless."
>
> —Jean Anthelme Brillat-Savarin, *The Physiology of Taste*, 1825

Servings: 4

PER SERVING:		
Total Carb: 9.3g	Fiber: 2.8g	Net Carb: 6.5g

RUTABAGA HOME FRIES

Tips and Notes

Some sources list the carbohydrate count for rutabaga as being higher than that for turnips; some list them as about the same. If in doubt, you may make any of these recipes with turnips. The rutabaga is a bit milder, and the texture is more like potatoes.

Miss those potatoes O'Brien, hash browns, and home fries? Try this substitute. Of all my recipes, I consider this one to be the "diet-saver" and so perhaps the "life-saver!" I have served it to guests who were convinced that they were eating potatoes.

- Rutabaga Faux Potatoes (about 1 pound before cooking), p. 167
- 2 tablespoons clarified butter or a combination of butter and oil
- 1 small onion (½ cup), peeled and diced
- 3 slices bacon
- Salt and pepper

Partially precook the bacon in the microwave or use precooked, packaged bacon. Cut the bacon into small pieces and reserve. Melt the butter in a skillet. Sauté the cooked rutabaga until it just starts to brown. Add the reserved bacon and onion to the skillet with the rutabaga and sauté until the onion is soft and the bacon is crisp. Add salt and pepper to taste.

VARIATION: Add chopped mushrooms and/or red or green pepper with the onions.

Servings: 4

PER SERVING:		
Total Carb: 11.0g	Fiber: 3.2g	Net Carb: 7.8g

"There is nothing so tragic on earth as the sight of a fat man eating a potato."

—Vance Thompson, *Eat and Grow Thin*, 1914

MINTED RUTABAGA

Try this with duck, chicken, or lamb.

- Rutabaga Faux Potatoes (about 1 pound before cooking), p. 167
- Olive oil
- 1 teaspoon Wax Orchard™ Fruit Sweet® (or use honey and add 0.6 net carbs per serving)
- 1 teaspoon granular Splenda®
- 1 tablespoon chopped fresh mint

Preheat oven to 350° F.

Drain the rutabaga and blot dry. Toss with a little olive oil in a roasting pan and bake in the oven until it starts to brown, about 20 minutes. Remove from the oven, sprinkle with Splenda®, and drizzle with Fruit Sweet® or honey. Mash the rutabaga with a fork or potato masher to a rough texture and stir in the chopped fresh mint. Return to the oven until heated through.

Servings: 4

PER SERVING:		
Total Carb: 10.0g	Fiber: 2.8g	Net Carb: 7.2g

> "If more of us valued food and cheer and song above hoarded gold, it would be a merrier world."
>
> —J. R. R. Tolkien

MEXICAN OMELET

- Oil for the pan
- 1 cup rutabaga, cooked as for Rutabaga Faux Potatoes, p. 167
- ¼ cup onion, chopped
- ¼ cup red or green pepper, chopped
- 4 eggs
- ½ cup cheese, shredded (Use more if desired.)
- ½ cup salsa
- Salt and pepper

Drain the cooked rutabaga, blot dry, and fry in oil until browned. Add onion and pepper and fry until the onion is softened. Pour eggs over the vegetables, stir, and cook until set. Top with cheese and serve with salsa.

Servings: 4

PER SERVING:		
Total Carb: 6.9g	Fiber: 1.3g	Net Carb: 5.6g

Rutabaga Fried in Duck Fat:

This makes rutabaga taste a lot like the classic French potato dish.

Slice small, fresh rutabagas into thin rounds. Simmer in water, to which you have added one or two walnuts in the shell, until tender. Drain well. Fry slices in duck fat, p. 38, turning to brown both sides. Add sliced onions and chopped bacon, if desired, when the rutabaga is almost done. Stir until onions are soft, bacon is crisp, and the rutabaga is brown.

ROASTED RUTABAGA WITH PEPPERS, ONIONS, AND MUSHROOMS

See also the variation using rutabaga under the Roasted Cauliflower recipe.

3   small rutabagas (about 1 pound before cooking)
½   small onion, diced
½   red bell pepper, diced
3   fresh mushrooms, chopped
•   Olive oil
•   Salt and pepper

Heat oven to 350° F.

Wash, peel, and dice the rutabagas. Put them in a roasting pan with the other vegetables and sprinkle with the olive oil. Toss to coat. (You may also spray them with no-stick spray to be sure they are all coated.) Sprinkle with salt and pepper. Cover the pan with foil and bake for 30 minutes or until the vegetables are soft. Uncover, stir, and roast for 15 minutes more or until brown.

Servings: 6

PER SERVING:		
Total Carb: 8.0g	Fiber: 2.4g	Net Carb: 5.6g

ROASTED VEGETABLES

1 or 2 small rutabagas, peeled and cut into chunks
     (about ½ pound before cooking)
½   head of cauliflower, separated into small florets
2   fennel bulbs, sliced into eighths
3   shallots, peeled
1   medium onion, peeled and cut into wedges
5 or 6 cloves garlic, peeled
•   Olive oil
•   Salt and pepper

Preheat oven to 400° F.

Mix the vegetables together in a roasting pan. Drizzle with olive oil and toss to coat. Season with salt and pepper. Bake uncovered, stirring occasionally, for 30 to 40 minutes or until brown.

Servings: 6

PER SERVING:		
Total Carb: 12.1g	Fiber: 3.7g	Net Carb: 8.4g

SMOKED CHEESE AND RUTABAGA CASSEROLE

Tips and Notes

4 or 5 small rutabagas (about 2 pounds)
2   walnuts in the shell
2   slices lemon with peel
2   cloves garlic, peeled and chopped
2   teaspoons olive oil
³/₄ cup shredded smoked Gouda or Edam cheese, divided in half
3   tablespoons butter, softened
6   ounces cream cheese, softened
2 to 3 drops Tabasco®
²/₃ cup cream
•   Salt and pepper to taste

Preheat oven to 350° F.

Peel and cube the rutabaga and cook with the walnuts and lemon by directions for Basic Rutabaga Faux Potatoes. Rinse and drain well. Sauté the garlic in olive oil until slightly softened. Cream together in a large bowl: the sautéed garlic, half of the smoked cheese, the butter, cream cheese, and Tabasco®. Stir in the cream and the salt and pepper. Add the rutabaga and stir until it is evenly coated. Place in a greased casserole and top with the remaining smoked cheese. Bake at 350° F for 30 to 35 minutes or until well browned.

Servings: 8

PER SERVING:		
Total Carb: 7.9g	Fiber: 2.3g	Net Carb: 5.6g

Tips and Notes

The only part of a potato that comes close to being low-carb is the skin. When my order in a restaurant comes with a baked potato, I scoop out the inside, pile on the toppings and eat just the skin. This is not something I could do often, but it's a lot better than eating the whole thing.

"An onion can make people cry, but there has never been a vegetable invented to make them laugh."

—Will Rogers

PUMPKIN TAMALES

Tips and Notes

Cotija cheese may be called queso añejo or añejo de Cotija. It is a dry, salty, crumbly, aged cheese. Cotija was the name of the town in Mexico where it was originally made. Look for it in the cheese display or with the Mexican foods at the grocery store. If you cannot find it, substitute Romano cheese.

Masa harina (Mexican cornmeal made from hominy), the main ingredient in tortillas, is generally something to avoid or use sparingly at twenty-one net carbs in one-quarter cup. This recipe, a take-off on the traditional fruit tamales of Mexico, also includes pumpkin purée, butter, and cheese, which cuts down on the carbs. I'm including a recipe for a savory one, with some variations, and a sweet one. They are all delicious and very easy to make.

For wrapping:
• Dried Cornhusks (or cooking parchment)

For the dough:
½ cup butter, softened
¾ teaspoon baking powder
¼ teaspoon salt
2 ounces (one-half of a 4-ounce can) diced green chilies
1 cup canned pumpkin or cooked and puréed fresh pumpkin
¾ cup masa harina (recipe was tested with Maseca Instant Corn Masa Mix)
¼ cup (1¼ ounces) grated Cotija cheese
2 tablespoons cream

• Optional Fillings: fill each tamale with 2 teaspoonfuls of meat from Carnitas recipe (see p. 199), or with chicken or pork filling for Tamale Pie (see p. 174), or with cooked and drained ground beef.

Use purchased cornhusks if possible, as they are larger than what we typically get from fresh corn on the cob. Cover the husks with hot water and let them sit for several hours or microwave for a few minutes to soften. Choose a few of the longest husks and tear into narrow strips to use as ties. Cut off the narrow ends of the remaining husks so that they are more square in shape. Blot the husks with paper towels to dry thoroughly. Four- by eight-inch pieces of parchment paper can be used in place of the cornhusks, if desired.

Combine the butter, baking powder, and salt in the bowl of a mixer and beat until fluffy. Add the chilies, pumpkin, masa harina, cheese, and cream and beat to incorporate.

Spread about ¼ cup of the dough on each husk. Make the layer in the shape of a rectangle about ¼ inch thick that comes all the way to the edge on one side. Leave at least 1 inch on the other side and 2 inches or more on each end of the husk uncovered. If using a filling, place 2 teaspoons of filling down the center of the masa-covered section.

(continued on next page)

PUMPKIN TAMALES, CONTINUED

Fold the masa-covered part of the husk in half so that the filling is enclosed, leaving the extra inch or more of husk to overlap the seam. Fold the two ends toward the center and tie in place with the husk strips, leaving it loose enough for the dough to expand. (For quicker preparation, fold up and tie one end only and stand the tamales to steam with the open end up. If your steamer is too large for them to stand upright, crumpled foil can fill in the open spaces to keep them stable.)

Put a few inches of water in a large pot or steamer with a rack and heat on low. The rack should not touch the water. Place the tamales upright on the rack or in a single layer. Cover the pot and steam for about an hour. Check the pot every 15 minutes or so to be sure it doesn't boil dry. When done, the dough should be firm and it should pull away from the husk cleanly. Unwrap one to check for doneness.

Serve the tamales with salsa verde or enchilada sauce. Unfilled tamales are a nice accompaniment for chops or steaks; the filled ones can serve as a main dish for lunch or dinner.

Servings: 14

PER SERVING:		
Total Carb: 6.5g	Fiber: 1.1g	Net Carb: 5.4g

VARIATION:
TAMALE PANCAKES

If you don't have time for filling the cornhusks and steaming the tamales, here is a shortcut.

Form the dough into balls about the size of a walnut. Flatten into small pancakes and fry in butter or oil until brown and crunchy. Turn and brown the other side. Serve as a side dish or top with shredded cooked meat, cheese, chopped tomatoes, shredded lettuce, and salsa as for tacos.

Servings: 28

PER SERVING:		
Total Carb: 3.3g	Fiber: 0.6g	Net Carb: 2.7g

Tips and Notes

Salsa is always a carb bargain, but the green kind is especially so. It is made with tomatillos, the little green "tomatoes" encased in a papery husk. Embassa brand Salsa Verde claims to have one gram of carbohydrate with one gram of fiber, which cancels it out, for a net carb count of zero. (See Sources.)

Tips and Notes

The extra broth from cooking the meat can be used for soup to serve with the pie. See the recipe for Carnitas Soup, p. 84.

VARIATION:

TAMALE PIE WITH CHICKEN

- One recipe of Pumpkin Tamale dough

For filling:
1½ to 2 pounds fresh chicken
½ cup onion, chopped
1 clove garlic, chopped
¼ cup mild green chilies, chopped
¼ teaspoon dried oregano
- A pinch of cumin
- Salt and pepper to taste

Put chicken in a pot with water to cover. Add onion, garlic, chilies, oregano, and a pinch of cumin to the pot. Add salt and pepper to taste. Simmer on low heat for 1 hour or until very tender. Remove the meat from the bones and shred. Strain the broth.

Grease a 2-quart, oven-proof casserole. Preheat oven to 350° F.

Spread about two-thirds of the tamale dough on the bottom and sides of the casserole. Place the meat, moistened with a little of the broth, on top of the dough. Cover with remaining masa dough. Cover the casserole with a lid or with aluminum foil and bake for 1 hour.

Servings: 8

PER SERVING:		
Total Carb: 12.8g	Fiber: 2.2g	Net Carb: 10.6g

VARIATION:

DESSERT PUMPKIN TAMALES

Make Pumpkin Tamale dough, but omit the chilies, and add ½ cup of granular Splenda®. Fill with 2 teaspoons of sugar-free jam, drained Cranberry Sauce, or Mincemeat. (See Index for recipes.) Serve hot.

Servings: 14

MEXICAN-STYLE HOMINY

Juanita's Mexican Style Hominy®, with four net grams per half-cup, is surprisingly low in carbohydrates considering that most corn products, and even other brands of hominy, have from thirteen to twenty-five grams in the same half-cup amount.

Put it, straight out of the can, in soups instead of dumplings or noodles, and in chili instead of beans. Serve it with butter as a side dish or whirl it in the food processor and use it in place of rice, bulgur, barley, grits, or polenta. It tastes remarkably like risotto, but is much easier to make and I actually like it better! If you can't find Juanita's, there are other brands that are almost as low, just be sure it says "Mexican Style" on the label. They vary a great deal in carbohydrate content, so check the carb count. See the chapter on Soups, Chowder, and Chili for more recipes that use Mexican-style hominy.

BASIC RECIPE FOR HOMINY "RICE"

To use canned Mexican-style hominy as a substitute for rice:
Drain Mexican-style hominy and pulse it in the bowl of a food processor, fitted with the metal blade, until it is evenly chopped and has the texture of rice. Use in recipes or as a side dish like cooked rice.

To use Pinewood Products Dried Hulled Hominy as a substitute for rice:
Rinse the hominy and pulse it five or six times in the food processor. Place in a saucepan, cover with water, and bring to a boil. Put a lid on the pan and reduce the heat. Simmer for 1 to 2 hours or until puffed and tender. Drain the hominy and process it in the bowl of a food processor, fitted with the metal blade, until it is evenly chopped and has the texture of rice.

HOMINY "RISOTTO"

Tips and Notes

Pinewood Products sells hominy made from Iroquois white corn. Higher in fiber and protein than regular corn, it may be even better for low-carb dieters than Mexican-style hominy, since it does not cause a sharp rise in blood-sugar levels. See Sources.

Pinewood Product's dried hominy still has the pedicles attached, which prevents the kernels from rupturing. Pulsing it a few times in the food processor will nick the kernels allowing them to pop and get tender when cooked.

1   can (1 pound, 13 ounces) Mexican-style hominy, drained
½   cup chopped shallots
4   large fresh mushrooms, chopped
2   tablespoons butter
½   cup chicken broth
½   cup white wine
½   cup fresh parsley, chopped
½   cup heavy cream
½   cup Parmesan cheese, grated
½   teaspoon salt
•   Pepper to taste

Process the hominy in the bowl of a food processor until it is evenly chopped. Sauté the shallots and mushrooms in the butter. Add the hominy, broth, and white wine, and simmer until liquid is absorbed. Add cream and parsley and heat through. Add Parmesan and heat and stir until melted. Add salt and pepper to taste and serve.

Servings: 8

PER SERVING:		
Total Carb: 10.3g	Fiber: 4.8g	Net Carb: 5.5g

"Cheese that is required by law to append the word food to its title does not go well with red wine or fruit."

—Fran Lebowitz

CHEESE POLENTA

This is my favorite recipe using hominy. Serve it as a side dish for roast chicken, duck, or ham with Shallot and Peach Chutney or Cranberry Relish for an impressive presentation. (See Index for recipes.)

2   cups Mexican-style hominy
$^3/_4$ cup cream
2   tablespoons butter
$^1/_2$ cup (2 ounces) grated Gruyere cheese, plus 6 teaspoons more for the tops
$^1/_2$ cup (2 ounces) grated Parmesan cheese
$^1/_4$ cup sugar-free Dried Cranberries. See p. 105. (Plump them in hot water with a little Splenda® if they are unsweetened. Dry them well or the polenta will be pink.)
$^1/_8$ teaspoon ground nutmeg
$^1/_2$ teaspoon salt
$^1/_4$ teaspoon pepper

Butter six $^1/_2$-cup baking dishes or a muffin tin and a shallow baking pan.

Process the hominy in the bowl of a food processor until evenly chopped and similar to rice in texture. Place the hominy, cream, and butter in a heavy saucepan. Cook, stirring, until it bubbles and thickens. Stir in the $^1/_2$ cup of Gruyere and all the Parmesan cheese, the cranberries, nutmeg, and salt and pepper. Cook and stir a few minutes more until it forms a smooth mass that pulls away from the pan. Press the mixture into the buttered baking dishes or muffin tin. Chill for a minimum of 15 minutes. It can be made ahead and refrigerated at this point.

Preheat the oven to 450° F. Loosen the edges of the polenta with a knife and unmold onto a buttered baking pan. Place one teaspoon of Gruyere on top of each serving and bake for 5 to 10 minutes, then run under the broiler briefly, just until golden brown on top. Serve hot.

Servings: 6

PER SERVING:		
Total Carb: 6.8g	Fiber: 3.5g	Net Carb: 3.3g

Tips and Notes

Polenta originated in Ancient Rome, where "pulmentum" was a staple food of the Roman Legions. The traditional coarse-ground pulmentum was made from wild grain or wheat and was preferred for porridge and flat cakes by peasants and soldiers for centuries even after improved milling techniques allowed for bread.

Buckwheat from the Middle East and then maize from the new world replaced the original grains, but the method of making polenta in a round bowl stirred with a wooden spoon for up to an hour, has not changed among traditionalists since the time of the Roman Empire.

In America, corn meal gruel was called nasamp by the Indians, shortened to samp by the English. Other regional names for it were grits, mush, and hasty pudding.

"…Thee the soft nations round the warm Levant
Polanta call; the French, of course, Polante.
E'en in thy native regions, how I blush
To hear the Pennsylvanians call thee Mush!…"

—Joel Barlow, "The Hasty Pudding," 1793

HOMINY AND GREEN CHILI CASSEROLE

VARIATION:

Hominy and Mushroom Casserole

Leave out the chilies and oregano. Sauté ¾ cup of chopped, fresh mushrooms briefly with the onion.

Makes 8 servings.
Per Serving:
Total Carb: 9.4g
Fiber: 4.8g
Net Carb: 4.6g

1   (28-ounce) can Mexican-style hominy, drained and rinsed
2   tablespoons olive oil
½   cup chopped onion
½   teaspoon dried oregano
1   (4-ounce) can diced green chilies, mild or hot, drained
1   tablespoon fine cornmeal or masa harina
½   teaspoon salt
1   teaspoon garlic paste
1   egg, slightly beaten
1   cup shredded Cheddar cheese, plus extra for topping

Preheat the oven to 350° F.

Process the hominy in a food processor until evenly chopped. Sauté the onion and oregano in the oil until the onion is soft. Stir the onion and all other ingredients into the hominy. Place in a greased baking dish and sprinkle with the extra cheese. Bake for 20 to 25 minutes or until the cheese starts to brown. Serve hot.

Servings: 8

PER SERVING:		
Total Carb: 10.2g	Fiber: 4.8g	**Net Carb: 5.4g**

CAULIFLOWER AND CELERY ROOT

CAULIFLOWER "MASHED POTATOES"

This makes a convincing mashed potato dish. I cook cauliflower with lemon slices and walnuts to make it very mild, then add garlic, cream, and butter for flavor; the egg and Parmesan help thicken it. Serve this to an unsuspecting friend and see if they can tell you what it is! (Or rather, what it isn't!)

1   small head cauliflower (about 1 pound)
5-6 cloves garlic, peeled, but not chopped
2   whole walnuts in the shell
2   slices lemon with peel
1   egg
2   tablespoons cream
2   tablespoons butter
¼   cup finely grated Parmesan cheese
•   Salt and pepper

Wash and trim the cauliflower and separate it into florets. Cook the cauliflower with the walnuts and lemon slices in salted water for 20 to 25 minutes or until very tender. Rinse and drain; remove and discard the walnuts and lemon. Return the cauliflower and garlic to the pan and heat, stirring, for a few minutes to dry. Blot the cauliflower and garlic on paper towels, pressing out as much liquid as possible. Put it in the food processor bowl and blend until very smooth. (If the cauliflower weighed more than one pound, process it in two batches.)

In a separate dish, beat the egg with a fork and blend in the cream; add the cream and egg mixture and the butter to the cauliflower in the processor bowl and process until blended. Return the mixture to the pan. Heat, stirring, over low heat for about 10 to 20 minutes to cook the egg and to thicken and dry the mixture until it is the consistency of mashed potatoes. Add salt and pepper to taste. Serve hot.

Note: Garlic oil or paste can be substituted for the fresh garlic or used to correct the seasoning.

Servings: 4

PER SERVING:		
Total Carb: 7.4g	Fiber: 3.5g	Net Carb: 3.9g

Adding walnuts in the shell to the cooking liquid will neutralize the odor of cooking cabbage. I have discovered that it also helps counteract the turnip or cabbage flavor of similar vegetables, like cauliflower and rutabaga. Changing the water once while boiling makes them even milder. Lemon also helps to neutralize strong flavors.

This is an easy and tasty way to cook cauliflower with no cabbage-like overtones.

1 head cauliflower (about 1½ pounds as purchased, untrimmed)
• Olive oil
1 tablespoon grated lemon zest
½ teaspoon tarragon
2 tablespoons shallots, finely chopped

Heat oven to 400° F.

Wash and trim the cauliflower and separate it into florets. Put it in a roasting pan and sprinkle with the olive oil. Toss to coat. (You may also spray it with no-stick spray to be sure it is well coated.) Roast uncovered for 30 to 40 minutes, stirring occasionally, until brown. Sprinkle zest, tarragon, and shallots over top and continue to bake for five minutes more.

Servings: 8

PER SERVING:		
Total Carb: 5.0g	Fiber: 2.6g	Net Carb: 2.4g

VARIATION:

Roasted Rutabaga

Use 6 small, peeled rutabagas (about 2 pounds), diced, in place of the cauliflower.

Makes 8 servings.
Per Serving:
Total Carb: 9.8g
Fiber: 2.9g
Net Carb: 6.9g

FAUX POTATO PANCAKES

2 cups Celery Root "Mashed Potatoes," p. 181
1 egg
2 tablespoons onion, grated or finely minced
1 tablespoon potato flour (optional, adds 0.6 net carbs per serving)
• Butter or olive oil or a combination of both for sautéing

Make Celery Root "Mashed Potatoes" and let cool, or use leftovers. Beat the egg with a fork. Stir the egg and the onion into the celery root mixture. Heat the butter or olive oil in a skillet (use an oven-safe skillet if you want to brown them under the broiler, in other words, no plastic handles). Drop the mixture by tablespoonfuls into the hot pan. Brown one side and turn to brown the other side. Keep them small or they may be difficult to turn without breaking. If they are too soft to turn, you can put them under the broiler to brown the tops.

Servings: 16

PER SERVING:		
Total Carb: 1.6g	Fiber: 0.2g	Net Carb: 1.4g

Tips and Notes

If you can afford the extra carbs, the potato flour makes these crisper and more like the real thing (still with a fraction of the carbs for potato pancakes, which the USDA puts at 22 grams each).

Celery Root "Mashed Potatoes"

Creamy, puréed celery root is a gourmet side dish that is frequently served in trendy restaurants. Think of it as mashed potatoes with a pedigree.

- 4 cups diced celery root (about 1⅓ pounds as purchased, with roots and tops trimmed)
- 3 shallot segments, peeled (about 3 ounces)
- 2 tablespoons cream
- 1 egg
- 2 tablespoons butter
- • Salt and pepper

Wash the celery root well, peel it, and cut it into cubes. Cover it with water and cook it with the shallots in a covered pan until very tender, about 20 to 25 minutes. Rinse and drain. Blot dry on paper towels, pressing out as much liquid as possible. Purée the celery root and shallots in a food processor until smooth. In a small bowl, beat the egg with a fork and blend in the cream. Add the egg mixture and the butter to the processor bowl; scrape down the bowl with a spatula, and process until blended. Return the mixture to the pan and cook and stir over low heat until the egg is cooked and the purée has the consistency of mashed potatoes, about 5 to 10 minutes. Correct the seasoning and serve, topped with a pat of butter.

Servings: 4

PER SERVING:		
Total Carb: 10.6g	Fiber: 2.0g	**Net Carb: 8.6g**

Celery Root, also called Celeriac

Don't be intimidated by this weird-looking vegetable. Not really a root, it comes from a kind of celery grown for its edible corm. It is very popular in Europe where it is used both raw and cooked.

Choose firm, fresh celeriac and scrub it well to remove all the dirt that tends to cling to its hair-like roots. To prepare, slice it first and then peel it, so it is easier to get into all the convoluted spaces. Cut off the fibrous roots, but if some are large, you can peel and use them too.

See the chapter on salads for more uses for celery root.

VEGETABLES

SOME OF MY BEST FRIENDS ARE VEGETABLES

Unless you are new to low-carb dieting, you are probably already eating lots of low-starch vegetables like artichokes, asparagus, broccoli, cabbage, cauliflower, celery, cucumber, eggplant, green beans, lettuce, mushrooms, peppers, pumpkin, rutabaga, snow peas, sugar snap peas, spinach, summer squash, spaghetti squash, salad greens, turnips, and zucchini. Tomatoes and onions are a bit higher in carbs but are still allowed in most low-carb plans.

Carrots, sweet potatoes, sweet peas (shelled), beets, and fresh corn have a higher sugar content and are usually relegated to the "seldom or never" column. Here are some good low-carb vegetable recipes, including some that may be less familiar. (Cauliflower, corn, rutabaga, spaghetti squash, and pumpkin recipes are given in the chapter on Starch Replacements. Additional recipes are found in other chapters.)

BRAISED FENNEL

The Italians have a special fondness for fennel. This simple side dish is often served with fried fish.

2 fennel bulbs (about 1 pound, trimmed)
⅓ cup olive oil
½ cup water
• Salt
• Black pepper
• Grated Parmesan cheese

Cut off the stalks close to the bulb, reserving some of the feathery fronds to use as a garnish for the finished dish. Cut a thin slice off the root end and trim and discard any discolored parts of the bulb. Slice vertically into ³⁄₈-inch slices. Rinse the slices well with cold water and drain. Place in a large skillet and add olive oil and water. Place over medium heat and cover pan. Cook, turning slices over occasionally, for about 20 minutes or until tender. Add more water if necessary. (The fresher the fennel, the faster it will cook.) When the fennel is tender, uncover the pan. Turn the heat up and continue to cook until all the water is absorbed and the slices are deep golden brown, turning to brown evenly on both sides. Sprinkle with salt and pepper and top with Parmesan. Serve hot.

Servings: 4

PER SERVING:		
Total Carb: 8.5g	Fiber: 3.5g	Net Carb: 5.0g

Tips and Notes

Fennel, a mild cousin of anise, becomes even sweeter when cooked. It can be used raw in salads, or cooked with Pot Roast and soups, but it is especially delicious when braised, sautéed, or fried.

There are two kinds of fennel: Finocchio, or Florence fennel, has a bulbous base that is used as a vegetable. Fennel seeds that are used as a spice come from common fennel, which has no bulb. Fennel pollen, called "spice of the angels," is also used as a spice. The fern-like greens of either plant can be used as an herb.

SAUTÉED ASPARAGUS

The size of the spear is not an indicator of tenderness, but of the age of the root; older plants will produce thicker shoots. Look for asparagus standing upright in a tray of water on the produce counter. It should be firm and bright green with tightly closed tips. When you get it home, break off the lower part of the stalks. They will naturally snap at the point where they become tough. Discard the lower stem or reserve to use for puréed soup. Put the asparagus in a container of water as if it were a bouquet of flowers and use it within a day or two. As far as I'm concerned there is only one way to cook asparagus.

Snap off the tough ends of the asparagus stalks. Use a vegetable peeler to pare away the triangular scales, which collect a lot of sandy soil as the shoots push up through the ground. Wash well. Line the stalks up on a cutting board and slice on the diagonal into half-inch pieces until you reach the tips. Sauté the stalks in butter for a minute or two before adding the tips. Continue to cook until just tender-crisp. Season and serve.

Serving size: 4 spears

PER SERVING:		
Total Carb: 2.5g	Fiber: 1.0g	Net Carb: 1.5g

SAUTÉED BROCCOLINI

Remove the tops and slice the stalks diagonally into ½-inch pieces. Sauté in butter or olive oil for about 2 minutes before adding the tops. Continue to cook until tender but still crisp.

The net carb count for broccolini is 5 grams for 8 stalks.

Tips and **Notes**

Broccolini, or baby broccoli, is a new vegetable that is 100% usable, including the stem. It is billed as being like a cross between broccoli and asparagus, but milder than both. It can be steamed, sautéed, or used fresh.

Very few foods have the honor of being featured on the flag of a nation. The Mexican flag depicts an eagle, perched on a flowering nopal cactus, holding a snake in his talons. Legend tells of the founding of what is now Mexico City by the Aztec people. One of their gods had given them a sign; when they saw an eagle, sitting on a cactus, eating a snake, they would know that they had found their new homeland. They named the city Tenochtitlan, which means "place of the prickly pear cactus."

Nopal cactus is reputed to be effective for lowering cholesterol and blood sugar, and nopal capsules are sold in Mexico for treating type-2 diabetes. Research conducted in Mexico has shown nopal to be effective for animals, but in human studies only very high doses were helpful. In any case, it is extremely low in carbohydrates; Embassa brand's label lists the carb count for a two-thirds-cup serving as one gram and the fiber as two grams for a net carb count of minus one. (I don't know if it's possible to have a negative carb count. Do you think that means we can subtract one carb from something else that we eat? Hmmm.) Some other sources put it at one to two carbs per serving.

NOPALES WITH GARLIC AND CHILIES

The pads of the prickly pear (nopal) cactus are an important food in Mexico and are becoming more available in the US. The Mexican food section of the grocery will probably have canned nopales, either pickled or packed in water. Rinse them well and heat to serve as a green vegetable. They taste like green beans with a slight tang of citrus. You may find fresh nopales in the produce display at a regular grocery store, especially in areas with large populations of people of Mexican heritage, or in a Mexican specialty market. I lived in Palos Verdes, CA for many years where every undeveloped, sunny hillside was covered with them, but I tasted neither the cactus nor its fruit until I moved to Washington.

Fresh nopales taste better than canned, but they do look dangerous. Handle them carefully until you can shave off the thorns. The best way I've found to do that is to use one of the long skinny micro-graters, the kind used originally as a wood rasp, that is now sold in kitchen shops. The cactus pads tend to be concave and uneven so cutting them into narrow strips first makes it easier to get at the thorns. Wearing gloves is not a bad idea. I've read that nopales can also be candied, something I intend to try. (Candied nopales are called Acitrónes.*)*

1   pound fresh nopales, thorns removed (3½ cups, cubed)
2   tablespoons olive oil
2   cloves garlic, minced
2   green onions, chopped
2   jalapeño peppers, chopped, seeds and membranes removed, or 2 to 4 tablespoons hot or mild canned chilies
•   Salt to taste

Cut the nopales into ½-inch cubes. Heat the oil in a large skillet and sauté the garlic for a few seconds, but don't let it brown. Add the nopales, onions, and peppers. Cover the pan and cook on low heat, stirring occasionally, for 8 to 10 minutes or until the nopales have released their viscous juices. Uncover the pan and raise the heat to medium-low; cook for about 20 minutes, stirring and scraping the bottom of the pan frequently, until all the sticky liquid has evaporated. Correct the seasoning and serve. Use the nopales as a green vegetable or put in low-carb tortillas, top with cheese, and roll up. This cooks down to a little more than a cup of vegetables to make two servings as a side dish or four servings in tortillas.

Servings: 2

PER SERVING:		
Total Carb: 4.3g	Fiber: 0.5g	Net Carb: 3.8g

Note: Like many other fruits and vegetables, jalapeños are getting enormous. If they are more than 3 inches long, just use one, unless you really like the heat.

OKRA AND TOMATOES

My mother always grew okra in her vegetable garden. She tossed it in cornmeal and fried it in bacon fat. My sister and I considered it totally revolting with its hairy pods and slimy juice and refused to eat anything except the crispy cornmeal bits that fell off in the skillet (which were delicious). After reading a Paul Prudhomme cookbook I decided to give it another chance. His etouffèe recipe didn't work for me; it involved cooking the okra on high heat until it stuck to the pan, then scraping it off, and repeating the sticking and scraping, over and over, for more than an hour. My pan was Teflon, and the okra burned after about 30 minutes. But I did learn that if you cook it long enough, the slime goes away!

4   slices bacon, chopped
1   pound okra, trimmed and cut into ¼-inch slices
½   cup onions, chopped
½   cup green bell pepper, chopped
¼   cup celery, chopped
½   teaspoon garlic, minced
¾   teaspoon salt or to taste
⅓   teaspoon cayenne pepper
1   (14½-ounce) can diced tomatoes, including the liquid

Sauté the chopped bacon in a large, heavy skillet or Dutch oven to render the fat and crisp the bacon. Remove and reserve the bacon. Add the okra, onions, pepper, celery, garlic, salt, and cayenne to the pan. Cover the pan and cook on high heat for 5 minutes, stirring thoroughly, twice. Remove the lid and continue to cook for 5 minutes more, stirring frequently, and scraping the bottom and sides of the pan. Add one-half of the tomatoes and one-half of the tomato liquid and cook, uncovered, on high heat for 10 minutes, stirring and scraping the pan frequently to keep the mixture from burning. Add the rest of the tomatoes and liquid and stir and scrape the pan for 10 minutes more. Remove about three-fourths of the vegetables from the pan and reserve. Lower the heat to medium and continue to cook, scrape, and stir for about 15 minutes more, or until very well browned, but not burned. Remove the pan from the heat and scrape the bottom well to release all the browned glaze. Stir the reserved okra mixture and the bacon back into the pan and return to high heat for a few minutes until hot. Correct the seasoning and serve.

Servings: 8

PER SERVING:		
Total Carb: 8.0g	Fiber: 2.7g	Net Carb: 5.3g

Tips and Notes

A common vegetable in the southern states of the US, okra was introduced from Africa with the slave trade. It is popular today in North African and the eastern Mediterranean countries, where they prefer very tiny, tender pods, only an inch or so in length. We are unlikely to get it that small here unless we grow our own.

Choose small fresh okra and store it in a plastic bag at room temperature for no more than a day. Do not rinse it until you are ready to cook it, as the water will increase its sliminess. Just before cooking, rinse it and cut off the caps on the stem end.

Chayote Squash, also called Mirliton

An unusual summer squash, pale green and about the size of a fist with "knuckles" on one end. It is firm-textured and very mild with one large seed. It doesn't need to be peeled or pitted, just dice the whole fruit and eat it fresh or cook it until fork tender. Use it raw in salads (see p. 92 for Celery Root and Chayote Salad with Mustard Dressing) or sauté it in butter for a vegetable side dish. It is also delicious breaded and fried. (Use recipe for Fried Tomatillos.)

One medium (7.2-ounce) chayote has 11 grams of carbohydrate, minus 6.1 grams of fiber, for a net count of 4.9 grams in two servings.

CHAYOTE SQUASH WITH BACON

2   chayote squash (about 7 ounces each)
2   tablespoons olive oil or butter
2   shallots (1 ounce each), chopped, or use onion
3   strips bacon, cooked until crisp and crumbled
•   Lemon peel, grated
•   Salt and pepper

Dice the squash and sauté in olive oil or butter until tender. Add shallots or onion and continue to cook until it is softened. Stir in bacon. Sprinkle with grated lemon peel. Add salt and pepper to taste and serve hot.

Servings: 4

PER SERVING:		
Total Carb: 6.4g	Fiber: 1.5g	Net Carb: 4.9g

"Pray you sit down; For now we sit to chat as well as eat."

—Shakespeare, *Taming of the Shrew*

FRIED TOMATILLOS

Tomatillos are like small green tomatoes incased in a papery lantern. (Mexican salsa verde is made with tomatillos.) Fried, they are like fried green tomatoes, but less sour.

8   ounces fresh tomatillos
1   teaspoon salt
1   teaspoon black pepper
½   teaspoon garlic powder
⅓   cup Low-Carb Flour Replacement (see p. 116)
¼   teaspoon baking powder
•   Oil for frying

Remove the husks from the tomatillos and rinse them to remove the sticky coating. Slice into quarter-inch slices. Spread out on a flat surface and sprinkle with salt, pepper, and garlic powder. Let stand for 15 minutes; drain. Mix flour replacement with baking powder in a flat pan. Heat ½ inch of oil in a skillet on medium heat until hot. Dredge tomatillo slices with flour mixture and shake off excess. Fry slices about 5 minutes, turning once, to brown both sides. Drain and serve.

Servings: 4

PER SERVING:		
Total Carb: 6.0g	Fiber: 3.3g	Net Carb: 2.7g

count includes all the flour replacement, but some will be left over

HEARTS OF PALM

Available fresh in Florida and canned elsewhere, hearts of palm are usually served cold with vinaigrette or in salads, but they are also wonderful as a hot vegetable. Serve them with cream sauce, sautéed in butter, or au gratin with Parmesan cheese. The USDA lists them at 1.5 grams of carbohydrate for one piece (a little over an ounce) with 1 gram of fiber for a net carb count of 0.5 grams per serving.

Tips and Notes

Heart of palm is the inner stalk of the cabbage palm tree, the official state tree of Florida.

SAUERKRAUT

Most sources list sauerkraut as having 1 gram of carbohydrate and 1 gram of fiber, giving it a net count of zero. It can be used for a lot more than topping a hot dog!

Buy fresh sauerkraut in plastic bags or jars from the refrigerated cases at the grocery or from a delicatessen. Put it in a colander and rinse it well under cold running water. Put it in a deep pot. Add a little water to the pot and bury a cored apple and a peeled onion in the sauerkraut. Place several slices of bacon across the top. Cover the pan and place over low heat. Cook for about an hour or until the apple and onion are very soft, checking occasionally, and adding water if necessary. Remove the apple and onion before serving for the lowest carb count. Serve as a side dish or see below for a main dish version.

VARIATION:

CHOUCROUTE GARNI

Layer the sauerkraut with a variety of cured or smoked meats, such as ham, smoked pork chops, and sausages. Add a little white wine rather than water. Cook as above.

OVEN DRIED TOMATOES

Preheat oven to 200° F.

Cut fresh tomatoes in half and squeeze out the watery juice. Cut into thick slices. Sprinkle with salt and drain on paper towels. Line a baking sheet with foil or parchment and place tomato slices close together on the pan. Bake for 2 to 3 hours until they shrink to about three-quarters their original size. Serve with grilled eggplant, add to salads, or use as a side dish. The carbohydrate count will be slightly less than the amount for the fresh tomatoes you have at the start (each medium-sized tomato will have 5.7 grams of carbohydrate and 1 gram of fiber for a net count of 4.7 grams).

SOUTHERN GREENS

Here's a tasty way to eat your greens. Your mama will be so proud of you! Trader Joe's sells this mixture already rinsed and cut, but you can assemble your own combination from whatever is available. You may add kale, beet tops, and chard to the listed greens.

1 pound mixed greens (mustard greens, turnip greens, spinach, and collard greens)
3 slices bacon, chopped
1 clove garlic, minced
1 onion, chopped
2 tablespoons olive oil
1 (14.5-ounce) can chicken broth
1 (5.5-ounce) can tomato juice
2 tablespoons cider vinegar
½ teaspoon marjoram
• Salt and pepper to taste
• Parmesan cheese, grated

Wash the greens and slice crosswise into strips. In a large pot, sauté the bacon, garlic, and onion in the olive oil. Add the broth, tomato juice, and vinegar and bring to a boil. Add the seasonings and the greens. Cover the pot, reduce the heat, and simmer for 35 minutes or until tender. Sprinkle the greens with Parmesan cheese and serve.

Servings: 9

PER SERVING:		
Total Carb: 4.5g	Fiber: 1.0g	Net Carb: 3.5g

Tips and Notes

For home gardeners who grow their own vegetables, a complete list of vegetables and their carbohydrate content is available online at www.burpee.com.

BEANS

We're talking about the starchy beans, like pintos, limas, and great Northern beans rather than green beans in the pod, which count as a non-starchy vegetable. Although most beans are high in fiber and generally considered healthful, soybeans and tepary beans are the carb bargains.

Soybeans:
Green soybeans, what the Japanese call *edamame*, are served cooked and shelled as an appetizer in sushi bars. They are available in my area both frozen and fresh from Trader Joe's. Asian markets also sell them as well as many regular grocery stores. Cook them in water until tender and serve them in place of lima beans as a side dish or in soup.

Black soybeans are available canned (see Sources). They are not good plain, but make good Baked Beans with my recipe.

Roasted soybeans make a crunchy snack and can be used like peanuts. See Sources for chocolate-covered soybeans that are relatively low-carb even when there's sugar in the chocolate. Make your own using the recipe for Nut Clusters (see p. 262) in the chapter on candy for a low-carb, no-sugar treat.

Tepary Beans:
Native Seeds Search sells both the beans, and the seeds for growing them, from the kind of plants originally cultivated by Native Americans in the Southwest. They come in three varieties: white, which is described as being mild and sweet; brown, which has a more nutty flavor; and blue speckled, which is similar to brown, but with its own "distinctive taste." All are high protein, high fiber, and have a low glycemic index (they do not cause a sudden rise in blood sugar levels). I have not been able to get a carb count for them, but since the purpose of controlling carb intake is to prevent excess insulin production, which is the body's response to a high blood sugar level, it makes sense that we should be able to include these in our diet.

"I was determined to know beans."
—Henry David Thoreau,
The Beanfield, Walden, 1854

BAKED BEANS

My baked beans can be made with black soybeans or white tepary beans. Both kinds are high in fiber and protein and won't break down like starchy beans; in order to get them to absorb the sauce, they need to be mashed up a bit toward the end of the cooking time.

1   (14-ounce) can black soybeans or 1 cup of dry, white tepary beans
4   slices bacon, cooked until crisp, and crumbled
½   cup chopped onion
•   Olive oil for sautéing onion or use bacon fat
2   teaspoons Sugar Twin® brown sugar substitute
1   teaspoon granular Splenda®
½   cup sugar-free Ketchup (see p. 232)
2   teaspoons Worcestershire sauce
1   teaspoon dry mustard
1   teaspoon browning sauce such as Kitchen Bouquet®
½   teaspoon salt
⅛   teaspoon pepper

Preheat oven to 350° F.

To make with black soybeans:
Drain the beans and rinse with warm water to remove the gelatinous liquid, if necessary.

To make with tepary beans:
Wash and pick over the beans. Place them in a food processor and pulse five or six times to nick the outer seed coating. (This allows them to cook up softer and absorb more flavor from the sauce.) Cover with water to a depth of 1 inch over the top of the beans. Either soak the beans for 8 hours, or bring them to a boil and simmer for 3 minutes, turn off the heat, cover the pan with a lid, and let them sit for an hour. Drain. Cover the beans with fresh water and simmer for 1 to 2 hours, or until tender. (The fresher the beans, the faster they will cook.) Drain.

Cook the bacon and crumble. Sauté the onion in the olive oil or bacon drippings. Combine cooked edamame or tepary beans with the rest of the ingredients in a casserole dish and bake, covered, for 20 minutes. Remove the cover and mash the beans roughly with a fork or potato masher. Return to the oven and bake, uncovered, for an additional 10 minutes, adding a little water if needed to prevent burning.

Servings: 4

PER SERVING:
Total Carb: 13.8g   Fiber: 5.8g   Net Carb: 8.0g
when made with black soybeans; count for tepary beans is not available, but should be similar

Tips and Notes

Eden Organic Black Soybeans® have one net carb in one-half cup.

Raw soybeans are potentially dangerous. Cooked or fermented soybeans pose fewer risks.

According to Tohono O'odham legend, the Milky Way is made of white tepary beans scattered across the sky by Coyote.

MAIN DISHES

CENTER STAGE

This is the easy part for low-carb cooks. Grilled steak, braised chops, and roast turkey are fine, but many of our favorite dishes, like meat loaf, barbecue, casseroles, fajitas, and breaded meats need a makeover. Other recipes are included here because they have an integral high-carb component, such as the vegetables with the pot roast and the Yorkshire pudding and gravy with the rib roast.

Tips and Notes

You may find several different names for pork ribs. Usually the ones labeled as "baby back ribs" come from the loin, and the name doesn't refer to the age of the pig. This cut may, more accurately, be labeled as "back loin ribs."

Spareribs come from the lower portion of the ribcage, below the loin. Spareribs will include a flap of meat on the membrane side, a second set of smaller bones, and part of the breast bone that form the rounded hump on top of the ribs. If this flap (or skirt) and the extra bones have been trimmed away, it is called a St. Louis cut.

Baby back ribs are a more tender cut of meat, but spareribs are meatier and more flavorful. St. Louis style spareribs are easier to carve.

BARBECUED RIBS

To achieve the dark, shiny look that caramelized sugar gives to barbequed ribs, I've added gravy flavoring (like Gravy Master® or Kitchen Bouquet®) to my Barbecue Sauce, and I coat the ribs with no-stick spray before the last 15 minutes of baking and again at the end.

Allow 1 pound of ribs per person. Remove the tough, white, fibrous membrane from the back of the rack. Hold it with a paper towel and you can pull it away. If you are using spareribs, cut off the breast bone, the skirt, and the small bones that form the hump of the rack, leaving just the parallel rib bones. The pieces that are trimmed away can be roasted along with the ribs. Cut the racks into two-rib portions. Sprinkle with salt and pepper and rub with olive oil. Place in a roasting pan, concave side up; cover the pan tightly with aluminum foil and bake at 325° F for 2 hours. Remove the foil. Drain off the pan drippings. Brush the ribs with sugar-free Barbecue Sauce (see p. 218), spray with no-stick spray, and continue to bake, uncovered, for 15 minutes. Turn the ribs and baste the other side with sauce. (Convex side should now be up.) Spray the ribs with no-stick spray and continue to bake for an additional 15 minutes. Spray once more with no-stick spray and serve hot. (⅔ cup of sauce should be enough for 4 pounds of ribs.)

Serving size: 1 pound (before cooking)

PER SERVING:		
Total Carb: 3.6g	Fiber: 0.6g	Net Carb: 3.0g

PULLED PORK

For Pulled Pork sandwiches, cut low-carb pita pockets in half. Butter the inside and place in the toaster. Fill with Pulled Pork and serve with dill pickles and Cole Slaw. Popover cases are also good filled with Pulled Pork as in the recipe for Tuna Melts.

4 to 5 pound boneless pork roast
* Olive oil
2   cups sugar-free Barbecue Sauce (see p. 218)

Heat oven to 275° F. Grease a roasting pan.

Place the pork in a roasting pan, rub with olive oil, cover with foil, and bake for 1 hour. Brush liberally with barbecue sauce. Continue to cook, covered, basting with the pan juices every hour, for a total of 5 hours, or until the temperature tests 180° F with a meat thermometer. Cool the meat long enough to handle and pull it apart. Place the pieces on a cutting board and chop into roughly 1-inch chunks. Return the meat to the pan and add 1 to 1½ cups more barbecue sauce. Return to the oven and bake in the sauce for an additional 30 minutes.

Servings: 12

PER SERVING:		
Total Carb: 3.5g	Fiber: 0.6g	Net Carb: 2.9g

VARIATION:
BEEF OR PORK BARBECUE

This is a great way to use leftover pork from Carnitas (see p. 199) or leftover roast beef.

Shred cooked beef or pork and place in a saucepan. Add Barbecue Sauce to cover. Simmer until heated through.

Tips and Notes

How come they don't make barbecue like they used to? Modern pigs from factory farms, "the other white meat," are much leaner than old-fashioned porkers. Some producers, like Niman Ranch, raise hogs in open pastures without the use of antibiotics or growth hormones. Because the hogs live outdoors in the Midwest, they develop more fat for insulation from summer heat and winter cold, which promotes superior marbling, flavor, and tenderness. See Sources.

MOUSSAKA

Even though I usually cook for two, I make a big pan of Moussaka. We can reheat it for several quick lunches or suppers.

2   globe or 6 Chinese or Japanese eggplants (about 2 pounds)
5   tablespoons olive oil

For the sauce:
1   small onion, peeled and chopped (about ½ cup)
1   pound ground beef or lamb
1   tablespoon tomato paste
¼   teaspoon ground cinnamon
1   fresh tomato, peeled and chopped, or 1 cup diced, canned tomatoes
2   tablespoons fresh parsley, chopped
¼   cup beef broth or water
•   Salt and pepper to taste

For the custard:
2   tablespoons butter
1   cup heavy cream
•   A generous pinch of ground nutmeg
2   eggs, beaten with a fork
•   Salt and pepper to taste

6   tablespoons grated Parmesan cheese

Grease a 9- by 13-inch baking dish.

Peel the eggplant and cut into three-eighth-inch slices. Salt both sides of the slices and place in a colander set over a bowl. Put a heavy dish on top to press out the liquid. Let stand for 30 minutes. Rinse to remove the salt and blot the slices with paper towels until dry. Heat oil for frying in a large skillet and sauté the eggplant on both sides until golden brown. Remove the eggplant and set aside.

To Make the Tomato Sauce:
Add the onion to the pan. Sauté the onion until soft, add the meat, and continue to cook, stirring, until brown. Add the tomato paste, cinnamon, chopped tomato, parsley, broth, salt, and pepper. Simmer the sauce, covered, for 15 minutes.

To Make the Custard:
Heat the butter and cream on low in a small saucepan, while stirring, until smooth. Add the nutmeg. Remove the pan from the heat. Dip out a little of the hot cream mixture and mix with the beaten eggs to temper. Stir the egg mixture back into the pan and blend until smooth. Season with salt and pepper.

(continued on next page)

Fried Halloumi® with lemon slices (Saganaki)

Greek Salad
- -
Moussaka

Roasted Vegetables

Grilled fresh sardines, topped with butter
- -
Kumquats in Syrup and Greek Yogurt

Shortbread Cookies
- -
Wine and Greek Coffee
*

Tips and **Notes**

Visitors to a Greek home are welcomed with a spoonful of home-style preserved fruit presented in a small crystal dish. Spoon sweets, as they are called, are made with whole fruits but have more syrup than regular jam or preserves. The sweets are accompanied by a glass of ice-cold water and perhaps a cup of Greek coffee. This sweet treat may also be used as a topping for ice cream or stirred into yogurt.

MOUSSAKA, CONTINUED

Preheat oven to 350° F.

To Assemble the Moussaka:
Put one-third of the eggplant slices in the bottom of the greased baking dish, cover with one-half of the meat sauce, and sprinkle with 2 tablespoons of the cheese. Make a second layer of eggplant, the rest of the meat sauce, and another 2 tablespoons of cheese. Use the last one-third of the eggplant slices to make the top layer and sprinkle the remaining cheese on top. Pour the custard evenly over the dish and bake at 350° F for about 50 minutes or until brown. Let sit for 5 minutes before cutting.

Servings: 8

PER SERVING:		
Total Carb: 8.4g	Fiber: 3.0g	Net Carb: 5.4g

CARNITAS

- Bone-in, pork roast, 4 to 5 pounds, with a layer of fat on the outside
- Water to cover meat
- 2 teaspoons of salt
- ½ teaspoon dried oregano
- ½ teaspoon dried cumin
- 2 medium onions, roughly chopped
- additional salt and pepper to taste

Put the roast in a deep pot and cover with water. Add other ingredients. Cover, bring to a boil, reduce heat, and simmer on low for 2½ hours.

Remove the meat from the cooking liquid and place in a greased roasting pan. Bake at 350° F for 45 minutes to an hour or until very brown and tender. Take the meat off the bone, roughly chop it, and then tear it into shreds. Serve as barbecued pork or use as filling for tamales or tacos. Skim and reserve the broth to use with the leftover meat to make Carnitas Soup (see p. 84).

Makes 8 to 10 servings.

PER SERVING:		
Total Carb: 0g	Fiber: 0g	Net Carb: 0g

Tips and Notes

You may brush the eggplant slices with olive oil and put them under the broiler rather than sauteeing them in a skillet to speed up the preparation. Be careful not to let thinner slices burn.

It has been my good fortune to be on the receiving end of the legendary hospitality of the Greeks. My husband and I were invited to visit Greece by a Greek friend and his American wife. In addition to entertaining us in their hilltop home overlooking the Saronic Gulf, our friend treated us to a tour of the historic sites and artistic treasures of his native country. He knew all the best restaurants and tavernas on the route, most of them with panoramic views of the pristine coastline and the blue, blue waters of the Aegean. A typical meal started with plate after plate of cold appetizers: eggplant salad, marinated octopus, Greek salad, tzatziki, taramossalata, cheese, olives, bread, and wine. Next came the hot dishes: fried calamari, eggplant with tomatoes and onions, tiny grilled fish, vegetable dishes, cheese dishes, savory pastries, and more bread and wine. Then, after we had eaten our fill, our host would say, "Now, what would you like for dinner?"

EGGPLANT CASSEROLE

A lot like lasagna. I confess that I usually use canned pasta sauce to which I add browned ground beef. Omit the meat and add a little olive oil for a vegetarian version or to use as a side dish.

I find Dorot frozen garlic, ginger, and herbs to be a great time saver—no more measuring, washing, peeling, and chopping, and although the herbs are not exactly like fresh, they will do in a pinch. They are sold at Trader Joes stores in the US. Dorot sells frozen crushed garlic, chopped basil, chopped coriander, chopped dill, chopped parsley, and crushed ginger in trays of 20 cubes each. See Sources.

6   Japanese or Chinese eggplants or 2 regular ones
3   tablespoons oil

Tomato sauce with meat:
1   pound lean ground beef
1   small onion, peeled and chopped (about ½ cup)
2   cloves garlic, minced, or 2 teaspoons of garlic paste
2   (8-ounce) cans tomato sauce
1   (15-ounce) can chopped tomatoes
4   tablespoons fresh parsley, chopped, or 2 tablespoons dried
2   teaspoons fresh basil, chopped, or 1 teaspoon dried
1   teaspoon salt
½   teaspoon pepper

½   cup grated Parmesan cheese
1   cup shredded mozzarella cheese (4 ounces)
¼   cup shaved Parmesan cheese to garnish
    (or use more grated)
•   Fresh basil leaves, shredded, for garnish

Grease a 9- by 13-inch casserole dish. Preheat oven to 350° F.

Peel the eggplant and cut it into three-eighth-inch slices. Salt both sides of the slices and place in a colander set over a bowl. Put a heavy dish on top to press out the liquid. Let stand for 30 minutes. Rinse to remove the salt and blot the slices with paper towels until dry.

Cook the ground beef in a skillet until it is no longer pink. Add onion and garlic, if using, and cook until the onion is softened and the meat is brown. Drain. Add the tomato sauce and tomatoes, including the liquid, the garlic paste, if using, the parsley, basil, and salt and pepper. Simmer uncovered, stirring occasionally, until thick (like spaghetti sauce), about 45 minutes.

Meanwhile, heat the oil in a skillet or on a griddle and sauté the eggplant slices on both sides until golden brown, adding extra oil between batches if necessary. Or brush slices with oil and grill, turning to brown both sides. Eggplant slices can also be placed on a broiler pan and browned under the broiler.

(continued on next page)

To assemble:
Place a layer of eggplant slices in the bottom of the casserole dish. Spread with a layer of tomato sauce and sprinkle with mozzarella and Parmesan cheese. Repeat until all the slices are used, ending with sauce and cheese.

Bake at 350° F for 30 to 40 minutes or until bubbly and brown. Let sit for 5 minutes before cutting. Garnish with shredded fresh basil leaves and thin shavings of Parmesan cheese.

Servings: 8

PER SERVING:		
Total Carb: 13.2g	Fiber: 3.7g	Net Carb: 9.5g

MEAT LOAF

1   tablespoon olive oil
¼   cup onion, chopped
¼   cup red or green pepper, chopped
1   pound lean ground beef
1   wasa-type cracker, crushed or processed into fine crumbs
1   tablespoon cream
1   tablespoon water
2   cloves fresh garlic, chopped, or 2 teaspoons of garlic paste
1   large egg
2   tablespoons sugar-free Barbecue Sauce (see p. 218)
2   teaspoons Worcestershire sauce
1   teaspoon salt
½   teaspoon pepper
•   Additional ¼ cup Barbecue Sauce for top of loaves
•   No-stick spray

Cook the onion and pepper in the oil until slightly softened. Mix all ingredients together in a bowl. Shape into two oval mounds on a greased roasting pan. Spread additional barbecue sauce over the loaves to cover, and spray with no-stick spray. Bake at 350° F for 35 to 45 minutes or until brown.

Servings: 4

PER SERVING:		
Total Carb: 7.9g	Fiber: 1.1g	Net Carb: 6.8g

VARIATION:
Meatballs

Form the Meat Loaf mixture into small meatballs. Fry in oil, in several batches, for 3 to 4 minutes until brown and firm. Serve on wooden picks with warmed sugar-free Barbecue Sauce (see p. 218) for dipping.

Steaks and chops should be close to room temperature before grilling or they will not cook evenly.

A steak's internal temperature should not exceed 135° because beyond that it is losing moisture.

Food science writer Harold McGee used computer simulations to discover the best way to cook a steak. Contrary to popular opinion, he discovered that searing meat does not seal in the juices; it does just the opposite - it dries them out. He says the best way to cook a steak is to continually flip it as it cooks so the heat diffuses evenly. The optimal interval between turns in 15 seconds, but every 30 seconds is adequate. A study from Lawrence Livermore National Laboratory showed that steaks cooked in this way are also more healthful with a reduction in carcinogenic compounds of 75 percent.[1] Marinating meat before cooking also seems to prevent the formation of harmful chemicals.

1 Daniel Zwerdling, "15 Seconds of Flame - A Steaks Own Story," *Gourmet Magazine*, October 2001.

GRILLED STEAK WITH CHIMICHURRI SAUCE

This tangy, garlic and herb sauce from Argentina is the perfect compliment for smoky grilled meats.

Make Chimichurri Sauce and let stand at room temperature for an hour or two. Trim excess fat from tender steaks, such as strip, T-bone, or porterhouse, and bring steaks up to room temperature. Season both sides with salt and pepper. Heat grill to high.

Grill steaks, turning frequently, until cooked to desired doneness. Time will vary depending on thickness of steak and distance from heat source. (A one-inch-thick steak, 5 or 6 inches from hot coals, will take about 6 minutes total for rare or about 8 minutes for medium/rare.) Use an instant-read thermometer, inserted into the side of the meat, not touching fat or bone, to check doneness: 130° F indicates rare; 135° F (medium/rare) is the maximum for juicy, tender meat (140° and above—shoe leather). Tent meat with foil and let stand for 5 to 10 minutes to reabsorb juices. Serve with Chimichurri Sauce.

Chimichurri Sauce:
1   cup flat-leaf parsley
6   cloves garlic (about 1 ounce)
1   teaspoon dried oregano or 1 tablespoon fresh
½   teaspoon of freshly ground black pepper
1   teaspoon of red pepper flakes, or to taste
1   teaspoon of salt
½   cup of red wine vinegar
1   cup of extra virgin olive oil

Measure parsley after discarding thick stems. Peel garlic cloves. Place parsley and garlic in food processor and pulse until finely chopped or chop by hand. Add other ingredients and process until blended or whisk together until emulsified and smooth. Let stand for an hour at room temperature. Whisk again before serving. Use as a sauce or marinade for grilled meat or fish. Store extra sauce, covered, in refrigerator.

Makes 2 cups

SERVING SIZE: One steak with 2 tablespoons of sauce.

PER SERVING:		
Total Carb: 1.2g	Fiber: 0.3g	Net Carb: 0.9g

OVEN FRIED CHICKEN

This is a great way to make chicken for family picnics or barbecues. It is crunchy, juicy, delicious, and, best of all, easy!

5   ounces packaged pork rinds (2 cups of crumbs)
8   pieces chicken
•   Salt and pepper
3   egg whites
¼   cup cream
¼   cup oil
¼   cup butter

Process the pork rinds in the bowl of a food processor until finely ground. You will need about 2 cups of processed crumbs. Dry the chicken and sprinkle with salt and pepper. In a medium-sized bowl, beat the egg whites with a fork until foamy and beat in the cream. Dip the chicken in the egg white and cream mixture, and then roll in pork-rind crumbs until evenly coated. Place on a rack to dry for 15 minutes.

Preheat oven to 425° F.

Place the oil and butter in a 9- by 12-inch roasting pan. Put the pan in the preheated oven until the butter is melted. Place the chicken in the pan, skin side down, and bake for 30 minutes. Turn the chicken and bake for an additional 30 minutes, or until well browned and crisp.

Servings: 8

PER SERVING:		
Total Carb: trace	Fiber: 0g	Net Carb: trace

PAN SEARED DUCK BREAST

Score the skin on duck breasts in a diamond pattern, cutting through the skin but not into the meat. Season both sides of the duck breasts with salt. Place skin-side-down in a skillet, preheated to low to medium/low heat (300° to 325° F). Cook for about 10 minutes or until skin is starting to brown. Pour off the fat. Raise heat to medium/high (400° F) and cook for about 5 minutes more until the skin is very deep brown and crisp, and the fat is rendered, pouring off the fat as it accumulates. Turn breasts over, and cook for another minute for rare or slightly longer for medium-rare. Let stand for a few minutes to reabsorb the juices. Slice horizontally and serve hot. The meat should be red like a rare steak.

DINNER MENU:

Peanut Soup
--
Oven Fried Chicken

Cheese Polenta

Southern Greens

Baked Rhubarb with Strawberry Sauce
--
Peach Cobbler
*

Boneless, skin-on, duck breasts are available from Maple Leaf Farms (see Sources).

KOREAN BEEF IN LETTUCE CUPS

Many dishes from the Far East are served in a lettuce-leaf wrapper. The lettuce leaves should be well dried and ice cold. I prefer the Boston-type lettuce to the more traditional iceberg because it is a little softer and less likely to break.

1½ pounds boneless beef sirloin

Marinade:
1   tablespoon sesame seeds
1   clove garlic, peeled
4   tablespoons soy sauce
2   tablespoons water
3   tablespoons granular Splenda®
½   teaspoon fresh ginger, grated
2   tablespoons sesame oil
2   tablespoons oil for stir-frying

1   head of Boston or Bibb lettuce (6 leaves)

Bulgogi Sauce:
1   tablespoon hot bean paste (available with the Asian foods
    at some groceries or from an Asian specialty store.
    See Uwajimaya in Sources to order.)
1   tablespoon sesame seeds, toasted
1   tablespoon sesame oil
1   tablespoon granular Splenda®
2   tablespoons cider vinegar

Vegetables:
6   green onions
3   medium zucchini (about 1 pound)
1   tablespoon vegetable oil for frying
1   small onion, thinly sliced
1   clove garlic, minced
⅛   teaspoon crushed red pepper flakes

To prepare the meat filling:
Freeze the meat for 20 minutes to facilitate slicing. Cut it into thin slices. Lightly crush the sesame seeds and the garlic and combine with the soy, water, Splenda®, ginger, and sesame oil. Pour over the meat in a glass dish, cover, and refrigerate for 8 hours or overnight.

(continued on next page)

"Tomatoes and oregano make it Italian; wine and tarragon make it French. Sour cream makes it Russian; lemon and cinnamon make it Greek. Soy sauce makes it Chinese; garlic makes it good."

—Alice May Brock
Alice's Restaurant Cookbook, 1969

KOREAN BEEF IN LETTUCE CUPS, CONTINUED

To prepare the lettuce cups:
Remove the outer layer of leaves from a head of Boston or Bibb lettuce and reserve for another use. Cut through the thick mid ribs of the next layer of leaves where they join the core. Hold the head, core facing up, under running water, and let the water flow under the leaves to separate them from the head. Repeat for each layer. This way you can remove the cupped inner leaves intact without tearing them. Blot the lettuce leaves carefully with towels and refrigerate until needed.

For the sauce:
Mix the sauce ingredients together until smooth. Store, covered, in the refrigerator, but bring up to room temperature before serving.

For the vegetables:
Shred the green onions and reserve. Slice the zucchini crosswise into half-inch rounds, and then cut each slice into three pieces. Heat the vegetable oil over medium-high heat in a skillet and fry the zucchini until softened and brown. Remove the zucchini from the pan and set aside. Fry the sliced onions and minced garlic with the pepper flakes until tender. Add the green onions and combine the mixture with the reserved zucchini.

For the meat:
Remove the meat from the marinade with a slotted spoon. Drain on paper towels to reduce splattering when meat is added to the hot pan. Heat a large, heavy skillet over medium-high heat. Stir-fry the meat in several small batches for about 2 minutes or grill over hot coals for about 1 minute per side.

To serve:
Place some of the meat and vegetables on a lettuce leaf. Spoon a small amount of sauce over the filling and roll up.

Servings: 6

PER SERVING:		
Total Carb: 6.4g	Fiber: 1.7g	Net Carb: 4.7g

"My favorite animal is steak."
—Fran Lebowitz

LAMB CURRY

The leftover meat from a roast leg of lamb makes a dish whose second incarnation is even better than the first. If you prefer something more like the traditional rice accompaniment with this, use Mexican style hominy that has been chopped in a food processor. (See p. 175 for Hominy "Rice.") It looks and tastes remarkably like brown rice. Personally, I find the crunchy texture of Spaghetti Squash to be excellent with the lamb curry; in fact, real rice seems boring by comparison.

For the curry:
½ cup sugar-free Dried Cranberries (see p. 105)
2 tablespoons granular Splenda®
½ cup water
2 tablespoons butter
1 medium-sized tart apple, peeled and sliced
½ onion, peeled and sliced
1 clove garlic, crushed
1 tablespoon yellow curry powder
1 tablespoon lemon juice
• Grated zest (thin yellow skin) of ½ a lemon
10 ounces beef broth
1 teaspoon gravy flavoring (like Kitchen Bouquet®)
3 whole cloves
½ teaspoon cornstarch or ¼ teaspoon potato flour
2 cups cubed cooked lamb
• Salt and pepper to taste

Serve over:
4 cups prepared Spaghetti Squash (see p. 160) or Hominy "Rice" (see p. 175)

Condiments to spoon on top:
½ cup toasted, sliced almonds
½ cup toasted, unsweetened coconut
½ cup Shallot and Peach or Rhubarb Ginger Chutney (see Index for recipes)
2 star fruit, chopped, seeded, sprinkled with Splenda®, and sautéed in butter

Heat the cranberries in a saucepan or in the microwave with the water and Splenda® until they are plump and the water is almost absorbed. (If any water is left, add it to the pan when you add the cranberries.) Reserve.

(continued on next page)

"The very discovery of the New World was the by-product of a dietary quest."

—Arthur M. Schlesinger, Jr., *Paths to the Present*, 1949 (Columbus was seeking the spices of the Orient.)

LAMB CURRY, CONTINUED

In a large skillet, sauté the apple, onion, and garlic in butter until soft. Stir in the curry powder and cook, stirring, until the apple and onion start to brown. Stir in the reserved cranberries and any liquid, the lemon juice and zest, the broth, gravy flavoring, and cloves. Simmer for 20 minutes. Remove the garlic and cloves. Dissolve the cornstarch in a little cold water and stir in or add the potato flour. Simmer until slightly thickened. Stir in the lamb and heat through. Serve on Spaghetti Squash or processed Hominy "Rice." Pass the condiments in individual dishes to be spooned over the curry.

Servings: 4

> **PER SERVING:**
> Total Carb: 8.1g   Fiber: 1.7g   Net Carb: 6.4g
> count is for curry only —does not include squash, hominy, or condiments

STANDING BEEF RIB ROAST

- A 6- to 6½-pound rib roast (4-rib)
- Salt and pepper to taste

Take the roast out of the refrigerator and let stand at room temperature for 1 to 1½ hours.

Position oven rack in lower third of oven. Preheat oven to 450° F. Grease a roasting pan and rack well so it will release the browned glaze after cooking.

Rub roast with salt and pepper. Place, fat side up, on a rack in a roasting pan. Roast in preheated oven for 20 minutes. Reduce the heat to 350° F and continue to roast for about 1½ hours more or until an instant-read thermometer inserted into the center of the roast (not touching fat or bone) reads the correct temperature: 125° F for very rare; 130° F for medium rare. Remove roast from pan and place on cutting board; tent with foil and let rest for 15 minutes before carving.

Make Pan Gravy or Meat Gravy to accompany the roast. Yorkshire Pudding is a traditional accompaniment (see Index for recipes).

Serving size: ½ to 1 pound

> **PER SERVING:**
> Total Carb: 0g   Fiber: 0g   Net Carb: 0g

"My doctor told me to quit having intimate dinners for four. Unless there are three other people."

—Orson Welles

"When mighty roast beef was the Englishman's food, it ennobled our hearts and enriched our blood. Our soldiers were brave and our courtiers were good. Oh! The roast beef of England."

—Henry Fielding, Grub Street Opera (act III, scene 2)

SESAME PORK

VARIATION:

Citrus Pork

Replace the marinade for Sesame Pork with:

- Zest of 1 lime
- ¼ cup lime juice
- Zest of 1 lemon
- ¼ cup lemon juice
- 2 tablespoons balsamic vinegar
- 3 cloves of garlic, peeled and crushed
- 1 teaspoon of dried thyme
- Salt and pepper to taste
- ¼ cup olive oil

Garnish with lime wedges.

Makes 4 servings.

Per Serving:
Total Carb: 4.3g
Fiber: 0.1g
Net Carb: 4.2

1½ pounds pork tenderloin
½ cup soy sauce
2 tablespoons sesame oil
2 tablespoons balsamic vinegar
2 teaspoons fresh ginger, peeled and grated
3 cloves garlic, peeled and crushed
1 tablespoon granular Splenda®
¼ cup toasted sesame seeds

Soak twelve to fifteen wooden skewers in water for an hour or more. Place the pork in the freezer until partially frozen to facilitate slicing.

Cut the tenderloins in half across the grain, and then slice lengthwise into quarter-inch thick slices. Thread the meat onto skewers. Combine the rest of the ingredients in a large, non-reactive, rectangular dish. Add the meat skewers, turn to coat both sides, and cover with plastic wrap. Place in the refrigerator to marinate for three hours or overnight.

Preheat the grill.

Remove the skewers of pork from the marinade and drain, reserving the liquid. Grill them for 2 to 3 minutes on each side over hot coals, brushing with the marinade and turning once.

Bring the remaining marinade to a boil and serve as a sauce with the meat if desired.

Servings: 4

PER SERVING:		
Total Carb: 4.8g	Fiber: 1.3g	**Net Carb: 3.5g**
count includes all of marinade		

A Porcine Riddle:

Who am I,
My health
assured,
I'm always killed,
Before I'm cured.

—JBB

Pot Roast with Vegetables

This is like my mom's pot roast with rutabaga and pumpkin pretending to be the potatoes and carrots. Of course you can substitute any combination of non-starchy vegetables that are available.

- A 3- to 4-pound beef pot roast (chuck, rump, or round)
- Low-carb Flour Mix, see p. 116, or use half soy flour and half wheat bran
- Salt and pepper
- Olive oil

1 cup water or broth
1 teaspoon Worcestershire sauce
3 small rutabagas (about 1 pound), peeled and cut into 2-inch chunks
2 walnuts in the shell
2 wedges lemon with peel
1 bulb fresh fennel (or use 1 cup celery)
1 small onion, peeled and cut into quarters
6 to 8 cloves garlic or 3 or 4 shallots, peeled
2 cups fresh pumpkin, peeled and cut into 2- to 3-inch chunks
2 tablespoons sugar-free Barbecue Sauce or sugar-free Ketchup (see Index for recipes)

Dust the roast lightly with flour mixture, salt, and pepper. Brown it in olive oil in a large roasting pan. Add 1 cup of water or broth and the Worcestershire sauce to the pan; cover and place in a 325° F oven for 2 hours.

Meanwhile, simmer the rutabaga in a generous amount of water with the walnuts and lemon for 15 minutes. Drain. Discard lemon and walnuts.

After the roast has cooked for 2 hours, place drained rutabaga and other vegetables in the roasting pan with the meat. Spoon the barbecue sauce and pan drippings over the meat and vegetables. Continue to cook, covered, stirring the vegetables and basting occasionally, for 1 hour longer or until the vegetables are tender and browned. Correct the seasoning and serve.

Servings: 8

PER SERVING:		
Total Carb: 10.5g	Fiber: 2.9g	Net Carb: 7.6g

Tips and Notes

The low-carb flour substitute from Big Skies Farm (see Sources) works well as a coating for chops, roasts, and cutlets. It gives a crisp brown crust. (Don't use it to make the gravy —it doesn't thicken liquids.)

> "Vegetables are interesting but lack a sense of purpose when unaccompanied by a good cut of meat."
>
> —Fran Lebowitz

FISH AND SEAFOOD

Look at your hands—we are the only primates with webbed digits. It is clear that we are, by design or by adaptation, meant to live in close proximity to water. Fish and seafood have been staples in our diet since prehistoric times and continue to be important to a healthy diet today. One caveat: much of the world's supply of fish contains high concentrations of heavy metals and toxins. Because big fish eat little fish and the toxins add up, when it comes to fish, smaller is better.

Wild, cold-water fish are preferable to Tropical and farm-raised. The fish that need to store up fat for long migrations in cold water provide more Omega-3 oils. Perhaps it is their ability to stay flexible in icy water that makes fish oil so beneficial for arthritic joints. I keep a supply of frozen wild salmon patties in the freezer; they can be heated in a skillet without thawing to use like burgers or broken up for a stir-fry. Sardines from a can and fish oil capsules are another option if you don't have access to fresh fish.

Tips and Notes

Dermatologist, Dr. Nicholas Perricone, puts wild salmon at the top of the list of foods for total body rejuvenation. His Three-Day Nutritional Face-lift™ requires that you eat salmon twice a day for three days "for the effects of the DMAE, astaxathin and the essential fatty acids in the salmon to take effect."

PAN SEARED WILD SALMON

One of the advantages of living in the Northwest is our abundance of fresh, wild salmon. There is a world of difference in the taste as well as the health benefits of wild salmon compared to farm raised, which are fed on fish meal and grain products with artificial color and antibiotics added. See Sources for information about ordering fresh wild salmon for overnight delivery. Serve it with Rhubarb Ginger Chutney (see p. 231).

4   skin-on wild salmon fillets
1   tablespoon oil
•   Salt and pepper

Sprinkle the salmon with salt and pepper. Heat a heavy skillet over high heat for 3 minutes. Add the oil to the pan. When the oil starts to shimmer (but before it starts to smoke), add the fillets, skin side down, and cook without moving them for 30 seconds. Reduce the heat to medium-high and continue to cook until the skin side is well browned and the bottom half of each fillet is opaque, about 4 to 5 minutes. Turn and cook, again without moving, until the fillets are no longer translucent and they are firm, but not hard, to the touch, 3½ to 4½ minutes longer. Remove the fillets from the pan and let stand for a minute before serving.

Servings: 4

PER SERVING:		
Total Carb: 0g	Fiber: 0g	Net Carb: 0g

CREAMED SALMON

Not really "creamed" since I use Greek yogurt to make an instant sauce for this spicy and delicious dish. I keep salmon patties in the freezer so I can make this whenever I need a quick, healthful meal. I serve it over Dreamfields™ pasta.

2   tablespoons olive oil
½   cup chopped onion
½   cup chopped red bell pepper
1   pound salmon or other firm fish, boned and cut or broken into roughly 1-inch pieces
2   cloves garlic, minced
2   teaspoons red pepper flakes
1   tablespoon chopped fresh parsley
1   teaspoon salt
1   cup Greek yogurt (plain yogurt with live cultures)
½   cup grated Parmesan cheese

Heat the oil in a large skillet on medium heat. Add the onion and red bell pepper to the pan and cook until softened, about 2 minutes. Add the salmon and cook, stirring, for 3 to 5 minutes, or until fish is almost done. Add the garlic, red pepper flakes, parsley, and salt and cook and stir for a minute or two more. Turn heat to low and stir in yogurt. Cook, stirring, until smooth and hot. Sprinkle with grated Parmesan and serve.

Servings: 4

PER SERVING:		
Total Carb: 4.4g	Fiber: 0.8g	Net Carb: 3.6g

count excludes the milk sugar that has been converted to lactic acid by the live culture in the yogurt

Tips and Notes

Fermented dairy products with live cultures must list the same number of carbs as the milk that goes into them, but, according to Drs. Jack Goldberg and Karen O'Mara, authors of the Go-Diet[2], most of the sugar has been converted to lactic acid. The amount of carbohydrate remaining is about 4 grams per cup. Cultured dairy products such as buttermilk, yogurt, and kefir provide "good" bacteria for the digestive system that can usually be tolerated even by those who are lactose-intolerant.

2 Jack Goldberg, Ph.D., and Karen O'Mara, D.O., *GO-Diet: The Goldberg-O'Mara Diet Plan, the Key to Weight Loss & Healthy Eating*, Go Corp, 1999.

Let the salmon fillets rest at room temperature for about 15 minutes before cooking so they are not icy cold in the middle.

"Fish is the only food that is considered spoiled once it smells like what it is."

—P. J. O'Rourke

SLOW-COOKED WILD SALMON

Moist, tender, and delicate, and nothing could be easier. Bake and serve in an ovenproof dish and there's not even a pan to wash.

- Oil for the baking dish
- 4 salmon fillets, about 6 ounces each and $3/4$- to 1-inch thick
- Salt

Preheat the oven to 250° F. Grease an ovenproof baking dish.

Season both sides of fillets with salt. Put in baking dish and bake in preheated oven for about 25 minutes. The fish is done when it is just barely opaque. It should be slightly rare but uniform in color all the way through. (This preparation preserves nutrients and the flavor and texture are superb, but be aware that the FDA recommends cooking fish to an internal temperature of 145° F.)

Servings: 4

PER SERVING:		
Total Carb: 0g	Fiber: 0g	Net Carb: 0g

Note:

Fish advisories from the US Environmental Protection Agency are available at: http://epa.gov/waterscience/fish/states.htm. Click on the map to find a guide to fish safety in your area.

COURT-BOUILLON LOUISIANA

A roux is a mixture of flour and fat, cooked slowly over low heat. A white, blonde, or brown roux is the base for many Cajun and Creole dishes. Potato flour makes a delicious roux that tastes authentic, but because you need less, it contributes fewer carbs than flour.

2   tablespoons butter
1   teaspoon potato flour, or use 1 tablespoon of all purpose flour and add 0.6 net carbs per serving.
1   cup onion, chopped (4 ounces)
1   clove garlic, minced
½   teaspoon dried thyme
1   teaspoon dried parsley
½   teaspoon of allspice
1   Turkish bay leaf
½   teaspoon of crushed red pepper flakes (optional)
2   cups water
½   cup dry red wine
1   (14 ½-ounce) can of crushed tomatoes, including the juice
2   pounds of red snapper, boned, and cut into bite-sized pieces
1   tablespoon of lemon juice
½   teaspoon salt
¼   teaspoon pepper

Melt the butter in a heavy pot on low heat. Add the flour and stir until slightly colored, 10 to 15 minutes. Add the onions and continue to cook for a few minutes until the onion is softened. Add the garlic, thyme, parsley, allspice, bay leaves, and red pepper, if using. Cook and stir for a few minutes more. Add the water, wine, and tomatoes. Simmer for 1 hour. Add the fish, lemon juice, and salt and pepper. Simmer for 15 minutes. Serve over Hominy Rice (see p. 175) or Deamfields™ pasta, if desired.

Servings: 6

PER SERVING:		
Total Carb: 6.5g	Fiber: 1.1g	Net Carb: 5.4g

Tips and Notes

I keep a pair of tweezers in my kitchen drawer to use to remove the bones from fish before cooking. It takes only a few minutes: drape the filet over an up-side-down bowl so the bones will pop up; they are lined up neatly in a row, making them easy to remove.

HOT TUNA SALAD

VARIATION:

Hot Chicken Salad

Substitute 2 cups cooked chicken, cubed, for the tuna.

Hominy "Rice" (see p. 175) or Dreamfields™ pasta can be used instead of spaghetti squash in this hearty lunch or supper dish.

- ½ cup sliced almonds
- • Olive oil or butter to sauté the almonds
- 3 (6-ounce) cans of tuna, drained
- 1 cup sliced celery
- 2 Hard-cooked Eggs, diced (see p. 65)
- 1½ cups cooked Spaghetti Squash, roughly chopped (see p. 160)
- ¾ cup real mayonnaise
- ¼ cup cream
- 2 teaspoons onion, grated or finely chopped
- ¼ teaspoon dry mustard
- ½ teaspoon curry powder or more to taste
- • Salt and pepper
- 1 tablespoon lemon juice

Preheat oven to 350° F.

Sauté the almonds in oil or butter until just starting to brown. Reserve half for topping. Mix the rest of the ingredients together and place in a greased casserole. Top with the reserved almonds. Bake for 20 to 25 minutes or until bubbly and brown.

Servings: 6

PER SERVING:		
Total Carb: 4.8g	Fiber: 1.7g	Net Carb: 3.1g

MACADAMIA COCONUT CRUSTED SHRIMP

If you really want to impress someone, this will do it! This amount will serve two or three as a main course or four to six as an appetizer.

½ cup pork rind crumbs (¼ of a 5-ounce package)
⅔ cup unsweetened, shredded coconut
⅔ cup macadamia nuts, chopped
1 teaspoon granular Splenda®
1 pound raw shrimp, extra jumbo (16 to 20 per pound) or colossal (10 to 15 per pound)
• Salt and pepper
2 large egg whites
3 tablespoons cream
• Oil for deep frying

Process the pork rinds in the bowl of a food processor until fine. Toast the nuts for a few minutes in the oven, especially if they have been frozen. Chop the nuts by hand so they retain a little texture. Stir together the pork rinds, macadamia nuts, coconut, and Splenda®.

Peel the shrimp, leaving the last shell segment and tail intact. Make a cut down the center of the back that goes almost all the way through. Remove the black vein. Rinse and dry well. Spread open to butterfly the shrimp. Sprinkle with salt and pepper. Beat the egg whites with a fork until foamy. Beat in the cream. Dip the shrimp into the egg whites and roll in the nut mixture to coat. Place on a rack to dry for a few minutes. Deep fry a few shrimp at a time in oil heated to 360° F for about 3 minutes or until brown and crisp. Serve with Sweet and Spicy Sauce (see p. 224) for dipping.

Servings: 3 as a main course

PER SERVING:
Total Carb: 8.7g   Fiber: 5.3g   Net Carb: 3.4g
    count includes all of the crumb mixture

Tips and Notes

Fried pork rinds, also called chicharrones, can be found with the chips or on the Mexican food aisle at the grocery store. They have no carbs and almost no fat, just a small amount of protein. They can be used for munching, as a replacement for crackers with soup or chili, or as crunchy croutons for soup or salad, as well as breading for fried foods.

SAUCES

FLUID FLOURISHES

If food is an art, the French are the old masters. And what is it that they do so well? Sauces! It's the sauces that take a meal from ordinary to sublime, and all the classic ingredients for great sauces like cream, butter, cheese, oils, eggs, herbs, and spices are low carb. We can be extravagant with sauces that add color, depth, texture, contrast, and variety to turn a simple meal into a sumptuous feast.

Tips and Notes

There are several theories about the origin of the word barbecue, but it is generally agreed that it came from the native Taino people of the Caribbean who cooked game and fish on wooden racks set over fire pits. The Spaniards called it barbecoa. Barbecue has come to describe a method of slow cooking using indirect heat and smoke. Barbecue is never rare, but falling-off-the-bone tender, with the connective tissue and fat melted away. In northern Mexico, the meat was served in soft flour tortillas like tacos. The term has come to mean the meat, the apparatus for cooking it, the process of cooking in this way, and the social gathering where the meat is served.

BARBECUE SAUCE

The main ingredient in most barbecue sauces is sugar; if you read the label, you will find that even the "dry rubs" for ribs contain a lot of brown sugar. Here's a recipe for a basting sauce that is every bit as good that has no sugar. Without the gravy flavoring, it is bright red; with it, it looks more like what we're used to. I like to make a double batch of sauce and keep it in the refrigerator to use on pork chops, Meat Loaf, Pulled Pork, and of course, Barbecued Ribs. (See Index for these recipes.)

½ onion, finely chopped (about 3 ounces)
2   tablespoons olive oil
2   cloves garlic, chopped or 2 teaspoons garlic paste
2   (8-oz) cans tomato sauce
1   teaspoon Worcestershire sauce
2   teaspoons liquid smoke, hickory- or mesquite-flavored
1   teaspoon Tabasco® sauce
½ teaspoon gravy flavoring (like Kitchen Bouquet® or Gravy Master®)
¼ cup granular Splenda®
½ cup cider vinegar
½ teaspoon garlic oil (optional)
½ teaspoon salt
¼ teaspoon pepper

Sauté the onion in the olive oil. Add the chopped garlic, if using, and sauté a little longer. Mix in the other ingredients and simmer, uncovered, on low heat for 30 minutes. Purée in a food processor if you prefer a smooth sauce.

Serving size: 2 tablespoons

PER SERVING:		
Total Carb: 2.4g	Fiber: 0.3g	Net Carb: 2.1g

COCONUT CURRY SAUCE

Excellent served hot over poached chicken.

1   cup canned coconut milk
1   tablespoon yellow curry powder
1   tablespoon granular Splenda®
1/4 teaspoon salt
1/4 teaspoon crushed red pepper flakes
2   teaspoons lime juice
1   tablespoon chopped fresh basil

Bring the coconut milk and curry powder to a boil in a small saucepan. Simmer, while stirring, for 4 minutes. Add the other ingredients and simmer for 1 minute more.

Servings: 4 (1/4 cup each)

PER SERVING:		
Total Carb: 2.9g	Fiber: 0.8g	Net Carb: 2.1g

BROWN SAUCE

2   tablespoons butter or bacon fat
1   chopped shallot (about 1 ounce) or a little chopped onion
2 1/4 teaspoons potato flour (Add an extra 1/2 teaspoonful for a thicker sauce.)
1   cup beef stock
1/4 teaspoon salt
1/8 teaspoon pepper

Melt the butter or bacon fat in a saucepan, add the shallot or onion, and cook on low heat until the butter is browned. Stir in the potato flour. Gradually stir in the broth. Bring to a boil and simmer for 2 minutes. Taste and correct the seasoning. Strain to remove the shallot or onion. Keep hot on very low heat or in the top of a double boiler until ready to serve.

Servings: 4 (1/4 cup each)

PER SERVING:		
Total Carb: 2.1g	Fiber: 0g	Net Carb: 2.1g

Poached Chicken

4   skinless, boneless chicken breast halves, about 1 1/2 pounds
•   Salt
4   cups of water
3/4 teaspoon of salt

Sprinkle both sides of the chicken breasts with salt. Let stand at room temperature for 15 minutes. Heat water and salt to a boil in a large saucepan. Add chicken and reduce heat to simmer. Cook, uncovered, for 6 minutes. Remove the pan from the heat. Cover the pan and let stand for 20 minutes, or until the chicken is just cooked, but still very moist and tender. Cut into the thickest part of one of the pieces to check. If it is still pink, leave it in the hot liquid for another 5 minutes. Store in the refrigerator, covered with some of the poaching liquid, until needed. Use hot or cold for main dishes, salads, enchiladas, tacos, and soups.

Umami, also called the fifth taste, is a Japanese word that has no English equivalent, used to describe the taste of delicious protein foods. A savory pan gravy comes as close to a translation as we can get.

Grease the pan before cooking roast beef or turkey so it will release the pan juices and the browned glaze.

PAN GRAVY

Unthickened pan gravy, what the French call au jus, has become a popular choice to accompany roast beef.

After removing the roast from the pan, spoon off most of the fat. Add ¼ cup of boiling water to the roasting pan. Scrape and stir to incorporate the browned bits and caramelized drippings from the pan. Cook over low heat until blended. Add more hot water for thinner gravy. Season to taste with salt and pepper.

MEAT GRAVY

After removing the roasted meat from the pan, drain or spoon off the fat and reserve. Add ¼ cup of boiling water to the roasting pan and scrape and stir to incorporate the browned bits and caramelized drippings. Add more water if necessary to make 1 cup of liquid. Measure 2 tablespoonfuls of the reserved fat into a saucepan and heat on low. Add 2¼ teaspoonfuls of potato flour to the fat and stir on low heat until lightly browned. Gradually stir in the pan drippings from the roasting pan. Simmer for 2 minutes. Taste before adding salt and pepper to correct the seasoning. Keep gravy hot on very low heat or in the top of a double boiler until ready to serve.

Servings: 4 (¼ cup each)

PER SERVING:		
Total Carb: 1.7g	Fiber: 0g	Net Carb: 1.7g

BASIC CREAM SAUCE

For a really quick sauce, leave out the onion, celery, and spices and use a bullion cube dissolved in a cup of water instead of the broth. (Caveat: most bullion cubes contain MSG and sugar.)

1	cup chicken broth
1	small Turkish bay leaf
1	small celery stalk with leaves
1	small onion, peeled and cut into quarters
1	whole clove
2	whole peppercorns, crushed
½	teaspoon salt
1	cup cream
4	tablespoons butter
4½	teaspoons potato flour

Place the broth in a medium saucepan with the bay leaf, celery, onion, clove, peppercorns, and salt. Simmer for 15 minutes. Remove from the heat and stir in the cream. Return to the burner and heat just to a simmer; remove the pan from the heat and let stand, covered, for 5 minutes.

Melt the butter on low heat in another saucepan. Add the potato flour and cook, stirring, for a minute or so, but do not let it brown. Remove the pan from the heat. Strain the warm cream mixture and add it slowly to the pan with the butter and potato flour while stirring. Place the pan back on the heat and simmer for 5 minutes or until it is thickened, stirring frequently. Add additional salt and white pepper to taste.

Servings: 8 (¼ cup each)

PER SERVING:		
Total Carb: 1.5g	Fiber: 0g	Net Carb: 1.5g

Tips and Notes

Potato flour turns out to be one of the best choices for thickening sauces. It is higher in carbohydrates than wheat flour, but you need only one third the amount. It is also higher than cornstarch, but you need only half the amount, so there is still an advantage.

Use 1⅓ teaspoonfuls of potato flour to thicken 1 cup of liquid for a light sauce. Use more for a thicker sauce. Double the amount (to 2⅔ teaspoonfuls per cup of liquid) for one that will become almost firm.

Buy potato flour, made from whole potatoes, as opposed to potato starch, which is just the extracted starch. Some manufacturers label their product as "potato starch flour," but here the word "starch" is just a milling term, and it is, in fact, potato flour.

Some thickeners used in commercial products are available for home use. See Ingredients to read about xanthan gum, guar gum, and ThickenThin products. These have zero carbohydrates and can be added to hot or cold liquids.

CHEESE SAUCE

Use this sauce over Dreamfields™ macaroni (see Sources), and no one will believe that it is low carb.

Make Basic Cream Sauce and let it cool slightly. Stir in 2 tablespoons of white wine or lemon juice. (The acid keeps the cheese from getting stringy, which can be a problem, especially with Swiss cheese.) Add 1½ ounces (about ¾ cup, lightly packed) of mild or sharp cheese that has been grated or finely shredded. Stir until cheese is melted. To keep warm until serving time or to reheat: Place in the top of a double boiler over hot water set on very low heat. Stir gently just until smooth and hot.

Servings: 11 (¼ cup each)

PER SERVING:		
Total Carb: 1.2g	Fiber: 0g	Net Carb: 1.2g

CREAM OF MUSHROOM SOUP

The recipe for Basic Cream Sauce can be used to make delicious soups. Use dried wild mushrooms to make this soup extraordinary.

Make Basic Cream Sauce, but increase the chicken broth to 2 cups. Sauté 1½ cups of finely chopped, fresh mushrooms or rehydrated, dried mushrooms in 2 tablespoons of butter until they start to color. Stir them into the soup. Garnish with chopped fresh parsley.

Servings: 4 (1 cup each)

PER SERVING:		
Total Carb: 4.1g	Fiber: 0.4g	Net Carb: 3.7g

Potato Soup

I'm amazed that I can include a recipe for a truly delicious potato soup in my book. While working on my Basic Cream Sauce recipe, I realized that I could alter it to make cream soups, and since it was thickened with potato flour, I was already half way there. I like this hot, but I guess it would be Vichyssoise if you served it cold, wouldn't it?

Make Basic Cream Sauce (see p. 221) but increase the chicken broth to 2 cups and increase the potato flour to 3 tablespoons. Sprinkle each serving with grated cheese, crumbled crisp bacon, and minced fresh chives as desired.

Servings: 3 (1 cup each)

PER SERVING:		
Total Carb: 9g	Fiber: 0g	Net Carb: 9g

Vichyssoise as an Appetizer

Serve cold Potato Soup in a shot glass or a demitasse as a starter. No spoon needed!

Servings: 24 (1 ounce each)

PER SERVING:		
Total Carb: 1.1g	Fiber: 0g	Net Carb: 1.1g

"We'll not talk about business till we've had our supper. No man can be wise on an empty stomach."

—George Eliot, Adam Bede

Tips and Notes

There are two kinds of starches commonly used for thickening foods: the grain starches, like wheat flour and cornstarch, and the root starches, like arrowroot and tapioca. According to food scientist Shirley O. Corriher, potato flour has some of the best characteristics of both. It doesn't have to be precooked in a roux, like wheat flour, since it has no "raw" taste. It doesn't have to be dissolved in liquid before it is added to a sauce to prevent lumping, like cornstarch. Sauces made with it can be reheated without becoming thinner and can be stirred after cooling without becoming watery, like the root starches. It sets up to a firm gel like the grain starches, but while they are opaque, it is clear and glossy like the root starches. It freezes and thaws as well as arrowroot and tapioca. Potato flour thickens at 160 to 175° F and will become thin if allowed to boil.

Rubbing your hands on an object make of stainless steel will remove the odor of garlic. A spoon or a faucet will work as well as the gadgets sold for the purpose.

"Make hunger thy sauce, as a medicine for health."

—Thomas Tusser

To substitute Splenda® and liquid for sugar-free syrup in recipes:

For each tablespoon of syrup, use one tablespoon of water and one tablespoon of granular Splenda® (or 1½ packets). You may also add a few drops of flavor extract.

SWEET AND SPICY SAUCE

This is my interpretation of a Thai sauce for grilled or deep-fried foods. I serve this as a dipping sauce with Macadamia Coconut Crusted Shrimp (see p. 215).

½ cup granular Splenda®
¼ cup rice vinegar
¼ cup water
½ teaspoon salt
2 cloves garlic, peeled and minced
½ teaspoon crushed red pepper flakes
2 tablespoons sugar-free orange Marmalade (recipe was tested with Smucker's® Light Sugar-Free Orange Marmalade)

Place the Splenda®, vinegar, water, salt, and garlic in a small saucepan. Bring to a boil and simmer for 10 minutes. Strain to remove the garlic (this lowers the carb count a little; leave it in if you prefer). Add the pepper flakes and marmalade. Heat and stir until the marmalade is melted. Serve at room temperature. Store, covered, in the refrigerator.

Serving size: 1 tablespoon

PER SERVING:		
Total Carb: 2.1g	Fiber: 0g	Net Carb: 2.1g

TERIYAKI SAUCE

½ ounce (2 tablespoons) fresh gingerroot, coarsely grated
1 clove garlic, minced
⅓ cup granular Splenda®
¼ cup sugar-free peach-flavored syrup (see Sources)
¼ cup water
½ cup soy sauce

Combine ingredients in a small non-reactive bowl. Cover and refrigerate for 8 hours or overnight, stirring several times. Strain. Warm the sauce and serve hot with steak or chicken.

Serving size: 1 tablespoon

PER SERVING:		
Total Carb: 1.4g	Fiber: 0g	Net Carb: 1.4g

HOLLANDAISE SAUCE

I confess that I never make Hollandaise the traditional way, since it is so easy to do in a blender or food processor.

3   egg yolks or the equivalent made from powdered egg yolks and water
2   tablespoons lemon juice
¼   teaspoon salt
•   A pinch pepper
½   cup butter

Blender method:
Put the egg yolks, lemon juice, and salt and pepper in a blender and turn it on at low speed just until mixed. Cut the butter into pieces and melt it in a small saucepan. Heat the butter until bubbling hot, but do not let it brown. Remove the knob from the lid of the blender and turn the blender on to the high or blend setting. Take the butter from the stove and pour it, while still bubbling hot, in a thin stream through the lid into the yolk mixture. Continue to blend for a few seconds until smooth and thickened.

Food Processor Method:
Heat the butter until bubbling hot, but do not let it brown. Process the yolks, lemon juice, and salt and pepper for a few seconds to blend and, with the machine still running, pour in the hot butter. Continue to process for a few seconds until smooth and thickened.

Serving size: 1 ounce

PER SERVING:		
Total Carb: 0.4g	Fiber: 0g	Net Carb: 0.4g

Notes:

If the sauce should start to curdle, pour in 1 tablespoon of hot water with the blender running.

Use the yolks from pasteurized eggs in the shell or reconstituted, powdered egg yolks (see Sources) rather than fresh ones, if you are concerned about safety, since the yolks are cooked only by the hot butter.

BREAKFAST MENUS:

MENU I

Poached Eggs with Hollandaise Sauce on Waffles
Broiled tomato halves
Berry Slushie
*

MENU II

Mexican Omelet with cheese and salsa
Sliced avocado
Oven Bacon
Coffee and Tea
*

MENU III

Hot Cereal with walnuts, wild blueberries, and cream
Milk
*

MENU IV

Cherry Clafouti
Oven Bacon
Coffee and Tea
*

MENU V

Scrambled Eggs
Smoked sausage
Corn Muffins with Butter and Strawberry Jam
Coffee and Tea
*

MENU VI

French Toast
Warm sugar-free maple syrup
Strawberries and Cream
Coffee and Tea
*

CONDIMENTS

ACCENT MARKS FOR A MEAL

That little something extra that sparks up a plate like an edible exclamation point.

It is not necessary to thaw frozen cranberries before cooking.

CRANBERRY SAUCE

Cranberries have so much pectin that this sauce will set up nicely even with no sugar.

1   cup granular Splenda®
1   cup water
1   (12 oz) package fresh or frozen cranberries
•   A few grains of salt

Mix the Splenda® and water in a saucepan and bring to a boil. Add the cranberries. Return to boiling, reduce the heat, and simmer for 10 minutes, stirring occasionally, until the cranberries burst. Cool to room temperature and then cover and refrigerate. Makes 3 cups.

Serving size: ¼ cup

PER SERVING:		
Total Carb: 5.5g	Fiber: 1.0g	Net Carb: 4.5g

CRANBERRY ORANGE RELISH

1   (12 oz) package fresh or frozen cranberries
1   slice fresh orange (about ⅛ medium orange with peel)
¾   cup granular Splenda®
2   tablespoons orange-flavored, sugar-free syrup, or use 2 tablespoons more Splenda®
2   teaspoons Grand Marnier (optional)
¾   cup chopped walnuts

Process the cranberries and the orange slice in the bowl of the food processor until evenly chopped. Stir in other ingredients. Store in refrigerator or freeze. Makes about 4 cups.

Serving size: ¼ cup

PER SERVING:		
Total Carb: 4.7g	Fiber: 1.1g	Net Carb: 3.6g

FRUIT AND NUT COMPOTE

This is a wonderful tart-sweet accompaniment to poultry, ham, or pork, and it can also be served with desserts.

1¼ cups granular Splenda®
³/₄ cup water
½ pound kumquats, seeded and cut into ¼-inch slices
½ pound fresh or frozen cranberries
1 teaspoon fresh ginger, peeled and chopped
½ cup pistachios, shelled

Stir the Splenda® into the water in a saucepan. Add the kumquats and bring to a boil. Lower the heat and simmer until the syrup is thickened, about 10 minutes. Cool, and then remove the kumquats with a slotted spoon. Bring the syrup to a boil and add the cranberries. Lower the heat and simmer until the cranberries pop. Return the kumquats to the mixture and add the ginger. Stir in the pistachios just before serving. Makes about 4 cups.

Serving size: ¼ cup

PER SERVING:
Total Carb: 4.9g   Fiber: 0.9g   Net Carb: 4.0g

PRESERVED GINGER

Serve as a garnish for poached salmon or other fish. (Ginger is traditionally served with seafood in Chinese dishes to neutralize fishy odors.) It can also be chopped and used in desserts.

1 cup thin-sliced fresh ginger
½ cup Da Vinci® Simple Syrup or ½ cup granular Splenda® plus ½ cup water
1 teaspoon white vinegar
• A pinch of salt

Peel the ginger and slice with a vegetable peeler or mandolin into very thin slices. Place in a saucepan and cover with water. Simmer for 3 minutes. Strain and repeat two more times in fresh simmering water. Place the ginger in the simple syrup and simmer for 30 minutes, stirring occasionally. Add the vinegar and salt and let stand in the syrup until cool. Refrigerate in the syrup.

Serving size: 1 tablespoon

PER SERVING:
Total Carb: 0.8g   Fiber: 0.1g   Net Carb: 0.7g

Tips and Notes

Simmer a few cranberries with the ginger to give it a delicate pink color.

The name, shallot, for this member of the onion family, is probably derived from Askalon, an ancient port city in Palestine; the "Ascalonian onion" was introduced to Europe by crusaders returning from the Holy Land. It looks like a cross between onion and garlic, but its taste is more delicate and subtle than either. The most common shallot in the US, the French red, has pink-tinged skin, but the gray shallot is said to be superior in flavor.

"Nothing would be more tiresome than eating and drinking if God had not made them a pleasure as well as a necessity."

—Voltaire

SHALLOT AND PEACH CHUTNEY

This chutney is adapted from a recipe on a package of Frieda's shallots. It is excellent on Lamb Curry (see p. 206).

3   cups fresh peaches, peeled and chopped. Frozen peaches, thawed and well drained, can be used instead.
2   shallots (about 2 oz.), peeled and finely chopped
1½ cups cider vinegar
¼   cup lemon juice
1   cup granular Splenda®
½   cup sugar-free Dried Cranberries (see p. 105)
1   tablespoon fresh ginger, peeled and minced
2   cloves garlic, minced
½   teaspoon salt
½   teaspoon cinnamon

Combine the fruit, shallots, vinegar, and lemon juice. Bring to a boil, reduce the heat, and simmer for 5 minutes, stirring occasionally. Add remaining ingredients. Simmer, stirring often, for 15 minutes more. Store in the refrigerator. Makes about 3 cups.

Serving size: 2 tablespoons

PER SERVING:		
Total Carb: 4.9g	Fiber: 0.7g	Net Carb: 4.2g

"PLUM" SAUCE

This "plum" sauce is made with peach or berry jam (no plums) for a sweet Chinese-style sauce to serve with duck or pork. Brush it on Crêpes (see p. 124) and fill with crisp, roast duck meat and slivered green onions for a take-off on Peking duck.

Process equal parts of Shallot and Peach Chutney (above) and sugar-free Peach or Strawberry Jam (see Index) in the bowl of a food processor until smooth. (Use my jam recipes or buy sugar-free prepared jam.)

Serving size: 1 tablespoon

PER SERVING:		
Total Carb: 3.8g	Fiber: 0.5g	Net Carb: 3.3g

Rhubarb Ginger Chutney

I had a fantastic piece of grilled wild salmon at McCormick's restaurant in Seattle that was served with rhubarb chutney, an unexpected, but totally successful combination. They used raisins while I use cranberries, but otherwise it is very similar.

4   cups fresh rhubarb (about 1½ pounds fresh), diced
2   shallots (about 2 oz. or ¼ cup), peeled and finely chopped
1¼ cups raspberry vinegar
1   cup plus 2 tablespoons granular Splenda®
½   cup sugar-free Dried Cranberries (see p. 105)
1   tablespoon fresh ginger, peeled and minced
2   cloves garlic, minced
½   teaspoon salt
½   teaspoon ground cinnamon

Combine all ingredients in a large saucepan. Bring to a boil, reduce the heat, and simmer for 20 minutes, stirring occasionally. Taste and add more Splenda® if it's too tart. Store in the refrigerator. Makes about 3½ cups.

Serving size: 1 tablespoon

PER SERVING:		
Total Carb: 3.2g	Fiber: 0.7g	Net Carb: 2.5g

see p. 105

"Hunger is the best seasoning for meat, and thirst for drink."

—Cicero

"Let the stoics say what they please, we do not eat for the good of living, but because the meat is savory and the appetite is keen."

—Ralph Waldo Emerson

KETCHUP

1 small onion, chopped
1 (15-ounce) can tomato sauce
¼ cup granular Splenda®
1 teaspoon each of the following whole spices:
   allspice, cloves, celery seed, and peppercorns
½ -inch piece stick cinnamon
• A pinch of dry mustard
1 small chopped clove garlic (or ½ teaspoon of garlic paste)
½ a Turkish bay leaf
• Salt and pepper or cayenne pepper to taste
¼ cup cider vinegar

Bring all ingredients except the vinegar to a boil in a 3-quart saucepan. Simmer until reduced by half. Add the cider vinegar. Simmer 10 minutes more. Add more salt and pepper or cayenne to taste. Strain. Store in the refrigerator. Makes about 1 cup.

Serving size: 1 tablespoon

PER SERVING:		
Total Carb: 2.5g	Fiber: 0.4g	Net Carb: 2.1g

SOUR CREAM DIP

Tips and Notes

Plain yogurt can be substituted in almost any recipe that calls for sour cream.

Mix 8 ounces of Crème Fraîche (see p. 51) or sour cream with 2 tablespoons of chopped chives or chopped green onion (tops only). Add enough cream to make the consistency like that of a cream-style salad dressing. Optional: add 1 tablespoon of crumbled, cooked bacon. Makes about 1 cup.

Serving size: 2 tablespoons

PER SERVING:		
Total Carb: 0.2g	Fiber: 0g	Net Carb: 0.2g
when made with Crème Fraîche		
Total Carb: 1.0g	Fiber: 0g	Net Carb: 1.0g
when made with sour cream		

Tea Eggs, page 66

Tortilla Chips, page 142 (sidebar)

Chili, page 82

Fruit and Nut Compote, page 229 and
Cheese Polenta, page 177,
Citrus Pork, page 208 (sidebar)

Kumquats in Syrup, page 110

Barbecued Ribs, page 196

Popovers, pages 118-19

Mixed Flour Bread, pages 144-145

Fillo Nut Cookies, page 313

Creamy Cheesecake, page 269

Snow Cones, page 284 (sidebar)

Dee Dee with (sugar-free) Ice Cream

French Vanilla Ice Cream, page 282

Sangria, page 341

Great Hot Chocolate, page 337

Brandon and Aidan making Silly Drinks, page 338

White Tea, page 333

JAM AND JELLY

Sugar-free jams can be found at the grocery store, ordered by mail (see Sources), or you can easily make your own. The water bath sterilization method normally used for making jam and jelly to be stored in the pantry may be a bit risky without sugar, which acts as a preservative. I prefer to make mine in small batches and keep it in the refrigerator. Reheating it to boiling every few days will prolong its storage life. You can also store it in the freezer.

Note: Purchased sugar-free jams, jellies and preserves will be lower in carbohydrates than home made because they can be made with zero-carb liquid sweeteners instead of the ones available for home use which have bulking agents. You may still prefer to make your own, since it is cheaper and tastier and made without maltitol or aspartame. My favorite of the brand name preserves is Hero Preserves. They are sweetened with sucralose, they are available at most groceries, and they are not expensive. See Sources.

STRAWBERRY JAM

Bright, clear, and delicious. (The butter reduces the amount of foam.)

3   cups chopped ripe strawberries
2¼ cups granular Splenda®
2   tablespoons lemon juice
½   teaspoon butter
½   teaspoon Wax Orchard™ Fruit Sweet® (optional, adds 0.1 carbs per serving)
•   A few grains of salt

Wash and chop the berries. Place in a small saucepan with the Splenda®, lemon juice, the butter, the optional Fruit Sweet®, and the salt. Bring to a simmer over low heat. Cook, stirring occasionally, for 15 minutes or until reduced to the proper consistency for jam, skimming the foam as necessary. Refrigerate or freeze. Makes about one cup of jam.

Serving size: 1 tablespoon

PER SERVING:		
Total Carb: 5.7g	Fiber: 0.8g	Net Carb: 4.9g

VARIATION

Strawberrry Jam Made With Pectin

There are powdered pectins on the market that can be used for making sugar-free jam and jelly. Ball®, Sure-Jel, and Certo all have one. They seem to be readily available at grocery stores. Pectin has 4 grams of carbohydrate per teaspoon, but the carb count for jams and jellies made with pectin won't be much higher than those without, since it thickens the jam with less fruit.

Stir 2 teaspoons of no-sugar-needed pectin (I used Ball® brand) into other ingredients from Strawberry Jam recipe and simmer, stirring occasionally, for 5 minutes. (Add 8 grams of carbohydrate for the whole batch, or 0.5 grams per tablespoon.)

Tips and Notes

See p. 111 for Kumquat Marmalade and Preserves as a variation under Kumquats in Syrup.

VARIATION: PEACH JAM

Substitute ripe peaches, peeled and chopped, for the strawberries in the Strawberry Jam recipe. Makes about one cup of jam.

Serving size: 1 tablespoon

PER SERVING:		
Total Carb: 7.0g	Fiber: 0.5g	Net Carb: 6.5g

VARIATION: TOMATILLO JAM

Spoon this sweet/hot jam over a block of cold cream cheese and serve with Parmesan Sesame Crackers, Tortilla Chips, or Pepperoni Chips as an appetizer. (See the Index for recipes.)

Substitute tomatillos (about 1 pound) for the strawberries in the Strawberry Jam recipe. Remove the husks, but do not peel. Wash to remove the sticky residue. Dice the tomatillos. Add ¼ cup of water. Add 1 tablespoon of diced chilies, mild or hot. Add other ingredients from Strawberry Jam recipe and cook until reduced to proper consistency for jam. Makes about 1⅓ cups

Serving size: 1 tablespoon

PER SERVING:		
Total Carb: 3.2g	Fiber: 0.3g	Net Carb: 2.9g

MINT JELLY MADE WITH PECTIN

1   cup plus an additional ¼ cup fresh mint leaves
1   cup water
½   cup granular Splenda®
2   teaspoons pectin (Recipe was tested with Ball's® Fruit Jell, No Sugar Needed Pectin.)
¼   cup water
1   teaspoon mint extract, optional

Put one cup of chopped fresh mint leaves and one cup of water in a saucepan. Stir together the Splenda® and the pectin. Add pectin and Splenda® to the pan, bring to a boil, and simmer for 5 minutes. Add one teaspoon of mint extract (optional). Strain out the mint leaves and add an additional ¼ cup of chopped, fresh mint leaves. Cool and store in refrigerator. Makes about 1 cup.

Serving size: 1 tablespoon

PER SERVING:		
Total Carb: 1.3g	Fiber: 0g	Net Carb: 1.3g

MINT JELLY MADE WITH GELATIN

1   cup chopped fresh mint leaves (1¼ cup total for the recipe)
1   cup water
½   cup granular Splenda®
½   packet of gelatin
¼   cup water
1   teaspoon of mint extract, optional
¼   cup additional chopped, fresh mint leaves

Put 1 cup of mint leaves and water in a saucepan. Add Splenda®. Simmer for five minutes. In a small bowl, soften the gelatin in an additional ¼ cup water. Stir gelatin into hot mint mixture and continue to cook until the gelatin in dissolved. Add mint extract, if using. Strain out the mint leaves, and add the additional ¼ cup of chopped, fresh mint leaves. Let cool and store in the refrigerator. Makes 1¼ cups.

Serving size: 1 tablespoon

PER SERVING:		
Total Carb: 0.6g	Fiber: 0g	Net Carb: 0.6g

Tips and **Notes**

Although I love lamb, it has very solid fat that can be cloying; the fresh clean taste of mint cuts through the grease.

DESSERTS

CAKE MAKES ANY DAY A PARTY

If I knew you were com-in I'd've baked a cake,
Baked cake, baked a cake,
If I knew you were com-in I'd've baked a cake,
How-ja do, How-ja do, How-ja do.

—Bob Merrill, Al Hoffman, and Clem Watts

DINNER PARTY MENUS

MENU I

Anitpasto Platter

--

Citrus Pork

Hominy "Risotto"

Mixed Greens with
Glazed Pecans

Cranberry Dressing

--

Flourless, Sugarless
Chocolate Torte

*

MENU II

Quail Eggs in a Nest

--

Grilled Wild Salmon

Fried Artichokes

Rhubarb Chutney

Celery Root and Jicama
Salad

--

Crêpes Suzette

FLOURLESS, SUGARLESS CHOCOLATE TORTE

This is an incredibly rich bittersweet dessert that is very dense and fudgy when cold but more cake-like when warm.

½ cup finely chopped walnuts or other nuts
4 ounces unsweetened chocolate, chopped into small pieces
1 tablespoon butter
8 ounces mascarpone cheese (Italian cream cheese),
    softened to room temperature
½ cup granular Splenda®
4 egg yolks
• A few grains of salt

Generously butter a 7-inch pie or tart pan. Sprinkle the bottom with nuts. Preheat the oven to 350° F.

In the bottom pan of a double boiler, bring one-half inch of water to a simmer. Reduce the heat so the water is hot but not bubbling. Place the chocolate and butter in the top of the double boiler and set over, but not touching, the hot water. Stir until melted and smooth. Remove from heat and leave until cool but still liquid.

Meanwhile, beat together in a bowl with an electric mixer: the mascarpone, Splenda®, egg yolks, and salt. Beat in the melted and cooled chocolate and butter mixture. Spread the batter in the pan. It will be like thick frosting. Smooth the top. Bake for 15 to 18 minutes at 350° F or just until the center feels firm to the touch. Serve warm or cold, topped with sugar-free Whipped Cream, sugar-free ice cream, Crème Anglaise (see Index), or fresh berries. Store in the refrigerator.

Servings: 8

PER SERVING:		
Total Carb: 7.2g	Fiber: 2.5g	Net Carb: 4.7g

CHOCOLATE CUPCAKES

3   ounces unsweetened chocolate, chopped
½   cup butter (8 tablespoons or one stick), cut into pieces
3   eggs, at room temperature
3   egg yolks, at room temperature
1   cup granular Splenda®
1   teaspoon vanilla extract
3   tablespoons oat flour
¼   teaspoon baking soda
•   A pinch of salt

Heat the oven to 350° F. Butter an 8-cup muffin pan or individual ovenproof ramekins. Line the bottom of the cups with a circle of parchment paper and butter the paper as well, or use non-stick pans.

Place one-half inch of water in the bottom pan of a double boiler. Bring to a simmer. Turn the heat to low so that the water is hot but not bubbling. Place the chocolate and butter in the top of the double boiler and set over, but not touching, the hot water. Stir until melted and smooth. Let cool. (Chocolate should be cool but still liquid when added to the batter.)

Beat the eggs, egg yolks, Splenda®, and vanilla together on high speed with an electric mixer until tripled in volume and the mixture holds soft peaks when the beater is lifted, about 7 minutes. Add the chocolate mixture in three batches and fold in until just blended. Mix the dry ingredients together and sift over the batter, a little at a time, folding in lightly with a spatula or wire whisk. Spoon the batter into the cups.

Bake until the top feels firm and the edges of the cakes pull away from the sides of the pan or until a wooden pick inserted in the center comes out clean, about 12 minutes. Let cool for 3 minutes. Run a rounded knife around the edges to loosen the cakes from the pan. Invert onto a serving plate. Serve warm with sugar-free Whipped Cream or ice cream or let cool to room temperature and frost with Cream Cheese Frosting (see Index for recipes). Store in the refrigerator. Unfrosted cakes can be warmed in a preheated 350° F oven for about 5 minutes or in the microwave for a few seconds to freshen. Frosted cakes taste better if removed from the refrigerator for a few minutes before serving. Unfrosted cakes can be frozen.

Servings: 8

PER SERVING:		
Total Carb: 7.5g	Fiber: 1.7g	Net Carb: 5.8g

VARIATION:

Chocolate Layer Cake

The recipe for Chocolate Cupcakes can be used to make one 8-inch layer.

Butter an 8-inch cake pan, line with parchment paper, and butter the paper as well, or use a nonstick pan. Preheat the oven to 350° F.

Spread the batter evenly in the pan and smooth the top, as cakes without sugar will not level out during baking. Bake for about 15 minutes or until a wooden pick inserted in the center comes out clean. Cool 3 minutes in the pan, then remove to a rack to finish cooling. Frost and serve, or wrap cake when completely cool and store in the refrigerator or freeze.

Servings: 8
Per Serving:
Total Carb: 7.5g
Fiber: 1.7g
Net Carb: 5.8g

Stir dry ingredients like flour and cornstarch before measuring to fluff them up in case they have settled. All my dry measurements are dip-level-pour, which means you fill the measuring cup or spoon by dipping it to overfill, and then leveling it off with a the straight edge of a knife or spatula. If you dip your measuring utensil and then press it against the side of the bag or box, you compress the contents and you may have too much.

CHOCOLATE SPONGE CAKE

For a gorgeous special-occasion cake, make three layers (triple this recipe); spread sugar-free raspberry jam between the layers and frost with Cream Cheese Frosting (see p. 253).

½ cup plus 1 teaspoon cake flour (65 grams)
1½ tablespoons Dutch-process cocoa powder
•   A pinch of salt
¾ teaspoon baking powder
1½ ounces unsweetened chocolate, chopped
3   tablespoons strong brewed decaf coffee or water
5   tablespoons butter, softened to room temperature
4   eggs, at room temperature, separated
¾ cup total granular Splenda®, divided into ¼ cup
     and ½ cup
2   egg whites
3   tablespoons water
½ teaspoon cream of tartar (omit if using a copper bowl)
2   teaspoons superfine sugar

Heat oven to 325° F. Butter an 8-inch round cake pan, line with a round of parchment paper, and then butter the paper also. Dust the bottom and sides of the pan with sifted cocoa; invert the pan and tap out the excess cocoa. Wrap the pan with insulating strips. (It is especially important that the cake layers be level if you make more than one layer and stack them. See Tip opposite.)

Measure out all ingredients before starting the recipe. Whisk the flour, cocoa, salt, and baking powder together. Put one-half inch of water in the bottom of a double boiler and bring to simmering. (Water should not touch the top pan.) Reduce the heat so that the water is hot but not bubbling. Place the chocolate and the 3 tablespoons of coffee or water in the top of the double boiler and stir until melted and smooth. Remove the top pan from over the water and then beat in the butter. Let cool.

Meanwhile, beat the egg yolks and the ¼ cup of Splenda® with an electric mixer until thick and light yellow. In a separate bowl, put the 2 extra egg whites with the 4 whites from the separated eggs (6 whites in all). Add the 3 tablespoons of water. With clean beaters, beat the egg whites until foamy and add the cream of tartar (if using). Gradually sprinkle on the sugar and the ½ cup of Splenda® while beating until stiff peaks are formed.

(continued on next page)

CHOCOLATE SPONGE CAKE, CONTINUED

Fold the chocolate mixture into the egg-yolk mixture in the first bowl. Gently fold in one-fourth of the egg whites. When partially blended, sift one-fourth of the flour and cocoa mixture over the top and fold in. Continue to fold in the egg whites and dry ingredients alternately, one-fourth at a time, until all are used. Be careful not to over mix the batter; it is better to leave a few streaks of whites than to deflate the mixture. Immediately spread the batter in an even layer in the prepared pan. Smooth the top, since a cake with almost no sugar won't level out. Bake on the center rack of the oven for 15 to 18 minutes. Test 1½ inches from the edge of the pan with a skewer or wooden pick. It should come out clean when the cake is done. Let cake cool in the pan for 10 minutes. Remove and place on a rack to cool completely before frosting. Fill and frost with Cream Cheese Frosting or serve with sugar-free Whipped Cream (see Index for recipes).

Servings: 8

PER SERVING:
Total Carb: 10.8g   Fiber: 1.1g   Net Carb: 9.7g

Note: Superfine sugar, also called baker's sugar, gives you more bang per carb when beating egg whites. The function of the sugar is to coat the egg proteins and keep them moist, so the finer the sugar, the more area it well cover. I have also added water to help keep the foam soft and moist since I am using so little sugar. You can usually find superfine sugar at the grocery store or you can order it from the *The Baker's Catalogue*® of the King Arthur® Flour Company (see Sources). If you prefer to make your own, just put regular sugar in the bowl of a food processor and process for a minute or two until fine. (Superfine sugar is not the same as powdered sugar, which contains cornstarch.)

Tips and Notes

To help keep cake layers level, wrap the pans with insulating strips sold for this purpose, or wrap them with a double layer of wet terrycloth. This insures even heating and prevents a hill from forming in the middle of the layer because the edges set faster than the center.

To use terrycloth:
Cut the strips to fit the height of the pan, dip in water, and secure them with paper clips or safety pins.

Chocolate Zucchini Muffins

My Chocolate Zucchini Cake recipe also makes great muffins. Replace ½ cup of the zucchini with an equal measure of sugar-free dried cherries and they become Chocolate Cherry Muffins.

Spoon batter into greased muffin cups. Bake for about 25 minutes, or until a wooden pick tests clean. Freeze some for later—they are best reheated in a convection or regular oven for a few minutes to re-crisp before serving. Split and top with butter.

Makes 24 muffins.

Per Serving:
Total Carb: 9.8g
Fiber: 2.4g
Net Carb: 7.5g

CHOCOLATE ZUCCHINI CAKE

My Aunt Lucille's favorite cake was a rich, moist, chocolate/apple bunt cake. I've tried to replicate the flavor and texture in my interpretation, but without the sugar and refined flour. (This is now my favorite cake.)

3	small zucchini or about 1 pound (2½ cups shredded)
3	eggs
2	cups granular Splenda®
1	cup whey powder
1	cup butter, softened to room temperature, or light olive oil
½	cup water
1	tablespoon vanilla extract
1	cup white whole-wheat flour
1¼	cups almond flour
¼	cup Dutch-process cocoa powder
2	teaspoons ground cinnamon
2	teaspoons baking powder
1	teaspoon baking soda
⅛	teaspoon salt
1¼	cups chopped walnuts
⅔	cup sugar-free Chocolate Chips, see p. 260, or use purchased sugar-free chocolate chips

Preheat the oven to 325° F. Grease a 9-cup bunt or tube pan (8- to 9-inches across), dust with cocoa powder and tap out excess. Measure all ingredients before starting recipe. Wash, trim and peel the zucchini and shred in the food processor or grate on the large holes of a box grater. Reserve.

Mix together in a large mixing bowl: the eggs, Splenda®, whey powder, butter or oil, water, and vanilla. Beat with an electric mixer until thick and smooth, about 5 minutes.

Sift together the flour, almond flour, cocoa, cinnamon, baking powder, baking soda, and salt. Beat the dry ingredients into the egg mixture. Stir in the reserved zucchini, the walnuts, and chocolate chips.

Bake for 40 to 45 minutes. Cake will pull away from the sides of the pan and a wooden pick will come out clean when done (test in a different place if it does not come out clean the first time, in case it hit a chocolate chip).

Servings: 24

PER SERVING:		
Total Carb: 9.8g	Fiber: 2.4g	Net Carb: 7.5g

ORANGE ALMOND TORTE

Everything goes into the food processor—quicker and easier than a cake mix.

- • Chopped almonds for the pan and the top of cake
- 1 orange (8 ounces)
- 1 cup plus 2 tablespoons almond flour
- 1 rounded teaspoon baking powder
- ½ teaspoon baking soda
- ½ cup whey powder
- 1 cup granular Splenda®
- ½ cup polydextrose, optional
- • A pinch of salt
- 3 large eggs, at room temperature
- 2 teaspoons orange or lemon extract
- 1 tablespoon of Grand Marnier, optional

Preheat the oven to 350º F. Butter a 7- or 8-inch pie pan, line with parchment paper, and butter the paper also. Sprinkle with finely chopped almonds.

Grate the rind of the orange directly into the bowl of the food processor. (If you don't have a kitchen scale, weigh the oranges at the grocery store. If your orange weighs more than 8 ounces, cut out a wedge and reserve for another use. If it weighs less, use part of a second orange.) Peel the orange and discard the white pith. Remove any seeds. Add the orange segments to the food processor and process until liquefied. Whisk the dry ingredients together. Add all ingredients and process. Scrape down the bowl and continue to process until blended and thick, for a total of about 5 minutes. Spread the batter in the prepared pan. Sprinkle the top with chopped almonds. Bake in a pre-heated oven for about 35 to 40 minutes or until well browned on top. (Do not under-bake or the cake will fall.) Let the cake cool in the pan. Frost with Confectioner's Icing or Chocolate Glaze, if desired (see Index for recipes).

Servings: 8

PER SERVING:		
Total Carb: 9.0g	Fiber: 2.1g	Net Carb: 6.9g

Celebrate!
Cake makes a day special,
Cake marks a date,
Cake means a party,
Cake for no reason at all,
Cake—because you can!

VARIATION:

Orange Almond Torte made with maltitol

Substituting powdered maltitol (see Sources) for part of the Splenda® in the Orange Almond Torte makes a very moist cake that browns well.

To make with part maltitol: Reduce the Splenda® to ¾ cup and add ¼ cup of powdered maltitol. Add an additional 5 to 10 minutes to the baking time. Makes 8 servings.

Per Serving:
Total Carb: 7.8 g
Fiber: 2.1g
Net Carb: 5.7g*
*Count excludes 4.5 grams of sugar alcohol per serving.

VARIATION:

Lemon Almond Torte

Make the Orange Almond Torte recipe, but replace the oranges with 8 ounces of lemons. Increase the Splenda® from 1 cup to 1 cup plus 2 tablespoons. Add other ingredients and process and bake as for Orange Almond Torte. This cake is good frosted with my Confectioner's Icing made with lemon juice (see p. 252). Makes 8 servings.

Per Serving:
Total Carb: 9.3 g
Fiber: 2.5g
Net Carb: 6.8g

SPONGE CAKE

This sponge cake can become the basis for endless variations, from a simple strawberry shortcake to an extravagant dessert for a party.

3   whole eggs
3   egg yolks
½   cup granular Splenda®
1   tablespoon superfine sugar, also called baker's sugar
1   teaspoon vanilla extract
1   teaspoon Wax Orchard™ Fruit Sweet® (see Sources)
    (or use honey and add 0.2 carbs per serving)
½   cup plus 1 tablespoon cake flour (70 grams or 2½ ounces)
¼   teaspoon baking powder
¼   teaspoon salt

Preheat the oven to 350° F. Butter an 8-inch square pan, line with parchment paper, and then butter the paper.

Place in a mixing bowl: the whole eggs, egg yolks, Splenda®, and sugar. Place the bowl over a pan of hot water and whisk until the mixture is lukewarm. Beat at high speed with an electric mixer until very pale and doubled in bulk, about 10 minutes. Beat in the vanilla and Fruit Sweet® or honey. Stir together the flour, baking powder, and salt. Sift over the batter while folding lightly, just until blended. Spread the batter into the pan and smooth the top.

Bake for 10 to 12 minutes or until the top is golden brown, the center is firm to the touch, and the cake has pulled away from the sides of the pan. A wooden pick inserted in the middle of the cake will come out clean when the cake is done. Turn the cake out of the pan onto a parchment lined rack to cool. Peel away the paper from the bottom of the layer. When cool, place upright on a serving dish. Refrigerate or freeze the cake if keeping for more than a day. Makes one 8-inch square layer.

Servings: 12

PER SERVING:		
Total Carb: 6.7g	Fiber: 0.2g	Net Carb: 6.5g

Note: The makers of Splenda® suggest adding a little honey or molasses to cookie recipes to keep them moist; I substitute Wax Orchard's™ liquid fructose called Fruit Sweet® (see Sources) in my cakes and cookies for the same reason. It is sweeter than sugar or honey so you need less, and it has 7.5 grams of carbohydrate in a tablespoon rather than the 15 in molasses, honey, or corn syrup.

VARIATION:

Sponge Cake made with part maltitol

If you can tolerate a small amount of maltitol, you can eliminate the sugar and Fruit Sweet® and simplify the recipe. It will also lower the carb count, make the cake higher, and improve the browning.

To make with part maltitol: Leave out the Fruit Sweet® and the superfine sugar. Add 2 tablespoons of powdered maltitol with the ½ cup of Splenda® and beat with the eggs. Increase the baking time to 15 to 20 minutes or until well browned and the cake has pulled away from the sides of the pan. Makes one 8-inch square layer or twelve servings.

Per Serving:
Total Carb: 5.5g
Fiber: 0.2g
Net Carb: 5.3g*
*Count excludes 1.5g of sugar alcohol per serving

VARIATION:
PEACH COBBLER

2 cups peaches, fresh or frozen
½ cup granular Splenda®
1 tablespoon butter
⅛ teaspoon ground cinnamon
• A pinch of salt
• Sponge Cake, ⅓ of one 8-inch layer (4 servings)

Peel, pit, and dice the peaches and put them, along with any juice, in a saucepan. If you are using fresh peaches, add a little water, if needed. If you are using frozen peaches, let them thaw and include the juice. Stir in the Splenda®, butter, cinnamon, and salt. Simmer until peaches are cooked and the juice is thickened, about 5 to 10 minutes. Pour the hot fruit over the cake slices. Serve warm with sugar-free Whipped Cream or Ice cream (see Index for recipes).

Servings: 4

PER SERVING:		
Total Carb: 19.2g	Fiber: 1.7g	Net Carb: 17.5g

VARIATION:
BOSTON CREAM PIE

• Sponge Cake, one 8-inch square layer
1½ cups Pastry Cream (see p. 256)
• Chocolate Glaze (see p. 255)

Split the cake layer and spread bottom half with 1½ cups of Pastry Cream. Replace the top half and spread ¾ of a cup of Chocolate Glaze over top. Cut into twelve portions.

Servings: 12

PER SERVING:		
Total Carb: 10.1g	Fiber: 0.7g	Net Carb: 9.4g

Tips and Notes

To make peaches easier to peel, place them in boiling water for a few seconds. Dip out with a slotted spoon.

Don't buy green peaches. They will soften but not ripen after they are picked.

French chef, Monsieur Sanzian, is credited with creating the Boston Cream Pie at the Parker House Hotel which opened in Boston in 1856. It was called chocolate cream pie or Parker House chocolate cream pie on the menu at the hotel. It seems to have been based on a local dessert called a Boston cream cake; Chef Sanzian's contribution was to use a chocolate glaze rather than powdered sugar on top and to call it a pie. Boston Cream Pie is the official state dessert of Massachusetts.

VARIATION: COCONUT AMARETTO CAKE

Also good with other flavors of sugar-free syrup; for example, sprinkle the layers with hazelnut syrup and top with chopped, toasted hazelnuts. For a few more carbs, Grand Marnier, amaretto, or other liqueurs could be used in place of the syrup.

- Sponge Cake, one 8-inch square layer
- ½ cup amaretto-flavored sugar-free syrup
- 2 cups unsweetened, shredded coconut, fresh or dried. (Fresh is best of course. If using dried coconut, mix it with an additional ¼ cup of sugar-free syrup and microwave it for a few seconds to moisten.)
- 2 cups sugar-free Whipped Cream (see p. 328)

Cut the cake into twelve squares. Split each piece horizontally with a serrated knife. Sprinkle both cut sides of each piece with 1 teaspoon of amaretto syrup. Cover the bottom half of each slice with Whipped Cream and replace the top half. Spread the top with Whipped Cream. Sprinkle the coconut over the top.

Servings: 12

PER SERVING:		
Total Carb: 10.1g	Fiber: 2.3g	Net Carb: 7.8g

VARIATION: RUM CAKE

Make Sponge Cake as directed. Cut the cake into 12 pieces and pierce the top all over with a fork. Reassemble the pieces into the shape of the original cake. Sprinkle with ¼ cup of rum. Spread with softly-whipped, sugar-free Whipped Cream. Serve at once.

Servings: 12

PER SERVING:		
Total Carb: 7.0g	Fiber: 0.2g	Net Carb: 6.8g

> "The most dangerous food is wedding cake."
>
> —James Thurber

VARIATION:

AMBROSIA CAKE

- Sponge Cake, one 8-inch square layer
- ½ cup amaretto or Grand Marnier liqueur
- Sugar-free Whipped Cream (see p. 328)
- Kumquats in Syrup (see p. 110)
- ¾ cup unsweetened coconut

Make sponge cake as directed and cut into twelve squares. Split each piece horizontally with a serrated knife. Sprinkle both cut sides of each piece with amaretto or Grand Marnier liqueur, using 1 teaspoon for each half of each piece. Cover the bottom half with Whipped Cream and replace the top half. Spread the top layer with Whipped Cream. Mix coconut into Kumquats in Syrup and serve over cake.

Servings: 12

PER SERVING:		
Total Carb: 14.0g	Fiber: 1.9g	Net Carb: 12.1g

VARIATION:

STRAWBERRY SHORTCAKE

- Sponge Cake, one 8-inch square layer
- 3 cups fresh strawberries, sliced
- ¼ cup granular Splenda®

Sweeten the strawberries with ¼ cup of granular Splenda®. Heat at full power in the microwave for a minute or two—not long enough to cook the berries, just long enough to draw out the juices. (Add a little strawberry-flavored sugar-free syrup if you like more juice). Cut the sponge cake layer into twelve pieces and pierce the top all over with a skewer or a fork. Pour the strawberries over the cake and top with sugar-free Whipped Cream or sugar-free ice cream.

Servings: 12

PER SERVING:		
Total Carb: 10.1g	Fiber: 1.2g	Net Carb: 8.9g

Tips and **Notes**

The Olympian gods ate a delicious food called ambrosia to ensure their immortality. We mortals use the name for a fruit dessert.

"Doubtless God could have made a better berry, but doubtless God never did."

—Izaak Walton, quoting William Butler

VARIATION: FRUIT PARFAIT

Use your prettiest crystal stemware to show off the colorful layers in this luscious fruit and cake dessert.

1   cup fresh, whole raspberries or sliced strawberries, plus 6 berries for garnish
½   cup fresh orange segments, seeds and membranes removed, cut into small pieces
1   kiwi fruit, peeled and cut into small wedges
4   slices fresh ginger, peeled and crushed
6   packets Splenda®
2   tablespoons Grand Marnier liqueur
•   Sponge Cake, half of one 8-inch square layer. Reserve other half of cake for another use.
6   tablespoons butter, melted
¾   cup unsweetened flaked coconut, fresh, frozen, or dried
•   Sugar-free Whipped Cream (see p. 328)

Preheat the oven to 400° F.

Mix the Grand Marnier with the fresh fruit and ginger and sprinkle with the Splenda®. Let the fruit macerate while toasting the cake.

Cut the cake in half and reserve half for another use. Cut the remaining cake into six portions; wrap and freeze to facilitate slicing into croutons. With a serrated knife, split each piece of frozen cake horizontally. Leaving the two halves stacked, cut each piece of cake in half, and then turn at a right angle, and cut into quarter-inch slices. (Each piece should make about 16 croutons.) Turn the cake croutons in the melted butter to coat. Spread on a greased baking sheet and bake at 400° F, stirring carefully two or three times, for about 5 minutes or until they just start to brown. Sprinkle the cake pieces with the coconut and continue to bake until the cake is well browned and crisp, and the coconut is toasted. Watch carefully so it doesn't burn.

Stir the fruit and remove the ginger slices. In six stemmed glasses, layer the toasted cake croutons, the fruit mixture with juice, and the Whipped Cream. Continue to alternate cake, fruit, and whipped cream, ending with Whipped Cream. Garnish the top with a berry.

Servings: 6

PER SERVING:		
Total Carb: 16.0g	Fiber: 3.5g	Net Carb: 12.5g

> "I've been on a diet for two weeks and all I've lost is two weeks."
>
> —Totie Fields

BROWNED BUTTER RHUBARB ALMOND CAKES

The menu for the dinner party hosted by Bill Gates for Chinese President Hu Jintao was printed in the Seattle Times. Just the name of the dessert set off a frenzy of calls and e-mails to the paper. When chef David Jue's recipe for Rhubarb Brown Butter Almond Cake appeared, I knew it had low-carb potential. Thank you, Bill! Thank you chef Jue!

2¼ sticks butter (1⅛ cups)
1¼ cups almond flour
1⅔ cups granular Splenda®
½   cup white whole-wheat flour, see Sources
•   a few grains of salt
½   cup whey protein powder
¾   teaspoon of baking soda
5   egg whites (½ cup plus 2 tablespoons)
1   pound rhubarb, chopped into roughly ¼-inch pieces (about 3 cups, chopped)
4   tablespoons of sugar-free orange, strawberry, or apricot jam

Place the butter in a saucepan and heat over low heat until butter is golden brown. It may take 15 minutes or so, but do not leave it unattended, as it can burn quickly. Strain the butter and discard the solids. Let the butter cool.

Whisk the dry ingredients together and add to the egg whites. Mix well. Mix in the butter, which should be cool but still liquid. Refrigerate, covered, for at least an hour or as long as several days. The mixture will be stiff, almost like peanut butter.

Preheat the oven to 375° F and butter a 12-cup muffin pan or 12 individual tart pans.

Place ¼ cup of the batter in each cup. Top with ¼ cup of the chopped rhubarb and push it lightly into the batter. Bake for about 15 minutes or until brown on top. Let cool. Heat the jam until melted and brush on the cakes to glaze.

Servings: 12

PER SERVING:		
Total Carb: 12.1g	Fiber: 2.6g	Net Carb: 9.5g

VARIATION:

Browned Butter Almond Tarts

Omit rhubarb. Put 1 tablespoon of batter into each of 36 mini-muffin cups. Press a blanched almond into the top of each (optional). Bake for about 15 minutes or until brown. Spread tops with sugar-free jam just before serving.

Makes 36 tarts.

Per Serving:
Total Carb: 3.5
Fiber: 0.6g
Net Carb: 2.9g

FRUITCAKE

Tips and Notes

I found that I could purchase unsweetened, dried peaches, apricots, and cherries, but I had to dry the cranberries and rhubarb and make all the sugar-free candied fruit and peels myself. Make your fruit-cake with candied watermelon rind, citrus peels, candied or dried cranberries, dried rhubarb, and nuts for the low-est carb count, but since this is a special occasion cake, you may want to add a few sugar-free dried cherries, peaches, and apricots. I had all the fruit and peels ready before the day I made the cake. Was it a lot of effort? Yes. Was it worth it? Yes! (I might even make it when it isn't Christmas!)

Did you see the 83-year-old man on Leno who claimed to have a fruitcake baked by his great grandmother in 1878? Every Christmas brings a new crop of fruitcake jokes—obviously, a lot of people have never tasted a good one! Too often what passes for fruitcake is a dry, brown brick with a few nuts and raisins. My version is halfway between fruitcake and fruit bread. It is mostly fruit and nuts with just enough batter to hold it together.

2   cups, total, nuts: walnuts, pecans, almonds, and macadamias
1   cup, total, sugar-free dried fruit: Cranberries, Rhubarb, (see Index for recipes), cherries, apricots, and peaches
1   cup, total, sugar-free candied fruit: Cranberries, Watermelon Rind, Citrus Peel, Cherries, Ginger, and Kumquats (see Index for recipes)
¼   cup whey protein powder (2 net carbs or less per serving), plus an additional 2 teaspoons
2   eggs, separated
¼   cup plus 2 tablespoons granular Splenda®
2   tablespoons Sugar Twin® Brown Sugar Replacement
2   tablespoons butter, melted and cooled
2   tablespoons cream
2   teaspoons vanilla extract
¼   teaspoon almond extract
½   cup almond flour
¾   teaspoon baking powder
½   teaspoon baking soda
2   tablespoons white whole-wheat flour (or use regular whole-wheat)
•   A pinch of cream of tartar (omit if using a copper bowl)

Preheat the oven to 325° F. Butter an 8½- by 4½-inch loaf pan and a piece of foil to cover the top. Line the pan with another piece of foil across the bottom and up the two long sides, leaving a little hanging over the sides to help with removing the cake from the pan. Butter the foil lining also.

If your dried fruit is moist and chewy, you can use it as it is; if it is dry and hard, you will need to soak it in a little hot water, or microwave it, covered with water, until it is plump. Taste and add a little Splenda® to the water for fruit that is very tart, such as cranberries. Drain well on paper towels.

(continued on next page)

FRUITCAKE, CONTINUED

Combine the fruit and nuts in a bowl with the ¼ cup of whey powder. Toss to coat, separating the pieces by hand if necessary.

Put the egg yolks, the sugar substitutes, and the additional whey powder in a mixing bowl. Beat until light. Beat in the melted butter, cream, and extracts. Whisk the almond flour, baking powder, baking soda, and whole-wheat flour together in a separate bowl and stir into the batter.

In a clean bowl, using clean beaters, beat the egg whites until foamy; add the cream of tartar (if using), and beat to the stiff-peak stage. Fold one-fourth of the egg whites into the batter to lighten, and then fold in the rest of the whites. Pour the batter over the fruit and nut mixture and stir until evenly coated. Spoon the batter into the prepared pan. Cover the pan with the piece of buttered foil and bake for 20 minutes. Remove the foil and bake for an additional 20 minutes, or until the cake is firm in the middle and brown on the edges.

Place the pan on a rack to cool. Remove the cake from the pan, peel off the foil, and cut into 16 slices. Store cake in the refrigerator, wrapped in foil. To freeze, separate the slices with sheets of waxed paper before wrapping.

Servings: 16

PER SERVING:

Total Carb: 9.5g   Fiber: 2.8g   Net Carb: 6.7g
when made with Dried Cranberries and Rhubarb; Candied
Cranberries; Lemon, Orange, and Kumquat Peels; and equal
amounts of walnuts, pecans, and almonds

"The dessert crowns
the dinner."

—Eugene Briffault

CHRISTMAS MENU:

French Onion Soup
- -
Standing Beef Rib Roast

Brown Sauce

Celery Root "Mashed Potatoes"

Fruit and Nut Compote

Hot Popovers with Butter

Baby Green Beans
- -
Fruitcake

Chocolate Truffles

Dessert Pumpkin Tamales

Nutty Fruity Candy
*

More cake recipes can be found as variations under Cheese Desserts: Tiramisu on page 271 and Raspberry trifle on page 272. See also: Berry Custard Cake, p. 322.

FROSTINGS AND FILLINGS

CONFECTIONER'S ICING

Tips and Notes

Maltitol is one of the sugar alcohols, which have been used for many years to make sugar-free products for people with diabetes. It can be used measure for measure like table sugar (sucrose), so recipes for candy and bakery products that use it do not need to be altered significantly. However, products made with any of the sugar alcohols must carry warnings that over-consumption may cause digestive problems, and maltitol is the worst offender in that regard. Most people can tolerate small amounts without distress.

Maltiol is available in granular form from Steel's Gourmet Foods (see Sources) under the brand name Nature Sweet. It has 6 calories (half the calories of sugar) and 3 net grams of carbohydrate per teaspoon, but it is counted as zero carbs since it has a minimal impact on blood sugar levels. Use it like powdered sugar for sprinkling on cookies or coating candy; use a paper doily as a stencil to make a decorative design on a plain cake.

Powdered maltitol can be used cup for cup like powdered sugar.

½ cup powdered maltitol
2 tablespoons cream or lemon juice, use more for thinner icing
• A few grains of salt

Sift or whisk the maltitol to break up lumps. Stir in cream or lemon juice and salt. Spread or pour over cakes or cookies.

Serving size: 1 tablespoon

PER SERVING:		
Total Carb: 0g	Fiber: 0g	Net Carb: 0g
when made with zero-carb cream		
Total Carb: 0.1g	Fiber: 0g	Net Carb: 0.1g
when made with lemon juice		
Counts exclude sugar alcohols.		

CONFECTIONER'S ICING WITH PART POLYDEXTROSE

The polydextrose cuts the amount of maltitol in half, adds fiber, and makes icing that tastes like it's made with real sugar.

1 tablespoon of water
2 tablespoons of cream or lemon juice
¼ cup of powdered maltitol
¼ cup of polydextrose (see Sources)
¼ cup of granular Splenda® or 6 packets
• A few grains of salt

Heat liquids until hot. Mix the maltitol, polydextrose, Splenda®, and salt together until well blended. Add dry ingredients to the hot liquid gradually, while stirring, to prevent lumps. Stir until dissolved. Thin with more liquids for thinner icing. Spread or pour over cakes or cookies.

Serving size: 1 tablespoon

PER SERVING:		
Total Carb: 0.8g	Fiber: 0g	Net Carb: 0.8g
when made with zero-carb cream		
Total Carb: 1.9g	Fiber: 0.8g	Net Carb: 1.1g
when made with lemon juice		
Counts exclude sugar alcohols.		

Cream Cheese Frosting, Cake Filling, or Pie Filling

Absolutely wonderful! Try it on the Chocolate Sponge Cake (see p. 240).

8   ounces whipped cream cheese
1¼ cups, total, granular Splenda®, divided into ½ cup and ¾ cup
•   A pinch of salt
1   teaspoon vanilla extract
1½ cups heavy cream

Beat the cream cheese with an electric mixer to soften. Beat in ½ cup of the Splenda®. Beat in the vanilla and then the rest of the Splenda® and a pinch of salt. Add the heavy cream and beat until stiff. Spread on completely cooled cake. Store cake in refrigerator. Extra frosting will keep for several days in the refrigerator. Makes about 4 cups.

Serving size: 2 tablespoons

PER SERVING:		
Total Carb: 1.1g	Fiber: 0g	Net Carb: 1.1g

VARIATION:
GRAND MARNIER FROSTING

Follow the directions for Cream Cheese Frosting, but reduce the vanilla to ½ teaspoon and add 2 tablespoons of Grand Marnier liqueur. Makes about 4 cups.

Serving size: 2 tablespoons

PER SERVING:		
Total Carb: 1.3g	Fiber: 0g	Net Carb: 1.3g

VARIATION:
CREAM CHEESE FRUIT PIE

Put a layer of Cream Cheese Frosting in the bottom of a baked pastry, meringue, or coconut pie crust or tart shell. Spread with a layer of fresh or cooked and cooled fruit, sweetened with Splenda®. Top with sugar-free Whipped Cream. (It's wonderful with blueberries.)

VARIATION:
Coconut Cream Cheese Pie

Stir ½ cup of unsweetened coconut into Cream Cheese Frosting. Spread in baked and cooled pastry, meringue, or coconut pie or tart shell to make a Coconut Cream Pie.

Servings: 16
Total Carb: 2.9g
Fiber: 0.4g
Net Carb: 2.5g

Tips and Notes

Serve these cream cheese pies in very small portions, as they are very rich.

Chocolate Cream Cheese Frosting, Cake, or Pie Filling

Serve this in small portions, as it is very rich.

4   ounces unsweetened chocolate, chopped
2   tablespoons Dutch-process cocoa powder
2   cups, total, granular Splenda®, divided into ½ cup and 1½ cups
½   cup brewed decaf coffee or water
8   ounces whipped cream cheese
1   teaspoon vanilla extract
2   teaspoons Kahlúa or crème de cacao liqueur (optional, add 0.1 grams of carbs per serving)
•   A pinch of salt
1½ cups heavy cream

Process the chocolate in a food processor until finely ground or chop fine with a chef's knife. Heat one-half inch of water in the bottom of a double boiler to a simmer. Reduce the heat so the water is hot but not bubbling. Stir together the cocoa and the ½ cup of granular Splenda® until smooth in the top of the double boiler. Stir in the chocolate and the ½ cup of coffee or water. Set over, but not touching, the hot water. Stir until smooth and melted. Let cool until the mixture is tepid.

Beat the cream cheese with an electric mixer to soften. Beat in half of the remaining Splenda®. Beat in the vanilla and chocolate liqueur (if using) and then the rest of the Splenda® and a pinch of salt. Beat the cooled chocolate mixture into the cream cheese mixture in the mixer bowl. Add the heavy cream and beat until stiff.

Spread on completely cooled cake layers to use as frosting and filling for a cake, or place in a baked pie shell for Chocolate Cream Pie and top with sugar-free Whipped Cream. Extra frosting will keep for several days in the refrigerator.

Makes about 5 cups, enough to frost and fill a double layer cake or fill a 9-inch pie shell.

Servings: 16 (as pie filling)

PER SERVING:		
Total Carb: 5.7g when used as pie filling	Fiber: 1.1g	Net Carb: 4.6g
Total Carb: 2.2g per 2 tablespoons when used as frosting	Fiber: 0.4g	Net Carb: 1.8g

"Too much of a good thing is wonderful."

—Mae West

CHOCOLATE GLAZE

This is a thin chocolate frosting that hardens when cool, perfect for Boston Cream Pie or cookies.

2 ounces unsweetened chocolate (2 squares)
1 cup granular Splenda®
3 tablespoons butter
2 tablespoons hot water
1 tablespoon vanilla
• A few grains of salt

Process the chocolate in a food processor until finely ground or chop fine with a chef's knife. Heat one-half inch of water in the bottom of a double boiler to simmering. Reduce the heat so the water is hot but not bubbling. Place the chocolate, Splenda®, butter, and the 2 tablespoons of hot water in the top of a double boiler. Stir in the vanilla and salt. Stir until chocolate is melted and the mixture is smooth. Add more hot water if necessary for proper consistency. Spread the glaze while warm. This glaze can be refrigerated and reheated. To reheat: Add a little more hot water, and microwave or heat in the top of a double boiler until melted. Makes about 1 cup.

Serving size: 1 tablespoon

PER SERVING:		
Total Carb: 2.5g	Fiber: 0.5g	Net Carb: 2.0g

QUICK CHOCOLATE GLAZE

Easy, but expensive.

Break low-carb chocolate bars, like Carb Safe or Atkins® Endulge™, into individual squares. Arrange on top of hot cake immediately after taking out of oven. Let the candy melt and then spread with a knife. You will need 1½ (3.54 ounce) Carb Safe bars or 5 (1.6 ounce) Atkins® Endulge™ bars to frost an 8- by 8-inch sponge cake layer or a pan of brownies.

Nutrition counts will vary with type of bar used.

4TH OF JULY MENU:

Pepperoni Chips and salsa

Buffalo Wings and Bleu Cheese Dressing

Barbecued Ribs

Baked Beans

Cole Slaw

Chocolate Cherry Zucchini Muffins with Chocolate Glaze

Assorted Bottled Beverages

*

PASTRY CREAM

This can be the filling for Boston Cream Pie or the base for a fruit tart. Put it in a pie shell and it becomes a cream pie. See the variations on the next page for Coconut and Chocolate Cream Pie or Pudding. If you really want to live dangerously, slice a small banana on the bottom for Banana Cream Pie.

See the variations on the next page

4   egg yolks from large eggs
½   cup granular Splenda®
1   tablespoon potato flour (or use 2 tablespoons of cornstarch and add 0.7 carbs per serving)
1   packet of Sweet One® (optional)
¼   teaspoon xanthan gum (optional)
½   cup milk
1¾ cup total heavy cream, divided into 1 cup and ¾ cup
1½ teaspoons vanilla extract
•   A pinch of salt

In a medium-sized heatproof bowl, beat the egg yolks with a fork and set aside. In a heavy saucepan, stir together the Splenda®, potato flour, and the optional Sweet One® and xanthan gum (if using). Gradually stir in the milk and one cup of the cream until smooth. Cook over medium heat, stirring, until the mixture just starts to bubble. Remove the pan from the heat. Stir half of the hot mixture into the yolks to temper, and then stir the yolk mixture back into the saucepan. Place the pan back over the heat and cook, stirring constantly, until the mixture thickens and starts to bubble, about 2 minutes. Remove the pan from the heat and stir in the vanilla and salt. To prevent a skin from forming on top, place a film of plastic wrap directly on the surface of the pastry cream or give it a squirt of no-stick spray. Cool to room temperature.

Beat the remaining ¾ cup of heavy cream until stiff and fold into the pastry cream. Place plastic wrap on top, as before, or spray with no-stick spray. Refrigerate until needed. Pastry cream will keep for several days. Makes 3 ½ cups.

Servings: 7

PER SERVING:		
Total Carb: 3.5g	Fiber: 0g	Net Carb: 3.5g

Tips and Notes

The optional xanthan gum helps produce a smooth and stable texture.

In "plain vanilla" recipes, using a small amount of acesulfame K with the Splenda® gives a more natural sweet taste. Two teaspoons of DiabetiSweet®, a blend of isomalt and acesulfame K, can be used in place of one packet of Sweet One®.

VARIATION:
CHOCOLATE CREAM PUDDING OR PIE FILLING

Put it in a crust or serve as a rich chocolate pudding.

Process 2 ounces (½ cup) of sugar-free Chocolate Chips (see p. 260) in a food processor until finely ground, or chop fine with a chef's knife. Add the chocolate after adding the egg yolks to the hot cream mixture in Pastry Cream recipe. Cook, stirring constantly, for 2 minutes on medium heat. Stir in the vanilla and add 1 tablespoon of crème de cacao (optional). If the chocolate is not completely smooth, cook and stir for an additional minute. To prevent a skin from forming on top, place a film of plastic wrap directly on the surface of the pastry cream or give it a squirt of no-stick spray. Cool to room temperature.

Beat the remaining cream and fold in the chocolate mixture. Serve as pudding or place the filling in a baked and cooled 9-inch pie crust and refrigerate. Makes about 4 cups.

Servings: 8

PER SERVING:		
Total Carb: 6.0g count is for filling only	Fiber: 1.0g	Net Carb: 5.0g

VARIATION:
COCONUT CREAM PUDDING OR PIE FILLING

Add ½ cup of unsweetened coconut with the vanilla in Pastry Cream recipe. Put the filling into a prepared pastry Pie Crust or Coconut Crust (see Index for recipes) or serve as coconut pudding. Sprinkle with toasted or plain unsweetened coconut. Makes about 4 cups.

Servings: 8

PER SERVING:		
Total Carb: 4.7g count is for filling only	Fiber: 0.8g	Net Carb: 3.9g

We say, "What's for dessert?"
The English say, "What's for pudding?"

Tips and Notes

You may substitute 2 ounces of purchased chocolate chips in this recipe.

The Hershey® Company makes Sugar-free Chocolate Chunks, made with maltitol (a sugar alcohol) and sucralose. They have 1 net carb per tablespoon. They are widely available in supermarkets.

Eat Well, Be Well™ makes semi-sweet, mini-sized chocolate chips that have 1 net carb in 2 tablespoons. They are sweetened with acesulfame K and sucralose and contain no sugar alcohols or trans fats. EWBW also makes chocolate bars (plain or almond) that have 2 net grams of carbohydrate in each 1.2-ounce bar. Some EWBW products are available nationwide in supermarkets and health food stores, and they can also be ordered online from www.netrician.com.

Big Skies Farm also sells mini-sized, dark chocolate chips sweetened with Acesulfame K and Splenda®. They have 1.5 net carbs in 2 tablespoons. They can be ordered online from www.lowcarbdietchefs.com. (Click on "chocolates.")

Use mini-sized chips by weight rather than measure since they pack together more closely.

CHOCOLATE

Silky, sensuous, and seductive, chocolate has been called "the plant Prozac®." The good news is that this is one addiction that can be indulged without fear of getting arrested, intoxicated, or fat (provided it's sugar-free, of course). It is low in carbohydrates and half of that is fiber, which doesn't count.

I use unsweetened chocolate, sugar-free chocolate syrup (like Da Vinci® or Atkins™), and Dutch-process cocoa powder. Occasionally I also use chocolate extract, crème de cacao, or Kahlúa liqueur. However, I find the most convenient form of chocolate, and the one I use most often, is Splenda®-sweetened Chocolate Chips that I make myself (see p. 260). I keep a stash for baking and for making quick snacks like Chocolate Cinnamon Tacos, p. 135.

CHOCOLATE TECHNIQUES:

Chopping:
The smaller the particles of chocolate, the faster and easier it melts. Large chunks need to be broken up and then chopped or grated, or ground in a food processor.

A chef's knife works well for chopping big chunks of chocolate into smaller pieces. A serrated knife is even better, but you have to put the chocolate on a cutting board with the handle extending over the edge to allow room for your knuckles. Use a rocking motion to shave the chocolate away in thin sheets from the edges of the chunk. There is a special tool called a chocolate fork that is made specifically for breaking up chunks of chocolate.

If you are preparing a large amount of chocolate, a food processor is faster than a grater. Break the chocolate up into one-inch chunks and process until finely chopped. A rotary cheese grater or a microplane grater will work for grating smaller amounts. My favorite chocolate is made by Guittard; it comes in flat, one-inch disks, which can be melted as it is or put directly into the food processor when necessary.

Melting:
Chocolate can be temperamental stuff. It must be melted, and then cooled slowly, while being stirred. It melts at 118° F and burns or separates if it gets much hotter than that.

Everything that touches the chocolate must be completely dry. Even a small amount of steam can cause it to seize and form a hard dry mass.

When used in cooking, the safest way to melt chocolate is to mix it with the liquids in the recipe, but there must be more than one tablespoon of liquid for each two ounces of chocolate. The liquid must be added at the beginning, before heating. If it is added afterwards, it will cause the chocolate to seize when the first drop touches it.

(continued on next page)

To melt over hot water:

Test your double boiler with cold water to see how much water it will hold without touching the bottom of the top pan. Put that amount of water in the bottom pan and bring to a simmer. Reduce the heat to its lowest setting, so that the water is hot but not bubbling. To be completely safe, cover the pan containing the chocolate with a lid when it is close to an open pot of hot water during the melting process. Do not leave the lid on once the chocolate is in place over the hot water or when it is a safe distance away, however, as there is a danger that moisture may condense under the lid and drip onto the chocolate. Place the chopped or grated chocolate in the upper pan and set over (but not touching) the hot water. Stir frequently and thoroughly until the chocolate is melted. Even a small amount of melted chocolate that is left too long in one place on the bottom of the pan can ruin the whole batch. You can use a saucepan and a heatproof bowl that fits snugly on top if you do not have a double boiler.

To melt in a microwave:

Be sure your microwave is dry inside before using it for melting chocolate. Place the finely chopped chocolate in a microwave-safe bowl and microwave at fifty percent power, stirring frequently. The stirring is important because chocolate tends to retain its shape; it may be completely melted without looking any different until it is stirred. If you continue to heat it, it will burn. Four ounces will take about 3 minutes, but the time may vary, depending on the type of oven and the kind of chocolate.

To melt in an oven:

Chocolate can also be melted in an oven, set on 225° F. Stir it often and remove it as soon as it is melted.

Chocolate repair:

Chocolate that has separated or scorched from overheating cannot be recovered. If it has seized from contact with moisture, it may be salvageable. As soon as it starts to thicken and lose its sheen, stir in a little oil or warm water until it is liquid once more.

Notes:

Callebaut premium chocolate is a good buy if you buy it in bulk by mail (see Sources), but be prepared to deal with a huge chunk of chocolate if you order it.

Guittard chocolate comes in 1-inch disks from *The Baker's Catalogue®* of the King Arthur® Flour Company. I have found it to be excellent, and it can be melted without being chopped, which makes it the clear winner in my book. See Sources under "chocolate."

Anytime you can substitute sugar-free chocolate syrup (like Da Vinci® or Atkins™) for part of the chocolate, liquid, and sweetener called for in a recipe, it will lower the carbohydrate count.

CHOCOLATE CHIPS

Tips and Notes

To help you judge the temperature of the chocolate, remember that body temperature is close to 100° F, so 80° will feel cool to the touch.

The slow cooling tempers the chocolate, making it dark, smooth, and shiny.

Splenda® won't dissove in chocolate; if used straight out of the box, the chocolate would have a grainy texture. Pulverize it in the food processor or use a rolling pin to crush it.

Be sure your microwave is dry inside before melting chocolate. Wipe it down if you have used it to heat liquid recently.

Splenda®-sweetened, semi-sweet chocolate chips are available by mail order and in some health food stores, but it is very easy to make your own if you follow the instructions below.

6   tablespoons granular Splenda®
4   ounces unsweetened chocolate

Chill a baking sheet lined with parchment, plastic wrap, or foil while preparing the chocolate.

Pulverize the Splenda® in the bowl of a food processor, fitted with the metal blade, until very fine. Chop the chocolate into 1-inch or smaller pieces. Add the chocolate pieces to the processor bowl and process until evenly ground. (If you don't have a food processor you can grate the chocolate and crush the Splenda® with a rolling pin.)

Put about one-half inch of water in the bottom of a double boiler (the water should not touch the top pan) and heat to a simmer. Reduce the heat to its lowest setting so that the water is hot but not bubbling. Place the chocolate and Splenda® in the top pan and set over the hot water. Stir until melted and smooth. Remove the top pan from over the hot water and let the chocolate cool, stirring thoroughly and frequently, until it is about 80° F. This may take 7 to 10 minutes. As soon as it feels cool to the touch, pour it out on the chilled baking sheet. Just pour it out in a heap, and then pick up and tilt the pan until the chocolate spreads to the a thickness of about ¼-inch.

When cold, peel off the paper or foil and chop the chocolate into chips. Store it in a covered container at room temperature. Use for cookies, cakes, or candy.

Microwave Method:
Follow the recipe above except place the grated chocolate and processed Splenda® in a microwave-safe bowl and microwave at 50 percent power, stirring several times, for about 2 minutes or until melted. Let cool, stirring frequently, until it is about 80° F. This may take 7 to 10 minutes. When it feels cool to the touch, pour it out on a waxed paper- or foil-lined, chilled baking sheet and tilt to spread to about ¼ inch thickness. Cool, and cut into chips.

Makes 1 cup (4 ounces)

Serving size: ½ ounce

PER SERVING:		
Total Carb: 5.0g	Fiber: 2.0g	Net Carb: 3.0g

CHOCOLATE DIPPED STRAWBERRIES

I like to use small strawberries for these so there is more chocolate in proportion to the berry. Long-stemmed berries are especially elegant if you can find them. The berries can be dipped the day before they are to be served. Store them, loosely covered, in the refrigerator. I don't really know if they will keep longer; I can never resist them long enough to find out!

- Fresh strawberries (Do not remove the caps.)
- Sugar-free Chocolate Chips

Wash and dry perfect strawberries. It is important that they be dry because any water that gets into the chocolate can cause it to seize. Line a baking sheet with waxed paper, put the berries on it, and chill them in the refrigerator until cold.

Heat one-half inch of water to boiling in the bottom of a double boiler. Reduce the heat to low so that the water is hot but not bubbling. Place the chocolate chips in the top of the double boiler and place over, but not touching, the pan of hot water. Stir until melted and smooth. Remove both pans from the heat source, but leave the melted chocolate over the pan of hot water while dipping the berries; be very careful not to allow any water or steam to contact the chocolate.

Hold the strawberries by the cap, or bend one end of a paper clip open and spear the berry crossways through the top. Dip the bottom two-thirds of each berry into the melted chocolate. Set on the chilled, waxed paper-lined pan to harden. Cover loosely with a second sheet of waxed paper and refrigerate until serving time. You can coat 3 to 4 small to medium berries per ounce of chocolate.

Serving size: 1 strawberry

PER SERVING:		
Total Carb: 4.2g	Fiber: 1.3g	Net Carb: 2.9g

Tips and Notes

Sweet Celebrations sells a maltitol-sweetened chocolate coating for candy making and dipping. See Sources.

Purchased sugar-free chocolate chips will have a lower carb count than ones you make yourself because commercial products are made with sweeteners without bulking agents. Eat Well, Be Well™ chips can be ordered from www.netrition.com.

VARIATION:

Chocolate Dipped Fruit or Citrus Peel

Substitute strips of sugar-free Candied Citrus Peel (see pp. 109–110) for strawberries. Dip half of each piece of peel in the melted chocolate.

CANDY

It's hard to recognize the destructive and addictive nature of concentrated sugar. It comes from Santa Claus and the Easter Bunny and from Mom and Grandma. It's a reward for a job well done, a thank you for a kindness, an apology for a transgression, and an expression of love from a sweetheart. The only negative connotation I can think of for the word is *Eye Candy* referring to entertainment that is shallow and worthless but seductive.

VARIATION:

Chocolate Soy Bean Clusters

Use roasted soybeans, sometimes called soy nuts, in place of nuts.

CHOCOLATE NUT CLUSTERS

This makes really fast and easy candy. It's also a good way to use every last bit of the chocolate left in the pan after dipping strawberries.

1   cup Sugar-free Chocolate Chips (see p. 260)
1   cup nuts: chopped walnuts, pecans, macadamias, almonds, soynuts, or other nuts

Heat one-half inch of water to boiling in the bottom of a double boiler. Reduce the heat to low so that the water is hot but not bubbling. Place chocolate chips in the top pan, set over hot water, and stir until chocolate is melted and smooth. Remove both pans from the heat. Stir the chopped nuts into the chocolate. Drop by rounded teaspoonfuls onto a waxed paper-lined sheet pan. Refrigerate to harden.

Servings: 24 pieces

PER SERVING:		
Total Carb: 2.4g	Fiber: 1.0g	Net Carb: 1.4g
when made with walnuts		

"I would stand transfixed before the windows of the confectioners' shops, fascinated by the luminous sparkle of candied fruits, the cloudy luster of jellies, the kaleidoscope inflorescence of acidulated fruitdrops—red, green, orange, violet: I coveted the colours themselves as much as the pleasure they promised me."

—Simone de Beauvoir

PEANUT BUTTER BALLS

If you're a fan of Reese's® peanut butter cups, you'll like these. Use the kind of peanut butter that lists just peanuts and salt as ingredients. It usually says, "stir before using." Almond or hazelnut butter would also be good and even lower in carbs.

⅓ cup crunchy peanut butter
1 tablespoon Wax Orchard™ Fruit Sweet® (or use honey and add 0.5 carbs per candy)
¼ cup whey protein powder (2 net carbs or less per serving)
2 packets Splenda®

For the coating:
1 ounce unsweetened chocolate, chopped
1 tablespoon butter, cut into pieces
2 packets Splenda®

Mix the Fruit Sweet® with the peanut butter until smooth. Blend in the whey powder and Splenda®. Shape the mixture into 1-inch diameter balls and refrigerate until firm and cold.

Heat one-half inch of water in the bottom of a double boiler until hot but not bubbling. Place the chocolate, butter, and Splenda® in the top of the double boiler and set it over the hot water. Stir until melted and smooth. Remove both pans from the heat source, but leave the chocolate over the hot water, being careful that no water touches the chocolate. Bend one end of a paper clip open and use to spear the peanut butter balls or use a fork. Dip the balls in the melted chocolate. Place on a waxed paper-lined baking sheet or put each candy in a fluted paper cup and refrigerate until hardened. Store in refrigerator.

Servings: 15 pieces

PER SERVING:		
Total Carb: 2.5g	Fiber: 0.8g	Net Carb: 1.7g

Tips and Notes

Wax Orchard™ brand Fruit Sweet® is a liquid fructose or fruit sugar that I use in place of honey or molasses to add moisture to cookies, cakes, and candies. It is sweeter than sugar or honey so you need less, and it has 7.5 carbs per tablespoon rather than the 15 in molasses, honey, or corn syrup. (See Sources)

Even if the peanut butter jar says "no trans fats", it may still have them. A product is allowed to make that claim if it contains 0.5 grams or less per serving. Read the label and if it lists partially hydrogenated oil, it may have up to 8 grams of trans fat in a 16-ounce jar.

There are lots of good low-carb candies to choose from. Whatever your favorite candy, you can probably find a dead ringer for it. Asher's®, Carb Safe, Atkins™, Russell Stover®, Whitman's®, and Doctor's Diet Carb Rite are just some of the brands available. Atkins' Endulge is sweetened with Splenda® as well as maltitol; most of the other brands are sweetened with maltitol or other sugar alcohols and carry warnings that "excess consumption can cause a laxative effect." One caveat: be sure to check the serving size—the carb count in large print may sound low for a whole candy bar, but it may really be the amount in a small portion.

CHOCOLATE TRUFFLES

For a velvety smooth, melt-in-your-mouth texture, let them warm up to room temperature before serving.

4   ounces unsweetened chocolate
¼   cup plus 3 tablespoons heavy cream
½   cup granular Splenda®
•   A few grains of salt
1   tablespoon butter
2   teaspoons vanilla extract
•   Cocoa powder, chopped nuts, or coconut for coating

Cut the chocolate into chunks and process in a food processor with the metal blade until finely chopped or grate by hand. Place the cream in a small saucepan and heat until it just starts to simmer. Remove from heat and add the Splenda®, salt, butter, and vanilla. Stir in the chocolate and beat by hand with a spatula or a wooden spoon until melted and smooth. Chill until firm enough to shape, about 1 hour.

Shape into 1-inch balls. To keep your hands from melting the chocolate mixture, dip them periodically in a bowl of ice water and dry them off as you work. Roll the truffles to coat in sifted cocoa, finely chopped nuts, or unsweetened coconut. Store in the refrigerator, but bring up to room temperature before serving.

Servings: 24 pieces

PER SERVING:		
Total Carb: 1.8g	Fiber: 0.6g	Net Carb: 1.2g

What goes best with a
food made from beans?
A drink made from beans!

Magic beans fill my cup,
Black and hot, I drink it up.
Magic beans make a sweet,
Dark and smooth and good to eat.
(chocolate and coffee)
—JBB

5 MINUTE FUDGE

Chocolate melts at body temperature, which is why it gives that pleasurable, cool sensation on the tongue as it dissolves into nothingness. The creamy smoothness of this fudge is enhanced by the mascarpone. If death by chocolate tempts you, here's your weapon!

1¼ cups plus 2 tablespoons granular Splenda®
- A few grains of salt
1 teaspoon vanilla extract
1 tablespoon water
4 ounces unsweetened chocolate, chopped into small pieces or grated
8 ounces mascarpone cheese, brought up to room temperature (If any water has separated out, drain it off.)
½ cup chopped nuts, optional

Place the Splenda® and salt in a small bowl and stir in the vanilla and water until the Splenda® is dissolved. Cream in the mascarpone cheese until smooth.

Bring one-half inch of water to a simmer in the bottom of a double boiler. Reduce the heat so that the water is hot but not bubbling. Place the grated chocolate in the top pan and set it over, but not touching, the hot water. Stir until the chocolate is melted.

Remove the pan with the chocolate from over the hot water. Scrape the Splenda® and cheese mixture onto the chocolate and use a heatproof spatula or a wooden spoon to work it in until it is smooth. Stir in the nuts, if using. Let cool for a minute or two.

Line a small, shallow container (about 6 inches square) or a candy mold with plastic wrap for easy removal. Scrape the fudge into the container. Chill until firm. Cut into ¾-inch slices. (The candy will cut more easily before it is completely cold.) Store in the refrigerator.

Makes about 14 ounces or 40 slices.

Servings: 40

PER SERVING:		
Total Carb: 1.7g	Fiber: 0.4g	Net Carb: 1.3g

Note: Mascarpone is Italian cream cheese. It has a higher cream content and fewer carbs than its American counterpart. Regular cream cheese can be used in this recipe, but premium chocolate and mascarpone make it luxurious.

VARIATION:

Peanut Butter Fudge

Reduce the mascarpone cheese to 4 ounces and add ½ cup of sugar-free peanut butter.
Makes 40 slices.

Per Slice:
Total Carb: 2.2g
Fiber 0.7g
Net Carb: 1.5g

Tips and Notes

Use the kind of peanut butter that lists just "peanuts" or "peanuts and salt" as ingredients. You are likely to find it with the organic foods and it will probably say, "stir before using." Smooth or crunchy is your call.

If you stir and refrigerate natural peanut butter, the oil will not separate.

To Toast Nuts:

Preheat oven to 300° F. Spread nuts in a shallow pan and bake for 5 minutes to crisp and dry them.

To substitute Splenda® and liquid for sugar-free syrup in recipes:

For each tablespoon of syrup, use one tablespoon of water and one tablespoon of granular Splenda® (or 1½ packets). You may also add a few drops of flavor extract.

A festive, no-cook candy to add to your holiday favorites.

¼ cup, total, mixed, sugar-free dried fruit. Use any combination Dried Cranberries, Rhubarb (see Index), cherries, apricots, and peaches

2 tablespoons sugar-free simple or vanilla syrup

¼ cup, total, of mixed, sugar-free candied fruit and peels Use any combination Candied Cranberries, Citrus Peels, Kumquats, Ginger, Watermelon Rind, and Cherries (see Index for recipes)

1 cup nuts (Pistachios and macadamias or sliced almonds look pretty with the brightly-colored fruit.)

½ cup unsweetened coconut, plus ⅔ cup more for coating the top and bottom of the candy

½ cup granular Splenda®

½ cup whey powder (2 net carbs or less per serving)

• A pinch of salt

½ teaspoon xanthan gum, optional (to help hold the candy together)

4 ounces (1 stick) butter, melted

Line an 8- by 8-inch square pan with waxed paper or foil. Butter the paper or foil.

Chop the dried and candied fruits and peels and combine in a small bowl with the vanilla or simple syrup. Cover and microwave for one minute. Let stand for a few minutes until the fruit is softened and the liquid is absorbed. Roughly chop the nuts.

Mix ½ cup of the coconut, all the fruits and peels, and the nuts together in a large bowl. Pulverize the Splenda® in a food processor or place between layers of plastic wrap and crush with a rolling pin. Stir the Splenda®, whey powder, salt, and xanthan gum (if using) into the fruit and nut mixture. Stir in the melted butter. Sprinkle the pan with ⅓ cup of coconut. Press the fruit and nut mixture firmly into the pan. Sprinkle the remaining coconut on top. Cover with a second sheet of waxed paper or foil and press down firmly to make the coconut adhere to the candy. Chill until firm; turn out of the pan and cut into 20 squares. Store in the refrigerator.

Servings: 20

PER SERVING:		
Total Carb: 4.5g	Fiber: 1.7g	Net Carb: 2.8g

when made with ¼ cup Dried Cranberries, ⅛ cup Candied Citrus Peel, ⅛ cup Candied Kumquats, ¼ cup sliced almonds, ¼ cup pistachios, and ½ cup macadamia nuts

Glazed Pecans

These are wonderful as a sweet treat or to use in salads. Chopped, they make a crunchy praline topping for ice cream.

2   cups raw pecan halves
1   egg white (2 tablespoons)
¼   cup granular Splenda®
2   teaspoons ground cinnamon
•   A pinch of salt

Preheat oven to 300° F. Spread nuts in a shallow pan and bake for 5 minutes to crisp and dry them. Let cool.

Place the egg white in a bowl and beat with a fork. Add the nuts and mix until all are coated and sticky. Mix Splenda®, cinnamon, and salt together and sprinkle the mixture over the nuts. Toss until nuts are completely coated. Spread in a single layer on a cookie sheet and bake for 12 minutes. Stir and break apart any nuts that stick together. Return to the oven for 5 minutes more. Store airtight.

Serving size: ½ ounce

PER SERVING:		
Total Carb: 3.1g	Fiber: 1.2g	Net Carb: 1.9g

VARIATION:

Walnuts or a mixture of different nuts can be substituted for the pecans. Stir in some dried cranberries, salted popcorn, and pumpkin seeds to make Trail Mix.

FOR THE LUNCH BOX:

MENU I

Ham and cheese cubes
Hard Cooked Egg
Slices of red and green bell pepper
Plain yogurt with sugar-free Strawberry Jam
Thermos of Milk
*

MENU II

Tuna salad
Parmesan Sesame Crackers
Fresh plum
Soy Nuts
Thermos of Hot Chocolate
*

MENU III

Corn Tortilla wrap (Poached Chicken, mayonnaise, tomato, and lettuce)
Dill pickle
Glazed Pecans
Orange segments
Thermos of Milk
*

MENU IV

Thermos of Chicken and Vegetable Soup
Tortilla Chips
Celery sticks with peanut butter
Chocolate Chip Cookies
Sugar-free Lemonade
*

CHEESE DESSERTS

To paraphrase Benjamin Franklin, "*Cheesecake* is proof that God loves us and wants us to be happy."

CLASSIC CHEESECAKE

Tips and Notes

Mascarpone is the Italian version of cream cheese. It contains more cream than its American counterpart and only 0.5 grams of carbohydrate per serving. Mascarpone will whip up like cream so it makes this cheesecake light and fluffy. You may substitute an extra 8 ounces of regular cream cheese for the mascarpone if you like.

Kaiser's Noblesse springform pan doesn't leak! It can be ordered from A Cook's Wares at www.cookswares.com.

16 ounces cream cheese at room temperature
8 ounces mascarpone cheese or use 1 additional 8-ounce package cream cheese
⅔ cup granular Splenda®, or more to taste
• A few grains of salt
3 large eggs at room temperature
1 cup sour cream
2 teaspoons vanilla extract
1 teaspoon almond extract
1 tablespoon amaretto (optional, adds 0.8 net carbs per serving)

Preheat the oven to 350° F.

Generously butter a 9-inch springform pan and wrap the outside with foil to prevent leakage. (Heavy-duty foil is wide enough to wrap a 9-inch pan with a flange. Crisscross two strips if you are using regular foil.) Have ready a large kettle of boiling water and a large roasting pan with a folded cup towel in the bottom to make a water bath.

Put cream cheese, mascarpone, Splenda®, and salt in the bowl of an electric mixer. Beat until very light and fluffy, scraping the bowl to be sure it is uniformly mixed. Add the eggs, one at a time, and beat well after each. Add the sour cream and extracts and beat until smooth. Put the batter into the prepared pan and set on the folded towel in the larger pan. Place in the preheated oven and pour the hot water into the outside pan to a depth of one inch. Bake for one hour. Turn off the oven and, without opening the door, let it cool for an additional hour. Remove the cheesecake from the water bath and run a dull knife around the edge to loosen it so that any shrinkage will cause the cake to pull away from the sides rather than crack in the center. Allow the cake to cool to room temperature, then cover with plastic wrap, and refrigerate in the pan. After several hours or overnight, remove the sides of the pan. Fresh berries or a drizzle of melted chocolate on top wouldn't hurt.

Servings: 10

PER SERVING:		
Total Carb: 4.3g	Fiber: 0g	Net Carb: 4.3g

VARIATION:
CITRUS CHEESECAKE

This is my favorite cheesecake. You have to try this one.

To the Classic Cheesecake recipe, add the grated zest of one orange and one lemon and replace the almond extract with 2 teaspoons of lemon extract. Replace the optional amaretto with 1 tablespoon of Grand Marnier. Garnish with thin slivers of Candied Citrus Peel (see pp. 109–110) or a dab of sugar-free orange marmalade, if desired. (For an even more intense citrus flavor, add $1/8$ teaspoon of lemon or orange oil.)

Servings: 10

PER SERVING:		
Total Carb: 4.4g	Fiber: 0g	Net Carb: 4.4g

CREAMY CHEESECAKE

A luscious no-bake cheesecake, fancy enough to serve your guests, but easy enough to make anytime.

¾ cup granular Splenda®
½ cup mascarpone cheese (4 ounces)
2 cups (one 15-ounce container) ricotta cheese
• Juice (3 tablespoons) and grated zest of one lemon
1 teaspoon vanilla
1 teaspoon amaretto liqueur (optional, adds 0.7 net carbs per serving)
1 teaspoon almond extract
½ teaspoon ground nutmeg
8 sliced seedless grapes for garnish

Process all ingredients except the grapes in a food processor until very smooth. Spoon into stemmed glasses and garnish each serving with 2 sliced seedless grapes. Refrigerate for 2 hours before serving.

Servings: 4

PER SERVING:		
Total Carb: 11.2g	Fiber: 0.3g	Net Carb: 10.9g

Tips and Notes

Double greasing the pan is recommended for foods that tend to stick, like cheesecakes.

To double grease:
Coat the bottom and sides of the pan generously with butter. Place the pan in the refrigerator until cold. Spray the interior of the pan with a no-stick spray over the butter.

Tips and Notes

Spice Island® and Trader Joe's® Tahitian Blend vanilla extracts have no sugar; many others have corn syrup listed in the ingredients, even when the label says "pure vanilla."

CHEESECAKE CUPS

This was my first sugar-free dessert recipe. Nothing could be easier.

16 ounces cream cheese (two 8-ounce packages)
3 eggs
½ cup granular Splenda®
1 teaspoon vanilla extract
¼ teaspoon almond extract

Preheat the oven to 350° F. Generously butter a 12-cup muffin tin or line with paper baking cups.

Soften the cheese to room temperature and beat in the eggs and Splenda® with an electric mixer until smooth. Beat in the vanilla and almond extract. Fill the muffin cups ¾ full with batter. Bake 20 to 25 minutes. Cool on a rack. The centers will fall; fill the depression with fresh fruit or sugar-free jam, if desired. Keep refrigerated.

Servings: 12

PER SERVING:		
Total Carb: 2.2g	Fiber: 0g	Net Carb: 2.2g

STRAWBERRY MASCARPONE DESSERT

An instant dessert that rivals anything you'll find on the menu at the best restaurants. Use whipped cream from an aerosol can and you can have this ready in 2 or 3 minutes. Sheer decadence!

For each serving:
Slice ½ cup of strawberries and sweeten with 4 teaspoons of granular Splenda® (or 2 packets). Drop ¼ cup of mascarpone cheese by teaspoonfuls over the berries. Top with whipped cream.

PER SERVING:		
Total Carb: 8.8g	Fiber: 2.0g	Net Carb: 6.8g

TIRAMISU

3   egg yolks or ¼ cup plus 2 tablespoons reconstituted powdered egg yolk or liquid whole egg replacement

½   cup granular Splenda®

1   cup, total, strong decaf coffee (Only 1 tablespoonful goes into the mixture, the rest is for soaking the cake.)

2   teaspoons cognac

1   cup (one 8-ounce container) mascarpone cheese

3   egg whites or the equivalent of 3 egg whites reconstituted from powdered egg whites

•   A pinch of cream of tartar (omit if using a copper bowl)

1   8-inch square layer of Sponge Cake (see p. 244)

2   tablespoons Dutch-process cocoa powder

Combine the egg yolks or substitute, the Splenda®, 1 tablespoon of the coffee, and the cognac in a bowl and beat with an electric mixer for 3 minutes. Add the mascarpone and beat for an additional 3 to 5 minutes until smooth.

In another bowl, combine the egg whites and cream of tartar (if using). With clean beaters, beat to stiff-peak stage. Gently fold the whites into the mascarpone mixture.

Cut the sponge cake layer into 9 squares. Split each square horizontally. Pour the coffee into a shallow dish. Dip the cut side of the bottom halves of the cake slices into the coffee. Place upright on individual serving dishes or reassemble the whole layer in a large bowl. Spread with the mascarpone mixture and dust with sifted cocoa. Dip the cut side of the top halves of cake slices in coffee. Place on top of first layer, cut side down, and spread the top with the remaining mascarpone mixture. Dust with sifted cocoa. Refrigerate for 1 hour before serving.

Servings: 12

PER SERVING:		
Total Carb: 10.0g	Fiber: 0.2g	Net Carb: 9.8g

Tips and Notes

When choosing egg substitutes, be sure to check the ingredients listed on the package. Some contain onion flavor, not a happy choice for a dessert.

You may find eggs in the shell which have been pasteurized, and although they are wonderful if you like your fried eggs with liquid yolks or want to make a classic Caesar salad, don't use them in any recipe that requires beaten whites. The whites have been thickened in the heating process and they will not achieve enough volume when whipped.

You may prefer to use powdered egg whites and yolks when a recipe requires raw eggs. They work beautifully, they sit patiently on the shelf until you need them, and they leave no odd whites or yolks to take up space in the refrigerator.

VARIATION:
TIRAMISU MOUSSE

Eliminate the cake and serve the mascarpone mixture as a mousse. Spoon into dessert dishes. Dust the top with sifted cocoa and top with sugar-free Whipped Cream (see p. 328).

Servings: 12

PER SERVING:		
Total Carb: 1.8g	Fiber: 0.2g	Net Carb: 1.6g

VARIATION:
RASPBERRY TRIFLE

Bake a Sponge Cake (see p. 244) in a 9-inch round cake pan. Slice the cake horizontally into two layers. Leave the coffee out of the mousse mixture and, instead of dipping the cake in coffee, sprinkle the cut sides of the cake layers with a total of ¼ cup of crème de cacao or Grand Marnier. Spread ¼ cup of sugar-free raspberry jam on the first cake layer. Top with the mascarpone mixture, then with the second cake layer, and then the rest of the mascarpone mixture. Decorate the top with dots of jam and sugar-free Whipped Cream, if desired.

Servings: 12

PER SERVING:		
Total Carb: 11.3g	Fiber: 0.6g	Net Carb: 10.7g

Tips and Notes

Trifle is an old-fashioned English dessert consisting of a layer of sponge cake or ladyfingers, soaked with wine, spread with jam and custard, and topped with syllabub or whipped cream. The top may be embellished with fruit, nuts, or grated chocolate. Trifle was typically served for Christmas, presented in a beautiful glass bowl to show off the colorful layers. It was also called tipsy pudding, tipsy squire, and tipsy parson. The Italians called it *zuppa inglese* (English soup).

"That most wonderful object of domestic art called trifle... with its charming confusion of cream and cake and almonds and jam and jelly and wine and cinnamon and froth."

—Oliver Wendell Holmes

MASTER THE COOKIE MONSTER

Commercial cookies provide a convenient, portable package for trans fats, refined flour, and sugar in the American diet. Keep a supply of home-made, sugar- and trans fat-free, low-carb cookies for the jar and the lunch box to tame the cookie monsters at your house.

BROWNIES

3   ounces unsweetened chocolate
½   cup butter, softened to room temperature
1   tablespoon sugar-free Strawberry Jam (see p. 233)
1   teaspoon vanilla extract
3   eggs
¾   cup plus 2 tablespoons granular Splenda®
3   tablespoons oat flour
1   tablespoon Dutch-process cocoa powder
½   teaspoon baking powder
•   A pinch of salt
½   cup chopped walnuts
½   cup sugar-free Chocolate Chips (optional)

Preheat oven to 350° F. Butter the bottom of an 8-inch square pan, or butter the bottom of the pan, line with parchment paper, and then butter the paper as well.

Chop the chocolate into small pieces. Heat one-half inch of water to a simmer in the bottom pan of a double boiler. Reduce heat so water is hot but not bubbling. Place the chocolate and butter in the top pan, and set over, but not touching, the hot water. Stir until melted and smooth. Stir in the vanilla and the jam. Let stand until cool but still liquid.

Beat the eggs with an electric mixer until fluffy, about 3 minutes. Beat in the Splenda®. Fold the chocolate mixture into the batter. In another bowl, whisk together the flour, cocoa, baking powder, and salt. Sift over the batter and fold in. Stir in the nuts (and chocolate chips, if using). Spread the batter in the prepared pan, smoothing the top. Spray the top of the batter lightly with no-stick spray before baking so the top will be crisp. Bake for 9 to 10 minutes or until the center is firm, but do not over-bake. Cut into 16 squares.

Servings: 16

PER SERVING:		
Total Carb: 4.4g without chocolate chips	Fiber: 1.2g	Net Carb: 3.2g
Total Carb: 5.7g with chocolate chips	Fiber: 1.7g	Net Carb: 4.0g

VARIATION:

Brownies Made with Flour Replacement and Maltitol

Using Big Skies Farm's Flour Replacement and maltitol makes very good Brownies and reduces the carbs a bit to boot.

Replace the oat flour with Big Skies Farm's Lite White Flour Replacement (see Sources). Use only ½ cup of granular Splenda® and add ½ cup of powdered maltitol (see Sources). Preheat oven, prepare pan, and melt chocolate with butter as in Brownie recipe. Mix the Splenda® and maltitol together. In another bowl, whisk together flour replacement, cocoa, baking powder, and salt.

Beat the eggs until stiff and beat in the Splenda® and maltitol. Fold in the chocolate and butter. Sift flour mixture over batter and fold in. Stir in nuts. Spread in pan, smoothing the top. Spray lightly with no-stick spray. Bake for 11 to 15 minutes or until the center is firm; do not over-bake.
Makes 16 servings.

Per Serving:
Total Carb: 3.8g
Fiber: 1.4g
Net Carb: 2.4g*
*Count excludes 4.6 grams of sugar alcohol per serving.

Tips and Notes

Nature Sweet powdered maltitol is available from Steel's Gourmet Foods (see Sources). It can be used like powdered sugar, but since it is one of the sugar alcohols, it can be excluded from the carb count.

Use an unsweetened, unflavored, whey protein powder with 2 grams of carbohydrate or less per serving if possible. Many brands of whey protein contain sugar, sweeteners, or pharmaceuticals. A little stevia or vanilla shouldn't be a problem, but don't use the kind with lots of additives. (You may have to adjust the Splenda® if you use sweetened whey.)

A wonderfully tart lemon curd on a cookie crust. The curd can also be used alone as a spread or placed in a Coconut Pie Shell or a Meringue Shell to make Angel Pie (see Index for recipes).

Shortbread Crust:
- ¾ cup gluten flour
- ½ cup whey protein powder (2 net carbs or less per serving)
- ½ teaspoon baking soda
- A pinch of salt
- 8 tablespoons butter, softened to room temperature
- ⅓ cup granular Splenda®

Lemon Curd:
- 1 cup plus 2 tablespoons granular Splenda®
- 4 large eggs
- 2 large egg yolks
- ¼ teaspoon xanthan gum, optional
- 1 cup lemon juice
- 4 tablespoons butter, at room temperature
- 2 tablespoons heavy cream
- 2 teaspoons grated lemon zest
- ½ teaspoon vanilla extract
- ¼ teaspoon salt
- A small amount of powdered maltitol or powdered sugar (optional)

To make the crust:
Preheat the oven to 350° F. Grease an 8-inch square pan.

Combine the gluten flour, whey powder, baking soda, and salt in a bowl and whisk together, breaking up any lumps. Beat the Splenda® and butter together in a large bowl with an electric mixer for 3 minutes. Add the dry ingredients and beat on low until evenly mixed. (The mixture will be crumbly.) Press the dough into the pan and bake for 10 to 15 minutes or until lightly brown. While the crust is baking, make the lemon curd.

(continued on next page)

Lemon Bars, continued

To make the lemon curd:

In a medium-sized bowl, whisk together the Splenda®, eggs, egg yolks, and the optional xanthan gum until smooth. Set aside. In a heavy saucepan, heat and stir the lemon juice, butter, and cream until the butter is melted and the mixture is just under the boiling point. Remove from the heat. Whisk some of the hot liquid into the bowl containing the reserved egg mixture to temper it, and then gradually whisk in the remaining mixture. Pour the mixture back into the pan. Cook on medium-low heat, stirring constantly with a flat spiral whisk or a heatproof rubber spatula, scraping the bottom and sides of the pan, until the mixture starts to thicken. This may take about 5 minutes. Remove from the heat. Strain if any lumps have formed. Stir in the lemon zest, the vanilla, and the salt.

To make the lemon bars:

Pour the hot custard over the hot crust and tilt the pan to make an even layer. Bake at 350° F until the curd topping has set, about 5 to 10 minutes. To keep the top from cracking, you may place a layer of heat resistant plastic wrap directly on the surface of the hot lemon custard as soon as you take it out of the oven. Let it cool to room temperature. Sift the powdered maltitol or sugar (if using) over the top. Cut into 16 squares. Store the lemon bars in the refrigerator. (The crust will soften if stored for more than a day.)

Servings: 16

PER SERVING:		
Total Carb: 5.1g	Fiber: 0.8g	Net Carb: 4.3g

Note: The optional xanthan gum will help produce a smooth and stable texture.

VARIATION:

Shortbread Crust

The crust from the Lemon Bar recipe can also be used for custard or cream pies.

To use with a filling that will be baked again, such as Lemon Coconut or Custard Pie (see Index for recipes): Pre-bake crust for 10 minutes in a 350° F oven. Cover the edges if necessary during the second baking time to prevent over-browning.

To use as a shell for cream pies: Continue to bake the crust until lightly browned. Let cool before filling.

Makes 9 servings.

Per Serving:
Total Carb: 4g
Fiber: 1.3g
Net Carb: 2.7g

COCONUT MACAROONS

1²/₃ cup unsweetened grated coconut
2   tablespoons Wax Orchard™ Fruit Sweet®, see Sources,
    or use honey (and add 0.8 net carbs each)
7   tablespoons granular Splenda®
1   egg white
1   teaspoon vanilla extract
•   A few grains of salt

If the Fruit Sweet® has been refrigerated, bring it up to room temperature. Bring one-half inch of water to a simmer in the bottom of a double boiler. Stir the coconut, Fruit Sweet®, and Splenda® together in the top pan of the double boiler. Set the pan over, but not touching, the simmering water for 5 minutes. Beat the egg white well with a fork and stir it into the coconut mixture. Add the vanilla and salt. Continue to cook just until the mixture sticks together when pressed between your fingers. Spread the mixture in a dampened pan, cover with moistened plastic wrap or waxed paper, and chill until cold.

Preheat the oven to 300° F.

Using wet hands, shape the chilled coconut mixture into small balls. Place on a nonstick cookie sheet and bake for 15 to 18 minutes or until lightly browned. Store the cookies in an airtight container in the refrigerator.

Servings: 24

PER SERVING:		
Total Carb: 2.9g	Fiber: 0.9g	Net Carb: 2.0g

Tips and Notes

See p. 309 for tips on egg white foams.

Unsweetened, dried coconut can be found in the health food section or the bulk bins at most grocery stores or from Bob's Red Mill® at retail stores or by mail order. It can also be ordered from the King Arthur® Flour Company (see Sources). Check an Asian grocery store for frozen, grated coconut that can be used like fresh.

SHORTBREAD COOKIES

The crumbs from these cookies can be used as a topping for Peach, Rhubarb, or Cherry Crisp (see Index for recipes).

- ¾ cup gluten flour
- ½ cup whey protein powder (2 net carbs or less per serving)
- ½ teaspoon baking soda
- A pinch of salt
- ¼ teaspoon xanthan gum (optional)
- 8 tablespoons butter (1 stick), softened to room temperature
- ⅓ cup granular Splenda®
- ¾ cup chopped almonds, walnuts, or pecans

Preheat the oven to 350° F. Butter an 8-inch square pan, line with parchment paper, and butter the parchment, or use a nonstick pan.

Combine the gluten flour, whey powder, baking soda, salt, and xanthan (if using) in a large bowl, whisk together and reserve. In another bowl, beat the butter and Splenda® together with an electric mixer for 3 minutes. Add the dry ingredients and the nuts to the mixer bowl and beat on low until evenly mixed. The mixture will be crumbly. Press the dough into the pan and bake for 10 to 15 minutes or until golden brown. Turn out on a cutting board and cut into 16 squares using a serrated knife to minimize breakage.

Servings: 16

PER SERVING:		
Total Carb: 3.2g	Fiber: 1.3g	Net Carb: 1.9g

Tips and Notes

The optional xanthan gum helps keep the cookies from crumbling.

GARDEN TEA PARTY MENU:

Salted Nuts

Blini with Crème Fraîche and smoked salmon

Cinnamon Nut Bread sandwiches with cream cheese

Jam Crêpes

Shortbread Cookies

Fresh strawberries with Devonshire Cream

Chocolate Covered Citrus Peel

White Tea
*

THUMBPRINT COOKIES

VARIATION:

Chocolate Filled Cookies

Instead of jam, fill the centers of the hot cookies with finely chopped sugar-free Chocolate Chips (see p. 260) or chopped low-carb chocolate bars (like Carb Safe or Atkins™ Endulge®). Return the cookies to the oven briefly if necessary to melt the chocolate. Makes 30 cookies.

Per Cookie:
Total Carb: 2.9g
Fiber: 1g
Net Carb: 1.9g

1   stick butter (½ cup), softened to room temperature
1   cup granular Splenda®
1   large egg yolk
1   teaspoon vanilla extract
¼   teaspoon baking powder
¼   teaspoon salt
2   cups almond flour or almond meal (See Sources)
⅓   cup finely chopped almonds
¼   cup sugar-free Strawberry or Peach Jam (See Index for recipes or use purchased sugar-free jam.)

Cream the butter and the Splenda® with an electric mixer, then blend in the egg yolk and vanilla extract. Whisk the almond flour together with the baking powder and salt. Stir into the butter mixture until smooth. Refrigerate for 1 hour. Shape the dough into 1-inch diameter balls and roll in the chopped almonds. Place on a large cookie sheet. Make an impression in each ball with your thumb. Return to the refrigerator for 15 minutes.

Preheat the oven to 350° F.

Bake the cookies for 18 to 20 minutes or until lightly browned and baked through. While still hot, fill the cavities with ½ teaspoon of sugar-free jam. Return to the oven for 2 or 3 minutes to melt the jam.

Servings: 30

PER SERVING:		
Total Carb: 3.3g	Fiber: 1.0g	Net Carb: 2.3g

CHOCOLATE CHIP COOKIES

The chocolate chip cookie, invented by Ruth Wakefield at her Toll House Restaurant in Whitman, Massachusetts in the 1930's, has become the most popular cookie in the US. These are very like the originals. (Got milk? See the chapter on Beverages.)

2/3 cup butter, softened to room temperature
1   cup plus 2 teaspoons granular Splenda®
1/3 cup sifted brown sugar or Sugar Twin® Brown Sugar Replacement or a combination of the two
2   eggs
1   tablespoon vanilla extract
1   tablespoon Wax Orchard™ Fruit Sweet® (or use honey and add 0.4 net carbs each)
1/2 cup plus 1 tablespoon oat flour
1/2 cup plus 1 tablespoon almond meal or almond flour
1   teaspoon baking soda
1/2 teaspoon salt
1   cup sugar-free Chocolate Chips (see p. 260)
1   cup macadamia nuts, roughly chopped (or use walnuts or pecans)

Preheat oven to 350° F.

Beat the butter with an electric mixer until fluffy. Beat in the Splenda® and sifted brown sugar and/or Sugar Twin® Brown Sugar Replacement. Add the eggs, one at a time, beating after each addition. Beat in the vanilla and Fruit Sweet® (or honey). Whisk the oat flour, almond meal (or almond flour), baking soda, and salt together and stir into the batter. Stir in the chocolate chips and nuts. Drop by scant tablespoonfuls onto ungreased cookie sheets. Moisten your finger and flatten the cookies down a bit if you used just Sugar Twin®. They won't spread out as much as they normally would with real sugar. Bake for about 10 minutes or until well browned. Let the cookies cool for a few minutes on the cookie sheet before removing with a spatula. These taste best when they are warm. To store, place in an airtight container and refrigerate or freeze; reheat them before serving in a 350° F oven for 3 to 4 minutes to crisp the outside and melt the chocolate.

Servings: 48

PER SERVING:		
Total Carb: 4.1g	Fiber: 0.8g	Net Carb: 3.3g
when made with brown sugar		
Total Carb: 2.9g	Fiber: 0.8g	Net Carb: 2.1g
when made with Sugar Twin®		

Tips and Notes

You can customize these cookies by substituting Sugar Twin® Brown Sugar Replacement for some or all of the brown sugar. I usually put 2 tablespoons of real brown sugar in a 1/3 cup measure and finish filling it with the Sugar Twin® Replacement. If you use no real sugar, they won't be quite as crisp, but they're still good.

Spraying cake and cookie batter with no-stick spray before baking produces a crisper crust.

See also Fillo Nut Cookies on 313 in section on Fillo.

Ice Cream and Frozen Desserts

I remember taking my turn sitting on top of the ice cream machine to hold it down while Daddy turned the crank. When your bottom was numb, it was time for one of the other kids to take a turn. The hardest part was waiting for the cream to harden, wrapped in layers of newspaper, before it was dished up. Even though it is possible to buy low-carb ice cream now (for several years we had to make it or do without), there is still something special about making ice cream outside on a hot summer night.

Ice Cream Techniques

Without sugar, ice cream mixtures freeze rock-hard around the edges, causing the motor of the ice cream machine to stall, while the center is still liquid. It took me years of trial and error to figure out how to make good sugar-free ice cream. Here are my solutions for making smooth, creamy ice cream without sugar:

1. Egg yolk acts as an emulsifier to produce a creamy smooth texture. (Don't skimp on the yolks and don't use egg substitute.)

2. Whipping both the egg whites and the cream incorporates more air and lightens the finished product.

3. A tiny bit of xanthan gum acts as a stabilizer and as an additional emulsifier. (See Ingredients and Sources.) It is not essential to the success of my recipes, but it makes them a bit more forgiving, as the frozen cream will hold its shape for a while before melting.

4. Polydextrose:
Polydextrose, a common ingredient in commercial low-carb and low-calorie products, can be purchased for home use. Polydextrose can replace the missing bulk of sugar in sugar-free ice cream, and it improves the texture and mouth feel.

I have included directions for several freezing methods. The simplest is still-freezing and it's not bad that way, but it will be icy. Beating it or whirling it in the food processor once or twice as it freezes can improve the texture. Churned ice cream requires a special machine, either the small countertop type or the old-fashioned tub kind. I've had better luck with a tub machine, the kind that uses ice and salt. Check the manual before using a countertop machine—you may need to cut my recipe in half. The tub machines will usually hold a double or even a triple recipe if you need to treat a crowd.

(continued on next page)

Ice Cream Techniques, continued

To still-freeze:
Method 1. Pour the mixture into shallow containers. Cover at once with waxed paper, parchment paper, or plastic film, and then cover with foil or a lid. Freeze for 1½ hours, or until frozen around the edges. Place the ice cream in a chilled bowl and beat with a fork or an electric mixer to break up the ice crystals. Return it to the freezer. Repeat several times to get the desired consistency. Cover as before and store in the freezer.

Method 2. Pour the mixture into a shallow container or ice cube trays and let it freeze until solid. Cut it into chunks and process it in two batches in a food processor until smooth. Serve at once as soft-serve ice cream or return it to the freezer to harden slightly.

To churn using a countertop freezer:
Place the canister in the freezer at 0° F overnight or until the liquid inside is solid and you can't hear a sloshing sound when you shake it. You may need to make only one-half the amount of ice cream mixture given in the recipes in this chapter. Pour the mixture into the canister and freeze according to manufacturer's directions. It will probably take about 15 minutes to freeze. You may need to scrape down the inside walls of the container several times in order to get the center to freeze. When the ice cream mounds up in the center, stop the machine and transfer it to a container, cover it with plastic film placed directly on top of the cream, and then cover with a lid or foil. Ripen the cream in the freezer for 2 to 3 hours before serving.

To churn using a motorized or hand-cranked freezer:
Pour the mixture into the canister of a motorized or hand-cranked freezer and freeze with ice and salt according to the manufacturer's instructions. Do not leave a motorized machine unattended, as my recipes will freeze much more quickly than cream containing sugar, and it will burn out the motor if it gets so hard that the dasher can't move. The ice cream is ready when it just holds its shape when mounded. Put it in a container, cover with plastic film placed directly on top of the ice cream, and then with a lid or foil. Let it ripen in the freezer for 2 to 3 hours.

To serve:
All home-made ice cream that has been stored in the freezer for more than a few hours needs to soften in the refrigerator before serving. The length of time depends on how solidly it is frozen and the thickness of the layer of ice cream in the container. One recipe of the French Vanilla Ice Cream, frozen in a 2-inch layer, may soften in as little as 10 minutes. If the layer is thicker, it may take up to 30 minutes or more. Set a timer and check it every 10 minutes until you learn how long it takes. Freezing the ice cream in several smaller containers will make it faster to bring one portion up to serving temperature and prolong the storage life of the rest of the batch, which will not then be subjected to repeated softening and refreezing.

"I doubt whether the world holds
for anyone a more soul-stirring
surprise than the first adventure
with ice-cream."

—Heywood Broun, *Holding a Baby,
in Seeing Things at Night*, 1921

Tips and Notes

Polydextrose improves the texture and mouth feel of sugar-free ice cream. Add ¹⁄₃ cup of polydextrose, stirred together with the Splenda®, to my recipe for French Vanilla Ice Cream, and you can freeze it in a countertop ice cream machine.

You may choose to use raw whites, but there will be a slight risk of exposure to Salmonella.

VARIATION:

Strawberry or Peach Ice Cream

Sweeten 1 cup of crushed fruit with ¼ cup of granular Splenda®. Purée in a food processor or blender. Stir the fruit into the hot custard. Optional: Add 2 tablespoons of strawberry- or peach-flavored sugar-free syrup. Makes 12 servings.

Per Serving for Strawberry:
Total Carb: 4.2g
Fiber: 0.3g
Net Carb: 3.9g

Per Serving for Peach:
Total Carb: 4.8g
Fiber: 0.3g
Net Carb: 4.5g

FRENCH VANILLA ICE CREAM

For the custard:
10 egg yolks
¹⁄₃ cup of polydextrose (optional)
3   packets of Sweet One®
1½ cups granular Splenda®
½   cup heavy cream (the recipe uses 3 ½ cups total)
¼   cup water
3   tablespoons vanilla extract
•   A pinch of salt

To finish:
•   The equivalent of 6 egg whites, either packaged, pasteurized whites made especially for whipping, or powdered whites plus water, reconstituted according to the directions on the container.
•   A pinch of cream of tartar (do not use cream of tartar if beating the whites in a copper bowl)
•   A scant ¼ teaspoon xanthan gum (optional)
3   cups heavy cream

Prepare a bowl of ice water to cool the pan after cooking the custard.

Heat one-half inch of water in the bottom of a double boiler to a simmer. Whisk the polydextrose, if using, and the Sweet One® into the Splenda®. Beat the yolks, the Splenda® mixture, ½ cup of the cream, and the ¼ cup of water with a whisk until well blended. Put the mixture in the top pan and place over, but not touching, the hot water. Cook, stirring constantly with a heat-resistant spatula, until thickened. The mixture may already look thick before it is cooked, but if you draw a flexible spatula across the bottom of the pan, the "track" that it leaves will close immediately. You want to cook it until the "track" stays clear long enough for you to get a glimpse of the bottom of the pan. This may take about 8 to 10 minutes. Scrape the sides of the pan often with the spatula and scrape off the custard that sticks to the spatula itself with a knife or a second spatula while cooking, to prevent any lumps from forming. (If you do get lumps, remove the custard from the heat and whisk vigorously until smooth or strain it when it has finished cooking.) Remove the pan from the heat and stir in the vanilla and salt. Cool the custard quickly by placing the pan in a large bowl of ice and water and stirring it until cold. Cover and chill the custard thoroughly in the refrigerator.

Whip the egg whites with the optional xanthan gum (and the cream of tartar if not using a copper bowl) until stiff but not dry. In a second bowl, with the same beaters, whip the 3 cups of cream until thick but not stiff. Gently fold the cream and egg whites into the custard. Freeze by one of the methods listed in Ice Cream Techniques.

Servings: 10

PER SERVING:		
Total Carb: 4.1g	Fiber: 0g	Net Carb: 4.1g

CHOCOLATE ICE CREAM

After a couple of failed attempts, I relegated chocolate ice cream to the "too hard" file. My daughter came to the rescue with this rich dark version. (Double this amount to freeze in a motorized or hand-cranked machine.)

6   tablespoons Dutch-process cocoa powder
½   cup granular Splenda® (1cup total for the recipe)
¼   cup plus an additional ½ cup half-and-half (¾ cup total for the recipe)
3½ ounces low-carb dark chocolate bar like
    Atkins™ Endulge® or Eat Well, Be Well™, chopped
5   egg yolks
½   cup granular Splenda®
1   tablespoon vanilla extract
2   tablespoons sugar-free chocolate syrup
3   egg whites or the equivalent from reconstituted powdered egg whites
1½ cups heavy cream

Combine the cocoa and ½ cup of Splenda®. Add ¼ cup of half-and-half and stir to make a paste. Heat the remaining ½ cup of half-and-half until it starts to boil. Pour it onto the cocoa paste and whisk until well blended. Return the mixture to the pan and bring to a simmer, stirring constantly. Simmer, stirring, for 6 minutes. Remove the pan from the heat and stir in the chopped chocolate bar. Stir until melted.

Have ready a large bowl of ice water to cool the custard.

In the bowl of an electric mixer, beat the egg yolks with ½ cup of Splenda® until pale yellow. Add the chocolate mixture to the bowl and beat vigorously, then return the combined mixture to the pan. Heat slowly to 185° F. Remove from heat. Add the vanilla and chocolate syrup. Set the pan in the ice-water bath and stir the custard until it is cool. Strain and refrigerate for several hours or overnight.

Beat 3 egg whites. In another bowl, whip the 1½ cups of heavy cream until stiff. Fold the cream and egg whites into the chocolate mixture. Freeze by one of the methods listed in Ice Cream Techniques.

Servings: 10

PER SERVING:		
Total Carb: 5.3g	Fiber: 1.2g	Net Carb: 4.1g

Tips and Notes

To prevent the formation of large ice crystals in ice cream while it is stored in the freezer, place it in a container, preferably polypropylene, to a depth of no more than 2 inches. Immediately cover it with a layer of plastic film or waxed paper, placed directly on top of the cream to exclude air, and then cover the container with foil or a lid. Freeze quickly.

The egg whites in this recipe are not cooked, so I prefer to use powdered or packaged whites. You may choose to use raw whites but there will be a slight risk of exposure to Salmonella. Powdered egg whites are available from many groceries or by mail from the King Arthur® Flour Company (see Sources). They also sell powdered yolks, which are not usually available in stores, and although the yolks do get cooked in the custard, you won't have extra whites leftover if you use the powdered ones.

Snow Cones

Scoop up fresh snow or shaved ice with a cup and invert into a chilled dish. Pour flavored sugar-free syrup over the snow or ice until it is saturated. Use about 1½ ounces (3 tablespoons) of syrup for 8 ounces (1 cup) of snow.

Total Carb: 0g
Fiber: 0g
Net Carb: 0g

AVOCADO LIME ICE CREAM

Unusual, smooth, and tart.

3   small or 2 large avocados (about 16 ounces total)
•   A pinch of salt
¾   cup granular Splenda®
5   tablespoons lime juice
•   The grated zest of one small lime
¾   cup heavy cream

Peel the avocados and remove the pits. Dice the pulp and purée it in the food processor with a little of the lime juice. (There should be about 2½ cups of avocado pulp.) Add the other ingredients and process until smooth. Freeze by one of the methods listed in Ice Cream Techniques.

Servings: 6

PER SERVING:		
Total Carb: 7.9g	Fiber: 1.6g	Net Carb: 6.3g

SNOW ICE CREAM

Here's a very simple and delicious ice cream that requires no freezer at all. All it requires is that you live in a place where it snows or that you have an ice-shaving machine.

⅓   cup granular Splenda®
1   whole pasteurized egg or ¼ cup liquid whole-egg replacement
¼   cup cream
1   tablespoon vanilla extract
•   Fresh clean snow or shaved ice

Mix the Splenda®, the egg or substitute, the cream, and the vanilla in a bowl and beat with a whisk or an electric mixer until smooth. Chill the mixture, as well as a cup for collecting the snow, and bowls for serving the ice cream, in the refrigerator for 15 minutes or more. Scoop up fresh snow or shaved ice with the cup and invert into the chilled dishes. Spoon the custard over the top. Stir briefly to blend. You can add additional custard if necessary to flavor the ice cream as it is eaten. This amount of custard will be enough for 2 or 3 bowls of ice cream.

Servings: 3

PER SERVING:		
Total Carb: 2.9g	Fiber: 0g	Net Carb: 2.9g

WHAT'S LIFE WITHOUT PIE?

Meat, fish, and fruit pies were common in England when the colonists came to America. Pie was so popular in early America that it was often eaten at every meal. This ultimate comfort food has achieved iconic status as the quintessentially American dessert.

APPLE PIE

At my house apple pie is one of the basic food groups. If apples happen to be fairly high in carbohydrates, so be it—this is one food that is not optional. The sugar, however, is.

- Pie Crust for a 9-inch double crust pie (see Index)
- 4 cooking apples (about 1½ pounds whole, or 4½ cups cut up)
- 2 tablespoons lemon juice in a large bowl of water
- ½ cup plus 1 tablespoon granular Splenda®
- ½ cup plus 1 tablespoon of polydextrose (optional)
- ½ teaspoon ground cinnamon
- 1½ teaspoons potato flour (or use 1 tablespoon of cornstarch and add 0.3 net carbs per serving)
- A pinch of salt
- 1 tablespoon butter

Preheat oven to 425° F.

Pare and slice the apples, dropping them into a bowl of water with the lemon juice added, to prevent darkening. Mix the Splenda®, polydextrose, if using, cinnamon, potato flour, and salt together. Drain apples well and toss with the dry mixture. Add a little lemon juice if the apples are bland or too sweet.

Put apple filling in a pastry-lined pan, dot with butter, and cover with the top crust. Make slits in the top to vent steam. Bake at 425° F for 35 to 45 minutes or until brown. Serve warm with sugar-free Ice Cream (see p. 282).

Servings: 10

PER SERVING:		
Total Carb: 17.9g filling only	Fiber: 1.2g	Net Carb: 16.7g

Tips and Notes

I always preferred under-ripe golden delicious apples for pies, but after moving to Washington, the apple capital of the world, I noticed that they were not quite the same. When a good friend from the Agriculture Department of West Virginia University came to visit, I found that it was not just my imagination. He said this variety originated as a spontaneous mutation in West Virginia, and that golden delicious apples grown in the eastern part of the country are superior to genetically identical apples from the Northwest. There was even an ad campaign that said: "Look for the freckles," a distinctive characteristic of the golden delicious apples from the eastern states.

Use Golden Delicious, as green and hard as you can find, Jonagolds, Northern Spy, or other tart apples for this pie.

FRIED APPLE PIES

When my mother was a child, she made fried pies for herself and her little sister to take to school for lunch. She used the leftover biscuit dough from breakfast, filled with sugar and butter. For us, she filled them with stewed, dried apples and fried them in bacon grease in an iron skillet. I re-created this old-fashioned treat using Carbquick™ baking mix, but you can use regular pie crust as well.

- Biscuit dough made with Carbquick™ baking mix
- 1 small apple (about 5 ounces)
- 2 tablespoons of Splenda®
- 1/8 teaspoon of ground cinnamon
- A few grains of salt
- 2 tablespoons of butter
- Butter, lard, or bacon grease for frying

For two pies you will need one fourth of the Buttermilk Biscuit dough made from the Carbquick™ recipe (the recipe on the box makes 16 biscuits). Roll dough into two 5½-inch circles, about the thickness of pie crust. (The whole biscuit recipe would be enough to make 8 fried pies). Alternately, make circles from regular Pie Crust.

Peel, core, and chop apple. Melt 2 tablespoons of butter in a skillet. Add the apple, Splenda®, 1/8 teaspoon cinnamon, and salt. Fry until apple is tender, about 5 minutes. Let cool. Place one half the apple mixture on one side of each circle of dough. Dampen one edge of dough with water and fold it over the filling. Press edges together and trim away excess. Fry pies in a heavy skillet until deep golden brown. Turn and fry other side. Serve with sugar-free vanilla ice cream.

Makes 2 pies.

PER SERVING:		
Total Carb: 23.8g	Fiber: 11.1g	**Net Carb: 12.7g**

"…with the merest drip of candied juice along the edges, (as if the flavor were so good to itself that its own lips watered!) of a mild and modest warmth, the sugar suggesting jelly, yet not jellied, the morsels of apple neither dissolved nor yet in original substance, but hanging as it were in a trace between the spirit and the flesh of applehood. . ."

—Reverend Henry Ward Beecher, describing the best time to eat a perfect apple pie.

DEEP-DISH CHERRY PIE

Even sour pie cherries are fairly high in carbohydrates, but cherry pie is such a favorite in my family that I make it anyway for special occasions. By using a top crust only, substituting almond flour for some of the flour, and rolling the crust thinner than usual, I can reduce the carbohydrate content considerably over what it would be with a regular double crust. Trader Joe's sells canned sour cherries. You can also use frozen pie cherries, but be sure they are unsweetened, tart cherries.

- Pie Crust for a single crust pie (see Index)
- 3 (14.5-ounce) cans pitted tart pie cherries (4 cups), drained, juice reserved
- ½ cup reserved cherry juice
- 1½ cups granular Splenda® (Add ¼ cup more if you like it sweet rather than tart.)
- ¾ cup of polydextrose, optional
- 1 tablespoon potato flour or 3 tablespoons of cornstarch (cornstarch adds an extra 1.3 net carbs per serving)
- A pinch of salt
- 2 tablespoons butter
- 2 teaspoons almond extract
- 1 tablespoon amaretto (Optional, but really good! It will add 0.9 net carbs per serving.)

Preheat oven to 425° F. You will need an 8- by 8-inch square pan with sides at least 2 inches high.

Drain the cherries in a colander over a bowl to catch the juice, pressing down on the cherries to extract as much juice as possible. Measure ½ cup of the cherry liquid. Discard the rest or use for another purpose. Stir the Splenda®, polydextrose, if using, potato flour or cornstarch, and salt together in a medium saucepan. Stir in ½ cup of the cherry juice. Cook and stir for a few minutes until thick and clear, but do not let it boil. Add the butter, almond extract, and the amaretto, if using, and stir until butter is melted. Mix in the cherries. Pour filling into an 8- by 8-inch square pan. Let the filling cool.

Cut pie crust one inch larger than the pan, and place over the filling. Fold edges under and crimp. Cut slits in top to vent steam. Bake at 425° F for 30 to 40 minutes or until crust is brown and filling starts to bubble. Cover edges after 20 minutes to prevent excessive browning. Serve warm with sugar-free ice cream.

Servings: 9

```
PER SERVING:
    Total Carb: 13.4g        Fiber: 0.8g        Net Carb: 12.6g
    filling only
```

Tips and Notes

Researchers at Michigan State University have discovered that tart cherries reduce the pain and inflammation of arthritis, gout, and fibromyalgia. There are other compounds in cherries that may inhibit cancer tumors and prevent heart disease. Melatonin, a sleep regulator and antioxidant that may help prevent brain deterioration, is also present in significant quantities. Studies are being conducted by Brunswick Laboratories, in Waring, Massachusetts, on the antioxidant capabilities of Montmorency cherries and by the USDA/Agricultural Research Service on the anti-inflammatory effects of fresh Bing cherries.

"Twenty cherries provide 25 milligrams of anthocyanins, which help to shut down the enzymes that cause tissue inflammation in the first place, so cherries can prevent many kinds of pain." Dr. Muraleedharan Nair, professor at Michigan State University and with the National Food Safety and Toxicology Center at MSU.

Longing for his favorite American pies after prolonged travels in Europe, Mark Twain wrote the following recipe for an English apple pie:

"Take a sufficiency of water and a sufficiency of flour, and construct a bullet-proof dough. Work this into the form of a disk, with the edges turned up some three-fourths of an inch. Toughen and kiln-dry in a couple days in a mild but unvarying temperature. Construct a cover for the redoubt in the same way and of the same material. Fill with stewed dried apples: aggravate with cloves, lemon-peel, and slabs of citron; add two portions of New Orleans sugars, then solder on the lid and set in a safe place till it petrifies. Serve cold at breakfast and invite your enemy."

Mark Twain
A Tramp Abroad, 1880

In France a galette can be a flat cake, a cookie, a biscuit, or a tart. In the US, a galette is a free-form, open-faced tart.

CRANBERRY PIE

- Pie Crust for a 9-inch single crust pie (see Index)
- 4 cups fresh or frozen cranberries
- 1½ cups granular Splenda®
- ½ cup water
- 2 tablespoons butter
- 2 eggs

Preheat oven to 350° F. Line a 9-inch pie pan with pastry.

Put the cranberries, Splenda®, and water in a saucepan and bring to a boil. Reduce the heat and simmer for 15 minutes. Stir in the butter. Remove from heat and let cool.

Beat the eggs with a fork and stir into the cooled cranberry filling. Pour into pastry-lined pan. Bake at 350° F for 30 to 40 minutes until filling is set and crust is brown. Serve with sugar-free Whipped Cream, if desired (see p. 328).

Servings: 10

PER SERVING:		
Total Carb: 9.3g filling only	Fiber: 1.6g	Net Carb: 7.7g

GALETTE

The easiest way to make a fruit pie is also one of the prettiest, just oozing with country charm. A rustic open-faced tart, called a galette, requires less effort and saves a few carbs as well, since it uses less pie crust than a regular double-crust pie with a fluted rim.

Prepare fruit pie filling and chill. Prepare Pie Crust for a 9-inch single-crust pie. Preheat oven to 400° F. Grease a baking sheet or line with a nonstick mat.

Roll out pastry into a rough circle; do not trim edges. Place on baking sheet. Put filling in center and spread out, leaving a 3-inch border of dough. Dot filling with butter. Gather up the edges of the dough and fold in evenly over the filling, leaving the filling exposed in the center. Bake until filling bubbles and crust is brown, about 30 minutes.

Note: This method works best with my fillings for apple, peach, or mincemeat pie. Don't attempt to bake a juicy pie, like cherry or berry on a baking sheet. You can still make a galette, just put it in a regular pie pan in case it leaks.

SHAKER LEMON PIE

I love to make this pie with sweet, thin-skinned Meyer lemons.

- Pie Crust for an 8-inch double crust pie (see Index)
- 3 Meyer lemons or use regular lemons
- 1 cup granular Splenda®
- 2 beaten eggs
- 2 teaspoons Grand Marnier liqueur, optional (adds 0.4 net carbs per serving)
- 1 teaspoon lemon extract
- 2 tablespoons water

Preheat oven to 450° F. An 8-inch pie pan is used for this recipe.

Slice the lemons very thinly, reserving the juice. Remove the seeds. (To substitute regular lemons, remove the thin yellow part of the skin with a zesting tool or a grater before slicing. Peel away the white pith from the lemon. Discard the pith and add the zest with the lemon slices.)

Place the lemon slices in a bowl with the Splenda®, extract, water, and the optional Grand Marnier. Stir and let stand for 20 minutes.

Line an 8-inch pie pan with pastry. Add the beaten eggs to the lemon mixture and stir to blend thoroughly. Pour the filling into the pie shell. Cover with top crust, fold edges under and crimp. Cut slits in the top crust to vent steam. Bake at 450° F for 5 minutes. Reduce heat to 350° F and bake 35 to 40 minutes more, or until top is well browned (cover edges with foil if necessary to prevent over-browning), and a knife inserted in the center comes out clean. Serve warm with sugar-free ice cream.

Servings: 8

PER SERVING:		
Total Carb: 8.4g filling only	Fiber: 1.0g	Net Carb: 7.4g

Tips and Notes

Eight-inch pie pans may be hard to find in the stores, but if you buy a take-out pie from a restaurant, it will probably come in an 8-inch pan. Also, when you buy a frozen pie crust in a foil pan, it may say "9-inch crust" on the package, but it will usually measure 8 inches inside the flange. If the pan was used for a cream pie, so that the crust was baked empty, it may have small holes in the bottom to improve the browning. Be sure to use those only for pies that won't leak through.

Cheese Plate

A cheese plate can be served after the main course or instead of dessert. Choose three to six varieties with contrasting tastes and textures, from soft to firm and from mild to sharp. Allow about 1 ounce of each per person. Arrange the portions around the rim of the plate and place accompaniments, such as Dried Cranberries, Candied Kumquats, fresh blueberries or strawberries, nuts, olives, or cornichons in the center. Serve with thin slices of toasted Mixed Flour Bread and Parmesan Sesame Crackers.

KUMQUAT PIE

This is similar to the Shaker Lemon Pie but not so tart. Serve it warm with sugar-free ice cream.

- Pie Crust for 8-inch double crust pie (see Index)
- 11 ounces kumquats, sliced very thinly and seeded (2 cups, sliced) For a faster method: cut kumquats in half, remove seeds, and chop by hand or pulse a few times in a food processor.
- 1 cup granular Splenda®
- 1 teaspoon orange extract
- 2 teaspoons Grand Marnier liqueur, optional (adds 1 net carb per serving)
- 2 beaten eggs

Preheat oven to 450° F. An 8-inch pie pan is used for this recipe.

Place sliced kumquats in a bowl with the Splenda, orange extract, and Grand Marnier. Stir and let stand for 20 minutes.

Line an 8-inch pie pan with pastry. Add the beaten eggs to the kumquat mixture and stir to blend thoroughly. Pour the filling into the pie shell. Cover with top crust, fold edges under and crimp. Cut slits in the top crust to vent steam. Bake at 450° F for 5 minutes. Reduce heat to 350° F and bake 35 to 40 minutes more, or until top is well browned (cover edges with foil if necessary to prevent over-browning), and a knife inserted in the center comes out clean. Serve warm with sugar-free ice cream.

Servings: 8

PER SERVING:		
Total Carb: 9.5g filling only	Fiber: 2.5g	Net Carb: 7.0g

"The magnificence of the dessert should not allow one to forget the cheese. Cheese complements a good dinner and supplements a bad one."

—Eugene Briffault

PEACH PIE

- Pie Crust for a 9-inch double crust pie (see Index)
- 4½ cups peeled and pitted fresh peaches or sugar-free frozen peaches, thawed and drained
- 1 cup granular Splenda®
- ½ cup of polydextrose, optional
- 2 teaspoons potato flour or 2 tablespoons of cornstarch (cornstarch adds 0.8 net carbs per serving)
- ½ teaspoon ground cinnamon
- A pinch of salt
- 1 tablespoon sugar-free peach syrup (optional)
- 2 tablespoons butter

Preheat oven to 425° F.

Slice or chop the peaches and put in a bowl. Mix the Splenda®, polydextrose, if using, potato flour or cornstarch, cinnamon, and salt together and sprinkle over the peaches. Add syrup (if using). Stir gently until blended. Scrape the peach filling into a 9-inch, pastry-lined pie pan. Dot with butter. Cover with top crust; fold the edges under and crimp. Make slits in the top crust to vent steam. Bake at 425° F for 25 to 30 minutes or until brown. Cover edges if necessary to prevent excessive browning. Serve warm with sugar-free ice cream, if desired.

Servings: 10

PER SERVING:		
Total Carb: 12.9g filling only	Fiber: 1.6g	Net Carb: 11.3g

"You lean over the sink to make sure you don't drip on yourself. Then you sink your teeth into the flesh and the juices trickle down your cheeks and dangle on your chin. This is a real bite, a primal act, a magical sensory celebration announcing that summer has arrived."

—Mas Masumoto, describing a juicy peach in *Epitaph for a Peach*.

VARIATION

Deep-dish Peach Pie

Make 1½ times the recipe for peach pie filling and use a top crust only. Follow directions for Deep-dish Cherry Pie to bake.
Makes 9 servings.

Per Serving:
Total Carb: 18.1g
Fiber: 2.4g
Net Carb: 15.7g
(filling only)

Tips and Notes

Adding polydextrose to my fruit pies, gives me glossy, thick juices that caramelize around the edges as if they were made with real sugar. I add ½ cup for each cup of granular Splenda® called for in the recipe. (This is in addition to the Spenda®, not a replacement for it, as the poly-d is not sweet.) Polydextrose has the texture and mouth feel of sucrose and adds missing bulk in recipes made with high intensity sweeteners. It also browns and caramelizes like regular sugar, but it behaves like soluble fiber when ingested. It is widely used in commercial products to allow a reduction in the amount of sugar or fat needed and to add beneficial fiber. See Ingredients for more information and Sources to order. My recipes were tested with polydextrose from Honeyville Grain.

Tips and Notes

When the colonists came to America, they developed new recipes using the local ingredients and simple cooking methods that fit their new circumstances. They gave their new desserts new names, reflecting the homemade, rustic character of these humble dishes.

Cobbler, from the word cobble, meaning, "to put together hastily," was a deep-dish fruit pie with a biscuit, crumb, or pastry topping, baked in an oven.

Crisps had fruit on the bottom, topped with bread or cookie crumbs, sugar, and butter.

Brown Betty had layers of fruit between layers of buttered crumbs.

A grunt and a slump were fruit pies with biscuit toppings, cooked on top of the stove. A Cape Cod grunt, made of berries, was put in a mold and steamed in a kettle. Louisa May Alcott's recipe for apple slump was cooked, covered, over low heat.

A pandowdy was a fruit pie with a biscuit topping. You "dowdy" the pie by cutting the pastry down into the juices partway through the baking time.

A buckle was a cake with fruit or berries stirred into the batter, giving it an uneven or buckled appearance.

VARIATION:
PEACH CRISP

Try this with rhubarb, cherry, or other pie filling as well.

1   recipe Shortbread Cookies (see p. 277)
1   recipe Peach Pie Filling
•   Butter

Preheat oven to 350° F.

Bake cookies as directed. Place pie filling into eight individual six-ounce ramekins. Crumble some of the cookies and spread 2 tablespoons of crumbs over each ramekin. Dot with butter. Bake until filling is bubbly and top is crisp, about 15 minutes, at 350° F. Serve warm with cream or sugar-free ice cream, if desired.

Servings: 8

PER SERVING:		
Total Carb: 20.7g	Fiber: 4.2g	Net Carb: 16.5g

Daddy makes a pie:

When my parents were first married, my mother went to work in the local peach harvest to make a little extra money. On her first day, she was given a bag of fresh peaches. The next day was Saturday, and my dad decided to surprise her by making a peach pie. When she came home, she was definitely surprised; there was flour everywhere, even on the outside of the front door. She never went back to work, and as far as I know, my dad never tried to cook again.
—JBB

KEY LIME PIE

- Shortbread Crust or Pie Crust for a 9-inch single crust pie, baked and cooled (see Index)
1 packet (¼ ounce) granulated gelatin
3 tablespoons cold water
2 cups granular Splenda®
- A pinch of salt
¾ cup butter, cut up
½ cup lime juice (2 large limes, about 9 ounces as purchased)
8 large eggs
1 teaspoon lime extract (see Sources) or use lemon extract

Bring about one-half inch of water to a simmer on low heat in the bottom of a double boiler. Have ready a bowl of ice and water and a baked and cooled 9-inch pie shell.

Soften 1 packet (¼ ounce) of granulated gelatin in 3 tablespoons of cold water.

Stir together the Splenda® and salt in the top of the double boiler. Add the butter and juice and place over, but not touching, the hot water. Heat until the butter is melted, stirring frequently.

Break the eggs into a bowl and whisk until smooth. Whisk the eggs into the lime juice mixture and continue to cook, whisking constantly, until the mixture thickens enough to coat the back of a spoon (about 5 minutes). Stir the gelatin and extract into the hot mixture. Remove the top pan from over the hot water and place it in the bowl of ice and water. Stir until chilled. Pour the lime filling over the prepared crust. Cover with plastic wrap, placed directly on the curd, and refrigerate for 2 hours before using. Serve with sugar-free Whipped Cream (see p. 328).

Servings: 10

PER SERVING:
Total Carb: 6.4g   Fiber: 0g   Net Carb: 6.4g
filling only

Tips and Notes

It is not necessary to search out real key limes for Key Lime Pie. If you have ever done so, you know that they are tiny and seedy and contain about one drop of juice each. Key lime juice can be had from a bottle if you want to be authentic, or you can make do quite nicely with ordinary limes.

VARIATION:

Lime Angel Pie

After cooling the lime filling in an ice bath, place it in a Meringue Crust (see p. 310). Serve at once with sugar-free Whipped Cream.

Makes 10 servings.
Per Serving, Including Meringue:
Total Carb: 8.6g
Fiber: 0g
Net Carb: 8.6g

VARIATION:

Rhubarb-Strawberry Custard Pie

Replace 2 cups of the rhubarb with 2 cups of fresh strawberries that have been cut in half or quartered. Reduce the Splenda® by 1 tablespoon.

Makes 10 servings.
Per Serving:
Total Carb: 5.9g
Fiber: 1.4g
Net Carb: 4.5g
filling only

Tips and Notes

Rhubarb leaves are toxic. Trim away any green leaves from the tops of the stalks.

RHUBARB CUSTARD PIE

Rhubarb is a Godsend for low-carb dieters. Not a rhubarb aficionado? Try this recipe. The soaking takes out some of the sourness and eliminates the astringency that some people find objectionable; the lemon juice keeps the bright red color from leaching out and prevents the rhubarb from becoming mushy. If you still don't like it, try replacing half the rhubarb with strawberries.

- Pie Crust for a 9-inch single crust pie (see Index)
- 1 pound fresh rhubarb stalks (4 cups, sliced)
- 3 eggs, well beaten
- 1 cup granular Splenda®
- A pinch of salt
- ¾ cup heavy cream
- 1 tablespoon butter, melted and cooled
- 1 teaspoon lemon juice

Wash the rhubarb and trim the ends. Cut into 4-inch lengths and cover with cold water. Let soak for 30 minutes.

Place the pastry in a 9-inch pie pan and flute the edges. Prick the crust with a fork or use a perforated pan. Bake the crust in a 425° F oven for 5 minutes. Remove the crust from the oven and let it stand for three minutes. Beat the eggs with a fork in a small bowl. Spoon a small amount of the beaten egg into the hot crust and tilt the pan to coat the bottom and sides. Pour any remaining egg back into the bowl with the rest of the eggs. If the hot crust does not cook the egg, return it to the oven for one or two minutes until the egg is set. (This keeps the crust from getting soggy.)

Remove the rhubarb from the water, drain, and blot dry. Cut it into ½ inch slices.

Position the oven rack in the lower third of the oven. Preheat oven to 425° F.

Mix the Splenda® and salt in a mixing bowl. Beat in the eggs, then the cream, butter, and the lemon juice. Put the rhubarb into the pastry-lined pan and pour the custard mixture over the top. Set the pie on the lower rack in the oven and bake at 425° F for 10 minutes. Reduce the oven temperature to 400° F. Bake for 30 to 35 minutes more or until puffed and golden and the center is set.

Servings: 10

PER SERVING:		
Total Carb: 4.8g filling only	Fiber: 1.2g	Net Carb: 3.6g

PUMPKIN PIE

The recipe on the Libby's® canned pumpkin label needed only a few alterations to go low-carb. See if you agree that this is as good as the original (maybe better).

- 9-inch Pie Crust, bottom crust only (see Index)
- ½ cup plus 3 tablespoons of granular Splenda®
- 2 tablespoons Sugar Twin® Brown Sugar Replacement
- ¼ teaspoon salt
- 1 teaspoon ground cinnamon
- ¾ teaspoon ground ginger
- ⅛ teaspoon ground cloves
- 2 large eggs
- 1½ cups canned pumpkin
- 1 teaspoon vanilla extract or 1 tablespoon of rum or brandy
- 1½ cups half-and-half

Prepare the crust for a single-crust pie. Preheat oven to 425° F.

Whisk the Splenda®, brown sugar substitute, and spices together in a small bowl. Beat the eggs with a whisk in a large bowl. (A bowl with a pouring spout is helpful.) Stir in the pumpkin and the Splenda® and spice mixture. Add vanilla and gradually stir in the half-and-half. Pour into the pie shell. Bake for 15 minutes. Reduce the heat to 350° F; bake for 30 to 40 minutes more, or until a knife inserted near the center comes out clean. It may be necessary to cover the edges of the crust to prevent over-browning. Use special pie-crust shields for this, or cut a 6-inch circle out of the center of a square of foil and lay it over the pie. Serve at once or place the pie on a rack until completely cool before covering or storing. Store in the refrigerator.

Servings: 10

PER SERVING:		
Total Carb: 6.3g filling only	Fiber: 1.5g	Net Carb: 4.5g

Tips and Notes

To keep the crust from getting soggy—prick it all over with a fork or weight it by lining it with foil and filling with dry beans or pie weights. Bake the crust for five minutes in the preheated oven. Remove the crust from the oven and let it stand for three minutes, then break an egg into the crust. Quickly tilt the pan to roll the egg around until the entire bottom and sides are coated with a thin layer of egg white. Tip the egg out of the crust. If the hot crust does not cook the egg white, return it to the oven for one or two minutes until the egg white is firm and opaque.

"What moistens the lip and what brightens the eye!
What calls back the past, like the rich pumpkin pie."

—John Greenleaf Whittier, *The Pumpkin*, 1844

THANKSGIVING DINNER MENU:

Potato Soup

--

Roast turkey and Dressing

Pan Gravy

Cranberry Sauce

Holiday Pumpkin Casserole

Brussels sprouts

Warm Mincemeat Pie French Vanilla Ice Cream

*

My mother could remember making mincemeat that really had meat in it. Old-fashioned mincemeat has a carb advantage over the all-fruit ones that are more popular today. I searched through old cookbooks for recipes that could be adapted and found several variations, going back as far as 1901 (by Fannie Farmer). Most of the old recipes are very cryptic and they make enough filling for 10 to 20 pies. I've tried to fill in the blanks, and I've reduced the amount to make one 9-inch pie. My husband says this tastes like the pies his grandmother made.

- Pie Crust for a 9-inch double crust (see Index)
- 1 cup stewing beef (about ½ pound before cooking), chopped
- 2 cups water for cooking the beef (to be reduced to 1 cup of broth)
- ½ cup beef suet, chopped (about 2 ounces)
- ½ orange or 3 ounces (about ¾ cup whole) kumquats
- 1½ cups tart apples, peeled, cored, and chopped
- 1 cup unsweetened, pitted, sour pie cherries (fresh, frozen, or canned)
- 3 tablespoons cider vinegar
- ½ cup sugar-free simple syrup (or use ½ cup more Splenda® plus ½ cup of water and add 0.6 carbs per serving)
- 1 cup granular Splenda®
- 1 cup sugar-free Dried Cranberries (see p. 105)
- 1 teaspoon lemon peel, grated
- 1 teaspoon ground cinnamon
- 1 teaspoon ground cloves
- 1 teaspoon ground allspice
- 1½ teaspoons ground nutmeg
- ½ teaspoon salt
- 1 teaspoon lemon extract
- ¼ teaspoon almond extract
- ¾ cup walnuts, chopped
- 3 tablespoons brandy (optional)

Simmer the beef in the 2 cups of water until tender. Drain, reserving the broth. Place the beef and the suet in the bowl of a food processor and process until finely chopped.

Boil the broth from the cooked beef until it is reduced to one cup.

If using half of an orange, remove and reserve the zest (the thin, orange-colored part of the peel). Remove and discard the white peel that remains and the seeds. Chop the orange segments or use seeded and chopped kumquats. Mix the chopped beef, the suet, and the broth with the chopped orange segments and zest or the chopped kumquats; put in a large saucepan. Add all the other ingredients, except the optional brandy. Bring the mixture to the boiling point. Reduce the heat and simmer, stirring occasionally, for an hour, or until thick. Stir in the brandy (if using). Let the mincemeat cool.

(continued on next page)

MINCEMEAT PIE, CONTINUED

Preheat the oven to 425° F.

Put the mincemeat filling in a pastry-lined pie pan and cover with a top crust. Trim the crust and fold under and crimp the edges. Make slits in the top to vent steam. Bake for 25 to 30 minutes or until brown. Serve warm with sugar-free ice cream, if desired. Makes 4 ½ cups of mincemeat.

Servings: 10

PER SERVING:		
Total Carb: 13.4g filling only	Fiber: 2.6g	Net Carb: 10.8g

Tips and Notes

Other uses for mincemeat filling include Mincemeat Strudel and Mincemeat Filled Pumpkin Tamales. See Index for these recipes.

PECAN PIE

After experimenting with polydextrose to make candied fruit, and seeing the beautiful caramelized syrup that was left in the pan, I suspected I had found the secret to making a sugar-free Pecan Pie, but I never expected it to be so easy and so utterly delicious.

- 8-inch pie crust or individual tart shells
- 1   cup of granular Splenda®
- 1   cup of polydextrose (see Sources and Ingredients)
- ½   teaspoon of salt
- ½   cup of water
- 3   tablespoons of butter, cut into pieces
- 2   eggs, beaten with a fork
- 1   cup of raw pecan halves

Mix Splenda®, polydextrose, and salt together until well blended. Heat water in medium-size bowl in microwave until hot. Stir in Splenda®, salt, and poly-d mixture. Microwave on high for 2 to 3 minutes until everything is dissolved and it makes a clear syrup. (You will see a slight film on top that wrinkles when you move the bowl.) Stir butter into syrup and let cool.

Preheat oven to 375° F. Stir eggs and pecans into pie filling. Pour into pie shell. Bake for 30 to 35 minutes until nuts are crisp and brown and filling is set. Serve slightly warm or let cool.

Makes 10 servings.

PER SERVING:		
Total Carb: 25.6g filling only	Fiber: 21.2g	Net Carb: 4.6g

Tips and Notes

Star fruit keeps its unusual crunchiness when sautéed and has a flavor reminiscent of apples. Serve it as a side dish, warm over ice cream, or make a beautiful tart by arranging the star-shaped slices over a cream filling in a tart shell.

Sautéed Star Fruit:

Slice the star fruit and remove the seeds. Sprinkle the slices generously with granular Splenda® and sauté in butter until they start to brown. Turn and sauté on the other side. Dust with cinnamon. Serve warm. One medium star fruit (4.7 ounces) has 9.9 grams of carbohydrate and 3.4 of fiber for a net of 6.5 grams of carbohydrate. (The Splenda® will add 1.5 net grams per tablespoon and the cinnamon will add 0.7 net grams per teaspoon.)

The Baker's Catalogue® from the King Arthur® Flour Company featured a recipe for a pineapple pie that looked so incredible that I had to give it a low-carb makeover. Star fruit is the low-carb stand-in for the pineapple. With pineapple extract, it is quite convincing, but this pie is also delicious with lemon flavoring.

For the Crust:
½ cup gluten flour
½ cup almond flour (or use ½ cup of finely chopped nuts)
½ cup unsweetened coconut
⅓ cup granular Splenda®
¼ teaspoon salt
4 tablespoons cold butter, cut into 4 pieces

For the Filling:
1 (¼-ounce size) packet unflavored gelatin
¼ cup water
¼ cup amaretto- or coconut- flavored, sugar-free syrup
  (or increase both the water and the Splenda® by ¼ cup and add 0.6 net carbs per serving)
8 ounces whipped cream cheese (it is sold this way), softened to room temperature
½ cup plus 1 tablespoon granular Splenda®
1 teaspoon vanilla extract
1 teaspoon pineapple extract (or use lemon extract)
1¼ cups (about 8 ounces) star fruit, chopped, seeds removed
  Reserve a few small slices for garnish.
1 cup heavy cream

For the Topping:
1 egg white
¼ cup granular Splenda®
2 cups unsweetened coconut

To Make the Crust:
Preheat the oven to 350° F. Combine all the crust ingredients in the bowl of a food processor and pulse to form coarse crumbs. Press the crumbs into the bottom and up the sides of a 9-inch pie pan. Bake for 10 to 15 minutes at 350° F, or until lightly browned. Remove from the oven and cool completely.

(continued on next page)

HEAVENLY PIE, CONTINUED

To Make the Filling:
In a microwave-safe bowl, combine the gelatin, water, and syrup. Heat in the microwave until the gelatin is dissolved. Let cool. In another bowl, beat together the cream cheese, Splenda®, and extracts until smooth, and then stir in the chopped star fruit. In the bowl of an electric mixer, beat the cream to soft-peak stage. Fold in the cooled gelatin mixture, then the cream-cheese mixture. Pour into the pie shell and refrigerate until firm.

To Make the Topping:
Preheat the oven to 350° F.

With clean beaters, beat together the egg white and Splenda® until stiff. Fold in the coconut. Spread the mixture on a nonstick or parchment-lined baking sheet and bake in a preheated oven for about 10 minutes or until it just starts to brown. Turn the pieces over and break them up. Continue to bake for another 5 minutes until golden brown. Remove from oven and cool completely.

To Serve:
Sprinkle the topping over the pie just before serving. Garnish each piece of pie with a slice of star fruit.

Servings: 10

PER SERVING:		
Total Carb: 12.7g	Fiber: 5.2g	Net Carb: 7.5g

Note: Star fruit vary in size, so buy however many it takes to weigh about 8 ounces for this recipe.

Tips and Notes

Star fruit seeds are said to be toxic, so be sure to remove them.

"To create a fine dessert, one has to combine the skills of a confectioner, a decorator, a painter, an architect, an ice-cream manufacturer, a sculptor, and a florist. The splendour of such creations appeals above all to the eye—the real gourmand admires them without touching them!"

—Eugene Briffault

LEMON COCONUT PIE

Tips and Notes

The lemon curd given as part of the recipe for Lemon Bar Cookies can also be used as the filling for a Lemon Pie.

- 8-inch single Pie Crust or use Shortbread Crust from Lemon Bar recipe (see Index)
- 1½ cups granular Splenda®
- ¾ cup unsweetened grated or flaked coconut
- 1 teaspoon potato flour
- ½ cup Crème Fraîche (see p. 51) or buttermilk
- ½ cup canned coconut milk
- 2 eggs
- 2 egg yolks
- 1 teaspoon vanilla extract
- 3 teaspoons of grated lemon zest (the thin yellow part of the rind)
- 3 tablespoons of lemon juice
- A pinch of salt

Preheat the oven to 350° F. Prepare an 8-inch pastry Pie Crust or Shortbread Crust. Pre-bake the crust for 5 minutes just before filling.

Stir the Splenda®, coconut, and potato flour together in a mixing bowl. Whisk in the remaining ingredients. Pour into prepared pie shell. Bake 35 to 40 minutes at 350° F or until filling is just set. Let pie cool to room temperature and top with fresh berries and sugar-free Whipped Cream (see p. 328). Store in the refrigerator.

Servings: 10

PER SERVING:		
Total Carb: 6.3g count is for filling only	Fiber: 1.0g	Net Carb: 5.3g

"Pie is the American synonym of prosperity, and its varying contents the calendar of the changing seasons. Pie is the food of the heroic. No pie-eating people can ever be permanently vanquished."

—From an editorial in the *New York Times*, 1902.

CHOCOLATE FUDGE PIE

Intensely dense and rich.

- Pie Crust for a 9-inch, single crust pie, baked and cooled (see Index)
- ½ cup (1 stick) butter
- 1 cup (6 ounces) of sugar-free, semi-sweet chocolate chips
- 1 cup granular Splenda®
- 1 tablespoon Dutch cocoa powder
- Pinch salt
- 3 eggs
- ¾ cup heavy cream
- 1 teaspoon of vanilla extract

Melt the butter in the top of a double boiler over hot water. Add the chocolate chips and stir until melted and smooth. Let cool slightly. Whisk together the Splenda®, cocoa, and salt in a bowl. In a separate bowl, beat the eggs with a fork and combine with the cream. Stir the egg and cream mixture into the dry ingredients, and then stir into the chocolate mixture in the top of the double boiler. Place top pan back over the water, put double boiler on low heat, and stir constantly for 5 to 7 minutes or until thickened, but do not boil. Remove from heat and stir in the vanilla. Pass the filling through a strainer to insure a silky-smooth texture. Let cool slightly, and pour into prepared crust. Top with sugar-free Whipped Cream. Serve in small slices, as it is very rich.

Makes 10 Servings.

PER SERVING:

Total Carb: 6.9g   Fiber: 1.7g   Net Carb: 5.2g
filling only, when made with my Sugar-Free Chocolate Chips

Total Carb: 9.2g   Fiber: 5.7g   Net Carb: 3.5g
filling only, when made with Eat Well, Be Well™ chips

Note:

The carb count will be less when using purchased sugar-free semi-sweet chocolate chips because Splenda® in both granular form and packets contains sugars (dextrose and maltodextrin) as bulking agents.

Tips and Notes

More pie recipes can be found in the Fruit chapter and under Frostings and Fillings:

Rhubarb Strawberry Pie (see p. 104 [sidebar])

Coconut Cream Cheese Pie (see p. 253)

Chocolate Cream Cheese Pie (see p. 254)

Cream Cheese Fruit Pie (see p. 253)

Coconut Cream Pie (see p. 257)

Chocolate Cream Pie (see p. 257)

PIE CRUSTS

MY FAVORITE PIE CRUST

Tips and Notes

Stir dry ingredients like flour and cornstarch before measuring to fluff them up in case they have settled. All my dry measurements are dip-level-pour, which means you fill the measuring cup or spoon by dipping it to overfill, and then level it off with a the straight edge of a knife or spatula. If you dip your measuring utensil and then press it against the side of the bag or box, you compress the contents and you may have too much.

The volume of flour will vary depending on its moisture content. Sifting and settling also changes the volume. Whether the flour is sifted before or after measuring can also make a difference. The most accurate way to measure it is by weight, so for recipes where an accurate measurement is important, I have included the weight, as well as the amount in cups. Package labels give you an accurate weight for a stated volume, so with a little math you can always figure out the weight for the amount called for.

There are two kinds of people: cake people and pie people. When I married a pie man, my first culinary challenge was to make good pie crust. I recently reworked my old recipe to eliminate the trans fats and to use whole-grain flour. The new incarnation uses white whole-wheat flour which has all the nutrition of regular whole-wheat but tastes more like all purpose flour. It makes a flaky, tender crust that tastes as good as ever but is much more healthful.

8½ ounces or 2 cups white whole-wheat flour
1   teaspoon salt
½   cup no-trans-fat shortening
¼   cup butter
⅓   cup water

Place the ingredients in the refrigerator until chilled. Preheat oven to 425° F.

Whisk or sift the flour. Stir in the salt. Take out ⅓ cup of the flour and salt mixture. Place it in a small bowl and stir in the ⅓ cup of cold water to form a moist paste. It should have a consistency like gravy. If it is too thick, add a little more water. Cut the shortening and butter into the remaining flour with a pastry blender (the kind with flat blades, not round wires) until the largest particles are like small peas. Drop the flour paste by small spoonfuls onto the dough, tossing to coat. Cut through the dough a few times with the pastry blender until incorporated. Work it together quickly with your hands to form a ball. Divide the ball into 3 or 4 portions and shape into flattened disks. Wrap separately in plastic film. Refrigerate for an hour or more so the dough can relax and the moisture can even out.

Put a layer of plastic wrap on the work surface. It will take two overlapping pieces for a regular size pie crust. A few drops of water under the plastic and under the edge where it overlaps will keep it from slipping. Dust the plastic wrap with flour. Place one ball of dough on it, dust with more flour, and cover with another sheet of plastic wrap. Roll out the pastry with a rolling pin, rolling from the center to the edges. Lift the top plastic and turn the dough over several times as you roll, dusting it with flour each time. Roll to a thickness of one-sixteenth of an inch. (This is half the thickness of my original recipe.) Remove the top layer of plastic and pick up the dough, along with the layer of plastic under it, and invert it onto the pie pan. (The plastic layer is now on top and the dough can be adjusted to fit in the pan without stretching or tearing.) Center the dough and gently push it into the pan. Remove the plastic.

(continued on next page)

Note: Stop immediately anytime the dough warms up or feels greasy. If the butter and shortening melt, your pastry will not be flaky. Refrigerate it until it firms up again.

For a one crust pie:
Trim the crust with kitchen shears, leaving a one-half inch overhang. Fold the edge under and crimp with your fingers to make a raised border. If the pie shell will be baked empty, prick it all over with a fork or weight it by lining it with foil and filling with dry beans or pie weights. This prevents the pastry from puffing up as it bakes. (See instructions on page 305 for docking the pan rather than the crust.) Bake at 400° F for 15 minutes. Cover the edges with pie shields or with a sheet of foil with a 6-inch circle cut out of the center and bake for another 5 minutes.

If the crust will be used for a custard or fruit pie, baked in the crust, see page 305 for tips to keep it from getting soggy. Bake according to recipe directions for specific pies.

For top crust only:
Put the pie filling in a pie pan or baking dish. Center crust over filling; trim with kitchen shears leaving a one-half inch overhang. Turn the edge under and crimp. Slash the top to vent steam, and bake according to specific recipe directions.

For double-crust pie:
Cut the extra dough away by running a knife around the outside edge of the pan. Roll out the dough for the top crust, put the filling in the pie shell, and center the top crust over the filling. Trim the top crust with kitchen shears, leaving a one-half inch overhang. Tuck the overhanging dough under the edge of the bottom crust and crimp edges together with your fingers. Slash steam vents in the top and refrigerate the pie for a few minutes. Bake according to recipe directions for specific pie.

Crust cookies:
My daughter suggested this method to use up extra pastry, to reduce the amount of crust per serving, and to keep it crisp.

Cut pastry into 3-inch squares, place squares on a cookie sheet, and prick them all over with a fork. Bake at 425° F for 10 to 12 minutes, or until brown. Place on top of prepared filling for individual servings of pie.

This recipe makes enough crust for two 9-inch double crust pies or four single if it is rolled to one half the normal thickness. Extra pie crust can be cut into squares and frozen for later use.

Servings: 8

PER SERVING:		
Total Carb: 5.5g for single crust	Fiber: 0.2g	Net Carb: 5.3g
Total Carb: 11.0g for double crust	Fiber: 0.4g	Net Carb: 10.6g

VARIATIONS TO LOWER THE CARB COUNT FOR PIE CRUST:

• Roll the pie crust to one-sixteenth-inch thickness rather than the usual one-eighth. You'll hardly notice the difference, but you'll cut the carbs in half.

• Use a top or bottom crust only or Crust-Cookie method rather than a double crust.

• For pie fillings compatible with a chocolate crust: Replace 2 to 3 tablespoons of the flour with Dutch-process cocoa powder. Subtract 1 net carb for each tablespoon of flour replaced in the recipe.

• Substitute ¼ cup of almond flour or finely ground almonds for an equal amount of the flour. Add 2 teaspoons of gluten flour so it isn't too crumbly. Reduce the net carb count by 16 grams for the whole recipe.

• Add ¼ cup of sesame seeds with the flour. Add 3 net carbs to the entire recipe. (It will make an extra serving.)

• Cut ½ cup of grated cheddar cheese in with the shortening—especially good for fruit or mincemeat pies. It will not add carbs to the total, but will add one or two extra servings.

• Use two or more of the above suggestions at once, for example: replace ¼ cup of the flour with almond flour, add ½ cup of grated cheese, and roll the crust half as thick.

Note: I use white whole-wheat flour for my pie crust. Try to find it at a regular grocery to avoid paying shipping. The flour itself is not expensive, but a 5-pound parcel will cost more to ship than the price of the flour. Bob's Red Mill® and the King Arthur® Flour Company sell white whole-wheat at retail stores and by mail order. See Sources to order or to find a retail store near you.

TIPS TO KEEP BOTTOM CRUST FROM GETTING SOGGY:

• Patch any holes or tears in the pastry to keep the filling from leaking out and soaking into the whole crust.

• Make several large slits in the top crust of a double-crust pie to let moisture escape.

• Thicken fillings before adding to crust.

• Chill crust and filling separately before assembly.

• Set the pie on a preheated baking sheet or baking stone and bake on the bottom rack of the oven. If your oven has a flat bottom, set the pie directly on the oven floor for the first 15 to 20 minutes of baking.

• Brush the bottom and sides of the crust with a coating of peanut butter, melted chocolate, or sugar-free jam.

• Sprinkle the bottom crust with a tablespoon of almond flour or low-carb bread crumbs to help soak up any moisture from the filling

• If you can spare a pie pan, it is better to make holes in the pan than to prick the crust. The reason for docking a crust is to allow the steam to escape and prevent bubbles. Holes in the pan allow the steam to evaporate from the bottom, preventing any subsequent problem with leaky fillings. Set a metal pan on a piece of scrap wood and use a small nail to pierce it in an overall pattern.

• Coat the bottom crust with a thin layer of egg white.

For a single-crust pie:
Prick it all over with a fork or weight it by lining it with foil and filling with dry beans, pennies, or pie weights. Bake the crust for five minutes in a preheated oven. Remove the crust from the oven, remove any weights, and let it stand for three minutes. Break a whole egg into the crust and quickly roll the egg around until the bottom and sides of the crust are coated with egg white. Tilt the pan to remove the egg. If the hot crust does not cook the egg-white coating, return it to the oven for one or two minutes until the egg white is firm and opaque.

For a double-crust pie:
Line the pie pan with pastry. Break a whole egg into the crust and roll it around until the bottom and sides are coated with egg white. Tip the egg out and refrigerate the crust for 15 minutes before adding the filling and top crust.

It may be necessary to cover the edges of the pie crust to prevent over-browning. When the edges are brown, cover them with pie-crust shields, or cut a 6-inch circle out of the center of a square of foil to lay over the pie.

A clear glass pie pan aids in browning and lets you see when the bottom of the pie is done.

PIE CRUST MADE WITH LOW-CARB FLOUR REPLACEMENT

My Low-carb Flour Replacement mix can be used to make a very good and very easy pie crust that you can enjoy when a whole-wheat crust would put you over your carb limit. I like to bake it empty and fill it with ice cream or make a fruit or cream filling separately and then assemble it just before serving so it stays crisp.

1	cup Low-carb Flour Replacement mix (see p. 116), plus more for rolling out the dough
1/4	teaspoon salt
1/4	cup no-trans-fat shortening, chilled
1/8	cup (2 tablespoons) butter, chilled
2	to 2 1/2 tablespoons cold water

Preheat oven to 425° F.

Whisk the flour replacement with the salt in a mixing bowl. Cut in the shortening and butter with a pastry blender (the kind with sharp blades, not round wires) until the largest particles are like small peas. Sprinkle the water over the mixture, one tablespoon at time, tossing with a fork to evenly moisten, until the mixture holds together when pinched. Form dough into a ball and flatten into a disk shape. Cover with plastic wrap and place in the refrigerator to rest for 10 minutes.

Put a layer of plastic wrap on the work surface. It will take two overlapping pieces for a 9-inch crust. A few drops of water under the plastic and under the edge where the two sheets overlap will keep it from slipping. Dust the plastic wrap with flour replacement. Place the dough on it, dust with more flour replacement, and cover with another sheet of plastic wrap. Roll out the pastry with a rolling pin, rolling from the center to the edges, to make a 9-inch circle. If the dough cracks as it is rolled, cut off pieces from the edge to patch. Lift the top sheet of plastic and turn the dough over several times as you roll, dusting it with flour mix each time. Remove the top layer of plastic and pick up the dough, along with the layer of plastic under it, and invert it onto the pie pan. The plastic layer is now on top, and the dough can be adjusted to fit in the pan without stretching or tearing. Center the dough and gently push it into the pan. Remove the plastic.

(continued on next page)

PIE CRUST MADE WITH LOW-CARB FLOUR REPLACEMENT, CONTINUED

Trim the pastry with kitchen shears, leaving a one-half inch overhang. Turn the edge under and crimp. Prick the crust all over with a fork, or weight it by lining it with foil and filling with dry beans or pie weights. Bake for 10 to 12 minutes or until crisp and brown. If the edges brown too quickly, cover with pie shields or with a sheet of foil with a 6-inch circle cut out of the center. Makes one 9-inch pie crust.

Servings: 8

PER SERVING:		
Total Carb: 4.4g	Fiber: 2.3g	Net Carb: 2.1g

COCONUT PIE SHELL

1   egg white
2   tablespoons granular Splenda®
1½ teaspoons Fruit Sweet® (see Sources) or use light corn
      syrup (add 0.9 net carbs per serving)
½   teaspoon vanilla extract
2   cups grated unsweetened coconut (if using shredded,
      whirl it in the food processor until finely chopped)

Preheat oven to 350° F. Grease a 9-inch pie pan.

Beat egg white until stiff. Beat in the Splenda®. Stir in the coconut and Fruit Sweet® or corn syrup. Press into well-greased 9-inch pie pan and bake for 15 minutes. Chill.

Servings: 8

PER SERVING:		
Total Carb: 5.7g	Fiber: 3.2g	Net Carb: 2.5g

Tips and Notes

To lower the carbohydrate count by half when using purchased pie crust: Thaw the crust or let it warm up according to the package directions. Turn it out on a sheet of plastic wrap that has been sprinkled with flour, almond flour, Low-carb Flour Replacement (see p. 116), sesame seeds, or finely chopped nuts. Sprinkle more over the top and cover with a second layer of wrap. Roll out the dough to half its original thickness.

Chocolate Coconut Candy

To make chocolate coconut candy rather than pie crust, drop mixture by rounded teaspoonfuls onto greased waxed paper or shape into 1-inch balls. Chill.

Makes about 32 candies.

Per Serving:
Total Carb: 1.9g
Fiber: 0.9g
Net Carb: 1.0g

CHOCOLATE COCONUT PIE SHELL

This is especially good filled with ice cream. It can also be used for cream pies.

2   ounces unsweetened chocolate, chopped
2   Tablespoons butter
²/₃ cup granular Splenda®
1½ tablespoons warm water
1½ cups unsweetened grated coconut

Butter an 8-inch pie pan.

Heat one-half inch of water in the bottom of a double boiler to a simmer. Reduce the heat so the water is hot but not bubbling. Place chocolate, butter, Splenda®, and water in the top of the double boiler and set over, but not touching, the hot water. Stir until melted and smooth, and then stir in the coconut. Press into an 8-inch buttered pie pan. Chill.

Servings: 8

PER SERVING:		
Total Carb: 7.6g	Fiber: 3.4g	Net Carb: 4.2g

SHORTBREAD CRUST

Use the shortbread crust recipe from Lemon Bars. (See p. 274.) Press into an 8-inch pie pan and bake for 15 minutes at 350° F or until brown. Let the crust cool and fill with cream pie filling or ice cream.

Servings: 9

PER SERVING:		
Total Carb: 4.0g	Fiber: 1.3g	Net Carb: 2.7g

NOTES ON EGG WHITE FOAMS

• Be sure all of your utensils are clean and dry. Separate the eggs into two bowls, one at a time, before adding to the mixer bowl, since a tiny speck of broken yolk will ruin your meringue. It's easier to keep it out than to remove it.

• Never beat egg whites in a plastic bowl. Plastic has an attraction for grease, and even after being well washed, it will reduce the volume of the meringue.

• A copper bowl really does have a positive effect on egg whites. They are more stable and less easily over-beaten in a copper bowl, and they will rise higher when baked. If you are using one, do not add cream of tartar as the acid will cause more of the copper to combine with the egg white and it could reach toxic levels. (Copper pans should not be used for heating or cooking foods unless they are lined with a non-reactive metal.)

• Eggs are easier to separate and egg whites will beat up better if allowed to come to room temperature first. Eggs whites that are three days old will produce a larger volume than very fresh ones, but fresh egg whites are more stable and will hold up better.

• Left-over egg whites can be frozen and will still beat up beautifully when thawed.

• Powdered egg whites work very well for beating, and they are safe to use in recipes that will not be cooked.

• Some packaged pasteurized liquid whites can be used for beating (check the label to be sure they are intended for whipping), but I have found the volume to be less than either powdered or fresh whites.

MERINGUE PIE SHELL

VARIATION:

Individual
Meringue Shells

Shape meringue into six 3-inch shells. After baking and cooling as directed, fill with fruit, ice cream, or pie filling. Invert a second meringue shell on top (optional) and garnish with whipped cream.

Makes 6 meringues.

Per Each Shell:
Total Carb: 3.9g
Fiber: 0g
Net Carb: 3.9g

If you use 1 tablespoon of ThickenThin Not/Sugar in this meringue, you can omit the superfine sugar and xanthan gum and reduce the net carb count per serving by 2 grams. See Sources and Ingredients.

¼ cup granular Splenda®
¼ teaspoon xanthan gum (optional)
4   teaspoons superfine sugar
4   egg whites, at room temperature
¼ teaspoon cream of tartar (omit if beating in a copper bowl)

Preheat oven to 200° F. Line a baking sheet with parchment paper or a nonstick liner.

Stir together: the Splenda®, the optional xanthan, and the sugar. Beat the egg whites with the cream of tartar (if using), to soft peaks. Add the mixture to the egg whites a little at a time, while continuing to beat until the whites are very stiff but still moist, about 5 minutes. Spread the meringue in an 8-inch circle with the back of a spoon, or pipe it on with a pastry bag fitted with a one-half inch plain tube. The bottom should be ½ inch thick with a rim around the edge about 1½ inches high. Bake the meringue for 2 hours or until it just starts to color slightly and feels firm to the touch. Turn off the oven and leave the meringue in the oven with the door closed for at least an hour longer or until totally dry and firm to the touch. If there is still a soft spot in the center on the bottom, remove the meringue, heat the oven to 200° F, return the meringue to the oven, and bake for an additional 10 minutes or so. Let cool in the oven for an hour or more as before.

Spread with a cream pie filling or fill with fruit or ice cream. Meringues can be stored unfilled in an airtight container after they are completely cool. They should stay crisp and fresh for quite a long time. They can be re-crisped in a 200° F oven for 5 to 10 minutes if necessary.

Servings: 8

PER SERVING:		
Total Carb: 2.9g	Fiber: 0g	Net Carb: 2.9g

FLORENTINE MERINGUE TORTE

A spectacular dessert for those very special occasions. To make ahead: Keep the meringue layers and cream mixture separate and assemble the torte close to serving time so the meringue will stay crisp.

- Triple the recipe for Meringue Pie Shell
- 1 pound mascarpone cheese
- 2 tablespoons amaretto-flavored, sugar-free syrup or use amaretto liqueur (add 1 net carb per serving)
- 1 cup sugar-free Chocolate Chips (see p. 260), finely chopped
- 4 cups heavy cream
- ½ cup amarettini cookie crumbs (see Sources)

Make a triple recipe of Meringue Pie Shell and shape into three 8-inch rounds. Bake as directed and cool completely.

Mix together: the mascarpone cheese, the chocolate, and the amaretto liqueur or syrup. Whip the cream to soft peak stage and fold into the cheese mixture.

Place a teaspoonful of the cheese and cream mixture on a cake plate and press a layer of meringue onto it to secure it in place. Spread a third of the filling over the top of the meringue. Repeat with the second and third layers, ending with the cream mixture. Sprinkle the cookie crumbs on top and serve at once or chill until serving time.

Servings: 16

PER SERVING:		
Total Carb: 8.4g	Fiber: 1.0g	Net Carb: 7.4g

Tips and Notes

This is one of the earliest recipes known for meringue.

"Snow eggs.
Boile some milk with a little flower water well allyed, then put it in more than half of one dosen of whites of eggs, and stir well all together, and sugar it. When you are ready to serve, set them on the fire again and glase them, that is, take the rest of your whites of eggs, beat them with a feather, and mix all well together; or else fry well the rest of your whites, and powre them over your other eggs. Pass over it lightly an oven lid, or the fire-shovell red hot, and serve them sured with sweet waters."

Francois Pierre La Varenne, *The French Cook,* translated into English in 1653 by I.D.G., with an introduction by Philip and Mary Hyman, Southover Press: East Sussex, 2001 (p. 98-99)

FILLO

Fillo is also spelled *filo* and *phyllo*. It comes from the Greek word for "leaf." The makers of fillo and Tess Mallon, who wrote *The Fillo Cookbook*, prefer the phonetic spelling. "Spell it as you say it," she advises.

FILLO TECHNIQUES

These large, tissue-thin layers of dough have 10 net carbs in each 12- by 17-inch sheet (from the Fillo Factory). Some traditional fillo pastries may have as many as 30 layers, but it is possible to get a similar effect using only a few. I use no-stick spray for the assembly because it is much faster than the standard method of brushing each sheet with melted butter. It also prevents tearing of the fragile layers with the brush.

Fillo that has been thawed improperly and re-frozen may develop spots of moisture that condense and cause the sheets to stick together. If you have tried to work with fillo before and found it difficult and frustrating, that was almost certainly the problem. Plan ahead when you purchase frozen fillo; take an insulated container with an ice pack to the store with you and put the fillo in the freezer immediately when you return home. Thaw it slowly in the refrigerator and you shouldn't have any problems with it.

You may be able to purchase fresh fillo dough from a Greek specialty shop or bakery if there is one in your area. Fresh fillo will keep for several weeks in your refrigerator and it can be frozen for longer storage. Fillo purchased frozen can be stored in the freezer for up to year. The unused portion of a thawed package can be refrigerated for 2 weeks or re-frozen for 3 months. It should be well wrapped and sealed with tape or stored in a sealed plastic bag before freezing.

• To use frozen fillo, thaw the unopened package in the refrigerator for 12 hours or overnight, and then bring it up to room temperature for two hours before opening the package. Refrigerated fresh fillo also needs to be brought to room temperature by removing it from the refrigerator for two hours before using.

• Prepare your filling according to the recipe you are using and set up your work area before opening the fillo package. Wet a cup towel and wring it out until it is just damp. Lay it out lengthwise, parallel to the counter. Place a dry towel over the damp towel. Prepare a second stack consisting of a dry towel, a damp towel, and a layer of plastic wrap and place it nearby to use to cover the unused fillo whenever you must leave it for more than a few seconds; it will dry out in a flash if left unprotected. (If it has been oiled, you can leave it uncovered for a brief period.)

• Open the fillo package. Remove the number of sheets that you need for the recipe and put them on the top (dry) towel. Rewrap the rest of the package and return to the refrigerator. Immediately spray the top layer of the stacked fillo sheets with no-stick spray, starting with the edges. As each layer is removed, spray the next layer underneath to prevent drying. The layers are very fragile; discard any pieces that stick together and use only pieces that are one layer thick. Broken pieces can be used, as long as they are only one thickness and oiled between every layer— just pile them up. A tear can be mended by placing a patch over it, as long as it is oiled first. Unbaked, finished pastries can be refrigerated for a day or so before baking.

FILLO NUT COOKIES

These ethereal little crisps are the perfect accompaniment to ice cream. Read Fillo Techniques on the previous page and the entire recipe before starting.

1 cup toasted almonds
¼ cup granular Splenda®
4 sheets fillo dough
• No-stick spray
¼ cup melted butter

Preheat the oven to 350° F. You will need a total of four large (12-by 17-inch) cookie sheets to bake all the cookies at once, two to hold the cookies and two to serve as weights to keep them flat. You can bake them consecutively with just two pans if you wash the pans between batches. Be sure the remaining fillo layers are well protected with oil or butter or covered with a dry towel, a damp towel, and plastic wrap until they can be baked so they won't dry out. (If you don't bother with the extra pan to weight the cookies, they will taste the same; they just won't look as nice.) Butter the inside bottom of two large cookie sheets and butter the outside bottom of two more large cookie sheets.

Put the almonds and Splenda® in the bowl of a food processor and process until coarsely ground or chop the almonds by hand. Put one sheet of fillo on a buttered cookie sheet. (You may need to trim the fillo to fit your pan.) Spray the fillo with no-stick spray and drizzle with melted butter, and then sprinkle evenly with about 2 tablespoonfuls of the nut mixture. Top with a second sheet of fillo, spray with no-stick spray, drizzle with butter, and sprinkle with nuts as before. Place a second cookie sheet, buttered side down, on top of the cookies to keep them flat. Bake for 10 minutes. Remove the top pan and cut the cookies into roughly 2- by 3-inch rectangles with a knife or a pizza wheel while they are still hot. Repeat for second batch. Store in an airtight container.

Servings: 60

PER SERVING:		
Total Carb: 1.5g	Fiber: 0.2g	Net Carb: 1.3g

Tips and Notes

For a close approximation of the classic French pastry called Napoleon, stack three Fillo Nut Cookies together with Pastry Cream or Whipped Cream and fresh raspberries or sugar-free raspberry jam between the layers. Spread the top cookie with Confectioners Icing and drizzle with Chocolate Glaze. (See Index for recipes.)

The name of the pastry apparently has nothing to do with Napoleon Bonaparte, since in France it is called *mille-feuilles,* which means thousand leaves, and it didn't make its appearance until the late 1800s. It is probably a corruption of Napolitain, meaning in the style of Naples, Italy, where multi-layered cakes with alternating layers of filling and cake were popular.

Tips and Notes

Read the instructions for working with fillo dough. If you have tried it before and found it difficult and frustrating, don't give up. Store it and prepare it according to the directions, and you will find it easy to use. Once you get into the rhythm of it, the assembly goes very quickly.

No-stick spray, like Pam® or Mazola®, makes the strudel assembly much easier and faster than the standard method of brushing every layer with melted butter. I recommend using the spray for the assembly and just using butter to brush the completed strudel for flavor.

This is really truly apple strudel. The traditional recipes use soft breadcrumbs to absorb the liquid from the fruit and keep the fillo layers apart so they will be flaky and crisp. I use chopped almonds instead to separate the layers, and I scatter the apple filling out over a wide area rather than having it in a single strip across one end of the pastry. This keeps the filling from saturating the fillo and making it soggy. I also dry my apples well and press them between paper towels after chopping to reduce the moisture as much as possible.

8	sheets fillo dough
•	No-stick spray
¾	cup sliced almonds

For the filling:

2	cups tart cooking apples (two medium apples)
½	cup sugar-free Dried Cranberries (see p. 105)
⅓	cup granular Splenda®
½	teaspoon ground cinnamon
½	teaspoon grated lemon peel
•	A pinch of salt
•	Melted butter for finished pastries, optional

If your fillo has been frozen, it needs to be thawed overnight in the refrigerator.

Remove the package of thawed fillo from the refrigerator. Leave the unopened package at room temperature for two hours. Prepare your filling before opening the fillo. Grease two cookie sheets.

Chop the nuts by hand or in the food processor until coarsely chopped. (The purpose of the almonds is to separate the layers of fillo so they stay crisp. If the nuts are ground to a powder, they won't do this.) Remove and reserve the almonds.

Peel, core, and chop the apples. Squeeze the apples in paper towels to remove as much moisture as possible. Roughly chop the cranberries by hand. Mix the apples, cranberries, Splenda®, cinnamon, lemon peel, and salt together.

Wet and wring out one large dish towel until it is just damp. Lay it out lengthwise, parallel to the counter, and put a dry towel on top of the damp one. Open the fillo and remove eight stacked sheets. Place on the dry top towel. Rewrap the rest of the fillo and return it to the refrigerator. Immediately spray the top sheet of fillo dough with no-stick spray, starting with the edges. You will be making one strudel at a time using the top layer of fillo while it is still stacked on top of the rest of the layers. One sheet of fillo will be folded in half to make each strudel.

(continued on next page)

Apple Strudel, continued

Sprinkle the left side of the top sheet of fillo with 2 teaspoons of the chopped almonds. Fold the sheet in half by lifting the right side and folding it over the left side as if you were turning a page in a book. Spray all the newly-exposed, dry fillo with no-stick spray. Sprinkle 2 teaspoons of chopped almonds on the new left "page." Scatter about ¼ cup of the apple filling over the almonds, leaving a 1-inch border uncovered on the sides and a 2- to 3-inch border on the top and bottom. (Remember not to put too much filling in one place or it will make the fillo soggy.) Roll up the fillo a turn or two, starting from the bottom edge, then tuck in both sides of the double sheet to enclose the filling. Spray the edges and the roll with oil and continue to roll. Spray the finished roll and the now-exposed fillo layer underneath with more no-stick spray. Place the roll on the greased baking sheet. Repeat for a total of 8 pastries, 4 on each pan.

Heat the oven to 375° F.

Cut diagonal slits down to the filling every two inches along the tops of the pastries. Enlarge the openings slightly by inserting a finger and lifting to open them up so the steam can escape. Sprinkle each strudel with a little melted butter for flavor, if desired, and bake for 15 to 20 minutes or until golden and crisp. Cut each roll into four slices.

Servings: 40

PER SERVING:		
Total Carb: 5.1g	Fiber: 0.7g	Net Carb: 4.4g

Note: The end slices of strudel will have more carbs than the middle ones since the fillo layers are doubled there.

Tips and Notes

If not served soon after baking, the strudel may need to be reheated in a 300° F oven for a few minutes to crisp it again before serving. A better way: Make only as many as you plan to use right away. Store the filling and the fillo, separately, in the refrigerator so that you can make up a fresh batch as needed.

VARIATION

Mincemeat Strudel

Follow instructions for
Chocolate Strudel but substitute ¼ cup of well-drained
Mincemeat (see p. 296) for
filling each strudel. Serve
warm.
Makes 4 servings per strudel.

Per Serving:
Total Carb: 4.8g
Fiber: 0.7g
Net Carb: 4.1g

CHOCOLATE STRUDEL

*This filling is adapted from one used in an Easter bread called gubana from
northern Italy. I've used it here for strudel but with a honey-flavored syrup like you
would use on baklava.*

8   sheets of Fillo dough
•   No-stick spray
¾   cup sliced almonds

For the filling:
½   cup sugar-free Dried Cranberries (see p. 105)
1¼ cups walnuts
¾   cup almonds
1   tablespoon granular Splenda® for chopping
    cranberries and nuts
2   tablespoons chocolate- or amaretto-flavored sugar-
    free syrup (or use 2 more tablespoons Splenda® and
    2 tablespoons water)
¼   cup plus 1 tablespoon Dutch-process cocoa powder
1   cup granular Splenda®
¼   teaspoon ground cinnamon
¼   teaspoon ground nutmeg
1½ tablespoons softened butter
2   egg whites
•   Melted butter (optional)

For honey syrup (optional):
¼   cup sugar-free vanilla syrup (like Da Vinci® or Atkins™)
1   teaspoon honey

Preheat oven to 375° F. Grease two cookie sheets.

Read the information about fillo dough in Fillo Techniques. If the
fillo has been frozen, it needs to be thawed overnight in the
refrigerator and allowed to come up to room temperature for two
hours. Prepare the chocolate filling before opening the fillo package.

Chop ¾ cup of sliced almonds by hand or in the food processor until
coarsely chopped. (The purpose of the almonds is to separate the
layers of fillo so they stay crisp. If the nuts are ground to a powder,
they won't do this.) Remove and reserve the almonds.

Chop the cranberries, walnuts, and the second ¾ cup of almonds in
the food processor with 1 tablespoon of Splenda® by pulsing until
roughly chopped, or chop by hand. Do not process too long—you do
not want them finely chopped.

(continued on next page)

CHOCOLATE STRUDEL, CONTINUED

Mix the chopped cranberry and nut mixture with the sugar-free syrup, cocoa, the cup of Splenda®, the cinnamon, nutmeg, and butter in a large bowl. In another bowl, beat the egg whites to soft-peak stage. Stir the beaten egg whites into the large bowl until all of the mixture is evenly moistened.

Wet and wring out one large dish towel until it is just damp. Lay it out lengthwise, parallel to the counter, and put a dry towel on top of the damp one. Open the fillo and remove eight stacked sheets. Place on the dry top towel. Rewrap the rest of the fillo and return it to the refrigerator. Immediately spray the top sheet of fillo dough with no-stick spray, starting with the edges. You will be making one strudel at a time using the top layer of fillo while it is still stacked on top of the rest of the layers. One sheet of fillo will be folded in half to make each strudel.

Sprinkle the left side of the top sheet of fillo with 2 teaspoons of the chopped almonds. Fold the sheet in half by lifting the right side and folding it over the left side as if you were turning a page in a book. Spray all the newly-exposed, dry fillo with no-stick spray. Sprinkle 2 teaspoons of chopped almonds on the new left "page". Place about ¼ cup of the chocolate filling in a strip about 2 inches from the bottom of the doubled sheet, leaving a 1-inch border uncovered on both sides. Roll up the fillo a turn or two, starting from the bottom edge, and then tuck in both sides of the double sheet so that the filling is enclosed. Spray the edges and the roll with oil and continue to roll. Spray the finished roll and the now-exposed fillo layer underneath with more no-stick spray. Place the roll on the greased baking sheet. Repeat for a total of 8 pastries, 4 on each pan.

Cut diagonal slits down to the filling every two inches along the tops of the pastries. Enlarge the openings slightly by inserting a finger and lifting to open them up so the steam can escape. Sprinkle each strudel with a little melted butter for flavor, if desired. Bake at 375° F for 15 to 20 minutes or until golden and crisp. Cut each roll into 4 slices.

Optional honey syrup:
Heat together the ¼ cup of vanilla-flavored, sugar-free syrup and 1 teaspoon of honey. Just before serving, pour the hot syrup over the cooled pastries. (If pastry is hot, use cold syrup instead.)

Servings: 32

PER SERVING:		
Total Carb: 6.8g	Fiber: 1.4g	Net Carb: 5.4g

Tips and Notes

Baklava is made with a honey syrup that preserves the fillo and keeps it crisp for a long time. There is not enough honey in this recipe to do that, so it must be poured over the strudels just before serving.

MOUSSES, PUDDINGS, AND CUSTARDS

Banana Pudding

The Southern twist on this distant cousin of the trifle is the browned meringue topping, probably the innovation of a frugal housewife who couldn't bear to waste the egg whites left behind from the custard.

Split a Sponge Cake (see p. 244) in half horizontally. Place on a baking sheet and bake at 400° F until slightly toasted. Place half of cake in a deep 8-inch square baking dish. Slice one half of a banana very thin and layer over the cake. Make Pastry Cream recipe (see p. 256), adding 1 Tablespoon of Crème de Banane, optional. Reserve egg whites. Cover cake with half the hot pastry cream. Put rest of cake in pan, cut-side-down, and pour rest of pastry cream over. Make soft Meringue (see page 154) with the reserved egg whites. Spread over warm pudding, sealing to edges. Bake in a 400° F oven for 3 to 5 minutes or until slightly brown. Serve pudding warm or let cool and refrigerate. Makes 9 servings.

Total Carb: 7.9g
Fiber: 0.3g
Net Carb: 7.6

AVOCADO MOUSSE

For this very delicate mousse, your avocado needs to be perfectly ripe and blemish free.

- 1   teaspoon gelatin
- ½   cup cold water
- 1   large ripe avocado (about 11 ounces)
- 2   teaspoons lime juice
- ⅓   cup granular Splenda®
- ½   cup heavy cream, whipped, plus extra for garnish
- •   Coconut or chopped pistachios (optional)

Place the gelatin and the water in a small saucepan. Set over low heat and stir until the gelatin is dissolved. Set aside. Peel and mash the avocado with the lime juice and Splenda®. You can use a food processor or strain the pulp to insure a velvety smooth texture. Whip the cream. Gently fold the gelatin and avocado pulp into the whipped cream. Pour into molds or serving dishes and chill. Top with sugar-free Whipped Cream and garnish with coconut or chopped pistachios, if desired, before serving.

Servings: 4

PER SERVING:		
Total Carb: 6.3g	Fiber: 1.6g	Net Carb: 4.7g

"Hallo! A great deal of steam! The pudding was out of the copper. A smell like a washing-day! That was the cloth. A smell like an eating-house and a pastrycook's next door to each other, with a laundress's next door to that! That was the pudding! In half a minute Mrs. Cratchit entered—flushed, but smiling proudly—with the pudding, like a speckled cannon-ball, so hard and firm, blazing in half of half-a-quartern of ignited brandy, and bedight with Christmas holly stuck into the top. Oh, a wonderful pudding!"

—Charles Dickens' *A Christmas Carol*

COCONUT PANNA COTTA

Panna Cotta is Italian for "cooked cream." The traditional recipe calls for a cup of cream and a cup of milk; by substituting coconut milk for the milk, we subtract a few grams of carbohydrates and add lots of flavor.

1 package plain gelatin (¼ ounce)
3 tablespoons water
1 cup heavy cream
¾ cup granular Splenda®
• A few grains of salt
1 (14 ounce) can unsweetened coconut milk
1 teaspoon vanilla extract
½ teaspoon coconut extract

Soften the gelatin in the 3 tablespoons of water for 5 minutes. Place the cream, Splenda®, and salt in a saucepan and bring to a boil over medium heat. Add the softened gelatin and stir until dissolved. Remove the pan from the heat and stir in the coconut milk and flavorings. Pour into six serving dishes and chill until set. Top with toasted unsweetened coconut or fresh fruit, if desired.

Servings: 6

PER SERVING:		
Total Carb: 3.0g	Fiber: 0g	Net Carb: 3.0g

MANY MOUSSES

Whipped cream, stabilized with a little gelatin, can become any mousse you can dream up. Spoon it up from a big glass bowl or mound it into pretty stemmed glasses.

Basic Mousse:
1 teaspoon of gelatin
2 tablespoons of water
1 cup of heavy cream
1 tablespoon of granular Splenda® or more to taste
1 teaspoon of vanilla extract

Soften gelatin in water for a few minutes then heat just until melted. Let it cool until it is barely warm. Beat the cream with the Splenda® and vanilla on high speed until it starts to thicken, then switch to low; whip just until it forms soft peaks. Add the softened gelatin and any flavoring ingredients and whisk into whipped cream. (The gelatin needs to be slightly warm or the cold cream will solidify it before it is blended.)

Makes about 2 cups or 4 Servings.

PER SERVING:		
Total Carb: 0.8g	Fiber: 0g	Net Carb: 0.8g

VARIATIONS:

Fruit Mousse
Warm ¼ cup of sugar-free jam and beat with a fork until smooth. Reserve. Make Basic Mousse (this page). Gently whisk jam into whipped cream with gelatin. Optional: add 1 teaspoon of compatible liqueur. Chill until set. Top with fruit or berries if desired. (Add 4.8 net carbs to Basic Mousse recipe.)

Chocolate Mousse
Melt ¼ cup of sugar-free chocolate chips with 2 tablespoons of water over hot water in the top of a double boiler, stirring frequently. Let cool until slightly warm. Reserve. Make Basic Mousse (this page). Gently fold the melted chocolate into the whipped cream with the gelatin. Optional: add 1 teaspoon of Kahlúa or crème de cacao. Chill. Top with berries or grated chocolate, if desired. (Add 1.5 net carbs to Basic Mousse recipe.)

Pumpkin Mousse
Make Basic Mousse (this page), but add an additional 2 tablespoons of granular Splenda® and a dash of cinnamon, nutmeg, and allspice. Gently fold in ¼ cup of pumpkin puree with the gelatin. Chill. Top with sugar-free Whipped Cream and chopped Glazed Pecans, if desired. See Index for recipes. (Add 1.2 net carbs to Basic Mousse recipe.)

Tips and Notes

Some cartons marked "heavy cream" contain milk, thickeners, and stabilizers, which add carbohydrates. Look for cream that says "zero carbohydrates," and lists only "cream" as an ingredient, or you could be adding as much as sixteen carbs per cup of cream to your recipe. You may be more likely to find a zero-carb cream on the organic foods aisle.

Put the roasting pan with the custard cups on the oven rack first, then pour in the hot water to prevent accidental burns.

Baked custard was my favorite of the desserts served in the lunchroom when I was in elementary school. Eggs and milk were considered perfect nutrition for children in those days, which was probably the reason so many of my friends wouldn't touch it. I would graciously volunteer to dispose of as many portions as I could get.

2   large eggs
1   egg yolk
⅓   cup granular Splenda®
1⅓ cups cream
⅔   cup water
2   teaspoons vanilla extract
•   Ground nutmeg

Preheat oven to 350º F. You will need four 6-ounce custard cups, a roasting pan that has been lined with a folded cup towel, and a kettle of boiling water.

In a medium-sized bowl, combine eggs, egg yolk, Splenda®, cream, water, and vanilla. Whisk for 1 minute or until smooth. Pour into four 6-ounce custard cups or ramekins. Sprinkle with nutmeg. Put a folded cup towel in the bottom of a large roasting pan. Arrange the custard cups in the pan so that they do not touch. Carefully pour boiling water into the pan to a depth of one inch. Bake for 45 minutes or until custards are set and a knife inserted near the center comes out clean. Remove from the water bath to prevent overcooking. Serve warm or chilled.

Servings: 4

PER SERVING:		
Total Carb: 2.4g	Fiber: 0g	Net Carb: 2.4g

VARIATION:
CRÈME BRÛLÈE

Prepare the custards as directed for Baked Custard. Sprinkle ½ teaspoon of sifted brown sugar evenly over each custard. Use a butane kitchen torch to melt the sugar, or place the custards under the broiler for 1 to 3 minutes until the sugar is bubbly and melted. Refrigerate until the caramel sets into a thin crisp crust.

Servings: 4

PER SERVING:		
Total Carb: 4.4g	Fiber: 0g	Net Carb: 4.4g

VARIATION:
CRÈME CARAMEL

For the caramel:

¼ cup sugar-free vanilla-, French vanilla-, or caramel-
   flavored syrup

1 tablespoon Fruit Sweet® (see Sources)

Prepare the custards as directed for Baked Custard and chill. In a small skillet, combine the syrup and Fruit Sweet® and simmer over low heat for about 5 minutes until thickened. Pour the warm syrup over the custards and serve at once. To make ahead, refrigerate the syrup and the custards separately. Reheat the syrup in the microwave for a minute or two at medium setting until it is warm. Pour it over the chilled custards.

Servings: 4

PER SERVING:		
Total Carb: 4.3g	Fiber: 0.1g	Net Carb: 4.2g

Da Vinci Gourmet ™ has the most flavors of sugar-free syrup. If you only stock one, get their simple syrup. You can always add vanilla extract to make vanilla syrup for this recipe.

CRÈME BRÛLÈE AND CRÈME CARAMEL MADE WITH EGG TOFU

Egg tofu can be found in Asian markets. It is a mixture of liquid eggs and tofu that is very much like a silky unsweetened egg custard. The label says a ⅓-cup serving has no carbohydrates. The instructions on the package say to slice and fry it, which makes it taste like scrambled eggs. It occurred to me that I could make instant Crème Brûlèe and Crème Caramel with it. I cut it into one-half inch slices and use it as the custard in these recipes. I use a bit more brown sugar or caramel sauce since there is no sweetener in the "custard." It is quite good for something so easy.

(The label for egg tofu lists hydrolyzed plant protein as an ingredient. That's another name for MSG. If you are sensitive to this additive, you should avoid the product.)

There are 1.8 net carbs per serving of Crème Caramel and 2 net carbs for the Crème Brûlèe.

BERRY CUSTARD CAKE

Tips and Notes

A folded cuptowel in the bottom of the pan insulates the ramekins so they don't overheat.

Put the roasting pan with the ramekins on the oven rack first, then pour in the hot water to prevent accidental burns.

This dessert separates into a sponge cake layer on top and a custard layer underneath with a warm berry center. Fabulous!

1   cup fresh strawberries or mixed raspberries, blueberries, and strawberries (or use frozen berries, thawed and drained)
2   tablespoons softened butter
½   cup granular Splenda®
2   eggs, separated
⅓   cup buttermilk
¼   cup heavy cream
¼   cup water
1   tablespoon all-purpose flour, sifted
•   Sugar-free Whipped Cream (see Index) for topping, optional

Preheat oven to 350° F. Have ready four 6-ounce ramekins, a roasting pan big enough to hold them, which has been lined with a folded cup towel, and a kettle of boiling water.

Put a few berries into each of the four 6-oz ramekins or bowls, reserving some for garnish. Set the ramekins aside.

In a mixing bowl, cream the butter with a rubber spatula until smooth. Add the Splenda® and cream the mixture until very light and well mixed. Add the egg yolks, one at a time, and beat well with a whisk or an electric mixer. Beat in the buttermilk, cream, water, and the sifted flour. In a second bowl, using clean beaters, beat the egg whites to stiff-peak stage. Fold ½ cup of the beaten whites into the batter to lighten. With a spatula, carefully fold in the rest of the whites until smooth. Line the baking pan with a folded cloth cup-towel so the bottoms of the dishes are not in direct contact with the pan. Place the ramekins in the baking pan and divide the batter equally among them. Carefully pour boiling water to fill the pan halfway up the sides of the ramekins. Bake until the cakes are puffed and golden brown, about 18 to 20 minutes. Serve warm or cold, garnished with the reserved berries and whipped cream.

Servings: 4

PER SERVING:		
Total Carb: 8.7g	Fiber: 1.1g	Net Carb: 7.6g

SOUFFLÉS

Soufflé comes from *souffler*, French for "to blow."

STRAWBERRY SOUFFLÉS

- Softened butter and granular Splenda® for coating the dishes
- 5 eggs at room temperature, separated
- 2 tablespoons warm water
- A pinch of cream of tartar (omit if using a copper bowl)
- A pinch of xanthan gum (optional)
- 4 tablespoons granular Splenda®
- ½ cup sugar-free Strawberry Jam (see p. 233), or use purchased sugar-free jam
- A pinch of salt

Butter six (7-ounce) soufflé dishes or a muffin tin. Place in the freezer until the butter is hard. Recoat with a second layer of butter and sprinkle generously with Splenda®, tapping out excess. Put dishes back into the freezer until ready to fill.

Preheat oven to 450° F. Place a baking sheet on the top rack of the oven to shield the soufflés from heat from the top. (They will rise better with heat coming only from the bottom heating element.)

Beat the egg whites with the warm water, cream of tarter, and xanthan gum (if using) to the soft-peak stage. Gradually beat in half of the Splenda® and continue to beat until the whites are firm but not dry. In another bowl, beat the egg yolks with the rest of the Splenda® until pale colored and thick. Fold in the jam and add the pinch of salt. Stir one-quarter of the egg whites into the yolks to lighten, and then gently fold in the rest. Divide the batter equally among the soufflé dishes and set them on a baking sheet. Bake in the lower third of the preheated oven for 8 to 10 minutes, or until well puffed and the top is firm. Serve immediately with Crème Anglaise (Custard Sauce) or sugar-free Whipped Cream, if desired (see Index for recipes).

Servings: 6

PER SERVING:
Total Carb: 8.3g   Fiber: 0.9g   Net Carb: 7.4g

Tips and Notes

No peeking! Never open the oven door while a soufflé is rising.

CHOCOLATE SOUFFLÉS

Tips and Notes

When beating egg mixtures, soft peak means the top of the point flops over when the beater is lifted; stiff peak means it stands up straight.

- Butter and granular Splenda® for coating the ramekins
- 4 ounces unsweetened chocolate, cut into chunks
- ½ cup heavy cream
- 3 large egg yolks, beaten with a fork
- 1 teaspoon vanilla extract
- A pinch of salt
- 5 large egg whites, at room temperature
- 2 tablespoons warm water
- A pinch of cream of tartar (omit if using a copper bowl)
- A pinch of xanthan gum (optional)
- ¾ cup plus 2 tablespoons granular Splenda®

Pulse the chocolate in the food processor until finely chopped or grate by hand. Put one-half inch of water in the bottom pan of a double boiler and bring to a simmer. Lower the heat so the water is hot but not bubbling. Place the chocolate and cream in the top of the double boiler, and set over, but not touching, the hot water. Stir until the chocolate is melted and the mixture is smooth. Let cool until tepid. (Chocolate should be liquid when yolks are added.)

Whisk egg yolks, one at a time, into the chocolate mixture until blended. Stir in vanilla and salt. (This part of the recipe can be done an hour or two ahead. Cover the mixture and let it stand at room temperature until ready to use. Warm over hot water until tepid when ready to continue.)

Preheat the oven to 425° F. Place a baking sheet on the top rack of the oven to shield the soufflés from heat from the top. (They will rise better with heat coming from the bottom heating element only.) Butter six (7-ounce) soufflé dishes or a muffin tin and place in the freezer until the butter hardens. Butter them again, sprinkle with granular Splenda®, and return them to the freezer until ready to fill.

Beat the egg whites with the water, cream of tartar, and xanthan gum (if using) in a medium-sized bowl to soft-peak stage. Gradually beat in the Splenda® and continue to beat until the whites are firm but not dry. Stir one-quarter of the egg whites into the chocolate mixture to lighten, and then gently fold in the rest of the mixture.

(continued on next page)

Chocolate Soufflés, continued

Divide the batter equally among the soufflé dishes and set them on a baking sheet. Bake in the lower third of the preheated oven for about 10 to 12 minutes, or until well puffed and the tops are firm. Pour Crème Anglaise (Custard Sauce) over the Soufflés, or top with sugar-free Whipped Cream, if desired (see Index for recipes), and serve immediately.

These hold up better than soufflés made with sugar. Refrigerate any extras and serve warm or cold the next day. They won't be quite as light, but still good.

Servings: 6

PER SERVING:		
Total Carb: 9.3g	Fiber: 2.7g	Net Carb: 6.6g

Who can eat dessert everyday?
We can!

Tips and Notes

See notes about egg white foams on page 309.

No peeking! Never open the oven door while a soufflé is rising.

See more recipes for Mousses and Puddings under other headings:

Chocolate Cream and Coconut Cream Puddings (see p. 257)

Tiramisu Mousse (see p. 272)

Pastry Cream (see p. 256)

DESSERT SAUCES

Too much is just right!

CHOCOLATE SAUCE

Tips and Notes

A chef's knife works well for chopping chocolate. I have a serrated Ginsu-type knife that is even better, but I have to put the chocolate on a cutting board with the handle extending over the edge to allow room for my knuckles. There is a special tool called a chocolate fork that is made specifically for breaking up chunks of chocolate. Chip the chocolate away in thin sheets from the edges of the chunk.

2   ounces unsweetened chocolate, finely chopped or grated
2   tablespoons butter, cut into several pieces
1   cup granular Splenda®
½   cup water
•   A few grains of salt
1   teaspoon vanilla extract

Chop the chocolate in a food processor or grate by hand until fine. Put one-half inch of water in the bottom of a double boiler and bring to a simmer. Lower the heat so the water is hot but not bubbling. Place the chocolate and butter in the top of the double boiler and set over, but not touching, the hot water. Stir until the chocolate is melted and the mixture is smooth. Stir in the Splenda®, water, and salt. Continue to cook, whisking constantly, until the sauce is smooth and thick, about 5 minutes. Longer cooking will produce a thicker sauce. Stir in the vanilla. Store in the refrigerator; reheat slowly over hot water.

Serving size: 1 tablespoon

PER SERVING:		
Total Carb: 2.5g	Fiber: 0.5g	Net Carb: 2.0g

QUICK HOT CHOCOLATE SAUCE

Add more or less xanthan gum to make the sauce as thick as you like or leave it out for a thin sauce.

⅓   cup sugar-free chocolate syrup, like Da Vinci® or Atkins™
2   teaspoons Dutch-process cocoa powder
•   A pinch of salt
2   tablespoons heavy cream
•   A scant ¼ teaspoon xanthan gum (optional)

Put cocoa, salt, and xanthan gum (if using) in a small saucepan. Stir in a small amount of the syrup to make a smooth paste. Stir in the rest of the syrup and heat on low until hot. Stir in the cream. Serve hot over ice cream or cream puffs.

Servings size: 1 tablespoon

PER SERVING:		
Total Carb: 0.2g	Fiber: 0.1g	Net Carb: 0.1g

COCOA FUDGE SAUCE

¼ cup Dutch-process cocoa powder
¼ cup granular Splenda®
• A pinch of salt
½ cup whipping cream
2 tablespoons water, if cream is very thick
1½ tablespoons butter, cut into pieces
½ teaspoon vanilla extract

Stir together the cocoa, Splenda®, and salt in a small, heavy saucepan. Stir in about half of the cream to make a smooth, thick paste. Stir in the rest of the cream, the water (if needed), and the butter. Stir over low heat until the butter is melted and the sauce is smooth and hot, but do not let it simmer. Stir in the vanilla. Serve warm or cold.

Sauce can be stored in a covered container in the refrigerator for up to a week or frozen for up to three months. To reheat or to thaw, put in the top of a double boiler over simmering water and stir occasionally until the sauce is warm, or microwave at 50% power in short bursts, stirring after each. Never let the sauce simmer or boil.

Serving size: 1 tablespoon

PER SERVING:		
Total Carb: 0.9g	Fiber: 0.3g	Net Carb: 0.6g

Tips and Notes

A rotary cheese grater or a microplane grater will work for grating smaller amounts of chocolate.

If you are preparing a large amount of chocolate, a food processor is faster than a grater. Break the chocolate up into 1-inch chunks and process until finely chopped. My favorite chocolate is made by Guittard; it comes in flat, 1-inch disks which can go directly into the food processor. You can order it from The King Arthur® Flour Company.

RASPBERRY SAUCE

10 ounces frozen, sugar-free raspberries, thawed and drained, reserving juice
3 tablespoons raspberry-flavored sugar-free syrup
¼ cup granular Splenda®
1 tablespoon framboise, Chambord, or other raspberry-flavored liqueur (optional - adds 0.3 net carbs per serving)

Purée the berries in the bowl of a food processor with the Splenda®. Put in a bowl and stir in the reserved juice and syrup. Strain, if you prefer a smooth sauce.

Serving size: 1 tablespoon

PER SERVING:		
Total Carb: 1.1g	Fiber: 0.5g	Net Carb: 0.6g

VARIATION:

Strawberry or Cherry Sauce

For Strawberry Sauce, use frozen strawberries and strawberry-flavored sugar-free syrup in place of raspberries and raspberry syrup. For Cherry Sauce, use pitted frozen tart cherries and cherry-flavored syrup. These will not need to be strained.

Serving size: 1 tablespoon
Made with strawberries:
Net Carb: 0.7g

Made with cherries:
Net Carb: 1.5g

You can buy dispensers for whipped cream that can be filled with fresh cream and sweetened to taste with Splenda®. They use an N₂O cartridge to aerate the cream. (Even the whipped cream in the aerosol containers from the supermarket has almost no carbohydrates, or fat either, for that matter, since it is mostly air.)

Some cartons marked "heavy cream" contain thickeners and stabilizers and are part milk, which adds carbohydrates. Look for a cream that says "zero carbohydrates," or you may be adding as much as 16 carbs per cup of cream to your recipe.

WHIPPED CREAM

1 cup heavy cream
1 tablespoon granular Splenda® or more to taste
1 teaspoon vanilla extract

Chill the mixing bowl and the beaters of an electric mixer. The cream should be 45° F or cooler or it will make butter. Beat it with the Splenda® and the vanilla on high speed until it starts to thicken, and then switch to low, watching carefully. Whip just until it forms soft peaks that droop over when the beaters are raised. Serve at once or refrigerate, covered, for an hour or two.

Variation:
For cream that holds up longer, soften 1 teaspoon of gelatin in 2 tablespoons of water for a few minutes, then heat just until melted. Cool it until it is barely warm before beating it into the whipped cream. (The gelatin needs to be slightly warm or the cold cream will cause it to solidify before it is blended.)

Serving size: 2 tablespoons

PER SERVING:		
Total Carb: 0.1g	Fiber: 0g	Net Carb: 0.1g

DEVONSHIRE CREAM

Use as a dip with fresh strawberries or spoon over cakes or puddings.

1 (8-ounce) package cream cheese, softened to room temperature
⅓ cup Crème Fraîche (see p. 51) or sour cream
1 tablespoon granular Splenda®

Beat the cream cheese until fluffy with an electric mixer. Fold in the Crème Fraîche or sour cream and the Splenda®. Chill and serve.

Servings: 10

PER SERVING:		
Total Carb: 0.8g	Fiber: 0g	Net Carb: 0.8g

CRÈME ANGLAISE (CUSTARD SAUCE)

- ¾ cup heavy cream
- ¼ cup water
- 5 large egg yolks
- 4 tablespoons granular Splenda®
- 1 tablespoon vanilla extract
- • A few grains of salt

Mix the cream and water in a heavy saucepan and place over medium heat. In a mixing bowl, whisk the egg yolks with the Splenda®, vanilla, and salt until pale yellow. When the cream and water mixture just begins to bubble at the edge of the pan take it off the heat. Slowly pour it into the eggs, whisking all the time. Pour the custard back into the pan, and return it to the heat. Cook at a bare simmer, not letting it boil, whisking constantly. When it thickens, take it off the heat and continue to whisk for a minute or two. Strain. While still hot, place a sheet of plastic wrap directly on the surface of the sauce or dot it with butter to prevent a skin from forming. Refrigerate or serve warm.

Serving size: 2 tablespoons

PER SERVING:		
Total Carb: 0.6g	Fiber: 0g	Net Carb: 0.6g

HARD SAUCE

A rich butter sauce that is part of English Christmas lore, Hard Sauce was traditionally served cold (so it was hard like butter), molded into decorative shapes, and placed on top of the steaming plum pudding. It works its magic equally well on hot Peach or Apple Pie or warmed up until it is soft and creamy and dolloped on a slice of Fruit Cake.

- ½ cup of butter (one stick)
- ½ cup of powdered maltitol
- • A few grains of salt
- 1 tablespoon of brandy
- ⅛ teaspoon of almond extract

Let the butter warm up to room temperature so that it is very soft, but not melted. Beat it with a spatula or a wooden spoon until it is very light and fluffy. Gradually beat in the maltitol and salt until smooth. Add the brandy and almond extract, a little at a time, and beat in. Store in the refrigerator. Serve cold or bring up to room temperature before serving. Makes about ¾ cup of sauce.

Net Carb count is zero.

"...The plum pudding is a national dish, and is despised by foreign nations because they never can make it fit to eat....In olden time a sprig of arbutus, with a red berry on it, was stuck in the middle, and a twig of variegated holly, with berries, placed on each side. This was done to keep away witches...If well made, Christmas plum pudding will be good for twelve months."
—*Cassell's Dictionary of Cookery with Numerous Illustrations*, 1875

More dessert recipes can be found as variations in other chapters:

Cream Puffs (see p. 121)
Jam Crêpes (see p. 127)
Chocolate Crêpes (see p. 127)
Cheese Blintzes (see p. 128)
Crêpes Suzette (see p. 129)
Cherry, Peach, Rhubarb, and Cranberry Clafouti (see p. 130)
Buñuelos (see p. 135)
Chocolate Cinnamon Tacos (see p. 135)
Dessert Pumpkin Tamales (see p. 174)
Baked Rhubarb with Strawberry Sauce (see p. 104)

BEVERAGES

BEVERAGES

Drink to your health.

FLAVORED COFFEE

A cup of flavored coffee satisfies like a rich dessert.

Add 1 to 2 tablespoons of sugar-free syrup for each cup of freshly brewed decaffeinated coffee. Some of the most popular flavors are vanilla, amaretto, and hazelnut, but Da Vinci's Gourmet® makes 52 different flavors. Check their web site www.davincigourmet.com for lots of coffee recipes.

Make Café au Lait with equal parts coffee and softly whipped cream rather than steamed milk. Use espresso, add chocolate flavored syrup, and serve in a tall glass mug for Café Mocha.

GREEN TEA

Green tea is widely used for its disease preventative antioxidants known as polyphenols. Many decaffeinated green teas are available.

For each serving, heat one cup of fresh cold water to just under boiling, add 1 teaspoon of loose tea or one tea bag, and steep for 3 to 5 minutes.

PER SERVING:		
Total Carb: 0g	Fiber: 0g	Net Carb: 0g

Tea and Coffee

Decaffeinated coffee and tea are acceptable for all low-carbohydrate diets. Caffeine has an effect on insulin production similar to sugar, according to Dr. Robert C. Atkins. The Hellers believe that caffeine acts as an anti-nutrient that eliminates potassium and thiamine from the body and increases carbohydrate cravings. The Eades are a bit more lenient toward caffeine but warn that elevated insulin levels can be problematic for caffeine-sensitive individuals.

Use real zero-carb heavy cream for your coffee, not the non-dairy creamers, which are mostly trans fats and sugar.

"If this is coffee, please bring me some tea; but if this is tea, please bring me some coffee."
—Abraham Lincoln

WHITE TEA

White tea is even higher than green in antioxidants, and it is naturally low in caffeine. While green tea may be an acquired taste, white tea is very mild and sweet, with none of the bitterness that many people find objectionable in green tea. White tea can only be harvested for two days a year—it is made from the new buds of the tea plant that have not yet unfurled. It is minimally processed so it retains more of its polyphenols.

For each serving, heat one cup of water to just below the boiling point, add 1 teaspoon of loose tea or one tea bag, and steep for only 60 to 90 seconds. I take mine with a packet of Splenda® and a pinch of cinnamon and ginger.

PER SERVING:		
Total Carb: 0g	Fiber: 0g	Net Carb: 0g

RASPBERRY OR PEACH ICED TEA

Use 2 ounces (4 tablespoons) peach or raspberry sugar-free syrup to each 8 ounces of tea. Serve over ice.

PER SERVING:		
Total Carb: 0g	Fiber: 0g	Net Carb: 0g

Tips and Notes

Cinnamon has a preservative effect, even at levels too low to taste.

True to my Southern roots, I drink iced tea year round, and since I don't always have room for a pitcher in the refrigerator, I add a tiny sprinkle of cinnamon to the bottom of the pot before adding the boiling water. It keeps the tea mold-free and fresh for an extra day or so. If you prefer to keep your tea sparkling clear, stir the hot tea with a stick of cinnamon rather than using powdered cinnamon. The stick can be dried and reused.

If you use the microwave to heat water for tea, put a stick of cinnamon in the cup and it will heat much faster.

"A cup of coffee—real coffee—home-browned, home-ground, home-made, that comes to you dark as a hazel-eye, but changes to a golden bronze as you temper it with cream that never cheated, but was real cream from its birth, thick, tenderly yellow, perfectly sweet, neither lumpy nor frothing on the Java..."

—Henry Ward Beecher, *Eyes and Ears*, 1862

Chinese Proverbs:

"Water is the mother of tea."

"Better to be deprived of food for three days than tea for one."

Berry Protein Shake

To make the Berry Slushy into a breakfast replacement shake, add ½ cup egg substitute, ¼ cup of low-carb protein powder, and 1 tablespoon of cream with the water. Makes 2 servings.

Per Serving:
Total Carb: 12g
Fiber: 2.5g
Net Carb: 9.5g

BERRY SLUSHY

In the book The Protein Power Lifeplan, *a drink made of frozen berries is suggested as a high-vitamin, high-fiber, high-antioxidant, but low-carb replacement for orange juice at breakfast. The authors, Drs. Michael and Mary Dan Eades, call it "Paleolithic Punch." This is my version. I'll take it over orange juice any day.*

1 cup frozen unsweetened berries, in any combination.
1 cup water
2 packets Splenda® or 4 teaspoons granular Splenda®

Purée the frozen berries in a blender until smooth. Add the water and Splenda® and blend until smooth.

Servings: 2

PER SERVING:

Total Carb: 9g   Fiber: 2.5g   Net Carb: 6.5g
nutrition information calculated using a mixture of blueberries, raspberries, blackberries and strawberries

---

LIME CARDAMOM SMOOTHIE

This is similar to India's popular yogurt-based lassi drinks, the perfect cool-me-down, pick-me-up on a hot summer day.

1   cup kefir
½   cup of cold water
2   tablespoons lime juice
2   tablespoons sugar-free simple syrup or use 2 tablespoons granular Splenda® and add 3 net carbs
½   teaspoon ground cardamom or nutmeg
•   A few grains of salt
½   cup of crushed ice or about 6 ice cubes

Blend kefir, water, lime juice, sweetener, and spice. Pour over ice in a tall glass and serve immediately.

Makes one serving.

PER SERVING:

Total Carb: 6.0g   Fiber: 2.0g   **Net Carb: 4.0g**
Count excludes the milk sugar that has been converted to lactic acid by the culture in the kefir.

EGGNOG

I'm playing it safe with this recipe and using egg substitutes. If you have a healthy immune system, you may choose to use the real thing.

- ¼ cup liquid egg replacement or reconstituted powdered egg yolks
- 2 tablespoons granular Splenda®
- ½ cup cream
- 1 teaspoon vanilla extract
- • A few grains of salt
- ¼ cup reconstituted powdered egg whites or packaged pasteurized egg whites
- ¼ cup rum, whiskey, or brandy (optional)
- • Ground nutmeg

Beat the egg substitute until light. Slowly beat in the Splenda®, cream, and salt. In a clean bowl, with clean beaters, beat the egg whites until stiff; fold lightly into the other ingredients. Add rum, whiskey, or brandy (if using). Spoon the eggnog into cups and sprinkle with a few grains of nutmeg.

To make with raw eggs: Use 2 egg yolks instead of the packaged egg substitute, and 2 egg whites instead of the egg white substitute.

Servings: 2

PER SERVING:		
Total Carb: 2.3g	Fiber: 0g	Net Carb: 2.3g

LEMONADE

For each serving:
1 cup water
2 tablespoons lemon juice
2 tablespoons granular Splenda® or Da Vinci® sugar-free
   simple syrup

Mix together and serve over ice.

PER SERVING:		
Total Carb: 5g when made with granular Splenda®	Fiber: 0g	Net Carb: 5g
Total Carb: 2g when made with sugar-free syrup	Fiber: 0g	Net Carb: 2g

Tips and Notes

Pasteurized eggs in the shells are now available. These are a safe alternative for dishes with liquid yolks, but the whites don't work well for beating. The heat that kills the bacteria partially thickens the whites so that they won't produce enough volume. Packaged liquid whole-egg replacements are another option to use in place of yolks, but be sure to read the label as some of them are onion-flavored and would not be suitable for use in a dessert. You can also use powdered egg yolks, but they are not so readily available. I order them from *The Baker's Catalogue®* of the King Arthur® Flour Company because I use so many for making ice cream.

There are also alternatives to raw egg whites. You can use packaged pasteurized whites, but if you plan to beat them, be sure the label says they are intended for whipping and for meringues. Powdered whites are also safe and they work beautifully. They are very convenient as well; they sit on the shelf until needed and leave no odd yolks in the fridge.

Chocolate Milk

2 teaspoons Dutch-process
 cocoa powder
2 tablespoons whey protein
 powder
• A few grains of salt
3 tablespoons heavy cream
2 tablespoons granular
 Splenda®

Mix the cocoa powder, whey powder, and salt. Add 3 tablespoons of cream and mix to form a paste. Add the water and Splenda® and whisk until smooth or mix in a blender. Chill or add ice. Makes 8 ounces.

Per Serving:
Total Carb: 2.3g
Fiber: 0.7g
Net Carb: 1.6g

Tips and Notes

Hood® Calorie Countdown™ makes a milk substitute with only 3 carbs per cup, compared to 12 for regular milk. Their fat-free dairy beverage is thin and watery, but the 2% tastes exactly like real milk. Calorie Countdown™ uses Splenda® and asulfame K to replace the natural milk sugar (lactose). See Sources.

MILK

When I made my Chocolate Chip Cookies my first reaction was, "Wow, chocolate chip cookies!" My second was, "Gotta have milk!" The problem with milk is the lactose, or milk sugar. By using the protein and cream components of real milk and replacing just the sugar, I thought I should be able to make something that would taste more like milk than the soy, almond, or rice based substitutes you can buy. It tastes best icy cold; I like to put an ice cube in the glass and use a straw. Also try it over strawberries or low-carb cereal.

2 tablespoons whey protein powder, 2 carbs or less per serving
• A few grains of salt
3 tablespoons heavy cream
1 cup water
1 tablespoon sugar-free simple or vanilla syrup or 1 tablespoon granular Splenda®

Stir the whey powder and salt into the cream and mix to form a paste. Add the water and syrup and whisk until smooth or mix in a blender. Chill until very cold or add ice to the glass. Makes 8 ounces.

Servings: 1

PER SERVING:		
Total Carb: 1g	Fiber: 0g	Net Carb: 1g

What's Wrong With Milk?

A study of more than 12,000 children nationwide found that the more milk they drank, the more weight they gained. Children who drank more than three cups of milk a day were 35% more likely to become overweight than those who drank one or two. The researchers expressed surprise that the findings applied even though most of the children were drinking low-fat milk.[3] Milk contains 11 to 12 grams of sugar per cup. Lactose, or milk sugar, tastes less sweet than other forms of sugar, but each eight-ounce serving of milk has the equivalent of 4 teaspoons of table sugar.

---

3 Rob Stein "The more milk kids drink, the fatter they tend to get, study says," *The Washington Post*, June 7, 2005.

GREAT HOT CHOCOLATE

The Aztecs put vanilla and chili pepper in their chocolate drinks. It's actually pretty good that way. (They didn't use sugar, but we don't have to be that authentic.)

1   teaspoon Dutch-process cocoa powder
1   teaspoon granular Splenda®
2   ounces sugar-free chocolate syrup (4 tablespoons)
⅓   cup heavy cream
⅔   cup water
•   A few grains of salt
•   A sprinkle of cinnamon

Mix the cocoa with the Splenda® in a microwave-safe cup. Add the syrup and mix to a paste. Stir in the cream, water, and cinnamon. Heat in the microwave for 1 minute. Stir; heat an additional 20 seconds. Top with sugar-free Whipped Cream (see p. 328).

Servings: 1

PER SERVING:		
Total Carb: 1.1g	Fiber: 0.3g	Net Carb: 0.8g

Tips and Notes

Dutch-process cocoas like Drosty® and Saco® brands are the lowest in carb count, only one gram per tablespoon, after you subtract the gram of fiber. I especially like Saco® cocoa; it is inexpensive and comes in a nice large round canister that makes dipping and measuring very easy.

For those of you who prefer your hot chocolate with marshmallows, La Nouba® makes zero carb, sugar-free marshmallows that melt just the way they should on top of a steaming cup of chocolate. See Sources.

"Fruit of all the kinds that the country produced were laid before him; he ate very little, but from time to time a liquor prepared from cocoa, and of an aphrodisiac nature, as we were told, was presented to him in golden cups...."
—Bernal Diaz del Castillo, describing a meal of emperor Montezuma in 1519

The Da Vinci Gourmet® Company originally developed its syrups to flavor coffee and tea. This is the brand used in many cafes and coffee bars. They make dozens of Splenda®-sweetened flavors that are available in stores or by mail order from their web site. They have more great drink recipes on their web site: www.davincigourmet.com. Atkins™ syrups can be substituted in some of my recipes, but Da Vinci® makes more flavors. Torani® brand can also be substituted; it has Splenda® for part of its sweetener, but also uses acesulfame K.

VARIATION:

Root Beer Float

Add a scoop of sugar-free ice cream to a glass of this root beer for a great root beer float.
Makes 1 serving.

Per Serving:
Total Carb: 5.9g
Fiber: 0g
Net Carb: 5.9g

SUGAR-FREE SOFT DRINKS

Have you ever had watermelon pop? Da Vinci® makes dozens of interesting and exotic flavored syrups. Just use the proportions below and turn them all into no-calorie, no-carb, and no-caffeine soft drinks.

2 ounces (4 tablespoons) sugar-free flavored syrup
8 ounces (1 cup) carbonated water

Stir together and serve over ice.

ROOT BEER

Extract makes a very delicious root beer. The directions on the McCormick's® root beer extract carton are for making 5 gallons of fermented root beer, but it won't work without sugar, so I tried using the extract in carbonated water. The result was quite satisfactory (it tastes like root beer barrel candies). Mine doesn't have the foam, but I think it tastes better than bottled sugar-free root beer.

½ teaspoon root beer extract (I used McCormick's®.)
1 tablespoon vanilla-flavored sugar-free syrup
2 packets Splenda® or 4 teaspoons granular Splenda®
8 ounces carbonated water

Mix in a glass and add ice.

Servings: 1

PER SERVING:		
Total Carb: 2g	Fiber: 0g	Net Carb: 2g

Silly Drinks:
When my grandchildren come over they love to make "silly drinks." I let them choose from my assortment of Da Vinci® sugar-free syrups to concoct soft drinks using any combination of flavors and carbonated water. The grown-ups have to sample their creations such as banana-green apple-root beer or peanut butter-lemon-gingerbread pop. Of course, we always respond "Mmmm, good!"—JBB

Italian Creme Sodas

Add an ounce of cream to any of the Sugar-free Soft Drinks on page 338 and it becomes an Italian creme soda. Below are some of my favorite combinations. All have zero carbs.

Fill a glass with ice. Pour 8 ounces of carbonated water over the ice. Add 1 ounce of heavy cream and 2 ounces of sugar-free syrup. Stir.

To make **Raspberry Truffle Italian Soda:**
Use 1 ounce (2 tablespoons) each of raspberry and chocolate sugar-free syrup.

To make **Chocolate-Covered Cherry Italian Soda:**
Use 1 ounce (2 tablespoons) each of cherry and chocolate sugar-free syrup.

To make **Vanilla Cream Italian Soda:**
Use 2 ounces (4 tablespoons) of vanilla sugar-free syrup.

To make **Dreamsicle Italian Soda:**
Use 2 ounces (4 tablespoons) of orange sugar-free syrup.

Cherry, Chocolate, or Vanilla Cola

Add 2 ounces (4 tablespoons) of sugar-free cherry, chocolate, or vanilla syrup to one can of diet cola.

Vanilla "Milkshake"

2 packets Splenda® or 4 teaspoons granular Splenda®
   or
4 teaspoons sugar-free vanilla or simple syrup
1 cup water
½ cup heavy cream
1 cup sugar-free French Vanilla Ice Cream, cut into
   1-inch chunks (See p. 282)

Put Splenda® or syrup, water, and cream in a blender. Add ice cream. Blend until smooth. Makes 2 cups.

Servings: 2

PER SERVING:		
Total Carb: 5.1g	Fiber: 0g	Net Carb: 5.1g
when made with granular Splenda®		
Total Carb: 4.1g	Fiber: 0g	Net Carbs: 4.1g
when made with sugar-free syrup		

Tips and Notes

To substitute Splenda® and liquid for sugar-free syrup in recipes:

For each tablespoon of syrup, use one tablespoon of water and one tablespoon of granular Splenda® (or 1½ packets). You may also add a few drops of flavor extract.

STRAWBERRY SHAKE

1   cup frozen unsweetened strawberries
2   packets of Splenda® or 4 teaspoons granular Splenda® or 4 teaspoons sugar-free strawberry or simple syrup
1   cup water
1   cup sugar-free French Vanilla Ice Cream cut into 1-inch chunks (See p. 282)

Put strawberries in a blender. Add Splenda® or syrup and water. Blend until evenly pureed. Add ice cream. Blend. Scrape down the sides of the container with a rubber spatula and blend until smooth. Makes 2 cups.

Servings: 2

PER SERVING:		
Total Carb: 10.9g	Fiber: 2g	**Net Carb: 8.9g**
when made with granular Splenda®		
Total Carb: 9.9g	Fiber: 2g	**Net Carb: 7.9g**
when made with sugar-free syrup		

CHOCOLATE SHAKE

1   teaspoon Dutch-process cocoa powder
1   teaspoon granular Splenda®
2   tablespoons sugar-free chocolate syrup, like Da Vinci®
½   cup heavy cream
½   cup water
1   cup sugar-free Chocolate Ice Cream cut into 1-inch chunks (see p. 283)

Put cocoa, Splenda®, syrup, cream, and water in a blender. Process to blend. Add ice cream. Blend. Scrape down the sides of the container with a rubber spatula and blend until smooth. Makes 2 cups.

Servings: 2

PER SERVING:		
Total Carb: 5.9g	Fiber: 1.4g	**Net Carb: 4.5g**
count excludes 4.4g sugar alcohols in ice cream		

SANGRIA

1   whole lime, sliced
½   orange, sliced
1   bottle red wine (25 ounces)
2   ounces Grand Marnier
½   cup granular Splenda® or ½ cup sugar-free simple syrup
16 ounces sparkling water

Place the sliced fruit in a pitcher and crush lightly with a wooden spoon. Add the wine, Grand Marnier, and Splenda® or syrup, and chill for 3 to 4 hours. Stir and add the sparkling water. Serve over ice. Makes 6 glasses.

Servings: 6

PER SERVING:		
Total Carb: 7g	Fiber: 0g	Net Carb: 7g
when made with granular Splenda®		
Total Carb: 5g	Fiber: 0g	Net Carb: 5g
when made with sugar-free syrup		

"It Ain't the Things You Don't Know That Hurt You, It's the Things You Know That Ain't So."

—Robert M. Solow

Wine

Most low-carb systems allow wine in moderation after the initial phases if you include the carbs in your total allowance. Dry or table wines contain from 1 to 1.5 grams of carbohydrate per ounce. Recent studies have shown red wine, in particular, to have a positive effect on health, and it has been suggested that wine consumption may explain why the French have lower rates of heart disease than we do, the so called French Paradox.

Resveratrol, a compound found mainly in red wine, has both antioxidant and anti-inflammatory properties. Not all red wines contain resveratrol, a natural fungicide produced by grapes that grow in humid areas. Grapes grown in a dry climate and those that have been sprayed to prevent fungal infection will have very little. Organically grown pinot noir has the highest levels of resveratrol.

SOURCES

*If there is only one item from a particular source, it is listed with the entry. Sources that have multiple entries are listed in the **Directory of Sources** at the end. Those entries are marked with an asterisk.*

For a while, low-carbohydrate foods and ingredients were almost as common as low-fat ones; many things that I originally had to order by mail were available in local grocery stores. Unfortunately, the rush to cash in on the low-carb craze produced a lot of products no one would buy twice. When merchants were left with shelves of foods that were hardly edible, let alone tasty, they assumed that the "fad" had passed and phased out *all* the low-carb products, even the good ones. So don't be shy about asking for low-carb items to convince store owners that there is a market for good products. I have included some of the best things I have found; you may have made your own discoveries that are as good or better.

This list may be helpful if you are unable to locate some of the products used in my recipes or want to purchase recommended items. You can contact a company or check its Web site to find a retailer in your area, or you may be able to order the items for home delivery. Another option is to ask your local grocer to stock a product for you. Make it easy for them by writing out the contact information for the manufacturer.

No time to Cook?

Home Bistro® offers frozen "chef-prepared" low-carb meals and side dishes for home delivery. Home Bistro Foods, Inc., 190 Banker Road, Plattsburgh, NY 12901; www.homebistro.com; phone: 1-800-628-5588.

Freshly prepared, low-carb meals can be ordered for weekly home delivery to many locations from Atkins at Home™. Meals are appropriate for either a 20- or 40-carb per day regimen. Sample menus are featured on the Web site. You can contact them at www.atkinsathome.com or by phone at 1-800-242-0076.

Beans

Soybeans
Eden® Foods sells canned, organic black soybeans. They have 8 grams of carbohydrate and 7 of fiber in ½ cup, for a net carb count of 1 gram. Many groceries and health food stores sell Eden products. There is a store locator on the Web site, and Eden products can be ordered online from www.edenfoods.com or from www.lowcarb.com.

Edamame (green soybeans) are available fresh and frozen at grocery and health food stores. Trader Joe's* sells several kinds.

Tepary Beans
Native Seeds Search is a nonprofit group that sells seeds and foods from plants used by early Native Americans. Their tepary beans, first cultivated in the Southwest by the native Hohokam people are high in protein, high in fiber, and have a low glycemic index. Native Seeds Search, 526 North Fourth Ave, Tucson, AZ 85705; Web site: www.nativeseeds.org.; phone: 520-622-5561.

Tepary beans are also available from Heritage Foods USA.* (Look on the Web site under "What We Sell, Fruits and Grains" for beans.)

Beverages and Soft Drinks

Jones Soda Company® sells Splenda®-sweetened, carbonated beverages in several flavors, including black cherry, root beer, and ginger ale. Their Web site, www.jonessoda.com, includes a store locator. Jones Soda Seattle, 234 9th Ave. North, Seattle, WA, 98109; phone: 1-800-656-6050.

Lorina® makes sparkling orangeade, lemonade, and pink lemonade sweetened with sucralose and natural flavors. It comes in a beautiful bottle with a wired stopper. I found all the flavors at Cost Plus World Market®.* It is imported from France by Lorina Inc., Gables International Plaza, 2655 Le Jeune Road, Suite 908, Coral Gables, FL 33134; phone 305-779-3085; Web site (it's in French): www.lorina.com.

SoBe® Lean® Diet drinks come in five flavors: cranberry grapefruit, mango melon, green tea, peach tea, and energy. They are sweetened with sucralose and acesulfame K. The different flavors contain herbs and nutraceuticals, such as vitamin C, chromium, and carnitine. An 8-ounce serving contains 1 gram of carbohydrate. The fruit flavors have no caffeine; energy has about as much as a cup of coffee, green tea has 3 mg., and peach tea has 15 mg. (Peach tea is my favorite.) SoBe® Lean® Diet drinks are recommended on the South Beach and Protein Power plans. Web site: www.sobebev.com.

Hanson's fruit-flavored sodas are sweetened with Splenda® and acesulfame K. Hanson's Ginger Ale is made with real ginger and lime juice. Hanson's products are widely available.

Colas
Diet Rite Cola®, introduced in 1958, was the first diet soft drink. In 2000, it became the first soft drink to be sweetened with Splenda®, although they have since added acesulfame K to the recipe. It contains no caffeine and no sodium. Diet Rite is available nationwide. Find more information at www.dietrite.com. Pepsi® One and Diet Coke® have no aspartame, but they contain caffeine.

White Tea
Celestial Seasonings® sells four flavors of white tea, including China White Pearl™, a decaffeinated white tea. Trader Joe's* has white tea in teabags (not decaf). Asian markets, like Uwajimaya*, will have many different brands, usually as loose tea, and reasonably priced. The Republic of Tea® sells 9 different flavors of white tea; only the kiwi pear flavor is decaffeinated. Cost Plus World Market®* and Starbuck's® carry The Republic of Tea® brand but may not stock all the varieties. The Republic of Tea®, 8 Digital Drive, Suite 100, Novato, CA 94949; phone: 1-800-298-4832; Web site: www.REPUBLICofTEA.com.

CAKES, PIES, COOKIES, AND MUFFINS

Amarettini di Saronno, miniature Italian cookies, have a little over 1 net gram of carbohydrate per tiny cookie, even though they are made with sugar. They are distributed by Eurofoods Inc., 51/15 35th Street, Long Island City, NY 11101. Cost Plus World Market®* usually stocks these.

Andre's Bakery™* makes coconut and chocolate macaroons and pecan and chocolate bite-size cookies, each with 2 net carbs per serving.

Controlled Carb Gourmet's classic brownie is a big cake-like brownie with 1 net gram of carbohydrate and 16 grams of sugar alcohol per 2-ounce serving. (Note that 2 ounces is *not* a whole brownie.) They are especially good if warmed in the microwave for a few seconds. The company also sells cakes, muffins, rolls, breads, and sugar-free syrups. Controlled Carb Gourmet, 8780 Charleston Blvd, STE 133, Las Vegas, NV 89117-5464; phone: 1-800-598-7720; Web site: www.controlledcarbgourmet.com.

Heavenly Desserts makes sugar-free, meringue kisses sweetened with Splenda® and modified malt (a sugar alcohol). They have no carbs after subtracting the sugar alcohol. The company also sells wheat and sesame crackers and frozen cheesecakes. A store finder is featured on the Web site. Manufactured by D-Liteful Bakery Co., 9012 NW 105 Way, Medley, FL 33178; Web site: www.d-litefulbaking.com.

Hill & Valley Inc. sells over 200 varieties of sugar-free and no-sugar-added baked goods. All the products are said to be trans-fat-free, but they are made with sugar alcohols. There is a nutrition chart on the Web site, but no list of ingredients. Their products are sold in many supermarket in-store bakeries. There is a store locator on the Web site, and you can order online at www.hillandvalley.net. Hill and Valley Inc., PO Box 6575, Rock Island, IL 61204; phone: 309-793-0161.

CANDY, CARAMEL POPCORN, AND MARSHMALLOWS

Asher's®, Carb Safe, Atkins™, Russell Stover®, Whitman's®, Carb Saver, and Doctor's Diet Carb Rite are just some of the low-carb candy brands available. Atkins™ Endulge is sweetened with Splenda® as well as maltitol; most of the other brands are sweetened with maltitol and carry warnings about excess consumption. One caveat: be sure to check the serving size—the carb count in large print may sound low for a whole candy bar, but it may really be the amount in a small portion.

D-LECTABLE makes D-lish chocolate bars and candy using an all-natural, high-fiber sweetener made from inulin. The products are available online from www.d-lectable.com.

Eat Well Be Well™ chocolate bars (plain or almond) contain no sugar alcohols or trans fats. They have 2 net grams of carbohydrate. EWBW also makes semi-sweet chocolate chips and cereal. Their products are available nationwide in stores and can also be ordered online from Netrition.*

York®, now owned by Hershey's®, sells sugar-free peppermint patties that are indistinguishable from the originals, but they are heavy on the maltitol. Phone: 1-800-468-1714; Web site: www.hershey ssugarfree.com. They can be ordered from www.low-carb.com.

Asher's® Chocolates makes wonderful cordial cherries with liquid centers that have less than 1 net carb in 3 candies. They are made with maltitol, sorbitol, and sucralose. Asher's also makes sugar-free chocolate bars, fudge, jellies, and caramels. Asher's® Chocolates, 80 Wambold Road, Souderton, PA 18964; phone: 800-438-8882 or 215-721-3149; Web site: www.ashers.com.

Brown and Haley® makes chocolate-coated Almond Roca®, sweetened with isomalt and sucralose. Each candy has 0.7 net carbs. Brown and Haley®, Tacoma, WA 98401; phone: 1-800-445-9020; Web site: www.brown-haley.com.

Judy's Candy Company makes delicious sugar-free caramels (made with maltitol, but real cream). Phone: 1-800-223-1642. They can be ordered from www.judyscandy.com or www.carbsmart.com.

Jelly Belly® makes sugar-free jelly beans. They are made with maltitol and Splenda®. Jelly Belly Company, One Jelly Belly Lane, Fairfield, CA 94530; phone: 1-800-522-3267; Web site: www.jellybelly.com.

Harry and David* makes sugar-free caramel popcorn called Moose Munch® chocolate cashew almond popcorn, sweetened with maltitol.

La Nouba® marshmallows are made in Begium. The company also makes a chocolate-covered version. They have zero net carbs and are sweetened with isomalt and maltitol. La Noruba® also makes low-carb candies, jams, and Belgian waffles (like big cookies). You must order them by the case if you place an order from the La Nouba® Web site. La Noruba Inc., Midland Park, NJ 07432; phone: 201-652-8369; Web site: www.lanouba.be. The marshmallows and many other low-carb items are available from the Lo Carb-U store at 5770 Melrose Ave., Los Angeles, CA 90038 or from their Web site at www.locarbu.com; phone: 877-562-2728. La Nouba® products are also available from Netrition.*

CHEWING GUM

Xylichew®, chewing gum is sweetened with only xylitol (it is 70% xylitol by weight). It may be beneficial in preventing tooth decay and ear infections. It is said to remineralize tooth enamel and it may help prevent osteoporosis. It is produced in Finland for Tundra Trading Inc., Glendale, CA 91204; Web site: www.tundratrading.com. It is available at many health and nutrition stores and can be ordered from the Web site. They also sell XyliBrush®, a toothpaste containing xylitol.

CHOCOLATE

Cocoa

Droste and Saco brand Dutch cocoa, available at many grocery stores, have 1 net gram of carbohydrate per tablespoon. Droste B.V., P.O. Box 5, 8170 AA Vaassen, Holland; Web site: www.droste.nl. Saco Foods Inc., Middleton, WI 53562; phone: 1-800-373-7226; Web site: www.sacofoods.com.

Chocolate Candy Coating

Chocolate candy coating, sweetened with maltitol, can be ordered from the Sweet Celebrations* catalog or from the Web site.

Chocolate Chips

Big Skies Farm sells mini dark chocolate chips sweetened with acesulfame K and Splenda®. They have 1.5 net carbs in 2 tablespoons. They can be ordered online from www.lowcarbdietchefs.com. (Click on "chocolates.")

Eat Well Be Well™* makes sugar-free, semi-sweet chocolate chips. They have 7 grams of fiber and a net carb count of ½ gram per tablespoon. They contain no sugar alcohols and are sweetened with acesulfame K and sucralose. They can also be ordered from Netrition.*

The King Arthur® Flour Company* lists maltitol-sweetened chocolate chips in their online catalog.

Unsweetened Chocolate

Callebaut unsweetened chocolate is a good buy if you buy it in bulk by mail from Sweet Celebrations.*

Scharffen Berger and Valrhona unsweetened chocolates are available from Chocosphere®.*

Guittard's unsweetened chocolate comes in convenient 1-inch disks that can be melted without chopping. Order it from *The Baker's Catalogue®* of the King Arthur® Flour Company* or from Chocosphere®.* (On Chocosphere's Web site, it is called "Guittard's Classic 'Oban' Cocoa Liquor Wafers.")

Although Nestlé regular semi-sweet chocolate chips are everywhere, their unsweetened baking bar is hard to find, and the company does not take mail orders. The baking bar is available online from www.netgrocer.com (search for Nestle Toll House Baking Bar), or it can be ordered by phone at: 1-888-638-4762. Nestlé USA, Inc., Solon, OH 44139; phone: 1-800-851-0512; Web site: www.Nestleusa.com.

Ghirardelli 100% cocoa unsweetened baking bars are sold in some groceries and drug stores as well as their own shops. Ghirardelli Chocolate Company, San Leandro, CA 94578-2631; Web site: www.ghirardelli.com. Ghirardelli does not sell the unsweetened baking bars on line, but they can be purchased at www.low-carb.com, www.clickbird.com, or www.perfectcoffeeshop.com.

CONDIMENTS

Mt. Olive no-sugar-added sweet relish is sweetened with Splenda®. It has 1 net carb per tablespoon. (The Web site lists zero carbs.) They also make no-sugar-added sweet gherkins. Mt. Olive Pickle Co., Inc., Mt. Olive, NC 28365-0609; phone: 1-800-672-5041: Web site: www.mtolivepickles.com. Order online from www.lowcarb.com or by phone at 1-888-339-2477.

Salsa Verde is available from most grocery stores or online from www.mexgrocer.com or www.amazon.com. The label for Embasa® brand lists 1 gram of carbohydrate and 1 gram of fiber for a net count of zero.

Steel's Gourmet Foods* sells ketchup, barbeque sauce, sweet and sour sauce, sweet ginger-lime dressing, and honey-mustard dressing sweetened with Splenda®.

CORN

Pinewood Products sells the kind of corn that was originally raised by the Iroquois in what is now New York State. It contains more protein and fiber than modern corn. They sell three products: roasted white corn flour, hulled hominy, and tamal flour. The minimum order is 5 pounds of one product. Pinewoods Community Farming, Inc., 214 Liberty St, Oswego, NY 13126. Their regular phone number was not working the last time I tried to call. You can order through Kevin White, the associate manager of the Iroquois White Corn Project, by cell phone: 315-430-4344; by fax: 315-207-0471; or by e-mail: kwhite33@verizon.net.

Iroquois corn can also be ordered through Heritage Foods USA™.* They donate a portion of their profits to nonprofit groups like Slow Food USA. (Look under "What We Sell, Fruits and Grains" for corn.) Co-founder, Patrick Martins, says, "Heritage Foods USA™ exists to protect small family farms and genetic diversity in the food supply by selling rare foods to mail order consumers and restaurant and retail outlets around the country."

Juanita's canned Mexican-style hominy has 10 grams of carbohydrate in ½ cup but 6 grams of fiber, which means only 4 net grams of carbohydrate per serving! It can usually be found on the aisle with the Mexican foods in the grocery store. Juanita's Foods, Wilmington, CA 90744; Web site: www.juanitasfoods.com.

BREAD, CRACKERS, AND TORTILLAS

Bread
Pepperidge Farm® very thin light wheat bread has 6 net grams of carbohydrate per slice. The slices are small, but it is real bread. Pepperidge Farm products are widely available. Pepperidge Farm, Inc., Norwalk, CT 06856.

Oroweat Lite 100% whole wheat bread, with 5.5 net carbs per slice, is also widely available. Distributed by Bimbo Bakeries U.S.A., Inc., 14401 Statler Blvd., Fort Worth, Texas, 76155; phone: 817-864-2500.

Low Carb Emporium's 7-grain fiber bread comes in several varieties with 3 net carbs per slice. They also sell bagels at 8 to 9.5 net carbs each, pita pockets at 3.5 net carbs, and lots of other breads and low-carb products. Look for "Low Carb Emporium" at www.deepdiscountnutrition.com.

Franz sells Smart Nutrition Net 4, reduced-carb, high-fiber bread. Franz Family Bakeries, 6405 Rosewood Street, Suite C, Lake Oswego, OR 97035-5286; Web site: www.usbakery.com.

Crackers
D-Liteful Bakery Co.®* sells Heavenly Harvest wheat or sesame crackers that have 1 net carb each and no trans fats. They are nice, thick crackers that are great for making snacks and appetizers or to go with soup.

Andre's Bakery™* makes low-carb baked goods and snacks. Their Carbo Save™ cheddar cheese crackerbread has slightly over 1 net gram of carbohydrate in each large cracker. The crackerbread comes in 10 flavors.

Falwasser™ wafer thin crispbread, tasty crackers from Australia, are so thin you can almost see through them. I discovered them at the gourmet cheese counter of my local Central Market, where they were offering them with the cheese samples. They come in 5 flavors. The poppy seed crackers have 17.5 net carbs in 16 crackers. Falwasser Australia, Central Plaza, Ashmore, Queensland 4211 Australia; phone: +16 (7) 55- 920-820; fax: +61 (7) 55-315-223; e-mail: sales@falwasser.co..au.

Soy Crisps, made by GeniSoy Products, have about 0.5 net gram of carbohydrate each. They come in several flavors, including ranch and apple cinnamon. (They also make a low-carb version, with more soy, which I do *not* recommend.) Genisoy Products Co, Fairfield, CA 94533; phone: 1-888-436-4769; Web site: www.genisoy.com.

Tortillas

La Tortilla Factory was the first company to make low-carb tortillas. They come in two sizes and several flavors. The original whole-wheat tortillas have 3 net carbs each; the large ones have 5. I especially like their new white flour wraps made with extra virgin olive oil. They taste like regular flour tortillas, but each large tortilla has only 7 net carbs. There is a store locator on the Web site, or you can order them online from www.latortillafactory.com or from many other low-carb sites. La Tortilla Factory, 3300 Westwind Blvd., Santa Rosa, CA, 95403; phone: 1-800-446-1516.

Cereal

Three flavors of breakfast cereal and individually packaged servings of hot cereal can be ordered from the Atkins™ Web site.*

Eat Well Be Well™ makes whole-grain cereal bars (10 net carbs), cereals (17 net carbs), and instant oatmeal (17 net carbs) with no sugar alcohols or trans fats. The cereal products may be too high in carbs for many of us, but a big improvement over what most children are currently eating. EWBW products are available nationwide in supermarkets and health food stores and can also be ordered online from Netrition* and other low-carb sites.

CHERRIES

Check at www.cherrymkt.org for a list of sources for cherries and cherry juice in your area.

Oregon canned pie cherries, available in most grocery stores, are the Montmorency variety. Oregon Fruit Products Co., P.O. Box 5949, Salem, OR 97304; phone: 1-800-394-9333; Web site: www.oregonfruit.com.

Remlinger Farms in Carnation, Washington, sells frozen Montmorency cherries in three-pound bags from their farm store and at QFCs, Albertson's, Thriftways, and many other stores in Western Washington and Northern Oregon. Web site: www.remlingerfarms.com.

Trader Joe's* sells canned Morello sour cherries and unsweetened, dried, tart cherries.

Flavonoid Sciences™, the makers of Cherry Flex™ capsules, have discovered a way to put the beneficial compounds of whole cherries in a softgel while eliminating most of the sugar. For more information, see www.cherryflex.com. Flavonoid Sciences™ is a division of Cherry Capital Services, Inc., P.O. Box 486, Eastport, MI 49627; phone: 1- 888-947-4047.

DAIRY PRODUCTS

For information about organic dairy products, check http://www.organicmilk.org/ or contact Northeast Organics Dairy Producers Alliance, 30 Keats Rd., Deerfield MA 01342.

Milk

Hood® Calorie Countdown™, originally called Carb Countdown, makes a milk substitute that uses Splenda® and acesulfame K to replace the natural sugar (lactose) in milk. It comes in 2%, fat-free, and 2% chocolate. The 2% tastes exactly like real milk. It has the same amount of calcium as regular milk, and it can be used like milk in recipes. Many stores carry only the fat-free one, but you can add a little cream to make it taste better. The 2% and fat-free versions have 3 net carbs per cup; the chocolate has 4 net carbs. Calorie Countdown™ products are widely available in stores, and home delivery is available in New England. HP Hood LLC Headquarters, 90 Everett Ave., Chelsea, MA 02150-2301; phone: 800-343-6592; Web site: www.hphood.com.

Cream

Trader Joe's* sells a zero-carb fresh cream and usually has good prices.

Organic Valley heavy whipping cream has zero carbs. The carton lists "pasteurized grade A organic cream" as the only ingredient. Distributed by CROPP Cooperative, La Farge, WI 54639; Web site: www.organicvalley.com.

Nestlé Media Crema canned cream can be substituted for fresh cream in recipes. It is made with light cream, but it has zero carbs anyway. Look for it with the Mexican foods at the supermarket or contact the company at 1-800-258-6727. Nestlé USA, Inc., Glendale, CA 91203; Web site: www.Nestleusa.com.

Cheese and Cheese Flour

Cheese flour is available from *The Baker's Catalogue*® of the King Arthur® Flour Company* and from Spices etc®.* King Arthur® sells only cheddar flour; Spices etc®. has cheddar, Parmesan, Parmesan/Romano, and blue cheese powders.

Cotija cheese, also called *queso seco,* can be used in Mexican dishes, and it can be fried like Halloumi®. You may find it in the cheese section or with the Mexican foods at regular grocery stores. Cacique®, City of Industry, CA, 91746, makes several kinds of Mexican cheese. Recipes and information are available at www.caciqueusa.com.

Shepherds of Cyprus Halloumi®, the Cheese That Grills, is available in supermarkets, delicatessens, and ethnic food stores. It is produced and packed by Pittas Dairy Industries LTD in Nicosia, Cyprus. To find where to buy Halloumi® in the US, contact Mr. Raffi Kradjian: phone: 1-818-502-1313; e-mail: *kraimpco@aol.com;* Web site: www.pittas.com. Distributed in the US by Kradjian Importing Co. Inc., 5018 San Fernando Road, Glendale, CA 91204.

BelGioioso® mascarpone cheese (Italian cream cheese) is not hard to find, but the price varies a great deal. Trader Joe's* usually has the best price for mascarpone and many other kinds of cheese. BelGioioso Cheese Inc., 5810 Country Road NN, Denmark, WI 54208; phone: 1-877-863-2123; Web site: www.belgioioso.com.

Ice Cream and Frozen Treats

TCBY frozen yogurt stores sell a low-carb, soft-serve ice cream in cones or dishes. (A cake cone has only 4 net carbs. Waffle cones are higher.) There is a store locator on their Web site: www.tcby.com.

Blue Bunny Carb Freedom ice cream, which comes in 4 flavors (chocolate almond fudge, butter pecan, peanut butter fudge, and vanilla bean), is one of my favorite brands. Blue Bunny also makes low-carb ice cream bars and other novelties. Phone: 1-800-331-0830; Web site: www.bluebunny.com.

Safeway stores sell Lucerne Carb Watch'n ice cream, which is also very good. My local Safeway carries it in chocolate, butter pecan, and vanilla. Different Safeway stores may have other selections.

Atkins™ Advantage* sells ice cream in many flavors in some retail stores.*

Breyers makes Carb Smart™ ice cream and ice cream bars, fudge bars, creamsicles, and ice cream sandwiches. Many stores carry Carb Smart™ products. Most of the ice cream flavors have 4 net carbs in ½ cup, but Neapolitan has zero. Breyers is part of Unilever Ice Cream, P.O. Box 19007, Green Bay, WI 54307-9007; Web site: www.icecreamusa.com.

EGG PRODUCTS AND SUBSTITUTES

I hesitate to recommend substitutes for fresh eggs. Eggs are a good source of natural protein and healthful fat, but for some people, an alternative may be a safer choice when a recipe requires raw eggs.

Liquid egg whites are available in cartons in the refrigerated case at grocery stores. They are useful for the times when you need just a little and don't want to sacrifice a whole egg or when you need a lot and don't want to waste the yolks. Check the label; some brands have been heated too much to whip properly.

All Whites® can't be used for whipping but will work for other purposes. Papetti Foods, Elizabeth, NJ 07206; phone: 1-877-727-3884; Web site: www.betterneggs.com.

Nulaid ReddiEgg® Real Egg Product, is a liquid, whole-egg replacement made from egg whites. (Not something I would use unless I needed to avoid raw eggs.) It does not contain real yolks, which are needed as emulsifiers in many recipes, such as ice creams and sauces. Phone: 1-800-7-NULAID; Web site: www.nulaid.com.

Powdered whole eggs, egg whites, and yolks, can be ordered from *The Baker's Catalogue®* of the King Arthur® Flour Company.* Reconstituted, powdered eggs can be whipped.

Egg tofu is available in the refrigerated case at some groceries, from Asian markets, and from Uwajimaya.*

EQUIPMENT

Home Marketplace sells 7-, 8-, 9-, 10-, and 12-inch pie pans in sets of two. They also have pie weights and pie crust shields. Home Marketplace, P.O. Box 3670, Oshkosh, WI 54903-3670; phone: 1-800-356-3876; Web site: www.thehomemarketplace.com.

The Roto Deep Fryer made by DiLonghi is available through *The Chef's Catalog** and Williams Sonoma.*

FISH AND SEAFOOD

The Pure Food Fish Market, in Seattle, WA, will ship overnight anywhere in the US. Phone: 1-800-392-3474; fax 206-622-2050; Web site: www.freshseafood.com.

Pike Place Fish, Seattle, WA, also ships anywhere in the US. Phone: 800-542-7732; fax: 206-682-4629; Web site: www.pikeplacefish.com.

Vital Choice Seafood sells frozen and canned, wild Alaskan salmon and halibut from their Web site: www.VitalChoice.com.

FILLO

The Fillo Factory sells all-natural, organic fillo with no trans fats. There is a store finder on their Web site or you can order through www.wellnessgrocer.com. Fillo Factory products are available at natural food stores and Whole Foods Markets®. Fillo Factory, P.O. Box 155, Dumont, NJ 07628; phone: 1-800-653-4556, extension 10; Web site: www.fillofactory.com.

Athens® and Apollo® frozen fillo is available in many groceries. Athens Foods, Inc., Cleveland, OH; Web site: www.athens.com.

Fresh fillo, imported from Greece, can be ordered from International Gourmet, 32907 Mesa Drive, Lake Elsinore, CA 92530; phone: 1-951-471-1969; e-mail: info@intlgourmet.com. There is a 5-box minimum order.

FLOUR REPLACEMENTS, FLOUR, AND BAKE MIXES

White whole-wheat flour is available in many stores and by mail order from the King Arthur® Flour Company* and from Bob's Red Mill® Natural Foods.* It is only slightly lower in carbs than all-purpose flour, but it has all the nutrients of whole wheat with a taste similar to white flour. To find a list of sources for white whole-wheat flour, check with the American White Wheat Producers Association, P.O. Box 326, Atchison, KS 6600; phone: 913-367-4422.

Oat flour, soy flour, and gluten flour are widely available at regular and health food stores and by mail order from Bob's Red Mill® Natural Foods* and the King Arthur® Flour Company.*

Carbalose™ is a low-carb flour substitute made by Tova Industries, LLC. It makes a crispy coating for fried foods, and it can be used like all-purpose flour in most recipes with a few changes. Carbquik™ Bake Mix is a low-carb biscuit mix (similar to Bisquik™) made with Carbalose™ flour. It contains 90% fewer net carbs than Bisquik™ and has no trans fats. Most recipes have 3 net carbs or fewer per serving. The Web site, www.carbalose.com, has lots of recipes and a store finder. Both Carbolose™ and Carbquik™ can be ordered online from Netrition.* (Look under Tova Industries.)

Lite White Flour Blend from Big Skies Farm has 6 net carbs per ¼ cup serving. It can be used cup for cup to replace all-purpose flour in most recipes. I like the whipping cream biscuit recipe on the Web site. They also sell a Lite Whole Wheat Flour Blend with 6 carbs and a Golden Flour that has 4 net carbs per serving, but the golden one contains soy flour, so it won't taste as good as the others. There are recipes on the Web site and you can order online: www.lowcarbdietchefs.safeshopper.com.

HERBS, SPICES, EXTRACTS, AND FLAVORINGS

Dorot sells frozen chopped basil, coriander, dill, and parsley, and crushed garlic and ginger in trays of 20 cubes each. They are sold in the US only at Trader Joe's* stores. Dorot Garlic and Herbs, kibbutz Dorot, D.N. Hof Ashkelon 79175, Israel; phone: +972-8-6808095; fax: +972-8-6808715.

Lime, orange, and many other extracts are available from Spices etc®.*

Vanilla without Corn Syrup or Sugar
Spice Islands vanilla, distributed by World Finer Foods, Inc., Bloomfield NJ 07003, is available at grocery stores and from www.spiceadvice.com.

Simply Organic vanilla, distributed by Frontier Natural Brands Inc., Boulder CO 80301, is available at www.ftrontiercoop.com.

Cook's™ Choice vanilla extract can be ordered online from www.cooksvanilla.com.

Trader Joe's* Tahitian blend pure vanilla extract is sugar-free. (Trader Joe's sells several kinds of vanilla, so be sure to get the one that lists only "bourbon and Tahitian vanilla beans, alcohol, and water" as ingredients.)

JAM AND JELLY

Harry and David* sells sugar-free Wild and Rare® preserves made with Splenda®. They come in strawberry, peach, raspberry, and marionberry.

Hero sugar-free preserves are imported from Switzerland. They are all-natural and sweetened with Splenda®. They make strawberry, raspberry, black cherry, apricot, and orange preserves. Hero products are heated for only a short time, to ensure that the nutrients, flavors, and textures are preserved. They are available at retail stores and can be ordered from www.heronorthamerica.com. Hero North America, 808 S. W. 12th Street, Ocala, FL 34474; phone: 1-352-368-1002.

Sugar-free jams, jellies, dessert toppings, pie fillings, and syrups are available from Steel's™ Gourmet Foods.*

Smucker's® makes light sugar-free orange marmalade. All the major grocery chains carry Smucker's® products. If they don't stock the orange marmalade, they can order it for you, or you can order it from www.smuckers.com. It is made with Nutrasweet or with Splenda® and Nutrasweet. The low-sugar version is also good, with only a slight increase in carb count.

MEATS AND POULTRY

Eat Wild's Web site gives grass farmers a place to advertise their products. Over 700 suppliers offer pastured beef, pork, chicken, lamb, goat, bison, venison, and rabbit. The site also lists sources for dairy products from grazing cows and eggs from pastured chickens. Check www.eatwild.com for sources for grass-fed products in your area. Some farms will sell meat in bulk for your freezer, or you may find a farmer's market or butcher where you can buy individual cuts.

Laura's lean beef is raised on family farms without the use of antibiotics, hormones, or animal by-products. They raise Limousin and Charolais cattle, breeds that produce lean beef. The Web site has a store locator. Laura's Lean Beef Company, 2285 Executive Dr., Ste. 200, Lexington, KY 40505; Web site: www.laurasleanbeef.com.

Lasater grasslands beef cattle spend their entire lives grazing in open pastures; they are free of growth hormones, antibiotics, and pesticides. Phone in Colorado: 1-719-541-2855, outside Colorado: 1-866-4LGBEEF; Web site: www.lgbeef.com.

Maverick Ranch Natural Meats sells organic beef, pork, lamb, chicken, and cage-free eggs. They do not use hormones, pesticides, or antibiotics. Their bacon, franks, and sausages are nitrite- and nitrate-free. Maverick Ranch products are carried in over 2,000 stores nationwide. Maverick Ranch Natural Meats, 5360 North Franklin St., Denver, CO 80219; phone: 1-800-497-2624; Web site: www.maverickranch.com.

Niman Ranch raises hogs the old-fashioned way, on family farms in the Midwest, without antibiotics or growth hormones. Because they spend most of their lives outdoors, their hogs develop a thick layer of fat for insulation, which gives the meat superior marbling, flavor, and tenderness. Niman Ranch pork can be ordered online, and the Web site has a list of retailers and restaurants that sell their meat. Niman Ranch, 1025 E. 12th St., Oakland, CA 94606; phone: 866-806-0340; Web site: www.nimanranch.com.

Wellshire Farms thick-sliced, uncured, dry-rubbed bacon is minimally processed and contains no added nitrites or nitrates. It is made from all-natural pork raised without antibiotics. They also sell franks, burgers, hams, deli meats, cheese, sausage, and turkey. Welshire Farms, Swedesboro, NJ 08085; phone: 888-786-2331; Web site: www.wellshirefarms.com. The Web site has a store locator, or you can order online.

Hormel® Cure 81® hams list zero carbs per serving and do not have added water or sugar (they do have nitrites). Hormel Foods Corporation, 1 Hormel Place, Austin, MN 55912-3680; phone: 800-523-4635; Web site: www.hormel.com.

Maple Leaf® all-natural, smoked, uncured ham is not preserved, and the label states that it is minimally processed with "no nitrate or nitrite added." This delicious ham has zero grams of carbohydrate per serving (although the label lists turbinado sugar). Maple Leaf Consumer foods, PO Box 5091 Burlington, Canada L7R 483; phone: 1-800-268-3708; Web site: www.mapleleaf.com.

Maple Leaf Farms'™ all-natural, USDA grade A ducks are raised without antibiotics. Independent animal welfare experts audit their farms, and their products bear an Animal Well-being Assured seal. Phone: 1-800-348-2812. The Web site has a store locator, or you can order online at www.mapleleaffarms.com.

MUSHROOMS

Chinese black mushrooms can be found in Asian markets or ordered from Uwajimaya.* Panda brand sells shredded or whole dried black fungus. Warning: don't be alarmed by the carb count you may see on the label. I bought one that said 65.5 grams per serving. Assuming there was a translation problem, I checked other sources. (It probably should have said 6.55 grams.) Whole mushrooms from the same company listed a carb count of 10 grams, and 7 fiber, for a net of 3 grams. *The Carbohydrate, Fiber, and Sugar Counter* (Natow and Heslin, 1999) gives 20 carbs minus 20 grams of fiber per cup for a net of zero carbs for black mushrooms. *The Complete Book of Food Counts* (Netzer, 2000), gives the carb count for 3 ounces of Frieda's fresh black mushrooms at 4 carbs and 1 fiber, for a net count of 3. I think it's safe to say the carb count is somewhere between zero and 3 per serving.

NUTS, NUT MEAL, AND NUT FLOUR

Choose raw nuts over roasted when possible; they will retain more healthful nutrients. Search online to find the best prices for almond and nut flour and meal.

Almond flour is available by mail from *The Baker's Catalog®* of the King Arthur® Flour Company* or Bob's Red Mill® Natural Foods.* Although Bob's label says almond flour/meal, it is made from blanched almonds.

Almond flour is available from Honeyville Grain, Inc.* The minimum order is 5 pounds.

NOW natural almond flour, in a 10-ounce bag, can be ordered from Netrition.*

Shiloh Farms almond flour, in a 12-ounce package, can be ordered from www.glutenfreemall.com.

Nuts4U sells all kinds of nuts and nut flours at www.nuts4u.com.

Almond meal (made from unblanched almonds) can be found at Trader Joe's* or purchased from Bob's Red Mill.*

NUT BUTTERS

Trader Joe's* sells peanut butter with 3 net grams of carbs in 2 tablespoons. The ingredient label lists only "dry roasted peanuts, salt."

Smucker's® natural peanut butter lists just peanuts and salt as ingredients. Smucker's® is available nationwide.

Adam's peanut butter is another natural peanut butter that is widely available.

Twist® is a sugar-free version of Nutella™. It is sweetened with maltitol, but it has no trans fats (trans fats are not allowed in many European countries). DeBoer's Twist® sugar-free chocolate hazelnut spread is made in Holland. It can be ordered from Netrition* and www.carbsmart.com.

OIL

Rice bran oil is usually available at Asian markets. For information or distributors in the US, contact California Rice Oil Company®, Double 7 Products Inc.®, 138-Hamilton Drive, Novato, CA 94949; phone: 1-415-382-0297.

PASTA

Dreamfields pasta is made with real semolina flour and is indistinguishable from regular pasta. It has 5 digestible grams of carbohydrate in a generous two-ounce serving, compared to 40 or more for regular pasta. Dreamfields comes as spaghetti, linguini, macaroni, lasagna, rotini, and two sizes of penne. It costs about the same as regular pasta. There is a store finder on their Web site at www.dreamfieldsfoods.com. You can order by the case from their Web site or by the package from Netrition* and from many other sites, including www.carbsmart.com.

POLYDEXTROSE

Polydextrose (polyD or poly-d) is not very sweet, but it has many of the qualities of sugar that are missing in high-intensity sweeteners. It contains 1 to 2 net grams of carbohydrate and 25 grams of soluble fiber per ounce. I used Sta-lite® III polydextrose from Honeyville Grain* to test my recipes. It comes in five-pound bags. Netrition* also sells polydextrose; their Life Source Foods PolyD Fiber is similar to the one from Honeyville Grain, but they also have one sweetened with sucralose, called PolyD Fiber Plus, which has a significant carb advantage, since it has about the same count as the unsweetened one; when you add your own Splenda®, you add 24 carbs per cup, because commercial Splenda® contains sugar as a bulking agent. Both products are sold in one-pound bags.

POTATOES

SunLite™ potatoes have 30% fewer carbs than russets. They are available in groceries in the Southeast states and can be ordered from the growers. Sunfresh of Florida Marketing Cooperative, Inc., 1755 Lakeside Ave., St. Augustine, FL 32086; phone: 904-825-0700; Web site: www.sunfreshofflorida.com.

PURSLANE

Purslane is a succulent plant that is eaten as a salad green, steamed, or stir-fried. It is popular in Europe, especially in Greece. It grows as a weed in many parts of the world, including North America. It contains high levels of vitamin C and it has the highest known concentration of omega-3 fatty acids from a plant source. Seeds are available from Seeds of Change™, PO Box 15700, Santa Fe, NM 87592-1500. Order online at www.seedsofchange.com or by phone at 1-888-762-7333.

SHORTENING

Crisco® has introduced a no-trans-fat version; they have resolved the issue by fully hydrogenating one of the oils (cottonseed) in the formula so that it is completely saturated. It has about the same consistency as their standard shortening. Crisco® is widely available.

Spectrum® sells a shortening with no trans fats made of organic, expeller-pressed palm oil. Spectrum Organic Products, Inc., 5341 Old Redwood Hwy., Suite 400, Petaluma, CA 94954. There is a store locator on the Web site at www.spectrumorganics.com.

Earth Balance® shortening is an expeller-pressed natural oil blend (palm fruit, soybean, canola seed, and olive oils). Look for it at health food stores and with the organic foods at the grocery store. Distributed by GFA Brands, Inc., Heart Beat Foods Div., P.O. Box 397, Cresskill, NJ 07626-0397; phone: 201-568-9300; Web site: www.earthbalance.net.

SPAGHETTI SAUCE

All the sugar-free pasta sauces I have found are imported from Italy. Most American-made sauces contain sugar, starch, and lots of additives. Cost Plus World Market®* stores usually carry several Italian brands.

Alessi® marinara pasta sauce is made with olive oil and has only 2 net carbs in ½ cup. It is imported from Sicily by Vigo Importing Co., Tampa, FL 33614; Web site: www.vigo-alessi.com.

Don Pomodoro® marinara sauce is made in Italy from all-natural, organic ingredients. It contains 3 net grams of carbohydrate in ½ cup. My local Albertson's store carries it. Order online at www.beltesoro.com or by phone at 877-725-6437.

SWEETENERS AND SUGAR-FREE SYRUPS

DiabetiSweet® contains isomalt, a sugar alcohol, and acesulfame K. It is available with the diabetic supplies in drug stores and online from www.diabeticproducts.com. HP Health Care Products, HI-TECH Pharmacal Co., Inc, Amityville, NY, 11701.

Erythritol is one of the sugar alcohols. It can be ordered from www.lowcarbsuccess.com and from www.nowfoods.com.

Nature Sweet powdered maltitol is distributed by Steel's Gourmet Foods.* They also make a brown sugar version.

Miracle fruit plants can be ordered from Whitman Rare Fruit Nursery, Dept. TMEN, 23430 S.W. 122nd Ave., Princeton, FL 33032, or from Aloha Tropicals, P.O. Box 6042, Oceanside, CA 92052; phone: 760-631-288; Web site: www.alohatropicals.com. Miracle fruit seeds can be ordered from Trade Winds Fruit, P.O. Box 232693, Encinitas, CA 92023; Web site: www.tradewindsfruit.com.

Shugr is a blend of erythritol, maltodextrin, tagatose, and sucralose. Shugr is sold in packets or in a shaker. The Shugr website, www.shugr.com, lists the retailers who carry the product, or you can order online.

SweetPerfection™, from Low Carb Specialties, Inc.™, is made of oligofructose derived from chicory root. It can be used like sugar in recipes. It has zero net carbs and 122 grams of fiber per cup. It can be ordered online from www.lowcarbspecialties.com. They also sell dark and milk chocolate bars by the dozen. Phone: 800-332-1773.

Sweet One®, also called Sunett®, contains acesulfame K with a little sugar as a bulking agent. One packet is equivalent to two teaspoons of sugar. It is available at many groceries. Phone: 1-800-544-8610; Web site: www.sweetone.com.

Sweetzfree, called liquid Splenda®, is concentrated sucralose without sugar added as a bulking agent. One drop has the sweetening power of 1½ teaspoons of sugar; a 4-ounce container equals 96 cups of sugar. However, there is a limited supply of Sweetzfree, as it is a cottage industry. Orders are only taken during monthly windows that are posted on the Web site: www.sweetzfree.com.

Fiberfit contains liquid sucralose and a little soluble fiber (guar gum and Irish moss). It is much less concentrated than Sweetzfree, but 1 teaspoon of Fiberfit has 8 teaspoons of "sweetening power." It is available online from Netrition*.

Whey Low™ is a blend of natural sugars. The manufacturer claims that fructose, lactose, and sucrose interact in a way that blocks the absorption of some of the sugars. Whey Low™ comes in seven varieties: granular, powdered, packets, maple, golden, Whey Low D (for diabetics), and one to use in ice cream. They can be ordered online from www.wheylow.com or from www.bigskiesfarm.com. The manufacturer and distributor of Whey Lowª is VivaLac¨ Inc., P.O. Box 264, Ashton, MD 20861; phone: 1-888-639-8480.

Wax Orchard™ makes Fruit Sweet® liquid fructose. Many grocery and drug stores in the Northwest carry Wax Orchard™ products, or they can be ordered from The Country Store and Gardens, 20211 Vashon Hwy. SW, Vashon Island, WA 98070; phone: 1-888-245-6136. It can be ordered online at: www.vashoncountrystore.com or www.zhealthinfo2.com/wax_.html.

X-W8 is a sweetener made from a sweet fiber called inulin. It tastes like cane sugar and can be used in the same way. It is now available in candies and as a sugar replacement called D-Lish. It is sold on the Web site at www.d-lectable.com. (Not everything on the Web site is made with the inulin sweetener.)

Atkins'™ syrups are sweetened with Splenda®. Many stores carry the sugar-free vanilla and chocolate flavors and they can be ordered from the Atkins* Web site.

Da Vinci Gourmet® sugar-free syrups come in 51 flavors, including peach, watermelon, and cola. Many grocery stores stock a few flavors, but all can be ordered online from www.DaVincigourmet.com or by phone: 1-800-640-6779. They are available in plastic bottles for shipping. Cash and Carry stores in the Northwest have a large selection of sugar-free flavors at discount prices. Cash and Carry is a division of Smart and Final, 600 Citadel Drive, Commerce, CA 90040; phone: 1-800-793-9344; Web site: www.smartandfinal.com.

Torani® makes sugar-free syrups that contain acesulfame K and Splenda®. Torani® syrups are widely available in stores and at Cost Plus World Markets®.*

THICKENERS AND STABILIZERS

Xanthan gum and guar gum are available from Bob's Red Mill® Natural Foods.* Many groceries have a display of this brand with the flour or in the organic foods section. Their products can also be ordered by mail or online from Bob's Red Mill® Natural Foods.* *The Baker's Catalogue®* of the King Arthur® Flour Company* also sells xanthan gum, in a smaller quantity, by mail order. Guar gum and xanthan gum are sold at Pilgrim's Natureway Nutrition Centers in the Northwest, in health food stores, and from many low-carb Web sites.

ThickenThin Not/Sugar, Not/Cereal, and Not/Starch are mixtures of vegetable gums used to thicken and add volume and texture to foods. They contain zero carbs. Expert Foods, Inc., PO Box 1855, Ellicott City, MD 21041; phone: 888-621-9059. ThickenThin products are available at health food stores and from www.expertfoods.com, www.proteinpower.com/products.php, and www.carbsmart.com.

WHEY PROTEIN POWDER

Trader Joe's* sells Designer Whey™ protein powder. The French vanilla flavor has less than 2 net carbs per serving. It is made by Next Proteins™, PO Box 2469, Carlsbad, CA 92018; phone: 1-800-DESIGNER; Web site: www.designerwhey.com.

Biochem® Sports makes 100% whey protein with 1 net carb per serving. Biochem, Hauppauge, NY 11788; Web site: www.biochem-fitness.com.

*See Directory of Sources.

Directory of Sources

Andre's Bakery™
Forest Hills, NY 11375
www.carbosave.net

Atkins Nutritionals™ Inc.
1-800-6ATKINS
customerservice@buyatkins.com
www.atkinscenter.com

The Baker's Catalogue® of the King Arthur® Flour
Company
P.O. Box 876, Norwich, VT 05055-0876
1-800-827-6836
www.kingarthurflour.com

Bob's Red Mill® Natural Foods
5209 SE International Way, Milwaukie, OR 97222
www.bobsredmill.com

Chef's Catalog
P.O. Box 620048, Dallas, TX 75262-0048
1-800-338-3232
www.chefscatalog.com

Chocosphere®
5200 SE Harney Drive, Portland, OR 97205
1-877-992-4626
www.chocosphere.com

Cost Plus World Market®
The Web site has a store locator.
200 Fourth St., Oakland, CA 94607
1-877-967-5362
www.worldmarket.com

D-Liteful Bakery Co.®
The Web site has a product locater.
9012 NW 105 Way, Medley, FL 33178
www.d-litefulbaking.com

Eat Well Be Well Foods™, Inc.
The Web site has a product locator.
1100 East Marina Way, Suite 223, Hood River, OR
97031
Sales: 1-770-474-9400;
information: 1-541-387-3330
www.eatwellbewell.com

Harry and David
Medford, OR 97501
1-800-547-3033
www.harryanddavid.com

Heritage Foods USA
P.O. Box 827, New York, NY 10150
1-212-980-6603; fax: 1-212-980-6603
www.heritagefoodsusa.com

Honeyville Grain Inc.
11600 Dayton Dr., Rancho Cucamonga, CA
91730
1-888-810-3212, ext. 121
www.honeyvillegrain.com

Netrition, Inc.
20 Petra Lane, Albany, NY 12205
1-888-817-2411
www.netrition.com

Penseys Spices
P.O. Box 924, Brookfield, WI 53008-0924
1-800-741-7787
www.penzeys.com

Spices etc®.
P.O. Box 2088, Savannah, GA 31402-2088
1-800-827-6373
Web Site: www.spicesetc.com

Steel's™ Gourmet Foods
55 E. Front Street, Suite D-175
Bridgeport, PA 19405
1-800-6-STEELS
www.steelsgourmet.com

Sur La Table
To register for classes: 1-866-3218-5412
For a catalog: 1-800-243-0852
P.O. Box 34707, Seattle, WA 98124-1707
www.surlatable.com

Sweet Celebrations
P.O. Box 39426, Edina, MN
1-800-328-6722
www.sweetc.com

Trader Joe's
Monrovia, CA 91016
www.traderjoes.com

Uwajimaya
Perishable items shipped overnight.
Stores in Seattle and Bellevue, WA, and Beaverton, OR
1-800-889-1928 or 1-206-624-6248
www.uwajimaya.com

Williams-Sonoma®
P.O. Box 379900, Las Vegas NV 89137-9900
Mail order: P.O. Box 7456, San Francisco, CA 94120-7456
1-800-541-2233
Online catalog: www.williams-sonoma.com

INDEX

NOTES

NOTES

Notes

NOTES

NOTES